Theory of Literature

THE OPEN YALE COURSES SERIES is designed to bring the depth and breadth of a Yale education to a wide variety of readers. Based on Yale's Open Yale Courses program (http://oyc.yale.edu), these books bring outstanding lectures by Yale faculty to the curious reader, whether student or adult. Covering a wide variety of topics across disciplines in the social sciences, physical sciences, and humanities, Open Yale Courses books offer accessible introductions at affordable prices.

The production of Open Yale Courses for the Internet was made possible by a grant from the William and Flora Hewlett Foundation.

RECENT TITLES
Paul H. Fry, *Theory of Literature*
Shelly Kagan, *Death*
Dale B. Martin, *New Testament History and Literature*

FORTHCOMING TITLES
Christine Hayes, *Introduction to the Old Testament*
Ian Shapiro, *The Moral Foundations of Politics*
Steven B. Smith, *Introduction to Political Philosophy*

Theory
of
Literature

PAUL H. FRY

Yale
UNIVERSITY PRESS
New Haven and London

Yale University Press books may be purchased in quantity for educational,
business, or promotional use. For information, please e-mail sales.press@
yale.edu (U.S. office) or sales@yaleup.co.uk (U.K. office).

Excerpts from *Tony the Tow Truck* by Robert Kraus, © 1985
by Robert Kraus, are used by permission of Grosset & Dunlap,
A Division of Penguin Young Readers Group, A Member of Penguin Group
(USA) Inc., 345 Hudson Street, New York, NY 10014. All rights reserved.

Hans Holbein the Younger, *The Ambassadors* (1533) © National Gallery,
London / Art Resource, NY.

Set in Minion type by Westchester Book Group
Printed in the United States of America

Library of Congress Cataloging-in-Publication Data

Fry, Paul H.
Theory of literature / Paul H. Fry.
p. cm. — (The open Yale courses series)
Includes bibliographical references and index.
ISBN 978-0-300-18083-1 (pbk.)
1. Literature—History and criticism—Theory, etc.   2. Semiotics.
I. Title.
PN441.F79 2012
801'.95—dc23   2011045263

A catalogue record for this book is available from the British Library.

This paper meets the requirements of ANSI/NISO Z39.48-1992
(Permanence of Paper).

10   9   8   7   6   5   4   3   2   1

To all my Lit 300 Teaching Fellows, with fond gratitude

The trouble with most folks isn't so much their ignorance, it's knowin' so many things that ain't so.

—JOSH BILLINGS

Contents

THE SOCIAL CONTEXT

THEORY CON AND PRO

Preface

These chapters have passed through transformations that must be unusual in publishing, although the series the book appears in will probably change that. My twenty-six Open Yale Courses lectures in "Lit 300" for the Spring 2009 semester were videotaped, yes, but you could hear them as audiotape, too—while driving to work or going for a run—and on the assumption that the written transcripts might also appeal, the process then began that morphed at last into the written form of this book. I had delivered the lectures extemporaneously, guided for each one by a page or so of scribbled notes. The audiotape was sent to San Diego, where a machine wrote down what it thought it heard. The result was then given to a human being in New Haven who made what she could of it. That was the point at which I should have done what I've been doing for the last several months, but the incentive was then too low, and I took time only to glance through the transcripts and make a few quick changes—despite realizing that the written record was getting to look like a joke or a bit of gossip that has passed through too many hands.

In a way it then made sense to leave it alone, though, because these *were* supposed to be transcripts, not rewrites, and even though they had the accuracy of those instant captions for the hearing-impaired on television, nobody could say that any changes had intentionally been made. They are now to become a book, however: both digital and print, to be sure, but still a book. An editor at Yale University Press took the transcript in hand on first receiving it and made some cosmetic improvements. The lectures were then sent to me as a zip-file, the mark-up editing program already activated, and I went to work. At this point, I kept thinking about the first few paragraphs of a famous and famously difficult essay that I'd assigned for the course (discussed in Chapter 13), Jacques Lacan's "Agency of the Letter in the Unconscious." His paper, he says, is a written version (*écrit*, in a volume called *Écrits*) of a seminar presentation. He feels that the orality of that occasion is important to retain if he is to convey to the fullest what he wants to say about the role of language in the unconscious. At the same time (though Lacan doesn't say this), it's quite obvious to any reader with experience as a listener that information conveyed in spontaneous speech is perhaps adequate to its occasion but not registered in at all the same way when it's taken in during a reader's more leisurely focus on a written text. Because this book is for readers, therefore, I have modified such parts of the lectures as seemed to me to need a more careful exposition, while hoping to retain a sense throughout of what the lectures sounded like. I am, notoriously, an impromptu speaker of "prose," so when you encounter a long sentence, please don't think it was any shorter in the lecture.

Without the extensive and indispensable help of my assistant, Stefan Esposito, I wouldn't have been able to focus on the unexpected challenge I have described. Stefan was one of the teaching fellows for this videotaped version of the lectures and is an important emerging scholar and theorist in comparative literature. To him I happily entrusted a last read-through and correction of the chapters—for each of which my subject line was always "revised revision, #x"—when I sent them to him in Boston. He composed the bibliographical essay, "The Varieties of Interpretation," with suggestions for further reading on each of our topics, which will be found at the end of the book. He has also furnished the references that we deemed necessary (as few as possible), and arranged in an appendix the handouts with passages to be discussed that I had circulated at some lectures or posted online.

Although references to the photocopied material I assigned have posed a challenge and at least conjecturally introduced a fussy element we had hoped in general to avoid, references to our main textbook were easy. I very strongly suggest that readers consider investing in this excellent volume, which stands out in the field for its judiciously and copiously chosen materials (including selections covering the entire history of criticism) and for its sensible introductions: David Richter, ed., *The Critical Tradition: Classic Texts and Contemporary Trends* (3rd ed.: Boston: Bedford/St. Martin's, 2007). All quotations from that volume are keyed in parentheses to the third edition.

The first two chapters are introductory and offer a good many of the apologies, disclaimers, and boasts that one might expect to find in prefaces, so I shall say very little here about what the ensuing tour through this vast subject matter includes. I am conscious, however, that there are certain recently influential names and ideas that the syllabus did not stretch to cover, although here and there some oblique or proleptic mention of these trends will be found. The "ethical turn," for example, encompasses late Derrida, as I point out, but I do not discuss the work of Giorgio Agamben or of neo-Marxists like Jacques Rancière and Alain Badiou. Also current is the brilliant

Marxist attention devoted to textual surface in England, with Simon Jarvis, Keston Sutherland, and others micro-reading in the spirit of founder J. H. Prynne, which has only reached American shores as yet in the shape of their promising students.

Literary sociology is an emerging field, but my discussion of John Guillory (and mention of Pierre Bourdieu in that context) is not supplemented by any discussion of the important work, for example, of the sociolinguist Michael Silverstein. A formative influence on Silverstein is the semiotics of C. S. Peirce; and it must be said that as neo-pragmatist views like those of Knapp and Michaels (discussed here) converge today with attention to the social and cultural circulation of literary knowledge and taste that is modeled on Jürgen Habermas's concept of the "public sphere" even more than on Bourdieu's concept of "habitus," something like a Peircean tradition of the socially indexical sign has emerged in rivalry with the Saussurian tradition to which these lectures devote most of their attention. A general introduction to the Peircean tradition has yet to be written, and I hope it will quickly appear. The reader will find a few thoughts on this topic at the beginning of my twenty-fifth chapter.

Theories of the circulation of knowledge other than those of Foucault, discussed here, and Antonio Gramsci, mentioned in passing, have recently carried scholars into the interrelated fields of systems theory (notably Niklas Luhmann), history of media, remediation, and media theory (the classics in this field being works by Marshall McLuhan and Friedrich Kittler), and more specifically within these last fields the history of the book (as in the work of Peter Stallybrass and David Kastan). All of this and more, then, remains to be covered in another course, and another book.

The challenge of acknowledging my intellectual debts—my personal ones, I mean, as the written ones find their way for the most part into the bibliographical essay—is overwhelming. I can name here only a few of the people whose conversation and teaching over the years have shaped my understanding of the subject, whether they knew it or not: Jeffrey Alexander, Johannes Anderegg, Marshall Brown, Margaret Ferguson, Stanley Fish, Hans Frei, Harris Friedberg, Paul Grimstad, John Guillory, Benjamin Harshav, Geoffrey Hartman, John Hollander, Margaret Homans, Helmut Illbruck, Carol Jacobs, Barbara Johnson, Jeremy Kessler, Eric Lindstrom, Alfred MacAdam, David Marshall, Irving Massey, Rainer Nägele, Ana Nersessian, Edward Nersessian, Cyril O'Regan, Brigitte Peucker, Anthony Reed, Joseph Roach, Charles Sabel, Naomi Schor, David Simpson, Peter Stallybrass, Garrett Stewart, Henry Sussman, Steve Tedeschi, Michael Warner, and Henry

Weinfield. It pains me even more than it has on similar occasions in the past, educating oneself in these matters (and allowing oneself to be educated) being such a crucial yet delicate business, that despite having made what began to seem a rather long list of acknowledgments, I have undoubtedly forgotten so many who deserve a place on it. I can only hope they are relieved to have escaped guilt by association. My debt to my teaching fellows, from my first involvement with the course in the 1980s (when Paul de Man's students brought their edge and zeal to our proceedings), is recorded in my dedication. For advice and encouragement along the way, in addition to Stefan Esposito I thank Diana E. E. Kleiner, the founder and tireless sustainer of Open Yale Courses, and, at Yale University Press, Laura Davulis, Christina Tucker, Sonia Shannon, Ann-Marie Imbornoni, and Aldo Cupo. My thanks also go to Wendy Muto and Brian Desmond at Westchester Book Group and to Julie Palmer-Hoffman, the copyeditor.

CHAPTER 1

Introduction

The Prehistory and Rise of "Theory"

Readings:

Passages from Marx, Nietzsche, Freud, and Paul Ricoeur.

Let me begin with a few remarks about the title of our course because it has some big words in it: "theory" and "literature," clearly, but it's worth saying something about the word "introduction" as well.

The word "theory" has a complicated etymological history that I won't linger over except to point out what can make its meaning confusing. The way the word has actually been used at certain periods has made it mean something like what we call "practice," whereas at other periods it has meant something very different from practice: a concept to which practice can appeal. This latter is the sense of theory that prevails today, but perhaps we accept it too quickly. Whereas for us the difference between theory and practice goes without saying, there's a less obvious difference between theory and methodology. Yes, it's probably fair enough to say that methodology is "applied theory," but that makes it like practice—call it disciplined practice—in the sense I just used. Theory, on the other hand, does not always have an immediate application. Theory can be a purely speculative undertaking. It's a hypothesis about something, the exact nature of which one needn't necessarily have in view because theory itself may serve to bring it into view. Whatever the object of theory might be, if it even has one, theory itself requires—owing to whatever intellectual constraints may be in play—a large measure of internal coherence rather more urgently than a given field of application.

Of course there is no doubt that most existing forms of theory do exist to be applied. Very frequently, courses of this kind have a kind of proof text—*Lycidas, The Rime of the Ancient Mariner,* a short story—and then once in a while the exposition of the lecture will pause, the text will be produced, and whatever type of theory has recently been talked about will be applied to the text; so that you'll get a postcolonial reading or a trauma theory reading of *The Rime of the Ancient Mariner*—there have been a lot of good ones, by the way—and so on throughout the course.

Now although I'm reluctant to say that theory should always have an application despite knowing that that's what usually happens, I won't depart from this custom; but I'll poke a little respectful fun at it by making it seem, at least at times, like breaking a butterfly on a wheel. *Our* text is a story for toddlers called *Tony the Tow Truck.* It's a little book made of thick cardboard pages with a line of text at the bottom, each page a picture of vehicles with human expressions and a row of houses with human faces expressing approval or disapproval in the background. We won't come back to this text for a while, but it's mercifully short, and as time passes we will do various tricks with it. As others revert to *Lycidas*, we shall revert to *Tony the Tow Truck* for the purpose of introducing questions of applied theory.

In this choice there is hardly any condescension toward theory and none at all toward literary texts. It's much more a question of reminding you that if you can apply theory to *Tony*, you can apply it to anything; and also of reminding you that, after all, reading—reading just anything—is a complex and potentially almost unlimited activity. That's one of the most important things that theory teaches us, and I hope to be able to prove it in the course of our varied approaches to *Tony the Tow Truck.*

Theory resembles philosophy, especially metaphysics, perhaps in this: it asks fundamental questions and also at times builds systems. That is to say, theory aims at a general description of what can be thought that resembles or rivals philosophy. But literary theory as practiced in the twentieth century and beyond differs in most instances from most philosophy in that to a surprising extent it entails skepticism. In literary theory there seems to be a pervasive variety of doubts about the foundations of what we can think, and it is certainly doubt that characterizes its modern history. Not all theory that we read in this course is skeptical. Some of the most powerful and profound thought that's been devoted to the theory of literature is positive in its intentions and its views, but by and large you will be coming to terms—happily or unhappily—with the fact that much of what you're going to find in the recommended readings accompanying this course is under-girded, or perhaps I should say undermined, by this persisting skepticism. It's centrally important, the skepticism of theory, and I'm going to be coming back to it over and over, but now I mention it just in passing to evoke what we might call the atmosphere of theory.

Turning to the word "literature," this is not a course in theory of relativity, theory of music, or theory of government. This is a course in theory of literature, and theory of literature shares in common with other kinds of theory the need for definition. Maybe the most fundamental and, for me, possibly the most fascinating question theory asks is, what *is* literature? Much of what we'll be reading takes up this question and provides us with fascinating and always—each in its turn—enticing definitions. There are definitions based on form: circularity, symmetry, economy of form, lack of economy of form, and repetition. There are definitions based on imitation: of "nature," of psychological or sociopolitical states, definitions appealing to the complexity, balance, harmony, or sometimes imbalance and dishar-mony of the imitation. There are also definitions that insist on an epistemo-logical difference between literature and other kinds of utterance: whereas most utterances purport to be saying something true about the actual state of things in the world, literary utterance is under no such obligation, the argument goes, and ought properly to be understood as fiction—making things rather than referring to things.

All of these definitions have had currency. We'll be going over them again and discovering their respective merits as we learn more about them; but at the same time, even as I rattle off this list of possibilities, you're probably thinking that you could easily find exceptions to all such claims. Well and good, that's properly ecumenical of you, but at the same time your tough-mindedness raises the uneasy sense, does it not, that maybe literature just isn't anything *at all*?—in other words, that literature may not be sus-ceptible to definition, to any one definition, but is just whatever you think it is or, more precisely, whatever your interpretive community says that it is. But even if you reach that conclusion, it won't seem disabling as long as you remember that certain notions of literature do exist in certain communities, that those notions in themselves reward study, and that after all you yourself know perfectly well, and for practical purposes agree with, what counts as literature among your peers. I have just outlined the so-called neo-pragmatist view of literature and of definition in general, but it doesn't excuse us from delineating an object of study. Definition is important to us, even if it's provisional, and we're certainly not going to give it short shrift in this course.

In addition to defining literature, literary theory also asks questions that open up the field somewhat. What causes literature and what are the effects of literature? As to cause, we ask: What is an author? And what is the nature of literary authority? By the same token, if literature has effects, it must have effects on someone, and this gives rise to the equally interesting and vexing question, what is a reader? Literary theory is very much involved with questions of that kind, and the need to organize these questions is what rationalizes the structure of our course. You'll notice from the contents that we move in these lectures from the idea that literature is formed by language to the idea that literature is formed by the human psyche to the idea that literature is formed by social, economic, and historical forces. There are corollaries for those ideas with respect to the kinds of effects that literature has, and the course moves through these corollaries in the same sequence.

Finally, literary theory asks one other important question, the one with which we'll begin before turning to form, psyche, and society. This question is not so much "What is a reader?" but "How does reading get done?" That is to say, how do we—how does anyone—form the conclusion that we are interpreting something adequately, that we have a basis for the kind of reading that we're doing? What is the reading experience like? How do we meet the text face-to-face? How do we put ourselves in touch with the text, which may in many ways be remote from us? These are the questions that are asked by what's called *hermeneutics*, a difficult word that we will be taking up soon. It derives from the name of the god Hermes, who conveyed language to man and who was, among many other things, the god of communication.

So much then for *literature* and its contexts in theory. Now let me pause quickly over the word "introduction." I started teaching this course in the late 1970s and 1980s, when literary theory was a thing absolutely of the moment. I had a colleague who was only half joking when he said he wished he had the black leather concession at the door. Theory was both hot and cool, and it was something about which, following from that, one had not just opinions but very, very strong opinions. In consequence, a lot of people thought that you couldn't teach an "introduction" to theory. They meant that you couldn't teach a survey, saying, "If it's Tuesday, it must be Foucault. If it's Thursday, it must be Lacan." It was a betrayal to approach theory that way. What was called for, it was thought, was a radical effort to grasp the basis for all possible theory. You were a feminist or a Marxist or a student of Paul de Man, and if you were going to teach anything like a survey you had to derive the rest of it from your fundamental conviction.

That's the way it felt to teach theory in those days. It was awkward teaching an introduction. While I was teaching this course, which was then called Lit Y and required for our literature major then as now, Paul de Man was teaching Lit Z, the art of interpretation as he practiced it. That course did indeed cast its shadow across every other form of theory, and it was extremely rigorous and interesting, but it wasn't a survey. It took for granted that everything else would derive from a fundamental idea, but it didn't for a minute suppose that a whole series of ideas, each considered fundamental in turn, could jostle for attention and get mixed and matched in a cheerfully eclectic way—which perhaps we will be seeming to do from time to time in our introductory course.

Do I miss the coolness and heat of that moment? Yes and no. As Wordsworth says, "Bliss was it in that dawn to be alive," and I hope to convince you that it's still advantageous for us too to be "into theory." We still have views; we need to have them and above all to recognize that we have them. We still have to recognize, as literary journalism by and large does not, that whatever we think derives from theoretical principles. We have to understand that what we do and say, what we write in our papers and articles, is grounded in theoretical premises that, if we don't come to terms with them, we will naively reproduce without being fully aware of how we're using them and how, indeed, they are using us. So it is as crucial as ever to understand theory.

Yet there's an advantage too in realizing that the cachet of theory has waned and the heat of the moment has passed. (I am not speaking here of methodology, which is as much as ever a matter of urgent dispute today.) We have the vantage point of what we can now call history. Some of what we'll be studying, indeed much of it, is no longer considered essential groundwork for today's methodologies. Everything we'll study has had its moment of flourishing and has remained indirectly influential as a paradigm that shapes other paradigms, but much of it is no longer lingered over as a matter for ongoing discussion—which gives us the opportunity for historical perspective. Hence from time to time I'll be able to be reasonably confident in explaining why certain theoretical issues and ideas pushed themselves into prominence at certain historical moments. With this added dimension an *introduction* becomes valuable not only for those of us who simply wish to cover the high points. It's valuable also in showing how theory is, on the one hand, now a historical topic, yet is, on the other hand, something that we're very much engaged in and still committed to. All that then by way of rationale for teaching an introduction to the theory of literature.

How does literary theory relate to the history of criticism? The history of criticism is a course that I like to teach, too; usually I teach Plato to T. S. Eliot or Plato to I. A. Richards or some other important figure in the early twentieth century. It's a course that shares one important feature with literary theory: literary criticism is, like theory, perpetually concerned with the definition of literature. Many of the issues that I raised in talking about defining literature are as relevant for literary criticism as they are for literary theory. Yet we all instinctively know that these are two very different enterprises. For one thing, literary theory loses something that literary criticism just takes for granted. Literary theory is not concerned with *evaluation*. Literary theory just takes evaluation, or appreciation, for granted as part of the responsive experience of any reader and prefers, rather, to dwell on questions of description, analysis, and speculation, as I've said. Or to be a little more precise: how and why certain readers under certain conditions value literature or fail or refuse to do so is indeed an object of literary theory, or at least of theory-inflected methodology, but why we *should* or should not value literature or individual works belongs only in the domain of criticism. I should say in qualification, though, that theory sometimes implies value even though it never lays claim to it. Sir Philip Sidney's "poetry nothing affirmeth and therefore never lieth," with which Paul de Man would agree completely, speaks both to theory and criticism.

So that's what's lost in theory; but what's gained in theory that's missing in criticism? Here I return to the topic that will occupy most of my attention for the remainder of the lecture. What's new in theory is the element of skepticism that literary criticism—which is usually affirming a canon of some sort—does not share for the most part. Literary theory is skeptical about the foundations of its subject matter and also, in many cases, about the foundations of its own arguments. How on earth did this come about? Why should doubt about the veridical or truth-affirming possibilities of interpretation be so widespread, especially in the twentieth century and beyond?

Here by way of answer is a dollop of intellectual history. I think the seeds of the sort of skepticism I mean are planted during what often is called "modernity." Modernity should not be confused with modernism, an early twentieth-century phenomenon. Modernity refers to the history of modern thought as we trace it back to the "early modern" time of Descartes, Shakespeare, and Cervantes. Notice something about all of those figures: Descartes in his First Meditation wonders how he can know for sure that he isn't mad or whether his mind has been taken over by an evil genius. Shakespeare is preoccupied with figures like Hamlet who may or may not be crazy. Cervantes makes his hero a figure who *is* crazy—or at least we're pretty sure of that, but Quixote certainly isn't. He takes it for granted that he is a rational and systematic thinker. We all take ourselves to be rational, too, but Cervantes makes us wonder just how we know ourselves not to be paranoid delusives like Don Quixote.

All these doubts about the basis of thought in reason arise in the seventeenth century. Why then do we get this nervousness about the relationship between what I know and how I know it arising at this moment? Well, I think it's characterized at least in part by what Descartes goes on to say in his *Meditations*. Descartes answers the question he has posed about how he can know himself to exist, which depends in part on deciding that an existing alien being doesn't exist as it were in his place—he answers this question to his own satisfaction by saying, "I think. Therefore, I am"; and furthermore, as a concomitant, I think, therefore all the things that I'm thinking about can be understood to exist as well.

Now this "Cartesian revolution" establishes a central premise for what we call the Enlightenment of the next 150 years. Thenceforth it was given that there is a distance between the mind and the things that it thinks about. At first this distance was considered highly fortunate. After all, if you look too closely at a picture or if you stand too far away from it you don't see it clearly—it's out of focus—but if you achieve just the right distance from it, it comes into focus. The idea of scientific objectivity, the idea that motivates the creation of the great *Encyclopedia* by the figures of the French Enlightenment—that idea depends on maintaining this objective middle distance between the perceiver and the perceived. Gradually, however, the supposition that this distance is neither too great nor too small begins to erode, so that in 1796 Kant, who isn't enlisted on the side of the skeptics by most of his serious students, nevertheless does say something equally as famous as the "cogito" of Descartes and a good deal more disturbing: "We cannot know the thing in itself." To be sure, Kant erected such a magnificent scaffolding around the thing in itself—the variety of ways in which, although we can't know the thing, we can triangulate it and come to terms with it obliquely—that it seems churlish to enlist him on the side of the skeptics. Yet at the same time there's a sense of danger in the distance between subject and object that begins to emerge in thinking of this kind.

By 1807, Hegel in *The Phenomenology of Mind* is saying that in recent history and in recent developments of consciousness something unfortunate has set in. We have "unhappy consciousness," an estranged state of mind that drives us too far away from the thing that we're looking at. We are no longer certain of what we're looking at, and consciousness, therefore, feels alienated. Here you see a development in the mainstream of intellectual history that opens the door to skepticism. But the crucial shift hasn't yet come about, because in all of these accounts, even that of Hegel, there is still no doubt about the authority of consciousness to think what it thinks. It may not think clearly enough about objects, but it is still the origin of its own thoughts, uncertain as they may be. But then come three great figures—there are others but these are considered the foundational figures—who begin to raise questions that complicate the whole issue of consciousness. They argue not only that consciousness doesn't clearly understand what it's looking at and is therefore alienated from it but also that consciousness is alienated from its own underpinnings, that it doesn't have any clear sense of where it's coming from any more than what it's looking at. In other words, consciousness is not only estranged from the world but deracinated from the sources of its own thoughts.

Marx, in the famous argument about commodity fetishism in *Das Kapital*, describes the way in which we take a product of human labor and turn it into a commodity by saying that it has objective value, not the value of the labor that produced it. He compares commodity fetishism with religion: God is a product of human intellectual labor that we objectify and posit as the producer of ourselves, having the timeless, immutable value of a commodity. One aspect of Marx's argument is that consciousness, the way in which we believe things, is deluded because it is determined by factors outside its control: social, historical, and economic factors that shape what we suppose to be our own authentic ideas, creating what Marx calls ideology.

So by the mid-nineteenth century the challenge to consciousness is twofold: it struggles not only with its inauthentic relationship with the things it looks at, distorted by ideology, but also with its inauthentic relationship with its own underpinnings, the "real existing conditions" that shape the bourgeois outlook and make it seem universal. The argument is a parallel one for Nietzsche, but he shifts the ground of attack. For Nietzsche, what makes the operations of consciousness inauthentic is the nature of language itself. When we think we're telling the truth, we're actually using worn-out figures of speech. "What then is truth? A mobile army of metaphors, metonymies, anthropomorphisms—in short, a sum of human relations which became poetically and rhetorically intensified . . . and are now no longer of account as coins but are debased." That word *now* is very interesting and not always noticed by those who have since wished to enlist Nietzsche for polemics against truth claims in language. Nietzsche appears to imagine a time when perhaps language was capable of naming reality, when the coin of the verbal realm had real exchange value, arguing that language has *now* reduced itself to a conquering invasion of worn-out figures, all of which dictate what we believe to be true. We speak in a figurative way about the relationship between the earth and the sky and soon believe there's a sky god. We slide from speech into belief, unwittingly using figures of speech that are not—or not any longer—verifiable.

Freud finally argues for a parallel relationship between consciousness— what I think I am thinking and saying from minute to minute—and what determines it, in his case the unconscious, which perpetually undermines what we think and say from minute to minute. In *The Psychopathology of Everyday Life*, Freud reminded us that the Freudian slip isn't something that happens just sometimes—and nobody knows this better than an ad-libbing lecturer—it's something that happens all the time. The Freudian slip is something that one dimly recognizes as the slipping of consciousness under the influence of the unconscious, yet for Freud it represents the perpetual, inescapable subjection of reason to desire.

Paul Ricoeur, a modern philosopher in the hermeneutic tradition who didn't fully believe Marx, Nietzsche, and Freud, retorted in the third passage in the appendix that these great precursors of recent thought—and particularly of modern literary theory—together dominate a "school of suspicion." *Suspicion*, like skepticism, is a word that can also be understood as negation. That is to say, whatever seems manifest or obvious or patent in what we are looking at is undermined for this kind of mind by a negation that is counterintuitive. Because it is dialectical, the reversal of what has been posited, negation does not just *qualify* what we suppose ourselves to know for certain (anyone might agree by the way that socioeconomic influences, language, and the unconscious exert *some* influence on thought), but undermines it *altogether*. The reception of Marx, Nietzsche, and Freud as strong negative thinkers has been tremendously influential. When we read Foucault's "What Is an Author?" for the next lecture, we'll return to the question of how Marx, Nietzsche, and Freud have been received and what we should make of that in view of Foucault's idea that it's dangerous to believe that there are authors because we soon turn them into authorities. But if it's dangerous to believe that there are authors for that reason, what about Marx, Nietzsche, and Freud, all of them powerful precursors of Foucault himself? Foucault confronts this question in "What Is an Author?" and responds, as we'll see, with a striking turn of thought. For us, the aftermath of the very passages I have just discussed, and certainly of the oeuvres of their three authors, can to a large degree be understood as accounting for our topic—the phenomenon of literary theory as we study it. In other words, literary theory, because of the influence of these figures, is to a considerable degree a hermeneutics of suspicion, an exercise in negation recognized as such both by its proponents and, at one time vociferously, by its enemies.

During the period when I was first teaching this course, a veritable six-foot shelf of diatribes against literary theory was being written, many for popular audiences, some with academic credentials. Today you can take or leave literary theory without much fuss being made about it; but the incredible outcry against it at that time reflected its dynamic appeal. For many, many people, most of whom for a while seemed to be writing books, literary theory had something to do with the end of civilization as we know it. The undermining of foundational knowledge, which seemed to motivate so much that went on in literary theory, was seen as the main threat to rationality emanating from the academy and was attacked for that reason in countless lively polemics. That the counterinsurgency against literary theory arose in part from theory's characteristic skepticism is what I have thought it best to emphasize at the present time, because today the humanities are still under fire but with a different emphasis. The main theme of the attacks on the humanities is no longer their negativity but—sometimes as an implied result—their uselessness.

I think that one influence Ricoeur leaves out of his negative pantheon, one that we can expect to become more and more important for literary theory and other kinds of theory in the twenty-first century, is that of Darwin. Darwin could very easily be considered a fourth hermeneutist of suspicion. He himself was not interested in suspicion, seeing in natural selection no real threat to religion broadly conceived, but he was certainly the founder of ways of thinking about consciousness that see it as determined, sociobiologically determined or determined in the realm of cognitive science, determined as artificial intelligence, and so on. All of this thinking descends from Darwin and will be increasingly influential in the twenty-first century. What will alter the shape of literary theory as it was known and studied in the twentieth century is, I think, an increasing emphasis on cognitive science and sociobiological approaches both to literature and to interpretive processes that will derive from Darwin in the same way that strands of thinking of the twentieth century derive from the three figures that I've discussed.

But what the hermeneutics of suspicion gave rise to first is something like an uneasy feeling in the air, contributed to also by sweeping historical changes; and this brings me finally to a preview of the passages from Henry James's 1903 *The Ambassadors* and from Chekhov's 1904 *The Cherry Orchard*. I am at pains to remind you that this is a specific historical moment. In both cases the speaker argues that consciousness—the feeling of being alive and being someone acting in the world—no longer involves agency: the feeling that somehow to be conscious is merely to be a puppet, that there are severe limits to our scope of activity. Strether in *The Ambassadors* and Yepihodov in *The Cherry Orchard* speak for a point of view that echoes the doom and gloom in the air, yet strikingly anticipates texts that are much more systematically informed. I want to begin the next lecture by taking up the passages from James and Chekhov before plunging into the question "What is an author?"

CHAPTER 2

Introduction Continued

Theory and Functionalization

Readings:

Foucault, Michel. "What Is an Author?" In *The Critical Tradition*, pp. 904–914.

Barthes, Roland. "The Death of the Author." In *The Critical Tradition*, pp. 874–877.

Passages from Henry James and Anton Chekhov.

In the first lecture we discussed the reasons why literary theory in the twentieth century is shadowed by skepticism, but as we were talking about that we actually introduced another issue that isn't quite the same as skepticism—namely, *determinism*. In the course of intellectual history, we said, first you encounter concern about the distance between the perceiver and the perceived, a concern that gives rise to skepticism about whether we can know things as they really are. But then as an outgrowth of this concern in figures like Marx, Nietzsche, and Freud, you get the further question, not just how we can know things as they really are but how we can trust the autonomy of that which knows. How can we be certain that consciousness is independent if in fact there's a chance—a good chance, according to these writers—that consciousness is in turn governed by, controlled by, "determined" by, hidden agencies? Determinism is at least as important in the arguments of literary theory as skepticism. They're plainly interrelated in many ways, but I want to focus in this lecture on the question of determinism.

In the last lecture, following Ricoeur, I mentioned Marx, Nietzsche, and Freud as key figures who inaugurated the negative mood of theory, and then I added Darwin. It seems pertinent to think of Darwin when we begin to consider the ways in which, in the twentieth century, human agency comes under siege. Circumstances of every kind have threatened the idea that we have autonomy, that we can act independently or, at least, that we can act with a sense of integrity and not just with a sense that we are being pulled by our strings like puppets. In the aftermath of Darwin in particular, our understanding of genetic hardwiring and other such factors made us begin to wonder how we could consider ourselves, each of us, to be free agents. Thus as scientific voices in addition to voices across the humanities responded to historical cataclysms that seemed as inescapable as divine thunderbolts, the crisis of agency intensified.

At the dawn of this epoch, we find the two passages by Anton Chekhov and Henry James that I introduced in the last lecture. Let's begin with the Chekhov. As you know, *The Cherry Orchard* is about the threat to a landed estate arising from the socioeconomic conditions that soon led to the Menshevik Revolution of 1905, with the characters' varied reactions—including avoidance—to this threat. One of the more interesting reactions comes from a family retainer who is not really a protagonist: the house servant Yepihodov, who is something of an autodidact. In a completely undisciplined way, that is, he is aware of intellectual currents. He is full of self-pity, and his speeches are more characteristic of Chekhov's gloomy intellectual milieu than are almost anyone else's. He says, "I'm a cultivated man. I read all kinds of remarkable books and yet I can never make out what direction I should take, what it is that I want, properly speaking." As I quote bits of this monologue, pay attention to the way he constantly talks about language and about the way he himself is subject to the vagaries of language. He searches for a mode of "properly speaking." He is somewhat knowledgeable about books and thinks himself caught up in the matrix of book learning. He is preoccupied with his conditioning by language that is not his own, not least when perhaps unwittingly he alludes to *Hamlet*. "Should I live or should I shoot myself?"—or, properly speaking, "To be or not to be?" Thus he inserts himself into the dramatic tradition to which as a character he himself belongs and shows himself to be, in a debased form, derived from one of those famous charismatic moments in which a hero expresses a comparable concern.

Here then is a character who is caught up in the snare of language. "Properly speaking and letting other subjects alone, I must say . . ." He is *forced to say*, that is. He would be an egoist if the commonplaces of language would only let him have an ego of his own: "I must say, regarding myself among other things, that fate treats me mercilessly as a storm treats a small boat."[1] And the end of the passage: "Have you read Buckle?" Henry Thomas Buckle is a forgotten name today, but at one time he was just about as famous as Oswald Spengler, who wrote *The Decline of the West*. Buckle was a Victorian historian preoccupied with the dissolution of Western civilization, an avatar of the notion in the late nineteenth century that everything was going to hell in a handbasket. One of the texts, then, that in a certain sense *determines* Yepihodov is Buckle. "Have you read Buckle? I wish to have a *word* with you, Avdotya Fyodorovna." The saturation of these speeches with words about words, language, speaking, and books is just the dilemma of this character. He is book- and language-determined, and he's obscurely aware that this is his problem even though knowing books is a source of pride for him.

Let us turn, then, to a passage in a very different tone from James's *The Ambassadors*. An altogether charming character, the late middle-aged Lambert Strether, has gone to Paris to bring home the son of a friend, Chad Newsome, who is to take over the family business, manufacturing an unnamed household article in Woollett, Massachusetts—probably toilet paper. In Paris Strether has awakened to the sheer wonder of urbane culture. He sees that he's missed something. He goes to a party given by a sculptor, and at this party he meets a young man named Little Bilham, whom he takes aside and addresses in a long speech, saying: "Don't do what I have done. Don't miss out on life. Live all you can. It is a mistake not to." And this is why, he goes on to say:

> The affair—I mean the affair of life—couldn't, no doubt, have been different for me; for it's at the best a tin mould, either fluted and embossed, with ornamental excrescences, or else smooth and dreadfully plain, into which, a helpless jelly, one's consciousness is poured—so that one "takes" the form as the great cook says, and is more or less compactly held by it: one lives in fine as one can. Still, one has the illusion of freedom.[2]

At this point, Strether, who is infinitely smarter than Yepihodov, says something very clever that I think we can make use of. He goes on to say, "Therefore, don't be, like me, without the memory of that illusion. I was either at the right time too stupid or too intelligent to have it. I don't quite know which." Now if he was too stupid to have it, then of course he would have been liberated into the realm of action. He would have been what Nietzsche in a book about the uses of history calls "historical man." He simply would have plunged into life as though he had freedom, even though he would have been too stupid to recognize that his freedom was an illusion. On the other hand, if he was too intelligent to—as it were—bury this illusion and live as though he were free, if he was too intelligent to do that, he would be a prototype for the literary theorist. He would be the sort of person who can't forget long enough that freedom is an illusion to get away from the crippling preoccupations that characterize a certain kind of thinking in the twentieth century. And it's delightfully circumspect of him that he says at last—because how can a determinate being know anything?—"I don't quite know which."

So these are characteristic passages that can introduce us to this lecture's subject, which is the loss of authority: "the death of the author" in Roland Barthes's title and what is implied in Foucault's question, "What is an author?" With the denial of human agency, the first sacrifice for literary theory is the author, the idea of the author.

Now let me set the scene. Like Strether but seventy years later, we're in Paris. It wouldn't have to be Paris. It could be Berkeley or Columbia or maybe Berlin. It's 1968 or 1969, spilling over into the 1970s. Students and most of their professors are on the barricades, in protest not only against the war in Vietnam but also against the authoritarian resistance to protest that marked the 1960s. A ferment of intellectual revolt takes all sorts of forms in Paris but is largely organized by what quickly became a bumper sticker in this country: "Question authority." Hence the most prominent intellectual in France writes an essay at the very peak of the student uprising entitled "What Is an Author?"

Yet Foucault offers a series of historically inflected answers to this question that are by no means straightforward or simple. Maybe you anticipated what I've just been saying about the historical setting and about the role of Foucault and were therefore more confused and frustrated by what he actually says than you expected to be. Yet you also saw that "What Is an Author?" nonetheless is written as much in the spirit of critique as you had anticipated. Because this course is introductory, I won't spend a great deal of time with the more unexpected turns of Foucault's argument; I'll emphasize, rather, the parts you may have anticipated.

Now most of us are likely to raise our eyebrows and ask whether this Foucault person really doesn't think he himself is an author. After all, he's a superstar. He's used to being taken very seriously. Does he want to say that he's not an authority but just an "author function," that the textual field of his own essay is a set of structural operations within which one can discover, just as one discovers a plot or an element of grammar, an *author*? Well, this is an emperor's new clothes sort of question that we're going to take seriously in the long run, but there *are* ways of keeping the question at arm's length, even of disarming it, and they need to be explored.

So yes, this very authoritative-sounding person would seem to be an author. I never met anybody who seemed more like an author than Foucault, yet he's asking whether there is any such thing as one, or in any case how difficult it is to decide what it is if there is. Let me digress with an anecdote that may help us to understand this odd connection between a star author and the atmosphere of thought in which there is no such thing as an author. A former colleague of mine was taking a lecture course at Johns Hopkins in the 1960s. The course was given by Georges Poulet, a "phenomenological critic" whose important work I regret not having time to cover in our survey. He was, in any case, a star author. Poulet would be lecturing away, and the students from time to time would raise their hand and simply utter a name. One would raise her hand and say, "Mallarmé." And Poulet would say, "Mais oui! Exactement!" and then go on with his lecture. Then somebody else would raise his hand and say, "Proust." "Ah, précisement! Proust. Proust." Then back to the lecture. So my colleague decided to act on a hunch. He raised his hand and said, "Voltaire," a famous author but not one in whom theorists typically find anything of interest. Sure enough, Poulet looked puzzled and said "Quoi donc? . . . Je ne vous comprends pas," then returned in a state of bemusement to his lecture.

Now this ritual of dropping names actually shows that they are not just names, not even just the names of stars. They are plainly names that stand for something other than mere authorship, names that stand for domains or fields of interesting "discourse." Poulet was the kind of theorist who believed that the oeuvre of an author was a totality that could be understood as a structural whole, and his commentaries worked toward that end. He would speak of "le texte mallarméen" or "le texte proustien." In this context, to refer to an author is to name a domain. That's of course what my colleague—because he knew perfectly well that when he said "Voltaire," Poulet would have nothing to do with it—had figured out. There were relevant and interesting fields of discourse and there were completely irrelevant fields of discourse. We spontaneously make these distinctions, perhaps, but we need to be aware that when we accord authorship to such fields we may well be thinking *not* of some intending consciousness but of isolated textual effects, "signatures" amid many other textual features that are not necessarily authorial traces but—for example—transpersonal language effects or the constraints of an occasion.

Theorists in Poulet's and Foucault's time liked to speak of "discourse" or "discursivity," as opposed to authorial speech. I said last time that sometimes people just throw up their hands when they try to define literature and say that literature is whatever anyone says it is. Such people are more likely to use the word "discourse" or "textual field" or "discursivity" than the word "literature." Like much jargon, such circumlocution does have a rationale. The word "discourse," or "discursivity" understood as the potential of discourse to become an arena for discussion, suggests that the boundary is extremely porous both between authors and between types of speech. One can speak hesitantly of literary discourse, political discourse, anthropological discourse, but one doesn't want to go so far as to say literature, political science, anthropology; and by the same token, the names "Fanny Burney," "Maria Edgeworth," and "Jane Austen," "Georges Poulet," "Michel Foucault," and "Tzvetan Todorov" are open fields, not enclosed fiefdoms. These are habits of speech that arise from sensing the permeability of all forms of utterance with respect to each other; and such habits challenge the notion that certain forms of utterance can be understood as authorized pieces of private property.

Best to clear up a common, sometimes willful misunderstanding: no one, certainly not Foucault, has said or ever will say that a written document doesn't have an author, isn't written by some person or persons. Yes, Barthes talks about the "death" of the author, but even Barthes doesn't mean that the author doesn't exist. We are asked only whether we really do necessarily appeal to the authority of an author in making up our mind about the nature of a given field of discourse. We can as readily find the author somewhere within the textual experience, with the advantage that it is then a text we are reading and not a decree from above. The author is a set of practices, a virtual presence, not an actual one: what Foucault calls a "function." The important questions now are how we recognize the author's presence, first, and, second, whether in attempting to determine the meaning of a text—and this is something we'll be talking about in the next lecture—we should appeal to the authority of the author. If the author is a function, that function is something that appears, perhaps problematically appears, here and there across the field of the text, something that for one thing (and this is a turn of thought you've been familiar with since high school English) we need to distinguish from the speaker or the narrator, or, yet more obviously in the case of plays, from the characters.

For Foucault a text is an entity composed of interactive functions. For Barthes, too, a text is a system of functions, but he lays more emphasis on the permeability of this system to other systems. Barthes opens "The Death of the Author" (874) by quoting a short story by Balzac called "Sarrasine":

> In his story "Sarrasine" Balzac, describing a castrato disguised as a woman, writes the following sentence: "*This was woman herself, with her sudden fears, her irrational whims, her instinctive worries, her impetuous boldness, her fussings and her delicious sensibility.*" Who is speaking thus? Is it the hero of the story bent on remaining ignorant of the castrato hidden beneath the woman? Is it Balzac the individual, furnished by his personal experience with a philosophy of Woman? Is it Balzac the author professing "literary" ideas on femininity? Is it universal wisdom? Romantic psychology? We shall never know, for the good reason that writing is the destruction of every voice, of every point of origin. Writing is that neutral, composite, oblique space where our subject [and this is a deliberate pun] slips away ["our subject" meaning that we don't quite know what's being talked about sometimes, but also, and more importantly, *the* subject, the authorial subject, the actual identity of the given speaking subject, is what slips away] into the negative where all identity is lost, starting with the very identity of the body writing.

At the time he wrote this essay, Barthes was writing a whole book about "Sarrasine" called *S/Z*. In this book, Barthes, known until then as a leading "structuralist," became increasingly preoccupied with the mazelike shapelessness of what seems to be structural. Although both Foucault and Barthes are dethroning the same authority in the same antiauthoritarian climate, the author is eclipsed here more completely than in Foucault, for whom "disappear" would be an overstatement.

Foucault, who I think does take for granted that a textual field is more firmly systematic than Barthes had come to suppose, says that when we speak of the author function rather than the author, we no longer raise certain questions, such as the following (913): "How can a free subject penetrate the substance of things and give it meaning? How can it activate the rules of a language from within and thus give rise to the designs which are properly its own?" In other words, we no longer ask how the author exerts autonomous will with respect to the subject matter being expressed. We do not suppose the meaning to coincide with the meaning of the author. Foucault continues:

> Instead, these questions will be raised: "How, under what conditions, and in what forms can something like a subject appear in the order of discourse? What place can it occupy in each type of discourse, what functions can it assume, and by obeying what rules?" In short, [when we speak in this way of an author function] it is a matter of depriving the subject (or its substitute) [a character, for example, or a speaker, as when we say the speaker is not the author in "My Last Duchess"] . . . of its role as originator, and of analyzing the subject as a variable and complex function of discourse.

("The subject" in "discourse" of this kind always means the subjectivity of the speaker, not the subject matter.)

With this much said about what Foucault and Barthes do and do not mean in dethroning the author, it's probably time to say something in defense of the author. I will speak for all of you who want to stand up and defend the author by quoting a wonderful passage from Samuel Johnson's "Preface to *Shakespeare*," in which he explains why we have always paid homage to the authority of the author. It's not just a question—as obviously Foucault and Barthes are always suggesting—of deferring to authority as though the authority were the police laying about them with truncheons. We can also think of authorship as human accomplishment. This is what Johnson says:

> There is always a silent reference of human works to human abilities, and as the inquiry, how far man may extend his designs or how high he may rate his native force, is of far greater

dignity than in what rank we shall place any particular performance, curiosity is always busy to discover the instruments as
well as to survey the workmanship, to know how much is to be
ascribed to original powers and how much to casual and adven-
titious help.[3]

It's all very well to consider a textual field as a system, but at the same time
we want to remind ourselves of our worth. We want to say that a "work"
(somebody's work) is not just a set of functions—variables, as one might say
in the lab. It's produced by genius. It's something that allows us to rate
human ability "high." Especially in this vale of tears—and Johnson is very
conscious of this being a vale of tears—that's what we want to keep doing.
Clutching at such straws as we can, it is in the spirit of homage rather than
in cringing fear that we appeal to the authority of an author.

But we are speaking of different times, the vale of tears having perhaps
changed in character. This is 1969, and the purpose that's alleged for appealing to the author as a paternal source, as an authority, is, according to both
Barthes and Foucault, to *police* the way texts are read even within the academy. (A very angry don at the Sorbonne had written a book against Barthes
called *Nouvelle critique, nouvelle imposture.*) In other words, both of them
insist that the appeal to the author—as opposed to the submersion of the
author in the functionality of the textual field—is a kind of delimitation or
policing of the possibilities of *meaning.*

Let me just cite two passages to that effect, first going back to Roland
Barthes (877). Barthes says, "Once the Author is removed, the claim to decipher a text becomes quite futile." By the way, once again there's a rift
here between Barthes and Foucault. Foucault wouldn't say "quite futile." He
would say we can decipher it, but that the author function is just one aspect
of the deciphering process. But Barthes had entered a phase of his career,
again, in which structures seemed so complex that they ceased to be structures. This has a great deal to do with the influence of deconstruction, to
which we'll return later in the book.

In any case, Barthes continues:

To give a text an Author is to impose a limit on that text, to furnish it with a final signified, to close the writing. Such a conception suits criticism [criticism here is a lot like policing—"criticism"
means being a nasty critic, *criticizing*] very well, the latter then
allotting itself the important task of discovering the Author (or

its hypostases: society, history, psyche, liberty [i.e., agency]) beneath the work: when the Author has been found, the text is "explained"—a victory to the critic.

In other words, the policing of meaning has been accomplished and the critic wins, just as in the uprisings of the late 1960s the cops win. We can reinforce this attitude with the pronouncement by Foucault (913): "The author is therefore the ideological figure by which one marks the manner in which we fear the proliferation of meaning."

Now once again, we are likely to counter skepticism with skepticism. You may well say, "Why shouldn't I fear the proliferation of meaning? I want to know what something definitely means. I don't want to know that it means a million things. I'm here to learn what things mean in so many words. I don't want to be told that I could sit here for the rest of my life just parsing one sentence. Don't tell me about these vertiginous sentences from Balzac's short story. I'm here to know what things mean. I don't care if it's policing or not. Whatever it is, let's get it done." The reason I could feel sympathy if you were to respond in this grumpy way is that to a certain extent the preoccupation with the ideological misuse of the appeal to an author belongs very much to its historical moment, a time when you could scarcely say the word "author" without thinking "authority," and you could certainly never say the word "authority" without thinking about the police. I know—I was then a student at Berkeley. This is a structure of thought that perhaps pervades the lives of many of us even to this day and has always pervaded the lives of many people in many places, we mustn't forget that, but it is not quite as much the default point of view in the academic world today as it was in the moment of these essays by Barthes and Foucault.

With all this said, how can the theorist recuperate honor for certain names like, for example, *her own*? "You're not an author, but I am": let's suppose someone were dastardly enough to harbor such a thought. Could you develop an argument in which the thought might actually seem to make sense? After all, Foucault—setting himself aside, he doesn't mention himself— Foucault very much admires certain writers. In particular, he admires, like so many of his generation and other generations, Marx and Freud. It's perilous to reject the police-like authority of authors in general—in some of whom we may justly discover authoritarian tendencies—when we don't feel that way about Marx and Freud. How can Foucault mount an argument in which privileged authors—that is to say, figures whom one cites positively and without a sense of being policed—can retain a place of honor?

Foucault, by the way, doesn't mention Nietzsche here, but he might very well have done because Nietzsche's idea of "genealogy" is perhaps the most important influence on Foucault's work. Frankly, I think it's just an accident that he doesn't mention him. It would have been a perfect symmetry for us, because in the last lecture we quoted Paul Ricoeur to the effect that these authors, Marx, Nietzsche, and Freud, were—and this is Ricoeur's word—"masters." Whoa! Masters? That's the last word Foucault would want to hear. How, then, does he circumvent this problem? He invents a concept. He says that Marx and Freud aren't authors but "founders of discursivity." A founder of discursivity is someone whose discourse enables constructive and progressive responses to it over time. Here he makes a subtle distinction between founders of an intellectual legacy and influential innovators in the development of genres. He speaks of Anne Radcliffe (he should be speaking of Horace Walpole, but never mind) as a person who established certain tropes, *topoi*, and premises that govern the writing of gothic fiction for the next hundred years and, indeed, even up to the present, yet should *not* be called a founder of discursivity. She doesn't establish a discourse or sphere of debate, he claims, within which ideas, without being attributable necessarily, can nevertheless be developed. This seems to me rather anti-literary, as though negotiating literary influence were not precisely a matter of speaking or writing in the wake of a "founder of discursivity," but I won't belabor the point.

Foucault is concerned also to distinguish figures like Marx and Freud from scientists like Galileo and Newton. In defense of Foucault here, notice that whereas we speak of people as Marxist or Freudian, we don't speak of people as Radcliffeian or Galilean or Newtonian. We use the adjective "Newtonian" in just the author-neutral way that Poulet used such terms in my anecdote, but we don't speak of writers who are still interested in Newtonian mechanics as "Newtonian writers." This appeal to usage may indeed justify Foucault's understanding of the textual legacy of those author functions known as Marx and Freud—whose names might be raised in Poulet's lecture class with an enthusiastic response—as placeholders for Marxist and Freudian fields of discourse. It may, in some sense, reinforce Foucault's argument that "Marx" and "Freud" are special inaugurations of debate, of developing thought, that does not necessarily cringe under the influence of the originary figure. That's certainly debatable; of course there are a great many people who think of Marx and Freud as tyrants, but within the traditions that they established, it is quite possible to understand them as instigating ways of thinking without necessarily presiding over those ways of thinking authoritatively. That in any case is the special category that Foucault wants to reserve for those privileged figures whom he calls founders of discursivity.

Very quickly then to conclude: one consequence of the death of the author and the reduction of the author to author function is, as Foucault curiously says in passing (907), that the author "has no legal status." What? What about copyright? What about intellectual property? Surely to say that the author has no legal status puts us back in the eighteenth century. Notice once again, however, the intellectual context of which Foucault is fully aware. Copyright arose as a bourgeois idea, allowing me to say that I possess my writing, I am its owner. The disappearance of the author, in keeping with the disappearance of bourgeois thought itself, entails, in fact, setting aside notions of copyright or intellectual property. In Foucault's time, Jean-Luc Godard made this point in ceasing to be director (*auteur*) and disappearing into film communes. So there is after all consistency in what Foucault is saying about the author having no legal status.

But maybe at this point it really is time to dig in our heels. "I am a lesbian Latina. I stand before you as an author articulating an identity and finding a voice for the purpose of achieving freedom; not to police you, not to deny your freedom, but to find my own freedom. I stand before you, in pride, as an author. I don't want to be called an author function. I don't want to be called an instrument of something larger than myself because frankly that's what I've always been, and now, invested in the authority of my authorship, I want to remind you that I am not anybody's instrument but that I am autonomous and free."

The traditional idea of the author, call it a paternalistic idea—so much under suspicion in the work of Foucault and Barthes in the late 1960s—can obviously be turned on its ear in this way. It can be understood as a source of *newfound* authority, of the freedom of one who is only recently liberated and hopes to be received by a reading community with that understanding. It's hard to know how a Foucault might respond; and the issues entailed bring to the surface a problem that dogs much of what we're going to read during the course of these lectures—even and especially within the sorts of theorizing that are called cultural studies and concern the politics of identity. Within those disciplines there is a division of thought between people who affirm the autonomous integrity and individuality of the identity in question and those who say any and all identities are only "subject positions"—*functions*, in short—that are revealed through the matrix of social practices. This same split exists, too, within those forms of theory that don't directly have to do with the politics of identity. A dispute arises sooner or later between those for whom what's important is the discovery of autonomous subjectivity and those for whom what's important is the discovery of an effacement of the ego or freedom from selfhood within the very instability of any and all subject positions.

So much then for these introductory lectures, which have touched lightly on key topics that we'll keep circling back to. In the next lecture we'll turn to a more sharply delineated subject matter: hermeneutics, what hermeneutics is, and how we can think about the consequences of conflicting hermeneutic premises. Our primary texts will be the excerpt from Hans-Georg Gadamer and a few passages from Martin Heidegger and E. D. Hirsch.

First Reflections on Interpretation
and Reading

CHAPTER 3

Ways In and Out of the Hermeneutic Circle

Readings:

Gadamer, Hans-Georg. "The Elevation of the Historicality of Understanding to the Status of Hermeneutic Principle." In *The Critical Tradition*, pp. 721–737.

Passages from Martin Heidegger, E. D. Hirsch.

Despite the intimidating sound of the word, "hermeneutics" is easily defined as the science of interpretation. You would think hermeneutics had always been a matter of interest, but in fact it's of continuous interest only fairly recently. Aristotle did write a treatise called *De Interpretatione*, and the Middle Ages were much concerned with interpretation, so I suppose what I'm saying in part is that the word "hermeneutics" wasn't then available; but it's also true that at many times the idea that there ought to be a systematic study of how we interpret things wasn't a matter of pressing concern.

Although there had long been prodigious feats of interpretation in the Talmudic tradition, what gave rise in the Western world to what is called "hermeneutics" was the Protestant Reformation. There's a lot of significance in that, I think, and I'll try to explain why, because at the heart of this historical fact we can find the reason why people care about interpretation at some times and don't care about it at others. You don't really puzzle your head about approaches to interpretation, how we determine the validity of interpretation and so on, until (a) meaning becomes terribly important to you, and (b) the ascertainment of meaning becomes difficult. You may ask yourself whether it isn't always the case that meaning is important and that meaning is hard to construe. Well, not necessarily. If you are a person whose sacred scripture is adjudicated by the pope and the occasional tribunal of church elders, you yourself don't really need to worry very much about what scripture means. You are told what it means. But in the wake of the Protestant Reformation, when one's relationship with the Bible became personal and everyone was engaged—with the guidance of their minister—in understanding what is after all pretty difficult stuff (who on earth knows what the parables mean?—and the whole of the Bible poses interpretative problems), then of course worries about how to interpret scripture become prevalent. Needless to say, since it's your sacred text, the meaning of it is important to you. It's crucial to you to know exactly what it means and why what it means is important.

So as Protestantism gained currency, by the same token thinking about hermeneutics took hold, and people began to write treatises about interpretation—but it was always interpretation of the Bible. In other words, in hermeneutics, religion came first because for the laity sacred texts were the only texts that it was crucial to understand. Soon enough, though, constitutional democracies began to appear, and when that happened people became much more interested—as citizens or as persons with suffrage or as persons with rights conferred by a state or nation—they became much more interested in the nature of the laws they lived under. That's why hermeneutics gradually expanded beyond religion to the study of the law. The governing principles that had been developed in thinking about interpreting scripture were then applied to the interpretation of something the meaning of which had become almost as important. You know of course that hermeneutics is inescapable in the study of the law to this day: what are the grounds for understanding the meaning of the Constitution, for example? There are widespread controversies about it, and many of the courses you would take in law school are meant to arbitrate among them. So once again you see that hermeneutics enters a field when the meaning of the foundational documents in that field becomes more important to a community of readers than it had been before and when that meaning is recognized to be difficult to grasp.

As yet we haven't said anything about literature, and the fact is that (after the medieval preoccupation with reading secular texts, especially the Greek and Roman ones, as religious allegory had died away) there was no hermeneutic art devoted to literature during the early modern period and for most of the eighteenth century. Think about the writers you've studied from the eighteenth century. It's striking that they all just take meaning for granted. Alexander Pope, for example, and even Samuel Johnson reflect on literature and why it's important and what the nature of literature is without much concern for interpretation. They're concerned instead with *evaluation*, establishing the principles of what a poem should be like and try to accomplish, while raising questions along the way that are largely moral and aesthetic. They are not concerned about interpretation because to them *good* writing is writing that's unambiguously clear, writing the meaning of which is so transparent that it doesn't *need* to be interpreted. In fact, during this whole period playwrights were writing prologues to their plays abusing each other for being obscure—that is, abusing each other *for requiring interpretation*. "I don't understand what your metaphors are all about. You don't know what a metaphor is. All you do is make one verbal mistake after another. Nobody can understand you." This is the recurrent topic of the prose and verse prefaces to theatrical pieces in the eighteenth century, and from that you can see that interpretation is not only not studied but is considered unnecessary unless you wish to read bad literature. If you have to interpret it, it isn't any good.

Then as the eighteenth century wears on, with the emergence of Romanticism—as is well known and I think often overstated—there emerges a cult of genius. At this period, the best work is said to arise from the extraordinary mental acuity or spiritual insight of the author. And with this new emphasis on the transcendent faculty of imagination, the literary creator starts to seem like the divine creator and to a certain extent becomes a placeholder for the divine creator. Remember that secularization in Western culture was increasing during the course of the Enlightenment—during the course of the eighteenth century—and as sacred scripture in some circles receded in importance, works of literary genius began to rival it. Northrop Frye has called the characteristic work of the Romantic period a "secular scripture." The meaning of this sort of literature has become more difficult—as those of you who have tackled Blake and Shelley can attest—because it is deeply personal and no longer reflects the shared values that had made for the literature of "what oft was thought but ne'er so well exprest" in the age of Pope. Thus in the Romantic period, both the importance of meaning and the difficulty of meaning increased as literature began at least partly for some readers to take over the role of religion, and at that point a literary hermeneutics became necessary.

A theologian of the Romantic period, Friedrich Schleiermacher, devoted his career to an approach to hermeneutics that was meant to be applied as much to literature as to the study of scripture, and his work established a tradition in which literature was a central concern in hermeneutic thought. What followed directly from Schleiermacher was the work of Wilhelm Dilthey around the turn of the century, of Martin Heidegger in his *Being and Time* of 1927, and of Gadamer. There is a rival tradition that descends from Kant through Husserl to Emilio Betti and E. D. Hirsch, and we shall consider Hirsch's quarrel with Gadamer in due course.

So what is the basic problematic for hermeneutics in the tradition of Schleiermacher? Probably you have all heard of the "hermeneutic circle." It describes the relationship between a reader and a text or—in the view of certain students of hermeneutics but not that of Gadamer—of a relationship between a reader and an author. Hirsch, for example, thinks the hermeneutic circle is a relationship between a reader and an author, with the text a kind of a mediatory document pointing toward the meaning of the author. But for Gadamer and his tradition, the circle is very differently conceived, as we shall see when I point out Gadamer's perhaps surprising attitude toward "romanticism." In the meantime, though, all would agree that the circular relationship between a reader and a text or author can be described in a variety of ways. It's often put in terms of the relationship between the part and the whole, and here is how the problematic of circularity enters into it: I approach a text and of course the first thing I read is a phrase or a sentence. There's still a lot more of the text and so that first fragment is a *part*, but I immediately begin to form an opinion about this part based on an imagined or supposed *whole*, an opinion that I project from this part or else possess in advance of this initial reading. I then use this sense of what the whole must be like to continue to read successive parts—lines, sentences, whatever they may be. I keep referring those successive parts back to a sense of the whole, which after all *changes* as a result of knowing more and more of the parts. The circularity of this interpretative engagement involves moving from a part to a preconception about the whole, back to the next part, back to a revised sense of the whole, and so on in a circular pattern.

This circularity can also be understood as an interchange between the present and the past—between my particular historical horizon and some other historical horizon that I'm trying to come to terms with. I bring what I know about the world to bear on my engagement with the text; I consider what the text seems to be saying in relation to what I already knew while allowing the text to modify my knowledge by imparting its own. Finally, because hermeneutics isn't just a bridge across a historical gulf—because it also can come into play across a social or cultural gulf, maybe not even very much of a gulf—we are still performing a hermeneutic act when we simply engage each other in conversation. I have to try to understand what you're saying, referring my interpretation of your message to what I want to say, and the circuit of communication between us has to stay open to ensure a mutual and developing understanding of what we're talking about. It's the same thing, more obviously, with conversations across cultures. So hermeneutics doesn't always concern what Gadamer would call merging *historical* horizons. It's also about merging social and cultural and interpersonal horizons as well. All of that is entailed in what Gadamer means by *Horizontverschmelzung.*

Here is Gadamer's version of how the circularity of this thinking works (722):

> [The reader—Gadamer's word is "he"] projects before himself a meaning for the text as a whole as soon as some initial meaning emerges in the text. [In other words, as soon as he sees what the part is like, he projects or imagines what the whole must be that contains this part.] Again the latter [that is, the sense of the initial meaning] emerges only because he is reading the text with particular expectations in regard to a certain meaning. The working out of this fore-project [that is, the sense we have in advance of the meaning of what we are going to read], which is constantly revised in terms of what emerges as he penetrates into the meaning, is understanding what is there.

"What is there" is an expression that Gadamer inherits from Heidegger, and it corresponds with what Gadamer means when he frequently talks about *die Sache,* the "subject matter." In other words, the effort a reader makes in coming to terms with the meaning of a text is an effort to master the subject matter, what is there: I suppose it would be fair enough to say, as a colloquial paraphrase, "what the text is really about."

Anyway, you can see that in this passage Gadamer is describing the circularity of our reading in a way that may raise some concerns. We are given pause, here and elsewhere, by his harping on "fore-structure," "fore-project," "fore-having." Can't I view "what is there," as we might say, objectively? In other words, won't I be hopelessly prejudiced about what I read if I've got some sort of preliminary conception of what its meaning is? Why can't I just set aside my preliminary conceptions, especially as the text tells me more and more, so that I can understand precisely what is there? Even given that the text tells me more and more, how am I ever going to understand what is there if you tell me that each revision of what I think as a result of further reading nevertheless becomes in itself yet another fore-project or preliminary conception?

This claim is especially difficult to credit when Heidegger and Gadamer then insist that even though we always interpret within our preliminary conceptions—Gadamer boldly *calls* them "prejudices," as we'll see—there nevertheless are, as Heidegger puts it, two ways into the circle, a good way and a bad way. A circle, in other words, is not necessarily a vicious circle, as you are tempted to conclude it is if you can't escape preconceptions. Gadamer and Heidegger insist that the way into the circle can also be "constructive."

To understand this claim, take a look in the appendix at the second passage from Heidegger, just the first sentence of it, where he says, "In an interpretation, the way in which the entity we are interpreting is to be conceived can be drawn from the entity itself, or the interpretation can force the entity into concepts to which it is opposed in its manner of being." You might well ask how you can draw anything "from the entity itself" if you are trapped in preconceptions. Well, let me give you an example in support of Heidegger's distinction. In the eighteenth century, a poet named Mark Akenside wrote a long verse essay called *The Pleasures of the Imagination* (1744), where you will find a line about the "The Sovereign spirit of the world" raising "his plastic arm."[1] We modern readers are into polymers. We know what plastic is. Strictly from within our own horizons we don't hesitate to conclude that the creator raised a prosthetic limb. But, after all, we do know something about the horizon within which Akenside was writing his poem: we are aware that in the eighteenth century the word "plastic" meant "sinuous," "powerful," "flexible," so we can open our closed horizon and conclude that the great creator raised his sinuous, powerful, flexible arm—which, we can't help noticing, makes a lot more sense.

Here you have the difference between good and bad prejudice. The good prejudice is our *prior awareness*—still a "prejudice" (*Vorurteil*, prejudgment)—that plastic has changed its meaning. The bad prejudice is when we leap to the conclusion, without thinking for a moment that there might be some other historical horizon, that plastic is a polymer. If we invoke the eighteenth-century meaning, we immediately see that the line makes perfect sense; but if we bring our own meaning to bear, we have to admit that the line is nonsense.

I'll come back to this example later on when we read an essay called "The Intentional Fallacy" by W. K. Wimsatt, and I will then raise the possibility that there might actually be some value in supposing that the creator of the world raised his prosthetic limb. But for the moment it should be plain to you that this is a good way of understanding what the difference between a useful preconception and a useless preconception brought to bear on an interpretative act might consist in.

Now in giving the example, I've gotten a little bit ahead of myself, so let me go back and fill in some blanks. As you can tell from your reading of Gadamer—and also from the title of the great book from which this excerpt is taken, *Truth and Method* (*Wahrheit und Methode*), with its implicit suggestion that there is a *difference* between truth and method—as you can tell, the great objection of Gadamer to other people's way of doing hermeneutics is that they believe there is a *methodology* of interpretation. The basic methodology Gadamer is attacking in the excerpt you've read is what he calls "historicism."

"Historicism" is a complicated word for us because later in the course we're going to be exploring the New Historicism, which has nothing to do, or very little, with what Gadamer is objecting to here. What Gadamer means by "historicism" is the belief that you can set aside preconceptions, that you can completely factor out your own subjectivity, your own view of things, in order to enter into the mindset of some other time or place: that you can completely enter another mind, leaving your own behind. This is the "method" of achieving "historical objectivity," and as we'll see at the end of this lecture, there's a certain nobility about it that should be juxtaposed with the nobility of Gadamerian hermeneutics. Gadamer objects to historicism in this sense in the first place because he thinks it's impossible. You cannot factor out preconceptions. All you can do is acknowledge another horizon without attempting the impossible feat of "bracketing" or setting aside your own horizon altogether. You try to find common ground, to find some way of merging a present with a past, a here with a there, which can result in what Gadamer calls, again, "horizon merger." The positive result of horizon merger is what Gadamer calls "effective history," by which he means history that is useful—history that really can go to work for us, history from which we can learn, not just an archive that objectifies the past. Gadamer also thinks that there's something immoral about historicism, even if it were possible, because it condescends toward the past, presuming that the past is simply a repository of information and forgetting that it may have something to teach us. We'll return to this point in the end.

Perhaps in order to make this viewpoint seem plausible, we should study it more reflectively for a moment. After all, most of us are proud of our capacity for objectivity and don't wish to be shaken in our conviction that we can "bracket" our prejudices (as Husserl would say) and view the past or any other form of otherness for what it is. So let's look at a couple of passages from Heidegger's "analytic of the hermeneutic circle" in *Being and Time,* to see what Heidegger has to say about this claim. First:

> When we have to do with anything, the mere seeing of the things which are closest to us bears in itself the structure of interpretation and in so primordial a manner that just to grasp something free, as it were, of the "as" requires a certain adjustment.

What is Heidegger saying? Let me try a thought experiment. I look to the back of the room, where I see that sign that says "exit." I'm not interpreting it. I don't have any preconception about it. I'm just looking. But wait. How do I know it's a sign? How do I know it says "exit"? I bring a thousand preconceptions to bear on what I take to be a simple act of looking. Heidegger concedes that it's not at all uninteresting to imagine the possibility of "just seeing" something without seeing it *as* something ("free, as it were, of the 'as'"). It might be exhilarating just to have something before us. But he thinks that is well nigh impossible. It is a very difficult mental act to *forget* that I am looking at a sign that says "exit" and just to look at "what is there" without knowing what it is. In other words, I don't *not* know first that that's a sign that says "exit." There may be sensory stimulus but there is no prior act of consciousness. The very first thing I know, whether accurately or not, is that an object is some particular thing and not something else.

As Heidegger points out, then, the seemingly primordial moment of "just having something before us," if it can be experienced at all, *derives* from the forgetting of preconceptions. I am always already in possession of an interpretation of whatever object I look at, which isn't at all to say that my interpretation is correct. It's only to say that I can't escape the fact that the very first movement of mind, not the last movement but the first movement of mind, is interpretative. Continue the passage: "This grasping which is free of the 'as' is a privation of the kind of seeing [and you see how attracted

Heidegger is to it because he shifts his rhetoric] in which one merely understands." In short, it would be a remarkable experience *not* to understand. It's a kind of imprisonment, understanding, and when Heidegger says that it would be exciting not to have to *merely* understand, he's also insisting that this is an incredibly difficult, if not impossible, contortion of thought. So that's why we must realize that when we are interpreters (and we are always interpreters, every moment of our lives), we are always working with preconceptions, "prejudices."

Now what about Gadamer's word "prejudice"? He sees that it will be an affront to our sensibilities and is somewhat defensive about it, going into the appropriate etymologies. The French *préjugé* and the German *Voruteil* both mean "prejudgment" or "prior judgment." Prejudices in this sense can actually be used in courts of law, he says, as a stage in the process of arriving at a verdict. They needn't be thought of as vulgar prejudices (instances of entering the circle in a bad way). One of these latter by the way is the "prejudice against prejudice," which Gadamer considers the characteristic stance of the European Enlightenment—the prejudice that enables its claim to objectivity.

But prejudice is harmful. We know what prejudice has wrought historically and socially, so how dare we try to vindicate it in this way? It has to be admitted that what Gadamer does in the excerpt you have read is to perform an act of intellectual conservatism at the least. That whole section of the excerpt in which he talks about "classicism" may seem at first blush to be a digression. We should realize, though, that when he discusses classicism, which he later calls "tradition," he is establishing his claim that we really can't merge horizons effectively unless we have a very broad and extensive common ground to share with what we're reading. The great thing about classicism for Gadamer, or "tradition," is that he supposes it to be something we can share. The classical, Gadamer argues, is that which doesn't speak mainly to its own historical moment but speaks for all time, speaks to all of us in different ways but does speak to us, proffering its claim to speak true.

Certainly, we realize, Gadamer is entitled to an intellectually conservative canon. He is not sure people can understand the past or otherness unless they share a great deal of common ground. But without drawing any necessary inferences about Gadamer himself, we can see that right here is where the "vulgar," destructive aspect of prejudice has a chance to sneak in. Slavery was considered perfectly appropriate and natural to a great many of the most exalted figures working within the tradition that Gadamer rightly calls classical—classical antiquity, including a great many figures of the modern era who never stopped to question slavery. Gadamer doesn't talk about this, although political philosophers and historians of thought often do, but we recognize that this is an aspect of that prejudice that one might share with tradition if one weren't somewhat more critical, more self-distancing, than the gesture of sharing common ground might imply. While plainly we can understand "prejudice" simply to mean inescapable precon-ception, an acceptable and indeed necessary way into the hermeneutic cir-cle, it would be foolish to abandon our prejudice against prejudice altogether.

What I'd like to do in the rest of this lecture is to call your attention to two passages, one in Gadamer's text that I'm about to cite and the other the fourth passage in the appendix by an American scholar, E. D. Hirsch, whom you may know as the author of a dictionary of what every school child should know and as a hero of the intellectual right during the whole period when literary theory flourished. Hirsch was always a serious student of hermeneutics and conducted a long-standing feud with Gadamer about the principles of interpretation.

This by way of prelude: Gadamer is opposed not only to historicism but to what he calls "romanticism" in hermeneutics because, as I indicated ear-lier, romanticism is focused on the mind of the author. Gadamer thinks the encounter of the reader should be with a text, not an author, because what he calls the "subject matter" of the text (*die Sache*) belongs at least as much to its historical horizon as to an individual mind. Hirsch in contrast thinks that meaning is "an affair of consciousness not of words"; that is, meaning is to be found neither in a moment of intellectual history nor in the words of a text considered simply as words, but in reference to the mind of its author. Hirsch's appeal to "intention" is a matter to which we'll soon return.

These two passages juxtapose the viewpoints that I've been trying to evoke in describing Gadamer's position. The dignity and nobility of what Gadamer says is that it involves being interested in something "true," keep-ing open the possibility that there could be a connection between meaning, arriving at meaning, and arriving at something that speaks to us as true. Hirsch, on the other hand, is evoking a completely different kind of dignity. What I want you to realize as we juxtapose these passages is that it is impos-sible to reconcile them, yet they pose for us a choice that needs to be made and perhaps suggests differing forms of commitment.

Gadamer says (735; here again he's attacking historicism):

> The text that is understood historically is forced to abandon its
> claim that it is uttering something true. We think we understand

when we see the past from a historical standpoint, i.e., place ourselves in the historical situation and seek to reconstruct the historical horizon. In fact, however, we have given up the claim to
find, in the past, any truth valid and intelligible for ourselves.

This argument would also apply to cultural conversation. If I'm proud of
knowing that in another culture when I belch after dinner it's a compliment
to the cook but draw no conclusions from this knowledge (other than "but
not where I come from"), that would be the equivalent of historicism. It's just
a factoid for me, not an effort to come to terms with anything. Gadamer
continues: "Thus, this acknowledgment of the otherness of the other, which
makes him the object of objective knowledge, involves the fundamental
suspension of his claim to truth." This is a devastating and, I think, brilliant
argument that ought to remind us of what's at risk when we champion
objectivity.

All right, but now listen to Hirsch. This isn't an easy choice. What
Hirsch says, rightly invoking Kant, is this: "Kant held it to be a foundation
of moral action that men should be conceived as ends in themselves, not as
instruments of other men." In other words, you are a means and not an end
to me as long as I'm exploiting you and instrumentalizing you. That's Kant's
position, which Hirsch is leaping to defend. If I don't think I can come to
terms with the actual meaning of an entity *as* that entity, as an end in itself,
I am *appropriating* it for my own benefit. This turns the whole idea of being
open to the possibility that the other is speaking true upside-down. Does it
matter only if it teaches me something?

Hirsch continues:

> This imperative is transferable to the words of men because
> speech is an extension and expression of men in the social do-
> main and also because when we fail to conjoin a man's intention
> to his words, we lose the soul of speech, which is to convey mean-
> ing and to understand what is intended to be conveyed.

Notice that although the nobility of this in contrast with the nobility of
Gadamer's sentiment is obvious and makes us feel torn—notice, however,
that unlike Gadamer, Hirsch is not saying anything about truth. He's talking about securing meaning—which is surely a good thing—and he's making the notion of arriving at a correct meaning as persuasive as he possibly
can, but it remains significant that he's not talking about truth. For Hirsch

the important thing is the meaning. For Gadamer the important thing is that the meaning be true, and that's where the distinction essentially lies. Because of his belief in the inescapability of preconception, Gadamer is willing to sacrifice historical or cultural exactitude of meaning. He says there's always something of me in my interpretation, insisting, however, that the hermeneutic circle is a vicious one if I am not mindful of other horizons. I must not say that "plastic" means "polymer," but I need to remember that it's I, within my climate of education, who know that "plastic" once meant something different, and I who take a special interest in plastic precisely because its meaning has changed.

It is actually unfair to Hirsch, by the way, to say that he disregards truth. Certainly it matters to Hirsch whether the other speaks true (that's why he has since said that schoolchildren must learn a common core of truths), but that conviction is not implicit in the philosophical position he takes up in this passage. At least in part for this reason, for any scholar, for any reader, this is a choice between incommensurables that really does have to be made. It's a choice that looms over a course in literary theory and in coming to understand the tradition of literary theory. You have not seen anywhere near the last of the distinction between these two positions that I've been making today.

CHAPTER 4

Configurative Reading

Reading:

Iser, Wolfgang. "The Reading Process: A Phenomenological Approach." In
The Critical Tradition, pp. 1002–1014.

In this lecture we continue discussing approaches to interpretation. Before
we talk further about E. D. Hirsch and then move to Wolfgang Iser, I want
to go back to Gadamer and say something more about his implied taste in
books, about the kind of literary and intellectual canon that his approach
to hermeneutics establishes. You remember that Gadamer is concerned with
the norm of classicism, which later in your excerpt he begins to call "tradition." The reason tradition is so important for him is not quite the same as
the reason tradition is important for a political or cultural conservative;
Gadamer thinks the reader has a limited capacity to understand a remote
horizon. He doesn't think the reader can perform miracles in intuitively
feeling his or her way into the outlook of another time and place; hence the
value of classicism, or tradition, is that there is evident common ground in
the texts we call classical. Sometimes we refer to them as "great books," the
sorts of text that speak, or we feel as though they're speaking, to all places
and times. It's widely contested whether there is really any merit in talking
about texts that way when their historical differences remain so profound
and sometimes so inassimilable, but for the moment I repeat only that

39

Gadamer's conservatism about the canon is related to his doubt about the ability of readers to span enormous *gaps*. I use that word "gaps" advisedly here because it is the word to which Wolfgang Iser attaches a wholly positive value in talking about the advantage of distance between the reader and the text and also about the semantic distance between successive moments of a text, as we'll see.

Does Gadamer underestimate the mental leaps of which readers are capable? Perhaps so. In a footnote elaborating on this question (731), he says something peculiar: "just as in conversation, we understand irony to the extent to which we are in agreement on the subject with the other person." That is, if you are expressing an opinion that differs radically from my own, Gadamer thinks I will not be able to understand whether you're being ironic, or what your irony means if you are. This seems to me just patently false. Think about politics: political talk shows, political campaigns. When our political opponent is being ironic about our views, we understand the irony perfectly well. We're used to it, we have accommodated ourselves to it, and of course our opponent understands our ironies, too. There is a kind of symbiosis, ironically enough, between political opponents precisely in the measure to which their ironies are mutually intelligible, and surely this applies to conversation in general. It's quite easy to decode most forms of irony, and this facility surely doesn't depend on any necessary, underlying agreement.

Now if I'm right to think this, perhaps we have found a loophole in Gadamer's conservatism about the elasticity of the reader's mind. His premise is that in order to understand, there has to be a basis of agreement; but if what we've just said is true about understanding each other's ironies even where there is disagreement, that ought to apply also to our capacity to read texts with which we distinctly disagree, the value of which we therefore feel we can never affirm but which we nevertheless can understand. Hence if understanding is not predicated on agreement, the possibility of "opening up the canon," as we put it, conceding that it doesn't have to be a continuous traditional canon, is available to us once again and Gadamer's conservatism on this issue can be set aside.

It's not that Gadamer is insisting on *absolute* continuity, however. On the contrary. You'll remember what he says early in the excerpt: in order to recognize that we are in the presence of an expression or idea that isn't comfortably within our own historical horizon, we need to be "pulled up short." In other words, to go back to our previous example, we need to recognize that there's something weird about Akenside's word "plastic," and in being pulled up short we recognize the need also for the fundamental act of reading that

Gadamer calls a merger of horizons. In such moments, we knowingly confront a horizon not our own that has to be negotiated if understanding is to take place.

And we can do it, too, even according to Gadamer. In fact, he insists that if we don't have this experience of being pulled up short, our reading is imprisoned. We just take it for granted that what we're reading belongs exclusively to our own horizon and we don't make any effort at all to understand what is fundamentally or at least in some ways alien to it. Gadamer acknowledges this, even insists on it as I say, but he doesn't lay stress on it because the gap that is implied in the need to be pulled up short is not a big one. We can easily traverse it. Just to belabor the example of "plastic": if we don't understand the eighteenth-century meaning of the word, we still notice that the modern meaning is implausible, so we go to the *Oxford English Dictionary*, we see it meant something different then, our problem is solved, and we continue to read. But there may be other occasions for being pulled up short that in Gadamer's view exceed the imaginative grasp of a reader. As you'll see when we turn to Iser, this is the fundamental difference between Gadamer and Iser, who remains in some ways Gadamer's disciple. Where for Gadamer the gap between reader and text, between my horizon and the horizon of the text, must be perforce a small one, for Iser it *needs* to be a much larger one in order for what he calls the "act of the reader," the reading act, really to swing into high gear, and we'll see that this difference accounts for the obvious difference between their two implied canons.

At this point, however, I want to discuss the other passages by Hirsch that we cited at the end of the last lecture (see also the appendix). As to that passage, quickly to review, you remember Gadamer said that we must not try to suppress our own outlook in approaching the otherness of the past if we wish the past to "speak true" to us. If we simply bracket out our own feelings, that can't possibly happen, so we are enjoined to think of reading as an active conversation. Hirsch argues, on the other hand, borrowing from Kant, that past and culturally disparate authors should be an end and not a means for us, so we ought to understand them strictly on their terms.

I introduced Hirsch in that context, then, and now I want to go back to him briefly. First there is Hirsch's argument, also mentioned in the last lecture, that "meaning is an affair of consciousness and not of words." In other words, the text is what makes the ascertainment of meaning available to us, but meaning is not *in* the text. Meaning belongs to the intention of the author, and that is what we need to arrive at as we work through the text. We must refer the words on the page to an authorial consciousness.

To put it another way, we refer a verbal expression to a *thought*. What this means, as Hirsch argues in a book called *The Aims of Interpretation,* is that in understanding a text we should attempt to grasp it in paraphrase. The beginning of our response might go something like: "What the author means to say is . . ." Hence we do not look for what the *text* means——it might mean anything, according to Hirsch, if you appeal to the text alone: "I ran out of gas" could mean "I raced out of a cloud of argon." Rather we should attempt to discover what the author "means to say."

It's tempting to say that this is just absolute total nonsense. We use a text in that case, which is actual and ready to hand, to find meaning in something at best virtual, something we don't have available to us? Why don't we just find meaning in the text? That would make more sense. We have no choice but to construe the text. We can't possibly know what the author meant except on the basis of our determination of the sense of the words in the text, so why not just focus our attention on that sense as its meaning? "I raced out of a cloud of argon" is just as implausible if we appeal to verbal context—except perhaps an imaginable science fiction context—as if we appeal to the intention of an author. Hirsch was a student of W. K. Wimsatt, the author of "The Intentional Fallacy," but obviously a rebellious one, as we'll see when we turn to Wimsatt. Thinking in part of Wimsatt, Hirsch insisted that appealing to intention is the only thing you can do in order to establish—according to the title of his first important book on hermeneutics—"validity in interpretation."

It's very difficult, then, intuitively to assent to Hirsch's position, and I'll just let you know by the way that I don't, for reasons that will accumulate as these lectures continue; but I will say in defense of Hirsch that if we reflect on the matter, we must realize that for a great many practical purposes we do establish meaning as authorial intent through the test of paraphrase. For example, you've all heard your instructors tell you before you take an exam: "Don't just parrot the words of the authors you're studying. I want to know that you understand those authors." Think about it. You prove to your teacher that you understand the authors by being able to put their meaning *in other words.* In this way, you describe the author's intended meaning, not just what the text says, which you could demonstrate by making your exam one long quotation. The instructor wants explanation, not quotation, and the form of explanation is paraphrase. You can't have paraphrase unless you can identify a meaning that is interpersonal, a meaning that can be shared among a group that understands it and can express it in other words. What

Hirsch argues is that if you can put an author's words in other words, those other words will secure the intended meaning, the author's *thought*.

That's a rather important argument in Hirsch's favor, I think, yet even on this point an objection occurs to us: as we've already indicated, we *always* describe meaning "in other words." "I raced out of an argon cloud" may or may not be the meaning of "I ran out of gas" no matter whether we appeal to the sense of a text or the meaning of an author, but it is a paraphrase in either case. This much, however, we can concede (and it will matter to have done so when we come to consider whether there is any such thing as a "referent" for an utterance): we need to realize that, practically speaking, the necessity of appealing to paraphrase in order to guarantee mutual understanding certainly does entail presupposing that meaning is a *referred-to thought*.

A course of lectures on literary theory will inevitably show the ways in which paraphrase is inadequate to the task of rigorous interpretation, so—again—I won't say much about it now. Cleanth Brooks, a New Critic and critical ally of Hirsch's mentor Wimsatt, had written an essay called "The Heresy of Paraphrase," no doubt also on Hirsch's mind, insisting that literary interpretation is a wooden, mechanical, inflexible exercise if it reduces the complexity of a textual surface to paraphrase. And there I'll leave the question of paraphrase for the moment.

Hirsch argues in another passage I've given you—I'll paraphrase now!—that Gadamer fails to realize the difference between the *meaning* of a text and the *significance* of a text. This is Hirsch's other key position, and we can understand it as follows: The meaning of a text is what the author intended it to mean, which we can establish with a reliable paraphrase. The significance of the text, to which Hirsch does not deny interest, is the meaning *for us*—the way in which, for example, we can translate it into our own terms historically or can adapt it to a cause or to an intellectual outlook. Hirsch insists—and here, of course, is where his distinction becomes controversial—that it's possible to tell the difference between meaning and significance. If, good historicists that you may be, you can pin down accurately and incontestably the author's meaning, appealing to all the philological evidence available, throwing out irrelevancies, and becoming convinced that you finally have the meaning right, then, once you've done that, you can impose any sort of significance on the text that you wish.

Gadamer does not comment on the distinction, but he certainly would not agree that we can distinguish between meaning and significance with any reliability. Because the proper and necessary way into the hermeneutic circle is to arrive at a merger of horizons, our own horizon and the horizon of the text, we cannot know with clarity where meaning leaves off and significance begins. As a matter of definition, Hirsch's distinction is in itself clear enough and even rather bracing. Yet to secure the distinction in actual practice, to say that you know the author's meaning and will now, in a wholly distinct gesture, explain how the meaning is significant for you— well, that would be a feat.

Turning then to Wolfgang Iser: this theorist is concerned with what he calls the act of the reader, or of reading—*Der Akt des Lesens* is the title of one of his books—and with this emphasis he joins the tradition of phenomenology deriving from Husserl and more directly, in Iser's case, from an analyst of the way in which the reader moves from sentence to sentence in negotiating a text, the Polish scholar Roman Ingarden, who is quoted frequently in the essay you've read. (It is with Ingarden in mind that Iser speaks of the "gaps," of which Ingarden does not approve, between sentence-thought and sentence-thought—not, that is, the gaps between text and reader.) Those writers together with Gadamer are the primary influences on Iser, who has been tremendously influential in turn. His interest in the reader's experience helped found a school of thought at the University of Konstanz in the 1960s and 1970s, resulting in a series of seminars on what was called "reception history" or, alternatively, "the aesthetics of reception." One of Iser's Konstanz colleagues was Hans Robert Jauss, whom we will be discussing eventually. The influence of the so-called Konstanz School spread to the United States and had many ramifications here, especially in the early work of another critic we'll be turning to later in this book, Stanley Fish.

Reception history has been a partly theoretical, partly scholarly field, one that's still flourishing in recent movements, such as "the history of the book" and the study of media reception. Later in his career, Iser taught annually at the University of California, Irvine, and by that time he was pursuing a new aspect of his project that he called the anthropology of fiction, posing the fundamental questions of why we have fiction and why we tell stories to each other. All of Iser's work is grounded in the notion of literature as fiction. He's almost exclusively a scholar of the novel. In fact, an important difference between Iser and Gadamer is that whereas Gadamer is an intellectual historian whose canonical texts are works of philosophy, works of social thought, and classical works of literature, Iser has always been a student of literary narrative.

Yet despite these differences, you'll see as you read Iser that in tone and in his understanding of the way we negotiate the world of texts he much more closely resembles Gadamer than Hirsch. We can put this in two different ways. We can say for one thing that Iser reconstructs what Gadamer says—and Hirsch denies—about the merger of horizons. For example, he says (1002), "The convergence of text and reader brings the literary work into existence." Gadamer would speak of the merger of the reader's horizon with the horizon within which the text appears. "Convergence," "merger": It's not the text's horizon; it's not the reader's horizon; it's the effective history that takes place when those horizons merge that constitutes the "work"—partly someone else's work, partly the reader's. This amounts to saying that the space of meaning is "virtual"—the word Iser uses: "[A]nd this convergence can never be precisely pinpointed, but must always remain virtual, and is not to be identified either with the reality of the text or with the individual disposition of the reader."

In addition, Iser plainly shares with Gadamer the conviction that the construal of meaning cannot be altogether objective. He is no more of a historicist than Gadamer is but insists rather on the mutual exchange of prejudice between the two horizons in question (1005): "One text is potentially capable of several different realizations, and no reading can ever exhaust the full potential, for each individual reader will fill in the gaps in his own way." "Gaps," again, is an interesting term. I don't actually know whether Iser—to be Hirschian—*means* what I'm about to say about gaps, but apart from designating openings of finite width, "gaps" also call spark plugs to mind. For the electrical current to operate in a spark plug, the two points of contact have to be "gapped." They have to be forced apart to a certain degree but not too far. Too much, there's no spark. Too little, you short out and there's no spark. It seems to me, then, that the "ah-ha" effect of reading, the movement back and forth across the gap between the reader and the text, can be understood as though the relationship between the reader and the text were the relationship between the two points of a spark plug.

How then does Iser differ from Gadamer? There is one point of difference that is interesting in view of what we've just been saying about Hirsch, and there's another crucial point of difference, mentioned already, to which we need to return. First, then, Iser actually seems to distinguish (1006) between "reading" and "interpretation": "[T]he text refers back directly to our own preconceptions"—Gadamer would call those "prejudices"—"which are revealed by the act of interpretation that is a basic element of the reading process." There's a wedge in this sentence between reading and interpretation that seems to resemble the wedge Hirsch drives between meaning and significance. Meaning or reading is construal; significance or interpretation is the application of that construal. Iser doesn't make much of the distinction, however, so in this respect his divergence from Gadamer is slight.

The other divergence, though, is central to Iser's thought. To return, then, to this point, Iser stresses *innovation* as the principle of value governing the interpretive strategies of reading. Innovation is what Iser's canon values, and that's what makes it so different from Gadamer's continuous traditional canon. Iser's understanding of gapping the spark plug boldly affirms the imaginative powers of the reader. In order to illustrate how what Iser calls "virtual work" gets done in this regard, let me just run through a few passages quickly. Whereas Gadamer says, again, but without emphasis, that in order to become aware that there is a difference between your own horizon and the horizon of the text you need to be "pulled up short," to be surprised, Iser throws his whole emphasis on this element of surprise. If it doesn't surprise, it doesn't have value, it's what critics and Iser himself condescendingly call "culinary"—overly familiar like routine cooking. If the element of surprise is to play its key role in the reading process, the gap has to stretch to the utmost, and that's what Iser is saying in the passages I'm about to quote rapid-fire.

"In this process of creativity"—the way in which a text induces the feeling of surprise in the reader—"the text may either not go far enough, or may go too far" (1003). In this particular passage, admittedly, you get a hint of Gadamer's conservatism. The text may "go too far," making demands on us that are too great. *Finnegans Wake* strikes some readers this way. We can't get from sentence to sentence, and even within a sentence we have no idea what the words mean. Many readers do enthusiastically meet the challenge; but in Iser's terms this sort of text has at least risked going too far. Again: "[W]e may say that boredom and overstrain form the boundaries beyond which the reader will leave the field of play." If there are no surprises, there's no point in reading the text. If the surprises are too great, they induce overstrain and we throw the book away in frustration.

"[E]xpectations," says Iser, "are scarcely ever fulfilled in a truly literary text" (1004). "Expectations" mediate the hermeneutic circle as it applies to the reading process Iser describes. Reading consists, according to Iser, in the violation of expectations. Yet to offset this freedom from the predictable, there has to be a sense, moving from sentence to sentence, that *something* is likely to happen next, whatever it may be. If that underlying sense isn't there, then whatever happens is simply met with frustration, but if we have the expectation that something's going to happen next, and then something different happens, that's all to the good. This is the evaluative principle that completely revolutionizes Gadamer's implied canon. Not continuity but innovation, the expectation of violated expectation, is what imposes or establishes value in the literary text. We don't sense that across the abyss truth is being spoken to us; we sense rather that across the abyss we are being constructively surprised.

When Iser does mention "expository texts," he may be alluding to Gadamer, who has expository texts chiefly in mind: works of philosophy and social thought that aren't trying to surprise or trick us but trying instead to lay out an argument that is consistent and continuous, keeping surprise to a minimum. It's difficult, philosophy and social thought, but it's not difficult because of the element of surprise. It's the vocabulary and the complexity of the thought that make it difficult. Iser acknowledges this: "[W]e implicitly demand of expository texts . . . [that there be no surprise] as we refer to the objects they are meant to present—[but it's] a defect in a literary text." Here is the difference for Iser between nonfiction and fiction.

The word "defamiliarization" we will encounter soon when we take up the Russian formalists. "Defamiliarization" means, precisely, pulling you up short or taking you by surprise, making you feel that what you thought was going to be the case or what you thought was the state of affairs is not the state of affairs. The poet Wallace Stevens puts it beautifully when he says that poetry should "make the visible a little hard to see"; in other words, it should defamiliarize that which has become too familiar and predictable. It is to this aspect of the reading process that Iser refers in saying: "[The] defamiliarization of what the reader thought he recognized is bound to create a tension that will intensify his expectations as well as his distrust of those expectations" (1010).

This pronouncement transfers value at least in part to what might be called the psychology of reading. Reading requires the tension of simultaneously having expectations and feeling that they should be violated, that probably they will be violated, and being on the alert for how they're going to be violated. This kind of tension provides, for Iser, the psychological excitement of reading. In short, Iser thinks the healthy reader should work hard and forego relaxation. There's not enough work to do in either of two scenarios: if, on the one hand, the text just seems real, if there's no spin on the everyday and there's no sense of this being a fictive world. Here the gap isn't big enough. As an implied evaluation of what is being read, this is a disputable claim. The history of fiction recurrently favors fictional worlds that aspire to be identical to the way things are. Arguably, Jonathan Franzen's novels are well received for this reason. The violation of expectations is not the driving force behind this kind of fiction. Another kind of psychological pleasure is involved that Iser is perhaps not taking into account, the pleasure in imitation that causes us to exclaim, as Aristotle says, "Ah, that is he."

On the other hand, Iser says, neither is there any value in reading a text in which an illusion is perpetually sustained. In other words, a never-never land is created that we know to be an illusion, but we get to live in it so comfortably and with so little alteration of expectation once we're there that it becomes womblike and cozy. Here Iser is referring to what he calls "culinary fiction," subgenres of literature like nurse novels, bodice rippers, and certain kinds of detective fiction—although a lot of detective fiction is much better than that description would imply. The pauper rarely gets to marry the prince in life, but in culinary fiction it's an unviolated expectation that this will happen. Iser disapproves, then, of both these reading experiences because there's no reading work to be done.

The relationship between text and reader must be a collaboration, Iser argues. The polysemantic nature of the text—the fact that the text hazards many possibilities of meaning if it's a good text—and the allure of comfortable illusion for the reader are constructively opposed factors. In other words, there is something in any reader that does undeniably wish to settle comfortably into the fiction of untransformed reality or into the world of the nurse novel or the bodice ripper; but a good text is perpetually bringing the reader up short and preventing that comfort zone from establishing itself, so that the tension between the tendency on our part to sustain an illusion and the way in which the text keeps undermining the illusion is again that aspect of the psychological excitement, the "tension," of reading that Iser wants to promote.

Now a word about *Tony the Tow Truck*. I wanted to call attention to a few places where the issue of expectation and its possible violation arises. It's only fair to say that if we're going to read *Tony* seriously in this way we have to put ourselves in the shoes, or booties, of a toddler; as readers or auditors we have to regard the psychological excitement of experiencing the text as that of a toddler. It's not so very difficult to do. For example:

I am Tony the Tow Truck.
I live in a little yellow garage.

> I help cars that are stuck.
> I tow them to my garage.
> I like my job.
> One day I am stuck.
> Who will help Tony the tow truck?

This is a wonderful example of the tension between having an expectation, the expectation that someone will help Tony, and being in a state of suspense, not knowing who that someone will be. From the adult point of view, this is a culinary moment because we know that we're in the world of folklore and that in folklore everything happens three times. We know without reading farther that two vehicles are going to come along and refuse to help Tony and that the third vehicle will. Notice even the title: *Tony the Tow Truck*, with its alliterative triad. When we read the Russian formalists, we will encounter one of their early research findings: "repetition in verse is analogous to tautology in folklore." We have exactly that going on in *Tony the Tow Truck*, "t- t- t," and then the three events: Neato the Car, Speedy the Car, and Bumpy the Car coming along in sequence, with Bumpy resolving the problem.

In any case, then, we have an expectation. We have the dialectic of suspense: on the one hand, will this crisis be resolved?—and on the other hand, for the adult, the folkloric certainly that it will be resolved. For the toddler there is already a sense of expectation, no doubt, but it is offset by the fear that the expectation will be violated.

> "I cannot help you," says Neato the Car. "I don't want to get dirty."
> "I cannot help you," says Speedy the Car. "I am too busy."
> I am very sad.
> Then a little car pulls up.

I think it's wonderful that "pulls up" is just like Gadamer being "pulled up short"; and there is, it seems to me, another crisis of expectation in this line. As a toddler, I need to negotiate that expression idiomatically. I'm three years old and maybe I don't know what "pulls up" means. It's not very thoughtful writing for a toddler precisely for that reason, but at the same time it lends itself to our purposes because it poses a reading problem, a piece of virtual work that needs to be done before the reader can get on with the story. The toddler has to find out what "pulls up" means in the same way that the adult reader of *The Pleasures of the Imagination* has to find out what "plastic" means. As I say, it's a wonderful irony that this particular difficulty in reading is precisely what Gadamer calls being pulled up short.

So you solve the problem and then, lo and behold:

> It is my friend Bumpy.
> Bumpy gives me a push.
> He pushes and pushes and—I'm on my way.
> "Thank you, Bumpy," I call back.
> "You're welcome," says Bumpy.

Here there arises another expectation. This is the kind of story that has a moral. A sense of warm reciprocity is established between the tow truck and the helper that saves the tow truck from being stuck, so the expectation is that there will be a moral. What will it be? There are many ways in which—as in *The Rime of the Ancient Mariner*—a moral could be attached here. It's by no means clear that *The Rime of the Ancient Mariner* will settle on the moral "Love all things, great and small things." And so it is with *Tony*. It happens to end "Now that's what I call a friend," but because other morals were possible we must remain in suspense to find this out. Once again, there is that moment of suspense that the reader is able to survive as it were with a kind of pleasurable excitement until the moral is revealed. By some such means, then, *Tony the Tow Truck* can be approached in a way that sheds light on Wolfgang Iser's "act of reading."

I'll conclude by posing a question: if there exists this remarkable distinction between Gadamer and Iser, where Gadamer seems to impose on us a traditional canon and Iser seems to impose on us an innovative canon, isn't there some relief in historicism after all? Any effort to achieve objective historicism must let the canon evolve as it will. It's odd, perhaps, that hermeneutic principles do almost tacitly entail evaluative premises. Doesn't historicism by contrast open the canon and indeed make the process of reading, the experience of reading, archival and omnivorous rather than canonical?

Well, here's the hitch: this *would* be the liberatory consequence of avoiding hermeneutic strictures only if we *could* distinguish, in Hirsch's terms, between meaning and significance. If we really are sure that the historicist approach to reading is effective and works, then later on, if we wish, we can establish a canon by saying certain texts have certain kinds of significance and those are the texts that we care about and want to read; but that would always be a voluntary gesture and not a necessary one. If, however, meaning and significance bleed into each other, what I'm going to be doing is establishing a canon as it were unconsciously or semiconsciously. I'll tell myself that such and such is just what the text means, but at the same time, I'll be finding ways, without realizing it, of affirming certain kinds of meaning and discrediting certain other kinds of meaning.

So what we've shown perhaps from every standpoint is that values do follow from our assumptions about how to read. Evaluation would *seem* rather distant from simple considerations of how to read, but it has a way of speaking from within the historical horizons we can never escape altogether.

Text and Structure

CHAPTER 5

The Idea of the Autonomous Artwork

Readings:

Wimsatt, William K., and Monroe Beardsley. "The Intentional Fallacy." In *The Critical Tradition*, pp. 811–818.

Passages from Sir Philip Sidney, Immanuel Kant, Walter Pater, Oscar Wilde, John Crowe Ransom.

In this lecture we begin a series of approaches to twentieth-century "formalism." That's a big word, and has often been a *disparaging* pejorative one. At the end of our series of discussions, I hope it won't seem quite as daunting and that its varied settings and implications will have been made clear to you. The topic we take up now belongs as much to the history of criticism as to literary theory. I've said there's a difference between the history of criticism and theory of literature, one difference being that the history of criticism involves literary evaluation: the question of why we care about literature, and how we can find a means of saying that it's good or not good. This is an aspect of thought concerning literature that tends to fall out of literary theory but not out of the materials that we are reading at present. When Wimsatt and Beardsley talk about the "success" of a poem, they understand the whole critical enterprise, including its theoretical underpinnings—defining a poem, deciding how we should best read it—still to be geared toward literary evaluation. Although our present subject matter belongs within the practice of literary criticism, then, we're going to be reading it with a theoretical spin, focusing on how poems are defined and the criteria we should favor to read poems in the best way.

I'll probably just refer to "Wimsatt," but you should know that his friend and collaborator on this essay, Monroe Beardsley, was a philosopher specializing in aesthetics who taught at Temple University. For the book in which "The Intentional Fallacy" appeared, *The Verbal Icon,* Wimsatt collaborated with Beardsley on three essays, and this is one of them. Wimsatt taught at Yale, which is usually considered the home of the New Critics, with Wimsatt its theoretical leader. This group, which also includes Cleanth Brooks, consolidated a teaching method and attitude toward literature that turned out to be the first wave—the first of two waves—of involvement in literary theory with which the Yale English and Comparative Literature departments have been most closely identified. In truth, some of the New Critics did much of their important work before they arrived at Yale. Others never were at Yale, yet the movement is still closely associated with this institution; and if this were a course of another kind, one taught for example by John Guillory, one of the authors we shall discuss, the instructor could plausibly explain this association as an aspect of the sociology of literary education.

When I arrived at Yale, Wimsatt was still teaching, and Cleanth Brooks, recently retired, was still hosting the annual softball game, so I feel a personal connection with them. I can understand at first hand, as I hope all of us will eventually, the degree to which the style of "close reading" that evolved within the New Criticism left an important mark on much subsequent criticism and theory, typically hostile to it, that hasn't always acknowledged this debt. But the whole topic of the way the New Criticism has been indignantly repudiated by its successors almost continuously until this day, even as it continues to influence every critic who still believes in interpreting (not all do), is best left for later occasions.

If it weren't for the New Critics, probably none of you would have been able to sit patiently through any of your middle and high school English classes. When in 1939 Cleanth Brooks and the poet-novelist Robert Penn Warren (neither of them yet at Yale) published a book called *Understanding Poetry,* subsequently reissued again and again as it swept the country, suddenly schoolteachers had a way of keeping kids in the classroom for fifty minutes. "Close reading," the idea that you could take a text and do things with it—the belief that teaching a text isn't just a matter of reciting it, emoting over it, and then looking around in vain for something else to say about it—was first and foremost pedagogically revolutionary. It introduced complex fields of unfolding meaning to which students soon felt they could contribute their own insights. They saw patterns of thought and ways of elaborating patterns that the teacher was guiding them toward, and the next thing they knew the fifty minutes were over and everybody had had a pretty good time. Hard to believe from our point of view that that had never happened in an English class before.

Seriously, many people who now take an interest in courses like this one have long taken an interest in literature because of the New Criticism—especially if they went to private school; but close reading is a feature of public school teaching, too, whenever the teachers have actually taken English classes in college. Its merits aside, close reading always filled the time. If you had more than fifty minutes, you could still make ample use of it. T. S. Eliot, who was one of the intellectual forebears of the New Criticism, nevertheless took a somewhat dim view of it and called it "the lemon squeezer school." All he meant was that it was a painstaking process that drained the subject. But the process was wonderfully galvanizing intellectually because it made students notice how intricate what they had thought to be simple really was. The New Criticism created an atmosphere in which it was acceptable to notice that subtle, complex thinking was exhilarating, not a social embarrassment like bad breath, and that even *poets* (the good folks who brought us "Roses are red") might be credited with thinking carefully and well. It dawned on many students in these classrooms that better interpretation is just better thinking.

Close reading entails attention to form, which indeed from the beginning has never escaped the attention of good critics. When Plato devoted book ten of his *Republic* to an argument supporting the banishment of the poets from his ideal republic, part of his complaint was that poets are terrible imitators. Their imitations are three times removed from the ideal *forms* of the objects we encounter in reality. They get everything wrong. They think that a stick refracted in the water must be a crooked stick. They are subject to every conceivable kind of illusion, not to be trusted, and Socrates calls them liars. So for Plato, poetry is already defined as form: bad form distorting proper imitation.

When Aristotle writes the *Poetics*, he does so very consciously in refutation of Plato's arguments in the *Republic*, and perhaps the cornerstone of his refutation is simply this: whereas Plato says poets imitate reality badly, Aristotle says this is a category mistake because poets don't imitate reality, they reconstruct reality. Poets imitate things not as they are but as they should be. In other words, the business of poets is to organize, to bring *form* to bear on, the messiness of reality. This reality, by the way, is not Plato's reality, which is the realm of the ideal forms. What Aristotle's poet does is to realign, the better to regularize, the elements existing in the real world. This is really the origin of formalism.

In the Renaissance, the poet and courtier Sir Philip Sidney produced an elegant, splendidly written defense of poetry, called in one version *The Apology for Poesie*. Although he was a fervent admirer of Plato, in this "defense"—and defenses of poetry must always be defenses against Plato—Sidney develops Aristotle's concept of form with striking rhetorical ingenuity, impressively laying out the case that Aristotle first made. In your passage (see the appendix), Sidney is talking about the various kinds of worthwhile discourse: divinity, hymnody, science, philosophy, history, secular poetry—in other words, all the ways in which one can contribute to human welfare and betterment. He says that each discourse except one of them is a "serving science." That is to say, all but one, even hymnody, are subservient either to the natural world or to the realm of the divine; their importance lies in their faithful imitation or at least celebration of those unquestioned worlds. Thus the first sentence of your passage: "There is no art [but one] delivered to mankind that hath not the works of Nature for his principal object." Here is why even the arts that the devout Sidney thinks far superior to secular poetry–hymnody, and also divine knowledge or theology—even those sacred discourses are also "serving sciences." Sidney is saying something very special about the poet, who stands somewhere between divinity and the other sorts of discourse with which poetry is traditionally in rivalry: science, philosophy, and history. Here is what's unique about poetry:

> Only the poet disdaining to be tied to any such subjection [subjection, in other words, to things as they are], lifted up with the vigor of his own invention, doth grow in effect another nature. . . .
> He nothing affirms, and therefore never lieth.

Plato, then, is wrong. The poet is not a liar because he's not talking about anything that's verifiable or falsifiable. He confines himself to the parameters of the world he himself has brought into being. Sidney thinks of it as a kind of magic. He invokes, for example, the pseudoscience of astrology. The poet, he says, "ranges freely within the zodiac of his own wit." He also invokes the pseudoscience of alchemy when he says that the poet, like the rest of us, inhabits a brazen world, and of this brazen world—"brazen" means brass—he makes a golden world. In short, poetry is transformational. In representing not things as they are but things as they should be, it transforms reality. This argument then once again justifies the idea of literature as that which brings form to bear on the inadequacies of the real.

Now I don't mean to imply, as I continue this thumbnail account, that ideas of form just stood still after Sidney until you get to Kant. A great deal changed, of course, but one aspect of Kant's famous "Copernican revolution" in the history of philosophy is his thinking about the special faculty that mediates our aesthetic understanding of things, a faculty that he calls "the judgment." In *The Critique of Judgment* of 1790, he outlines among many other things a philosophy of the beautiful and of the means whereby "the judgment" perceives objects as beautiful (*schön*, or "beautiful," is the equivalent of the Latin *formosus*). To a large extent, Kant, without knowing anything about Sidney, nevertheless follows Sidney in this regard, as you'll see.

I'm going to read these passages with some perseverance, so all will become clear, I hope, but especially this: Sidney, as we've seen, actually ranks poetry somewhere between divinity and the other sciences. Poetry is not the supreme vocation that a person can pursue. Sidney believed this so passionately that when he knew himself to be dying, having been mortally wounded in a battle, he ordered that all of his own poems be burned. He had no doubt that poetry was inferior to a higher form of thought. In a way, that's what Kant's saying, too, though he is thinking not of divine science but of the moral imperatives posited by the faculty of reason. In the passages you'll read, you'll see that his point is not that art and the judgment of the beautiful are the supreme expressions of which humanity is capable. His point is only, like Sidney's, that they have a special characteristic that nothing else has. That's the point that this whole tradition is trying to make. Here is how Kant puts it in the second passage I've taken from his work:

> The pleasant and the good both have a reference to the faculty of desire [The pleasant is the way in which our appetency, our sensuous faculty—which Kant calls "the understanding," by the way—experiences objects. Things for the understanding are either pleasant or unpleasant. The good, on the contrary, is the way in which our cognitive and moral faculty—which Kant calls "the reason"—comes to terms with those same objects. Things are either to be approved of or not to be approved of; but in the case of either the understanding or the reason, as Kant argues, things exist in reference to the faculty of desire—I want, I don't

want; I approve, I disapprove], and they bring with them the former [that is to say, the pleasant] a satisfaction pathologically conditioned; the latter a pure practical, satisfaction which is determined not merely by the representation of the object but also by the represented connection of the subject with the existence of the object [in other words, by the way in which I want it or don't want it, approve of it or don't approve of it].

My wishes, in other words, determine the attitude toward objects of perception both of my understanding and of my reason. But my attitude toward an object perceived as neither pleasant nor good is *dispassionate* and views the object not for me but in and for itself. This is the attitude of the *judgment*, viewing the object not as pleasant or good but as beautiful.

Take the next passage, then: "*Taste* is the faculty of the judging of an object or a method of representing it by an *entirely disinterested* satisfaction or dissatisfaction." In other words, under the sway of the other two faculties, I still like it or don't like it as the pleasant or the unpleasant or the good or the bad, but now my liking has nothing to do either with desire or with approval. I like it or I don't like it according to principles that arise from the faculty of judgment and not from the faculty of the understanding, which is appetitive, or the faculty of reason, which is moral.

Hence the fourth passage: "*Beauty* is the form of the *purposiveness* of an object so far as it is perceived in it *without any representation of a purpose*." Here Kant makes a distinction between the purpos*ive* and the purpos*eful*. The purposeful is the practical purpose of the object. What can it do? What can it do for me? How does it go to work in the world? What is its function among other objects? What bearing does it have on—in particular—my life? This is true both for the understanding and the reason. But the purposiveness of the object as perceived by the judgment is the way in which the object is sufficient unto itself. It has its own inner purpose, which is not a purpose that has any bearing necessarily on anything else. It has, as one might say, an internal coherence. It has a dynamism of parts that is strictly with reference to its own existence. *It is a form.* That form, because we can see it has structure and because we can see it has organization and complexity, is purposive though not purposeful.

So that's Kant's famous distinction between the purposive, the inner organization of an aesthetic object, and the purposeful, which is the quality of any object—including the aesthetic object viewed appetitively or morally—insofar as it goes to work in the world or for us. As I've just indicated, an aesthetic object *can* be viewed as purposeful. I see a naked body, which the art historians call a nude. Let's say I don't accept that it's merely a nude. I want it or I disapprove of it and, presto, it's no longer aesthetic. I'll come back to that in a moment, but I hope you can see how this example shows the difference between the purposive and the purposeful.

In order to rephrase these important distinctions, I want to turn to a passage from Samuel Taylor Coleridge, who is, at least on this occasion, a disciple of Kant and is, I think, usefully paraphrasing the arguments of Kant that we have just been engaged with. Coleridge here emphasizes more strongly than Kant does the superiority of the moral faculty to the aesthetic one, even though the moral has in common with the appetitive one the motivation of desire. This is the fifth passage, most of which you'll find in the appendix:

> The beautiful [says Coleridge] is at once distinguished both from the agreeable, which is beneath it, and from the good, which is above it: for both these necessarily have an interest attached to them: both act on the will, and excite a desire for the actual existence of the image or idea contemplated, while the sense of beauty rests gratified in the mere contemplation or intuition regardless whether it be a fictitious Apollo or a real Antinous.

The judgment of beauty does not depend on the actual existence of the object for its satisfaction (it could be ranging freely within the zodiac of our wit), hence purports to show that the nature of this satisfaction does not arise from "interest," or desire. We admire it not as a possession but as a *form*.

Oscar Wilde—ever the wag and a person who generated more good literary theory in ways that didn't seem like literary theory at all, perhaps, than anyone else in the entire history of thinking about the subject—says in the series of aphorisms that make up his "Preface" to *The Picture of Dorian Gray*, "All art is quite useless." I hope that after reading these prior passages and enduring the explication of them, you can immediately see what Wilde means in saying all art is quite useless. He's appropriating a term of disgust in the utilitarian tradition—heaven forbid that anything might be useless!—and pointing out that art is *uniquely* useless; it appeals to no merely appetitive or exaltedly rational form of subjective interest, hence we have no instrumental use for it. We don't have to have an "interest" in it—in the sense of owning part of a company. We don't need to have an interest in it in order to appreciate it. We can distance ourselves from our subjective wants and needs and likes and dislikes, and we can coexist with art in a happy and constructive way that is good both for us and for the work of art, because if we recognize that there are things in the world that have intrinsic value and importance and what we call beauty, and yet are not the things that we covet or wish to banish, we recognize in ourselves the capacity for disinterestedness and at the same time we allow the work of art to be free from our designs on it. We thereby recognize in ourselves an attribute, freedom, that is the cornerstone of many systems of value.

To realize that we don't have to take an instrumental interest in things in order to recognize that they are self-sufficient and valuable shows us something crucially important about ourselves. Wilde's suggestion, but I think also Kant's suggestion before him, is important for our recognition of our own value as independent moral agents. Disinterestedness entails the realization that freedom is possible not just for me but for those things in which I have no instrumental interest. What's implicit then in this view of art and of human judgment is that once again—and this is not the first time we've brought this up in these lectures, nor will it be the last—it's a way of recognizing that in addition to all our other attributes, some of them wonderful, we are also free, autonomous. This discovery of our freedom, and by implication the freedom of other things from our desires, is what lends moral integrity to the formalist tradition; and you'll see that it needs this defense to ward off the countless objections that we'll be taking up in turn as need arises. Many of the charges against defenses of form as intrinsically valuable—as when Walter Pater at the end of the nineteenth century proclaimed the value of "art for art's sake"—arise from the failure or the angry refusal to distinguish between disinterestedness and indifference.

John Crowe Ransom, who was never at Yale but is nevertheless one of the founders or first members of a self-identified school of figures who called themselves the New Critics, published a book called *The New Criticism*, where the term comes from. You may have noticed that in Wimsatt's "Intentional Fallacy" there is a footnote to a Joel Spingarn, who wrote an essay called "The New Criticism" in 1924. Spingarn's topic has nothing to do with the New Criticism. He just means criticism that is recent, and while in a sense that's what Ransom meant too on the occasion of writing his book, the label soon attached itself to a particular viewpoint. Also, since the time of the New Critics, the work of Roland Barthes and some of his contemporaries—Poulet, whom I mentioned, Jean Starobinski, and others—was called in the French press *La Nouvelle Critique*, but that label too is not to be confused with our present topic.

The New Critics, the "American New Critics" as they are sometimes identified, were a school—and I use that term advisedly because they willingly identified themselves as a group—who refined upon the idea we've been tracing of the independent status of the work of art—Ransom calls it a "discrete ontological object"—and the means whereby it can be appreciated as independent in all of its complexity.

Our first foray into the thinking of this school will be our reading of Wimsatt and Beardsley's "The Intentional Fallacy," which I'll get to in a minute; but, simply as a reprise, take a look at the two passages from Ransom that complete what's in the appendix. They provide a link between the sort of thinking you've encountered in reading "The Intentional Fallacy" and the tradition that I've been trying to describe. The first of these ought to be completely transparent to you now because it is simply a paraphrase of the passages I have given you from Kant and Coleridge: "The experience [says Ransom] called beauty is beyond the powerful ethical will precisely as it is beyond the animal passion . . . and indeed these last two are competitive and coordinate." In other words, what they have in common with each other, ethical will and animal passion, is that they're both grounded in interest. That's the point of Sir Kenneth Clark's word, "nude," which is best pronounced "nyewd." For the naked human being, as viewed both by the appetite and by moral reason, the expression "naked body" is just fine as a common term from the standpoint both of what Kant calls "the understanding" and from what he calls "the reason"; but if we do believe there is another category, the aesthetic, viewed by an independent faculty called "the judgment," we need another word for what we're looking at. Modern painters of the body, like Philip Pearlstein and Lucian Freud, would strongly disagree, insisting on the presence of appetite and disgust in any visual perception as they do, but in a way that helps us to our point. When we're looking at a traditional *painting* of a naked body, we don't say, "Oh, that's a naked body." We say, "That's a nyewd," and that instinctive choice of terms bears out the semiconscious way in which all of us acknowledge that aesthetic judgment must somehow differ from appetitive and moral judgments.

And yet a lot of thoughtful people think this distinction is nonsense. The predominant view in the twentieth century has, in fact, been that there's no such thing as disinterestedness, that whatever we are looking at we have an interest in, and that this Kantian moment of dispassionate or disinterested contemplation is what the early twentieth-century critic I. A. Richards called a "phantom aesthetic state." In the lectures that follow, we'll spend more time agreeing with Richards than not. Just to do justice in passing to

Kant's noble idea, however: there is a certain sense, is there not, in which we suddenly find ourselves, without meaning to and without being merely the victims of any sort of cultural tyranny (this is the "Mona Lisa," I'd better look rapturous in front of it), standing in front of something, clasping our hands, tilting our head, and feeling somehow or another different from the way we feel when we typically look at things. And that, too, is an intuitive way of admitting that however difficult it may be to define or defend disinterestedness, something like that state of mind does seem to occur at certain moments of experience. We just feel different looking at a certain work of art or a certain landscape, let's say, than we feel looking at other sorts of things. Maybe we don't know why. Maybe we doubt that the difference is absolute in the way that Kant wants to insist it is. Nevertheless, *in tendency* we have feelings of this kind and there is no reason not to acknowledge them. At least it helps us understand why the tradition I have sketched in exists.

Let us turn now to Wimsatt. Immediately he attacks what he calls "the romantic understanding of literature." What does he mean by "romantic"? It's the attitude that supposes a "poem" (the New Critics used this term to mean "work of literature") to be an *expression* of some passion or profound genius working its way into a form, but that the important thing is the expression. This much, by the way, Wimsatt has in common with Gadamer, because Gadamer too disapproves of the author focus of romanticism. Gadamer is interested in what he calls the subject matter, *die Sache*. He's not interested in *your* expression of that essential content or *my* expression of it. He's interested in the way a reader can come to terms with a meaning conveyed by a text, and that much, as I say, despite the profoundly different nature of their projects, Wimsatt and Gadamer do have in common.

So a poem is not an expression but an independent object with a self-contained meaning, and if this meaning is not self-evident to the attentive reader, then we don't judge the poem a success. This is where evaluation comes in. The success or failure of a poem depends on the realization of meaning. It doesn't depend on our going to the archive, finding out what the author said in his letters about it, or what he told his friends, or what he told the newspapers. If the meaning is not clear in the poem itself, we judge it a failure. We don't refer to an authorial intention. We have no reason to appeal to one if we respect the autonomy of the poem.

Hence (811): "[T]he design or intention of the author is neither available nor desirable as a standard for judging the success of a work of literary art." It follows from this that even a short poem, even a short lyric poem passionately expressed, doesn't warrant an appeal to the author. Even a personal lyric should be understood dramatically, as though the poem were one of Browning's or T. S. Eliot's dramatic monologues. The speaker of any poem on Wimsatt's view is a speaker endowed with a certain character, a certain viewpoint, a certain argument to be put forward, and our sense of the way this character is elaborated has to be derived from the poem itself and not reinforced by biographical reference to the author, standing somewhere behind the poem.

So why should we focus on the "poem"? Notice that we never hear about "literature." We never even hear about "poetry." The object of attention for an analysis of this kind is *the* poem. The poem is, as John Donne puts it, a little world made cunningly. It's a microcosm, a distillation or quintessence. It is a model, in other words, for the way in which literature can be understood as world-making—a representation, again, not of things as they are but of things as they should be. Aristotle's "as they should be" is not in this case necessarily an ideal, but rather simply that which is formal, that which is organized, and above all that which has a coherence and makes sense self-sufficiently and within itself. That's why the poem, the lyric poem, is privileged among the forms of literary discourse in the New Criticism. All literature for the New Critics is by implication a "poem," but the actual lyric poem is the privileged site of analysis whereby this broader statement can be made to seem reasonably to account for everything that can be held in mind at once. The absence of the Romantic word "poetry" is also significant. "Poetry," as opposed to "the poem," is that which just spills out. It's the spontaneous overflow of powerful feelings. The New Criticism isn't interested in spontaneous overflows of powerful feelings. Wimsatt has his little joke about drinking a pint of beer and taking a walk, as A. E. Housman recommended. The New Criticism just isn't interested in the spontaneous overflow that might result from that.

In any case, Wimsatt goes on to argue that if we take our evidence of meaning from the poem itself, we should remember that there are three kinds of evidence, in order of importance descending to nil. What has the most bearing on what a poem means is "language"—that is to say, words in the public domain that all of us share and that we can understand fully (with recourse to a good dictionary if necessary) in order to come to terms with the exact meaning of the poem. A certain word—this is, of course, what kept you alert in your high school classes for so long—typically has five or six meanings. The New Criticism delights in showing how all five or six of those meanings do have some bearing on the meaning of the poem. That's all considered entirely legitimate evidence, which one uses to build up the interpretation of the poem. What is not relevant at all, at the other end of the scale, is the "evidence" I've mentioned already: what the author said about the poem in letters to friends, to newspapers, and so on. If such pronouncements aren't reflected in the poem or—what is more likely—clearly have no bearing on its success or failure as a coherent utterance, they cannot help with interpretation.

At this point, though, Wimsatt acknowledges that there's a rather messy third category of evidence in between that has to do with language, and is therefore legitimate to a point, but that also has to do with the author's idiosyncrasies—the way that particular author used language, for example, by sharing certain coterie words or even indulging a private misunderstanding of certain words. You've got to know when you're reading Whitman what he means by "camerado." It's not exactly what the rest of us typically mean when we speak of comrades or comradeship. The word is loaded in ways that—Wimsatt would probably acknowledge—need to be taken into account if we're going to understand what Whitman is up to. Now this is very tricky because it certainly does bring the author into play. Wimsatt spends the rest of this essay talking about the murky boundaries between types of evidence: type of evidence number two, which is out of play, and type of evidence number three, which may be in play but has to be dealt with in a gingerly way.

But I'm most interested in a footnote that arises from this argument about the idiosyncratic nature of language as a particular author may use it. This footnote (814–815n), is just about as devastating and counterintuitive a pronouncement as you'll find anywhere in our entire course, and certainly the most earth-shattering pronouncement that anybody could ever possibly have made within the New Criticism: "And the history of words *after* a poem is written may contribute meanings which if relevant to the original pattern should not be ruled out by a scruple about intention." Now *that* is bold. The creator "raised his plastic arm"—everybody knows Akenside didn't mean polymers, but now we're all into cyborgs and we take the capabilities of plastics very seriously. In a way, the implication that he has a prosthetic limb is a tribute to the creator and also an acknowledgment of the fact that the "Sovereign spirit of the world" lives in the Eternal Moment. He's not subject to history. This "spirit" knew in the eighteenth century that someday plastic would mean polymer. Therefore, if the creator of the world chooses to raise his prosthetic limb, that is simply a way of making us understand what it is like to be omnipotent and omniscient in the Eternal Moment. In short, if you take Wimsatt's footnote seriously, it gives you a legitimate way not to undermine Akenside's line ironically but to reinforce its meaning and to give it a formal richness that it would not otherwise have.

I'll begin the next lecture by talking about a poem of Yeats called "Lapis Lazuli," written in 1935, in which he says that people who build up things that have been destroyed are always "gay." If we invoke intention, Yeats doesn't mean that they're always gay in our colloquial sense. He is using the English translation of the German word *fröhlich* from Nietzsche's *The Gay Science*. Yeats is an astute and careful reader of Nietzsche, and in fact he is elaborating in "Lapis Lazuli" on what Nietzsche says in that book. At the beginning of the next lecture we will do the same thing with the word "gay" that we've just done with the word "plastic," then consider an essay by Cleanth Brooks alongside other aspects of the New Criticism and its antecedents.

CHAPTER 6
The New Criticism and
Other Western Formalisms

Readings:

Richards, I. A. "Principles of Literary Criticism." In *The Critical Tradition*, pp. 764–773.

Empson, William. *Seven Types of Ambiguity*. New York: New Directions Publishing, 1966, pp. 16–19.

Brooks, Cleanth. "Irony as a Principle of Structure." In *The Critical Tradition*, pp. 799–806.

In the last lecture, I started giving examples of what might happen if one takes seriously that extraordinary footnote in Wimsatt's "The Intentional Fallacy," where he says "the history of words *after* a poem was composed may well be relevant to the overall structure of the poem and should not be avoided owing simply to a scruple about intention." That *should* be truly shocking to hear, not just for anyone with a scruple about intention, but for anyone simply wondering what counts as evidence. Just imagine a *philologist* being confronted with the idea that the meaning of words at a certain historical moment can be augmented or even overridden in understanding the meaning of a poem. So to make the footnote seem just a little more plausible, I went back to the great creator raising his plastic arm and suggested that after all one might constructively complicate Akenside's meaning by conceding that the modern, anachronistic meaning of "plastic" would be relevant to the sense of the poem.

Here's another example a little closer to home from Yeats's "Lapis Lazuli" of 1935. It's a poem that begins, "I have heard that hysterical women say / they are sick of the palette and fiddle-bow, / of poets that are always gay."[1] The storm clouds of the coming war are beginning to gather. A lot of people are saying, "Enough of this effete culture. We need to think about important things, particularly about politics and the social order." Yeats disagreed, insisting with the help of a misogynistic cheap shot that there is a continuing role for art—as indeed after all there may well be, even in such times. So he's "sick of" everybody saying they don't want to talk about painting, about music, or about poets who are "always gay."

The poem involves a stone, a piece of carved Chinese lapis lazuli that has a flaw in it, a flaw that's like a "water-course," where one can imagine a monastic pilgrim climbing upward toward enlightenment. As the poem goes on, Yeats talks about the way civilizations crumble: all things fall, but then it's possible to build them back up. "All things fall and are built again / and those that build them again are gay." As I said last time, needless to say Yeats was not aware of the anachronistic meaning of "gay" that we may be tempted to bring to bear. Yeats is thinking of Nietzsche's word *fröhlich*, which in context you might translate as "energetically joyous." Yeats borrows that word from the translated title of a book by Nietzsche, *The Gay Science*.

Well and good, but if you were a queer theorist or if you were interested in making a strong claim for the importance of queerness in our literary tradition, you would be very tempted to say that the anachronistic meaning enriches the poem: those who build civilizations again are not just energetically joyous as creators, they are also openly or discoverably gay. (Maybe that makes even the chatter about hysterical women significant.) This text-based claim may or may not raise the hackles of the philologists, but it does lend a supplementary coherence to the poem. At least it might pass as what E. D. Hirsch, you'll remember, calls "significance."

In the second line of *Tony the Tow Truck*, we learn that "I live in a little yellow garage." Now of course, as Cleanth Brooks would put it, the *deno*tation of the word "yellow" is just that the garage is painted a certain color. The *conn*otation, which undoubtedly the author had no notion of—this is a book for toddlers—is the derogatory imputation of cowardice, possibly also the derogatory imputation of being Asian. Maybe the gentle Tony is really a

mistakenly placed in a line

when is does (not) belong!

cowardly Asian. Well, fine, but this has nothing to do with the text, we say; yet suppose it did. We could always put the author on the couch and ask why the garage is yellow and not some other color. Once again an implication that's irrelevant on nearly all counts can set the reader's mind racing, for better or worse.

So you see the extraordinary implications of Wimsatt's footnote. Our examples also show, perhaps in advance of today's discussion, how important the notion of *unity* is to the New Critics (a notion entailed in such terms I've used as coherence and complexity). Everything we have to say in this lecture will concern the evaluative norm of unity, which Kant would call the integrity of a purposive manifold that the judgment deems beautiful. Thus the connotation of a word is valuable and ought to be invoked even though it's philologically incorrect if it contributes to the unity, the complex building up of the unity, of the literary text. If, however, the philological transgression is merely what Gadamer would call a "bad prejudice"—some aspect of a particular reader's private investment that nothing could possibly be done with in interpreting the text—then it should be thrown out of play. So the criterion is this: the connotation must be relevant to the unified form that we as critics are trying to realize in the text. The criterion of unity is what governs interpretive decisions, not just for the sorts of semifacetious readings we can do on the strength of Wimsatt's footnote but also for readings that may have some marginal plausibility.

Now a word or two about the immediate antecedents of the New Criticism. In the first place, the 1930s and 1940s in the academic world bear witness to the rise of a canon of taste largely introduced by the great modernist writers, particularly by T. S. Eliot. You may notice that Brooks, for example, has a kind of Donne obsession. He gets that from Eliot's essay "The Metaphysical Poets," which in turn is a review essay of a volume of Donne's poems that made Donne overnight, for a great many readers, the central poet in the English tradition. In "The Metaphysical Poets," Eliot makes several remarks that had far-reaching consequences for the New Criticism. He says, "Poetry in our own time—such is the complexity of the world we live in—must be difficult." He says also that poetry has to reconcile all sorts of disparate experience: reading Spinoza, the smell of cooking, the sound of the typewriter. All of this needs to be yoked together in the imagery of a good poem, as is done in a poem by Donne or Herbert, and this model of complexity is what matters both for modern literature and for literary criticism. Other modernists like James Joyce also contribute to this idea of the independent unity of the work of art. In *The Portrait of the Artist as a Young Man*, Stephen in his disquisition on form and Aquinas and all the rest of it argues that the work of art is cut off from its creator because its creator withdraws from it and sits paring his fingernails, in the famous expression. You remember that Wimsatt argues—probably thinking of that passage in Joyce—that the work of art is "cut off" from its author at birth. Its umbilical cord is removed and it roams the world on its own, a unity unto itself.

Modernism is a source, then, but we need also to consider the state of academic criticism. In the 1930s, Ransom, in his polemical manifestos *The New Criticism* and *The World's Body*, singled out two main adversaries: first there was old-fashioned philology, which would always insist that "plastic" means what it meant in the eighteenth century. The philologists made up a large majority of the professors. This was the golden age during which literary scholarship reached its maturity. Standard editions were being created. The great learned journals were in their early phase, magisterially stockpiling contributions to knowledge. The basic facts of the literary tradition were still being established, although nearly all that mattered much had by then been accumulated, and that was one reason why some in the new generation were restless. The flourishing of philology in the very late nineteenth and early twentieth century had created for us the archive that we now use and take for granted today, but the New Critics saw a certain hardening of the arteries and felt that amid the accumulation of knowledge the challenges of interpretation had been forgotten.

The other dominant practice was what might be called "appreciative teaching." A contemporary and colleague of I. A. Richards at Cambridge had been the famous "Q," Sir Arthur Quiller-Couch, whose mesmerizing lectures had virtually no content at all. They were simply evocations, appreciative evocations, of great works of literature. At Yale, exactly contemporary with "Q" we had a similar figure, William Lyon—"Billy"—Phelps, who would enter the classroom, rapturously quote Tennyson, clasp his hands, and say that it was truly wonderful poetry. The students in turn were so appreciative that they gave hundreds of thousands of dollars to the university as long as they lived. In other words, this was *valuable* teaching—but the New Critics wanted no part of that either.

What they wanted—and in this their surroundings were similar to the academic atmosphere that you'll see the Russian formalists found themselves in—was a systematic and carefully considered approach to interpretation, so that the practice of criticism could become less pedantic and scattershot, or less effusive and scattershot. It was against this academic backdrop—itself influenced by the prevalent ideas of the British academy—that the New Criticism arose in the 1930s and 1940s.

The first figure whom you read for this lecture is I. A. Richards. Before he joined the English department at Cambridge, Richards was trained as a Pavlovian psychologist, which is why you read in his essay about "stimuli" and "needs." His sense of the way the mind reacts to experience, dividing reactions as he does into the uncomplicated, the resisting, and the adjusting, can likewise be traced to Pavlovian principles. These ideas derived from psychology govern Richards's understanding even of his literary vocation during the period when he wrote *Principles of Literary Criticism* (1924). For Richards, reading is experience, the way the mind is affected by what it reads. Thus even though his subject matter is literature, he's nevertheless constantly talking about human psychology: what needs are answered by literature, how the psyche responds to literature, what's good and bad about psychic responses, and so on.

Another aspect of his having been a scientist is that Richards really did believe, seriously believed, in *reference*—the ways in which language really can hook on to the world. Verifiable and falsifiable statement is for Richards the essence of scientific practice, and he cares very much about that. He does not, in other words, share with so many literary critics—perhaps even with Brooks, who follows Richards in making the fundamental distinction I'm about to describe—he does not share with the majority of literary critics and artists a measure of distaste for science. This is also true of his student, William Empson, who was a math major before he became an English major. Richards really did believe that literary studies could be put on a scientific footing.

Because Richards takes science so seriously, he actually reverses the idea that we talked about last time in Sidney, Kant, Coleridge, Wilde, and Wimsatt. He reverses the idea that it's exclusively art that's autonomous. He says science is autonomous (cf. 766), meaning that scientific facts can be described in statements without reference to any kind of psychological context or any dependency on the varieties of human need. Science is autonomous in the sense that it is a pure, uncluttered, and uninfluenced declaration of fact or falsehood.

Then he says:

> To declare Science autonomous is very different from subordinating all our activities to it. [Here's where poetry comes in.] It

is merely to assert that so far as any body of references is undistorted it belongs to Science. It is not in the least to assert that no references may be distorted if advantage can thereby be gained. And just as there are innumerable human activities which require undistorted references if they are to be satisfied [scientific activities], so there are innumerable other human activities not less important which equally require distorted references or, more plainly, fictions.

Here you see Richards's basic distinction between what he calls "scientific statement" and what he calls "emotive statement": the distinction between what is truly referential, what is incontrovertibly verifiable or falsifiable, on the one hand, and what is emotive, on the other. Later on Richards changes his vocabulary, no longer talking about scientific and emotive language. Even more dangerously from the standpoint of anybody who likes poetry, he talks instead of "statement," meaning science, and "pseudo-statement," meaning poetry. You are *really* out on a limb if you're going to defend poetry—which Richards kept doing—as "pseudo-statement," but of course "pseudo-statement" is just another expression for what he here calls "fiction."

Once we settle into this vocabulary, and once we get used to this unquestioningly scientific perspective, we may wonder why on earth we need pseudo-statement, or fiction, at all. We know very well, by the way, that there are many excellent scientists who simply cannot stand to read poetry because it's "false." As Richards says, there's always something archaic or atavistic about poetic thinking. It's not that it's not trying to tell the truth, as Sidney said (it "nothing affirms, and therefore never lieth"). It *is* in fact, Richards goes so far as to say, following Plato, *lying*. Poetry seems to get itself in trouble constantly: "It is evident that the bulk of poetry consists of statements which only the very foolish would think of attempting to verify. They are not the kinds of things which can be verified" (768).

It usually follows from this line of thought that somebody like that will remind us for example that although a democratic society is the best society to live in, poetry prefers feudal society because it makes better poetry. And likewise whereas we all know that the universe is of a certain kind—we can't even call it Copernican anymore—poetry has an odd preference for Ptolemaic astronomy. In other words, everything in poetry is a throwback to some earlier way of thinking. But Richards cheerfully embraces this idea without criticism. It's what he means by "fiction" or "pseudo-statement."

If that's poetry, why do we want it? Because, according to Richards, it fulfills needs in our psychological makeup that science can't fulfill. We are a chaos of desires. They include the desire for truth—what we can learn from science—but a great many of our needs require fanciful or imaginative fulfillment. The reason this fulfillment is important and should be valued is, he says, that unless our needs are organized or harmonized so that they work together in what he sometimes calls a "synthesis," they can actually tear us apart. Literature is what can reconcile conflicting or opposing needs, and Richards cares so much about this basic idea that in another text, not in the text you've just read, he says, shockingly, "Poetry is capable of saving us." In other words, poetry is capable of doing now what religion used to do. Poetry—remember this is a scientist speaking—is no more true than religion, but it can perform the function of religion and is therefore capable of saving us. Thus even despite the seeming derogation of the very thing that he purports to be celebrating in books like *The Principles of Literary Criticism,* Richards does hold it to be the mission of poetry to harmonize conflicting needs.

It's somewhat like Aristotle's idea of catharsis, which can be understood in various ways. Milton at the end of *Samson Agonistes* understands it as the homeopathic purgation of emotion through the expenditure of emotion: as a result of this tragedy, we can have "calm of mind, all passion spent." That could be the motto for Richards's work. The reconciliation of conflicting needs through the experience of poetry results in a kind of catharsis, a "calm of mind, all passion spent." Tragedy would serve Richards as a good paradigm for his idea. Although he doesn't say so, we can imagine him saying that tragedy reconciles the need for violence with the need for justice.

Richards's undergraduate student, William Empson, went to Richards and said he had an idea about ambiguity. He said he felt there was quite a bit that could be written about it, and so he wondered whether Richards would mind if maybe he worked on it. Richards said it sounded good and sent him off to work. A few months later Empson brought him the manuscript of one of the greatest books of criticism in the twentieth century, and one of the most incredibly surprising: *Seven Types of Ambiguity.* The brief excerpt from Empson in your list of readings is taken from *Seven Types of Ambiguity.*

I think Empson is the funniest person who has ever written literary criticism, with the deadpan skill and perfect timing of a good stand-up comic. I enjoy reading him so much that when I was asked to write a book about him, I did so. I hope you enjoy him, too. He's a page-turner, and his brilliance as a critic is really inseparable from the fun of reading him. I'm especially interested in the excerpt you have because of what he says there about "atmosphere." This is his way of responding to "enthusiastic" or appreciative criticism. One of the tricks of "Q" and Billy Phelps and all the other authors and lecturers of the appreciative school was to say that they read for "atmosphere," that there was something one just felt on one's pulse when one encountered great literature, and their purpose as lecturers and as critics was to evoke the atmosphere of things. Empson responds that atmosphere certainly does exist and we should certainly talk about it; but after all, what is the use of atmosphere if it doesn't serve an interpretive function? If there is atmosphere in the passage I'm about to quote from *Macbeth*, it must be atmosphere of a certain kind put there for a certain reason. What follows, it seems to me, is one of the most breathtaking riffs on a passage of literature that you'll ever encounter. I'm sorry if I sound like Billy Phelps (talking about mere criticism, not Tennyson!), but I do get excited, too.

As Empson says, the murderers have just left the room, and Macbeth is twiddling his thumbs, hoping it's getting dark because it's got to get dark before Banquo and Fleance can be killed. So naturally he looks out the window to see how the time is going, and this is what he says:

> . . .
> Come, seeling Night,
> Skarfe up the tender Eye of pitiful Day
> And with thy bloodie and invisible Hand
> Cancel and teare to pieces that great Bond
> That keeps me pale!

Empson doesn't mention that last word, "pale," but in juxtaposition with the crows and rooks it strikes me that it is an interesting moment in the passage.

To continue:

> *Light thickens, and the Crow*
> *Makes Wing to th' Rookie Wood.*

Empson italicizes those lines because while he has something to say about every part of the passage, they are going to be the true focus of what he'll say later.

> Good things of Day begin to droope, and drowse,
> While Night's black Agents to their Prey's do rowse.

Thou marvell'st at my words, but hold thee still [Lady Macbeth
has come into the room];
Things bad begun, make strong themselves by ill:
So prythee go with me.[2]

Empson is fascinated by this passage, and he gives you, in the next few
paragraphs, the amazing variety of grounds for his fascination. Throughout what he says, he indicates that this is what people mean when they
talk about atmosphere. It's not just something you feel on your pulse. It's
something that can be described and analyzed. I just want to touch on the
last part of what he says. He says, "*Rooks* live in a crowd and are mainly
vegetarian"—I am moved shamelessly to interrupt and to say that Empson's the person who says that the ancient mariner shot the albatross because the crew was hungry. In the 1798 edition of *The Rime of the Ancient
Mariner*, biscuit worms had gotten into the hard-tack, so naturally, Empson says, "The particular kind of albatross that the mariner shot, I am told,
makes a very tolerable broth."

So anyway, we begin here:

> *Rooks* live in a crowd and are mainly vegetarian; *Crow* may
> be either another name for *rook*, especially when seen alone, or
> it may mean the solitary Carrion crow. This subdued pun [this
> ambiguity—remember, this is a book about ambiguity] is made
> to imply here that Macbeth, looking out of the window, is trying to
> see himself as a murderer and can only see himself in the posi-
> tion of the crow: that his day of power now is closing; that he has
> to distinguish himself from the other rooks by a difference of
> name, *rook-crow*, like the kingly title, only; that he is anxious at
> bottom to be one with the other rooks, not to murder them; that
> he can no longer, or that he may yet, be united with the rookery;
> and that he is murdering Banquo in a forlorn attempt to obtain
> peace of mind.[3]

I'm not at all sure there's anything more to be said about that passage in
Macbeth. Empson insists on a complex mode of ambiguity that governs the
passage—not on atmosphere. Sure, call it "atmosphere" if you like, as long as
you're willing to subject it to verbal analysis, as long as you're willing to show
how and why the atmosphere is exactly of the nature that it is, and that it

arises—and here is the connection between Richards and Empson—out of a mental conflict: poetry, the poetry of this speaker, this speaker/murderer, is attempting desperately to reconcile and harmonize wishes, just as he is attempting desperately to be reconciled and harmonized with the society that he has alienated himself from and that he is betraying. Macbeth is not Shakespeare, we should add. Shakespeare is representing him attempting to do something that in the immediate psychological circumstances poetry can't do, but in the process evoking an extraordinary complexity of effort on the part of his own mind to reflect the tension of the moment through the medium of language. As I say, it is in this way that Empson follows Richards.

But there's something quite different about them as well. First of all, Empson doesn't settle into the assumption that criticism should focus on the reader's experience of the literary. Richards is actually an avatar of figures like Iser, together with Hans Robert Jauss and Stanley Fish—whom we'll be discussing in the future—who are interested in reader response, in the structure of reader experience. Empson sometimes thinks of the reader, but he never really says where he thinks meaning resides, unless perhaps it be in the sphere of authorial intention. He is seriously committed to fathoming intentions—much more so than Richards, and certainly more so than the New Critics, from whom he sharply diverges in this respect. Especially in his last books, he used a biographical focus to ascribe to authors the most outrageous meanings that other critics threw up their hands in despair about, but his appeal always had been to authorial intention. At the same time, however, Empson doesn't distinguish rigorously among author, text, and reader as though they were separate functions. For Empson, there's a fluid and easy movement back and forth between what for hermeneutics are three very different sources of meaning. Empson works with a synthetic mélange that's ultimately an appeal to the author but certainly involves both working on the text itself and also understanding its effects on the reader.

So all of this distances Empson from Richards to a certain extent, but the most important difference, I think, between Empson and the other figures we're discussing—a difference that makes it even a little problematic to say that he anticipates the New Criticism—is that Empson rarely concerns himself with the *whole* of a text. He isn't really interested in the unity of "the poem." He simply wants to say as much as he can about certain local effects, certainly with the implication, possibly, that what he says has a bearing on our understanding of, let's say, the whole of *Macbeth*; but he doesn't set about doing a systematic reading of the whole of *Macbeth*. He always zooms in on something, thinks about it for a while, and then zooms out and thinks about something else, leaving us to decide whether his local insights have a bearing on the entirety, the literary unity, of the text as a whole.

Another thing to say about Empson's perspective, which makes him differ sharply, I think, from Richards and from the later New Critics, is that Empson is perfectly willing to accommodate the idea that maybe—as in the psychology of Macbeth the character—that maybe poetry *doesn't* reconcile conflicting needs. Maybe, after all, poetry is an expression of the irreducible conflict among our needs. The last chapter of *Seven Types of Ambiguity*, his seventh ambiguity, is actually, as Empson said, about some "fundamental division in the writer's mind."[4] There, you see, he diverges from his teacher. He's fascinated by the way literature doesn't unify opposites or reconcile needs but leaves things as it found them, exposed now in all of their complexity. Paul de Man more than once invoked Empson as a precursor of deconstruction, not of the New Criticism. Because he's not concerned with unity or with the reconciliation of opposites, I think it true that he is a precursor of deconstruction. Deconstruction follows the New Criticism, too, in being a mode of close reading; and there has never been a more ingenious close reader than Empson.

Before turning away from Empson, whose influence was widespread despite his idiosyncrasies, it needs to be said that his interpretive purposes are very different from the purposes of the New Critics—the American New Critics, particularly Brooks, whose preoccupation with unity is something he freely confesses. In *The Well-Wrought Urn*, *Modern Poetry and the Tradition*, and the other books for which he's well known, Brooks uses a number of terms to describe the ways in which the complexity of literature is placed in the service of unity. In the essay you're reading here, he uses the term "irony." He admits that maybe he stretches the word "irony," but he does try to argue that all the complications of meaning he discusses in his essay can be considered irony. In another great essay, the first chapter of *The Well-Wrought Urn*, he talks comparably about "paradox," and elsewhere he takes up other ways of showing how complex feelings and thoughts are unified in poems.

Empson's word "ambiguity" continues to play an important role in the work of the New Criticism. And certainly it is a candidate to be an alternative term that one might use if one got tired of saying "irony" or "paradox." Yet another word proposed by the poet and critic Allen Tate, one of the founding figures of the New Criticism, is "tension"—that is, the way the literary text resolves oppositions as a tension, holding in suspension a conflict experienced as tension. Before leaving this idea, let me just say that all these words—irony, paradox, ambiguity, tension—concern effects that one locates within a text or "poem" as part of its meaning. It's just here that the New Critics differ sharply from Richards—as Wimsatt argued in his essay called "The Affective Fallacy"—who likewise stressed conflict but directed that conflict out of the text (without denying its origin in the text) into the drama of the reader's mind.

Wearing my New Critical hat, I'm prepared now to point out that *Tony the Tow Truck* features a complex pattern of imagery that reveals a conflict between pulling and pushing—as befits a story about a tow truck. We'll revert to the notion of "pushing" in other contexts in a later lecture (you can guess one of its implications for a toddler), but for the moment you can see that the tension between that which pulls and that which pushes is one of the story's motive forces. It is *ironic* that Tony is now stuck and instead of pulling—his own mode of assistance—he needs to be pushed, so we can easily see the situation in Brooksian terms.

But there's one way in which *Tony* is probably not a good proof text for the New Criticism. Brooks argues that poetry should be about moral things but that it shouldn't point to a moral. What the New Critic can admire about the story is the new moral horizon opened by the realization that there's more than one way to be helpful; but unfortunately *Tony the Tow Truck* points to a more abstract moral that seems tacked on, hence weakening the unity of the narrative.

The value to look for in literary unity for Brooks, and for the New Critics in general, is that it be complex, that it warp the statements of science through the "bias" or curving spin of paradox or irony, and that it bring to bear a tension between the denotation and the connotation of words. So the question again is—the question Empson raises in advance—why should these sorts of tension, these movements of complex reconciliation, necessarily result in *unity*?

Take, for example, Brooks's reading of "She Dwelt among Untrodden Ways" (quoted 808), the Lucy poem by Wordsworth, which emphasizes the irony of the poem. Brooks pretends to be on very thin ice talking about Wordsworth in relation to irony at all (after all, his whole point is that you can find irony in any poem of value), but he certainly succeeds. For instance, you can't really say Lucy is a flower and a star simultaneously. She's a flower, she's perishable, she's half hidden, and she's ultimately dead and in the ground—whereas a star would seem to be something that she just can't be mapped onto if she is this half-hidden thing. But after all she *is* a star to the speaker, though unnoticed by everyone else. The relationship between the depth of the speaker's feeling and the obscurity of Lucy in the world is the irony that the speaker wants to lay hold of and that reconciles what seem like disparate facts in the poem.

This interpretation is remarkable in itself, but the trouble is that close reading can always be pushed *farther*. It's all very well to say, "Look at me, I'm reconciling dissonances, I'm creating patterns, I'm showing the unifying purpose of image clusters," and all the rest of it, but by this means your reading may hold together only up to a point, and what you have yoked together risks becoming unyoked again. It falls apart, or at least it threatens to do so, because an overload of meaning sets in. An English contemporary of Brooks, F. W. Bateson, wrote an essay on this same poem, "She Dwelt among Untrodden Ways," in which he points out that the poem is full of oxymorons.[5] A "way" is a path, but how can there be a path if it's not trodden upon? What is the meaning therefore of an untrodden way, or of "there are none to praise" her but "very few to love"? Why call attention not perhaps so much to the odd difference between "few love her" and "none praise her," but to the notion in itself that *none* praise her? This is palpably false because here and now we find the poet praising her, as presumably he always did. Why does Wordsworth keep calling attention, in short, to logical disparities? "She lived unknown and few could know": how could she have been unknown if a few did know her? In short, the poem is full of complexities, but who says they're being *reconciled*? They're lingering oxymorons, arguably catachreses or even solecisms, which for whatever reason leave a good deal unresolved.

Thus Bateson appears to argue that Wordsworth is calling attention to a conflict of emotion or feeling that can't be reconciled, hence the pathos of the ending, "[O]h, / the difference to me"—the difference, precisely, that can't be reconciled. This kind of close reading, then, is not performed in the service of unity but recognizes that the very arts whereby we see an entity as a unified whole can just as easily be put to the purpose of blasting it apart again, and of calling our attention to that which can't be reconciled, just as the speaker can't be reconciled to the death of Lucy, and just as Empson's seventh type of ambiguity marks a fundamental division in the writer's mind.

The New Critics can, I think, be criticized for that reason. The close reading aftermath of the New Criticism does precisely that—supposing that one sees deconstruction as a response to the New Criticism. The deconstructive response consists essentially in saying that you can't just arbitrarily tie a ribbon around something and say, "Ah ha. It's a unity." The ribbon comes off if you keep tugging at it. Things fly apart, and it's not a unity after all. A question we'll come back to more than once is whether the preference for unity in one generation and disunity in the next is ontological (what exists is either coherent or chaotic) or psychological (the healthy mind seeks either harmony or dissonance), but we'll leave it at that for now.

This question does also have a sociopolitical dimension, however. There is another aspect of the thousand ways in which the New Criticism has been criticized for the last forty or fifty years that needs to be touched on now, though the others can wait. The notion of autonomy, the notion of the freedom of the poem from any kind of dependence in the world, is something that is very easy to undermine critically. Think of Brooks's analysis of Randall Jarrell's "Eighth Air Force." It concludes by saying that this is a poem about human nature under stress, and whether human nature is or is not good; arguments of this kind, Brooks says, set forth by the poem, "can make better citizens of us." In other words, the experience of reading poetry is not just an aesthetic experience. It's not just a question of the private reconciliation of conflicting needs, whether in the text or in the mind. It's a *social* experience, in this view, and the social experience of the New Critics is, unquestionably, a conservative one, though not reactionary. You can already see the insistence on the need to balance opinions, to balance viewpoints, and to balance needs, precisely in a way that is, of course, a vote for social and political centrism on behalf of unity. How, then, can literature in this view be constructively progressive? For that matter, if one's that way inclined, how can it be constructively reactionary? The New Criticism micromanages in the interest of a unity that is implicitly social.

That's actually a mild version of what has been a frequent source of irritation with the New Criticism in its afterlife over the last forty or fifty years. For various biographical reasons, the New Criticism has just as often been associated with reaction. The religious premise of this movement, too, has not been lost on its million critics. There's an implicit Episcopalian perspective in Brooks's essay when he's talking about the Shakespeare song, in which, under the aspect of eternity, inevitably things here on earth seem ironic. Naturally, one will think of things in ironic terms if one sees them from the perspective of the divine or of the eternal moment. And on that note, for the time being, we leave the New Critics.

CHAPTER 7

Russian Formalism

Readings:

Eikhenbaum, Boris. "The Theory of the 'Formal Method,'" in *Russian Formalist Criticism: Four Essays*. Ed. and Trans. Lee T. Lemon and Marion J. Reis. Lincoln: University of Nebraska Press, 1965.

Shklovsky, Victor. "Art as Technique." In *The Critical Tradition*, pp. 774–784.

Passage from Yuri Tynianov.

We now start a sequence that takes us through deconstruction, a sequence that has genuine continuity. I don't have to stretch to point out similarities and divergences because the ensuing series of theorists are themselves retrospectively working with all the interconnections I could see fit to mention. Nevertheless, for later developments, the relationship between the foundational Russian formalists and the foundational work of the linguist Ferdinand de Saussure is a rather complex matter that I'm going to postpone summing up for some time. Much will become clearer when we actually get into what's called "structuralism" and you read the essay by Roman Jakobson called "Linguistics and Poetics." Jakobson is the true point of intersection for everything that follows, both intellectually and internationally. Having spent the early part of his career as a key contributor to OPOJAZ, the journal of the Russian formalists, he then emigrated to Prague, where he joined a linguistic circle that proved to be the origin of structuralism; then moved on to Paris, where he collaborated with Claude Lévi-Strauss; and finally to the United States, where he taught at Harvard. His masterpiece, "Linguistics and Poetics," a lecture delivered at the University of Indiana and one of the most important documents in the entire history of literary theory, is important for us, too, as the crossing point or Venn diagram of Russian formalism and Saussurian semiotics, from which we can develop an understanding of what came after both.

But now we begin thinking about the Russian formalists. How can I explain what a decidedly new chapter this is for us? The novelty of it is lessened, I know, by my having decided to precede the Russian formalists a-chronologically with the New Criticism—another variety of formalism, to be sure, but at the same time continuous with our earlier study of hermeneutics because their concern had to do still with principles of interpretation. But for a while now we'll be leaving hermeneutics behind and discussing what's best called "poetics" (the study of the constitutive features of literary and other utterances), even though as we'll see evaluative agendas do peep through along the way.

Hermeneutics, just to dwell on the leap we're about to make, is devoted to the determination of meaning. Very frequently, as in Gadamer, this meaning is called "the subject matter" and focuses mainly on content. Even critics who focus on form, like the New Critics, see form as a means of complicating meaning, with meaning still the end in view. The Russian formalists differ very sharply in this regard because what they're interested in is precisely the way "literariness," as they call it—the devices of literariness—can be deployed so as to impede our arrival at meaning and indeed change our understanding, along the way, of what we mean when we speak of "meaning." If, in other words, hermeneutics is devoted to the possibility of communication and of understanding, the Russian formalists are interested in that special aspect of verbal communication, called "literariness," which actually disregards communication and understanding—not necessarily to prevent it altogether but simply to fulfill a separate objective. The roughening of the verbal surface—celebrated by Viktor Shklovsky as a key aspect of "defamiliarization"—is what slows us down, what gets in the way of our arriving at meaning, and does so for reasons the formalists devote their attention to.

Maybe what I'm saying about the radical break in approach we're embarking on doesn't completely convince those of you who have noticed that the New Critics and Wolfgang Iser, too, show us how literature slows down and complicates understanding. All of the above would seem to agree that in opposition to the shortest distance between two points we experience in a practical message, "literariness," as the formalists call it, or "poetic language," as they also sometimes call it and as the New Critics call it, too, is what slows us down. It creates a distance between two points—rather than a straight line, an arabesque. In other words, it makes us pause over what we're reading. The formalists profess to being exclusively concerned with the way literature is *put together*. Those titles that Eikhenbaum keeps talking about—*How Don Quixote Was Made, How Gogol's Overcoat Was Made*—reflect this preoccupation. Although the New Critics and Wolfgang Iser are likewise interested in the roughening of form, they value it for hermeneutic purposes. It slows us down, yes, but this slowing down allows us to arrive at a richer meaning. The formalists, on the other hand, are concerned only with what they consider to be a scientific understanding of how the parts of a literary text intersect formally. Temporarily, then, as we advance through the course, we'll suspend our interest in meaning and focus instead on how something literary is made.

Take, for example, *Tony the Tow Truck*. I mentioned that an interesting phenomenon in the text of *Tony* is the tripartition of the "t" sound: "Tony," "tow," "truck." Just after we read "Tony the Tow Truck," we encounter a triadic or triple encounter with vehicles: Neato, Speedy, Bumpy. Notice, then, the groups of three appearing at a variety of levels in the text of *Tony the Tow Truck*. They exactly correspond to the aphorism of Osip Brik quoted by Eikhenbaum: "repetition in verse is analogous to tautology in folklore."[1] In remarking upon these triads we have uncovered something about the form, the structure, of *Tony the Tow Truck*, but we haven't discovered anything about the meaning. Nothing appears to follow from the really rather striking observation that triadicity is pervasive in this text. Oh, maybe if you're clever enough you could parlay it into some sort of meaning, but that certainly wouldn't be the purpose of a Russian formalist. To notice that various textual levels are organized in parallel sets of three is an empirical observation about form, made in the interest of science.

The stress on taxonomy—the relationship among parts viewed as what are called "devices"—is one of the ways the formalists have of insisting that their enterprise is scientific. They seem to feel furthermore that the scientific attitude they embrace is embattled, even dangerous to assume. When reading Eikhenbaum's rhetorically rather bizarre essay, nobody can possibly miss his obsession with "struggle," with the fight, with doing battle. You say to yourself, "Good heavens. It's just literature. Relax, it can't be that important." But for Eikhenbaum, there's obviously a lot at stake. I'll soon sketch in some social and historical reasons why this is so, but in the meantime what he's struggling *for* is important to recognize, too.

In the very first sentence of the essay, you read the expression "the struggle for science."[2] As Eikhenbaum claims, this struggle takes place against the backdrop of the completely undisciplined and unsystematic thinking that he identifies as typical in the teaching of literature in the universities. It's a sad state of affairs, in his view, when the most rigorous thinking that's being done about literature is being done in popular journals.

That's part of the struggle, undoubtedly, but another part is simply to break through to some means of understanding the thing that you're talking about. You want to talk about it systematically, but how can you talk about anything systematically if you don't know what it is? You need to pin down an object of study, a first principle from which other principles can emerge. The first step for the formalists was to realize that "literature" could not be an object of study (just as we'll find Saussure realizing that "speech" could not be an object of study). Who knew what literature was? Nobody had ever really known how to define or delimit the objects that count as literature. Better, then, to isolate a phenomenon that can be observed and described comparatively in anything one reads, then coin for this data base, as we'd call it, the term "literariness." We can identify certain devices that perform certain functions, and by studying and adding to these we can perhaps evolve a theory grounded in observation that has more widespread implications.

I use the word "evolve" here deliberately. Behind Eikhenbaum's notion of a "struggle for science," there are two key figures. The first is obviously Marx, whose intellectual influence resulted in the Bolshevik Revolution of 1917, when the Russian formalist movement was at its height. In this atmosphere, the idea of struggle, as in "class struggle," was prominent. Eikhenbaum in 1927 would use such a word calculatingly, as we'll see, but at the same time it's very interesting that the kind of science he's thinking about is not just any science. It's Darwinian science; and after all, Darwin, as much as Marx, is focused on struggle: the struggle for survival, the struggle for dominance. Notice the comparable importance—and we'll come back to this, too—of the word "dominant": "the dominant" in the thinking of the Russian formalists and the struggle for dominance among species in a habitat. So if you think in terms of "literary evolution," as Yuri Tynianov does in the 1927 essay that your recommended reading concludes, you will consider literary history itself as a sequence of changes in which literary devices struggle to become "the dominant," the device that "motivates" or preselects the devices in a given textual system.

Thus in his very first sentence, it is simultaneously a Marxist and a Darwinian vocabulary that Eikhenbaum is invoking, and that's partly what accounts for the strenuousness of his rhetoric. Class struggle was the key used to unlock most mysteries in the Russia of 1927, itself perhaps struggling for explanatory cachet with a rival key, the interspecies and infraspecies struggle for survival. If the disorganized, unsystematic academics despised by the formalists weren't then attuned to the importance of these struggles—class struggle, the struggle for science, science as the science of struggle—if they weren't attuned to these currents, that in itself showed how obsolete they were.

On the other hand, however, "The Theory of the Formal Method," Eikhenbaum's essay that you've read for this lecture, was written in 1927, directly in the aftermath of a bombshell published by Leon Trotsky called *Literature and Revolution* in 1924. Trotsky's *Literature and Revolution* is an incisive book, an attack on many cultural currents, but in particular and very painfully an attack on the formalists. Trotsky argues that the preoccupation with form in and for itself is a kind of aestheticism—something, by the way, that Eikhenbaum denies during the course of his essay, which is a covert rebuttal of Trotsky—a kind of aestheticism that turns its back on history and turns its back, too, more precisely, on class struggle. Trotsky is not simple-minded in his literary taste, and he doesn't just spontaneously insist that everybody has to set aesthetic considerations aside and write socialist realism. (That didn't happen, by the way, until 1934, when socialist realism became mandatory at the International Soviet Writers Conference.) Trotsky's book aims at those particular forms of "aestheticism" that can be understood as self-involved and indifferent to history and class struggle, with the Russian formalists prominently featured among them.

It's 1927. Things are changing. It's been ten years since the revolution. Society and government are increasingly bureaucratized and subject to strict forms of surveillance and social engineering. Whether and to what extent the Russian formalists and their allies, the Futurists—among them the poet Mayakovsky and others—felt a kind of antagonism or growing threat from the government in 1927 is not wholly clear to me, nor does there appear to be any consensus on this topic among the experts. There is quite a bit of evidence that they did feel some anxiety, and we do know that within a few years they all disappeared, retooled themselves, or went into exile. Nonetheless, until roughly the period of Eikhenbaum's essay there was still a tremendous amount of intellectual ferment and excitement in the capitals of Russia. There was no wasteland of thought as yet by any means. Yet we do need to recognize that Eikhenbaum after Trotsky's book is drawing the official language of struggle over his essay as a protective cloak, a camouflage. Best not to acknowledge official criticism directly, then. Best to maintain that one's only "enemies" are the academicians and the Symbolists. There's one way in which he does allude to Trotsky's critique, however. That is the marvelous response of the formalist Viktor Shklovsky to the earlier "ethnographic" theorist Alexander Veselovsky, to which I'll return.

In the meantime, the enemies are figures like Potebnya the academician, who defended the argument of the Symbolists—the other very lively group of antagonists to the formalists—that poetry is made up of imagery, patterns of thought shaped by images. In the case of the Symbolists, this shaping arises from the unconscious and is reinforced by sound and by language. Thus in their view, language is subsidiary to imagery and thought, a kind of handmaiden to those materials. Language is the vessel, in other words, into which the energies of symbolic thought are poured. It's primarily to justify his strong disagreement with this idea that Eikhenbaum devotes the attention of the essay you have read.

Still, before we turn to the theoretical crux of this disagreement, it's hard to let go of the feeling that's made very clear in an essay from this period by Jakobson called "The Generation That Squandered Its Poets"[3]—the impression of bureaucratization that's taking hold, an atmosphere in which our perceptions of the things around us become automated. Shklovsky in particular is very much preoccupied with the automatization of perception, the way in which we no longer really see what's around us. Recently I quoted Wallace Stevens saying that poetry should "make the visible a little hard to see." Just so, Shklovsky and his colleagues insist that the roughening of textual surfaces by various devices can serve to defamiliarize automated perceptions, both to make us suddenly see again the nonsemantic features of the language that we're using and also to see the world itself anew by means of devices of language that tear the film of familiarity from the objects before our eyes. Thus one purpose of defamiliarization is to dispel that gray uniformity that Jakobson called "byt" in "The Generation That Squandered Its Poets."[4] One has to recognize, I think, that this motive stands behind the work of the Russian formalists; hence the claim to be strictly scientific needs to be qualified by the presence of a partly hidden aesthetic agenda, a secret return of value, to be understood as a reminder that life doesn't need to be as dull as it has lately become.

What, then, is literariness? It is the sense in which those devices of a text that call themselves to our attention are demonstrably innovative, or what Shklovsky calls "palpable": the way they shake up perception because we're not used to seeing them. The call for novelty was then worldwide; at the same time, there was Ezra Pound among the high modernists in the West taking "Make it new" for his slogan. There were the various observations of Eliot and Joyce and others whom I cited last time in talking about the background to the New Criticism—all of them insisting on the necessity of difficulty, of novelty, of coming to terms with the immediacy of one's particular circumstances, and of getting away from that which is familiar and ordinary and vague. It was a transnational idea, in other words, which nevertheless had, obviously, certain specific applications depending on where it appeared. The newness that the Russian formalists are interested in is only implicitly aesthetic, as we've said, and it's not just any newness. It has to do particularly with the palpable or roughened form, the intransitive materiality, of that which defamiliarizes.

We can no longer avoid grappling with the somewhat slippery word "form." "Form" as opposed to what? This is a crucial issue for the Russian formalists, at the heart of their "struggle" with the Symbolists, and in counterattack they approach the question of form very boldly indeed. Part of their platform is that *everything* is form. There is no proper distinction, in other words, between form and content. That's the fundamental mistake, as they see it, that their enemies of various kinds make in approaching literature. And yet, you may wish to argue, the formalists' own basic distinctions are dualistic, are they not? The distinction between poetic and practical language, the distinction between plot and story, the distinction between rhythm and meter—all seem implicitly to fall back into the divide between form and content. Surely, for example, "plot," which is the way a story is put together, and "story," which is what is narrated, must fall back into this division. Well, I actually think the Russian formalists can be defended against this charge, and I want to spend a little time developing a possible defense.

To begin with, "poetic" and "practical" language: you've already been hearing this distinction in I. A. Richards and in the New Critics. But the New Critics, even though they do insist that form is meaning, form is content, and so forth, are not really breaking down the distinction between form and content. The very fact that they understand poetic language to be that in which form is predominant and practical language to be that in which content is predominant shows the persistence of the distinction, which in any case they never deny except in rhetorical gestures. But the Russian formalists see the difference between poetic and practical in a different way. For them, so-called content is itself a function of poetic language. To put it another way, practical language coexists in any text with poetic language and assumes a function not in relation to reference but in relation to poetic language. Like any other device, practical language together with its referential baggage is a variable *within* a text and has to be understood as existing in a dynamic, functional relationship with those aspects of the text in which literariness is more self-evident. It's not a question, in other words, of poetry or of a novel being somehow or another strictly a matter of poetic language. In poetry or the novel, you can argue that the poetic function— and this is the term Jakobson will ultimately use for "poetic language" in his essay, "Linguistics and Poetics"—is the dominant; but that's not to say that practical language is absent or that it doesn't have its own function, differentially fixed in relation to the functions of other devices. If one wishes to isolate something called "content," in short, it turns out at bottom to be a device among other devices.

By the way, if we begin by talking about poetic and practical language, we're beginning where the Russian formalists themselves began. As Eikhenbaum explains, in 1914 the first publication of their journal was entirely devoted to poetic sound, to the way in which sound seems, indeed is, wholly independent from the elaboration of sense (i.e., it is not the form of a content). In this context, Eikhenbaum reminds us in passing that we should be on our guard against thinking that sound is intrinsically onomatopoetic— that is, that it reflects the meaning of what it's talking about. The formalists and also Saussure—this is one of the most important links between the formalists and Saussure—are very carefully on their guard against supposing that sound is by nature onomatopoetic because that would suggest once again, in keeping with Symbolist ideas, that sound is subservient to meaning, to the ideas about things that it seems to sound like. The importance of the earliest work of the Russian formalists was the establishment of the idea that sound goes its own way and is not subservient to anything, that it is a device independent of, though interacting with, other devices, and that it doesn't exist for any remotely hermeneutic purpose. In fact, it exists, amazingly, *in order to hinder understanding* in the kinds of texts that we're inclined to call "poetic." It's repetitive; it's anti-economical; it's retardant.

Language of this sort or any sort is a device, and in relation to other devices it's called a "function." That is to say, it *has* a function; it contributes to our understanding of the way in which a text has structure. Every aspect of the structure of the text can be understood as having a function.

Take, for example, "The rain in Spain falls mainly on the plain." Now this is an example of a text in which assonance is plainly the dominant. It is repetitive, and we readily understand it to be somehow different from the ordinary way in which a fact is communicated; but if we are not Russian formalists, we're tempted to say, "Well, it's a mnemotechnic device introduced for the purpose of—in other words it's subservient to—the task of memorizing a fact." By the way, I've never known whether it *is* a fact. A lot of mountains are rainy. The Pyrenees I suppose are dry. I really have no idea whether it's a fact, and it's significantly unimportant in *My Fair Lady* whether it's a fact. What's important in *My Fair Lady* is to repeat the repetitiousness of verse—"The **rain** in **Spain** falls **main**ly on the **plain**"—in order to bring out the tautology of the plot. Eliza Doolittle tries repeatedly to say more or less what I just said but, just like Neato and Speedy failing or being unwilling to push Tony out of his problem, Eliza repeatedly says instead: "The rine in Spine falls minely on the pline." That's not good enough, and so the repetition in the plot reinforces the repetition of the sound in question. Whether or not the statement is a fact is completely immaterial to Eliza, it's completely immaterial to Henry Higgins, and it's completely immaterial to the outcome of *My Fair Lady*. What's important in *My Fair Lady* is the functionality of repetition in the transformation of the principal character into a lady—analogous to the vowel shift from the possessive "I" in "My" to the long, smooth "a" in "Fair Lady." (Even onomatopoeia can be recognized as an infratextual device.) So in formalist terms, that's the way we need to understand what we might otherwise consider a mnemotechnical device for communicating something about the weather in Spain: a mere form for a content.

In any case, the first wave of Russian formalist thought had to do strictly with sound, but they knew that in the long run they would have to approach every aspect of the text, not just sound, in a similar spirit. Sound may sometimes reinforce sense, but as soon as it's clear that sometimes it doesn't, then we can see that its function is not essentially or intrinsically referential. Any other device, too, may sometimes refer, or seem to refer, yet its literary function as opposed to its communicative function appears only in relation to the function of other devices. Some parts of a text may seem to resist this treatment more than others, but that needn't be the case. For example, in the case of socialist realism or indeed realism of any kind, it is possible to call the subject matter of such texts their "society function." The society function in a realist text exists in relation to—indeed "motivates"— plain style, rich detail, and certain recessive traits (as Darwin might say) such as metaphor, symbol, and allegory. At a certain moment in the evolution of forms, one can see that the society function becomes the dominant. The form-content distinction is thereby avoided. What other people call content is a device like any other, and it engages in the struggle for dominance with all the other devices that one can identify as aspects of literature.

Take the distinction between "plot" and "story." There you would really think the formalists are on thin ice. We can all agree that plot is the constructedness of the story, the way the story is put together, how the overcoat is made. But as to story, that's what the plot is *about*, as we say, and in that case how can we avoid calling it content? Well, perhaps we can. In the first place, notice that sometimes story can be the dominant in obviously formal terms. I think of that story that all of you have probably read in school, "The Things They Carried" by Tim O'Brien. It's a list of the contents of a soldier's knapsack during the Vietnam War, just a list of the contents. Of course, all the items in the knapsack are evocative and suggest a plot that the reader can piece together. By the end of the story, in other words, an implied plot exists. It's just the opposite of the usual relationship between plot and story. Ordinarily, a plot constructs something that is implied—that which happens, that which we can talk about in paraphrase or as a subject matter seemingly outside the text; but here in O'Brien's story, you're given the subject matter. The subject matter itself becomes the dominant device. It implies a way to construct it, but the way to construct it is not the dominant. The dominant is the stuff in the knapsack, listed with as little artifice as possible. So that's an instance of the way in which you can see the relationship between plot and story as a relationship of devices, even though it's always tempting to say the story's the content and the plot's the form.

Any device can be the dominant at a given moment in literary history. In Longfellow's *Hiawatha,* as you know, meter is the dominant, roughly at the time Swinburne and Robert Bridges were experimenting with Greek meters. In Tennyson, sound is the dominant, "the moan of doves in immemorial elms, and murmur of innumerable bees." Tennyson thought the two most beautiful words in the English language were "cellar door," an expression that has absolutely no redeeming value, no content as one might say; and audible beauty of that kind very frequently had no referential function in the making of his poetry. So we can say that the dominant device in Tennyson's poetry, as in much Victorian poetry—certainly Swinburne's—is metrical sound. And in Keats, to move back fifty years, we can say that the dominant device is imagery, his famous emphasis on synesthesia (the way the various senses merge in the evocation of images). In Gertrude Stein, the dominant is repetition undoubtedly. In Wordsworth or Joyce and Woolf at a different period, the dominant is perhaps not "formal." Think of the feeling we have that Wordsworth's blank verse just kind of disappears into prose. I don't think that's quite true, but many people do believe, with Matthew Arnold, that "Wordsworth has no style."[5] In Wordsworth and also in Joyce or Woolf (who fairly bristle with style), the dominant across periods is perhaps the interiority of consciousness—that is, the way in which what we call stream of consciousness or the inwardness of thought motivates everything else that goes on in the text: ellipsis, word inversion, fragmentation in the modernists, the halting appositions of reflection and reverie in Wordsworth. In short, any number of aspects of literature, understood as "literary," can become the dominant.

Now as soon as we start talking about the becoming dominant of devices, we must consider likewise the evanescence of the dominant. What is culinary in one generation—and here I'm alluding to a passage quoted by Eikhenbaum—for example, the devices of crime fiction prior to the work of Dostoyevsky, become absolutely central in another. Eikhenbaum is thinking chiefly of *Crime and Punishment,* but this is true of other works of Dostoyevsky as well. The devices of the dime-store detective novel actually become the dominant of a mainstream literary form, but then they in turn are replaced by some other dominant and retreat back to genre fiction. What I'm driving at is that once you start thinking about the evanescence of the dominant, you're also thinking about *literary history.*

One of the most misleading charges, a charge leveled by Trotsky among many others, is that the Russian formalists ignore history—that being the charge so often leveled, too, against the New Critics. The Russian formalists don't at all ignore history. Almost from the beginning, but increasingly during the 1920s, they turned their attention to the problems of literary historiography, and they said some rather bracing things about it. In your text, we find Eikhenbaum citing Viktor Shklovsky's response to an earlier remark by the ethnographic critic Alexander Veselovsky:

> He [Shklovsky] had encountered Veselovsky's formula, a formula
> broadly based on the ethnographic principle that "the purpose
> of new form is to express new content" [new content, in other

words, being those social and historical and environmental forces that oblige literary techniques to change].[6]

That's the "ethnographic" approach of Veselovsky to literary study. It is obviously also the historical-materialist, or socialist, position: history produces literature; and not just literary history but social history produces literature. Shklovsky disagreed, advancing a completely different point of view:

> The work of art arises from a background of other works and through association with them. The form of a work of art is defined by its relation to other works of art to forms existing prior to it. . . . Not only parody [parody, by the way, is a very, very broad term in Russian formalist thought, in a way simply meaning change, the way in which one text inevitably riffs on another text in elaborating its own devices and emphases and in search of a new kind of motivation], but also any kind of work of art is created parallel to and opposed to some kind of form. *The purpose of new form is not to express new content, but to change an old form which has lost its aesthetic quality* [lost its power to defamiliarize, its power to take the film away from our eyes].[7]

No doubt you're saying this is all very bracing and daring, but Veselovsky is surely right. Surely we know that literature is produced by historical forces. What does it mean to say a new form comes about only to replace an old form that has ceased to be aesthetically viable? Something like this must be the spontaneous response of all of us to a pronouncement like Shklovsky's. It is to offset this response of ours that I give you an extraordinary passage from the end of Tynianov's "On Literary Evolution," written also in 1927—written also, that is, in response to Trotsky's *Literature and Revolution*. This is what Tynianov says:

> In formalist historiography, the prime significance of major social factors is not at all discarded. [In other words, we're not just playing a game here. We, too, understand the relevance of what we call "the society function."] Rather it must be elucidated in its full extent through the problem of the evolution of literature. This is in contrast to the establishment of the direct influence of major social factors [and here comes the truly remarkable part of the passage] which replaces the study of evolution of literature

with the study of the modification of literary works, that is to say their deformation.[8]

You see the distinction, I hope. In natural selection, certain things happen. There is mutation. New genes emerge as dominant, no longer recessive or latent, and organisms change. That's evolution, but organisms are also affected by changes in their environment. In comes the prehensile thumb, for example, a matter of evolution, but the next thing you know you get a colossal earthquake and the possessor of the prehensile thumb disappears from the earth—which is to say, very possibly the human species will never develop. That's the *modification* of a form, quite clearly distinct from, indeed inimical to, its evolution. It strikes me that Tynianov has here made a crucial distinction. This or that period may provide the sorts of impulses that give rise to socialist realism, but if you have a *ukase* from above telling you that if you're going to write, it has to be socialist realism, that's a modification, a modification of what would and does evolve in and of itself within the determinate field of literary historiography.

The distinction, it seems to me, is compelling. The only objection to be made to it perhaps is that much of the time it's just more trouble than it's worth to enforce it. It would drive us into such baroque circumlocutions and avoidances of the obvious to say that social factors have nothing to do with literary evolution that we are not likely to honor the distinction continuously, but I think it's very important always to have it in the back of our minds. Tynianov owes to Darwin the title of his essay, "On Literary Evolution"—not "revolution" but "evolution." I have little doubt, however, that Tynianov owes to the notion that literature should conform to certain standards in Trotsky's *Literature and Revolution* his own quiet protest that evolution is not modification.

Before we turn to Saussure next time, we shall pass quickly in review some possible grounds for critique of Russian formalist theory.

CHAPTER 8

Semiotics and Structuralism

Readings:

Saussure, Ferdinand de. Selections from *Course in General Linguistics*. In *The Critical Tradition*, pp. 842–847.

Additional passages from Saussure.

Let me begin by repeating my intention to postpone a comparison and contrast of the Russian formalists with Ferdinand de Saussure's concept of semiotics until we discuss Roman Jakobson's "Linguistics and Poetics," at which time I think the relationship between the two movements in which he himself was involved will come into focus more naturally than if I tried now to outline what the connection between the two movements is.

Semiotics is not in itself a literary theory. As we'll learn from Jakobson, the study of literature can be understood—that is, "poetics" can be understood—as a subfield of semiotics, but semiotics is not in itself a literary theory. Hence, perhaps to your frustration, what you read today has in itself very little to tell you about literature. This isn't the last time this will happen as we travel through our topics, but then of course it will continue to be our job to bring out the implications for literature of theoretical texts that don't have any direct bearing on literary study yet have influenced that field enormously. Saussure's version of semiotics, for example, has exercised a vast influence on a broad array of literary theories. Semiotics develops into what is called "structuralism," which in turn bequeaths its terminology and its set of issues and frameworks for thinking to deconstruction, to Lacanian psychoanalysis, to French Marxism, and to binary theories of race, colonization, and gender—in other words, to a great deal that we will be studying in the future.

Now as an anecdotal or conjectural aside—I've always found this so fascinating I can never resist talking about it—there are various texts in our field that are considered foundational but that curiously enough, à la Foucault, don't actually have an author. Aristotle's *Poetics* we believe not to have been written by Aristotle but rather to be a compilation of his lecture notes. This is one of the reasons why, during the golden age of Arabic scholarship in the Middle Ages, there was so much dispute about the *Poetics*. The manuscripts we find from this period are full of marginal notes in which the scholars are still trying to reconstruct passages that seem to them inconsistent. The *Poetics* is thus a disputed text without an author, but it's also a foundational text. Aristotle is considered the "father of criticism," and likewise what Foucault would call a "founder of discursivity," yet the author of the *Poetics* is not, strictly speaking, Aristotle.

Well, the odd thing is, it's much the same with Saussure, who can be considered the patriarch of many broad currents in literary theory, as I have indicated. Saussure's *Course in General Linguistics* was not written by Saussure but is a compilation of notes written by his students during a series of lectures that he gave from 1906 to 1911, notes that were then gathered together in book form by two of his disciples who were linguists. Here, too, we have a *virtual* founder of discursivity. Some scholars who go to Geneva for a look at the Saussure archive are predisposed to dislike the received wisdom of "Saussure" and hope that they can discredit semiotics by learning that Saussure didn't really hold the opinions that the text has canonized. Others admire Saussure and feel that he needs to be rescued from the misconceptions of his compositors, while yet others visit the archive as a shrine and hope that it will fully confirm the integrity of the text. But this is all really neither here nor there. I just find it amusing, given one of our points of departure in these lectures, that two people who are incontestably founders of discursivity in the field that we study are in fact not, strictly speaking, authors. We must turn in any case to the text as we have it.

What is semiotics? It's the study of existing, conventional, communicative systems. All of these systems we can call "languages," and verbal "language"—the system we use when we speak to each other—is one of them, but far from the only one. There are also the gestures that mimes use, nautical flags, railroad semaphores, and the stoplight—red, green, yellow. All are semiotic systems studied comparatively by the general science of semiology. All are systems of communication with which we function, the intelligibility of which allows us to negotiate the world around us. Semiotics has expanded into every imaginable aspect of thought, including regions where "communication" needs to be understood as "conditions for intelligibility." There is a Darwinian semiotics, for instance. Ecosystems are semiotic. In the very broadest sense, semiotics explains how any field of interrelated objects becomes intelligible *as* that field.

I turn now to a passage where something about the nature of such fields can be made clear. "Language," says Saussure, "is not a function of the speaker." (In this case, he is talking about verbal human language.) "It is a product that is passively assimilated by the individual." Now what does this assertion imply? The fact that human language is not my language—the fact that it doesn't originate in me, the fact that it's not, in other words, my private language—suggests a measure of loss. When I speak, when I use language in speech, I'm appropriating a tool that is not strictly my own. It's *conventional*—which is to say, it is available in the public sphere for all of us—and perhaps the romantic in us wishes that were not so. Wouldn't it be nice if language were my own?

But to offset this loss, the remarkable gain that makes language something like the object of science that Saussure is hoping, like the formalists, to secure, is that if language is not private, if it's not something that I can make up as I go along, and if then it is conventional, available to all of us, then that's precisely what allows language to be communicative. It is a system of conventional signs, in other words, that we recognize as signs because they are common to us all. This conventionality, then, is the object of Saussure's attention as a linguist and as a semiologist.

Language is something that we make use of when we communicate, but it is not itself the act of communication, or expression. The best and quickest way to say this is that I don't speak language, I utter speech *with* language. Language exists as an aggregate all at once, a database—this is something that's going to come up again and again as we come back to our diagram of coordinates—and what's more, this aggregate that we call language exists only virtually. We can't say where it is, except that it's a database "in the cloud." It's not at all just the lexicon in a dictionary because in order to be systematic, that lexicon must be structured as a system of rules that the dictionary doesn't give us. You remember that Freud said we have to infer the unconscious from the erratic behavior of consciousness. There's got to be something behind consciousness, we say, so we're going to call it "the un-conscious" and then try to describe it. It's very much the same with lan-guage, or *langue* in Saussure's French. What we *do* when we communicate is *speak,* and when we speak we say correctly that we "use" language, but we still need to remember that language and speech are distinct entities.

Now as I've implied, in a certain sense we can understand language as an amalgam of everything that's in the dictionary together with every-thing that could be codified in an ideal or utterly systematized set of rules of grammar, syntax, and idiom, compromising somehow—along some com-mon denominator—between descriptive and prescriptive attitudes toward such rules. But there is no actual amalgam of that kind. In other words, we posit that it exists, that it's there to be put together, partly as a matter of experiment and partly as a matter of conjecture, by the linguists; but as a composite thing existing in a spatial simultaneity, that is, *synchronically,* language is something that we can only infer from speech, in parallel with our inference of Freud's unconscious from conscious behavior. Speech, on the other hand, is not virtual but actual, it's what we do. Speech (*parole* in Saussure's French) is the way in which we appropriate, deploy, and make use of language. *Parole* is the unfolding in real time of a set of possibilities given in virtual space—that set of possibilities being what Saussure calls *langue.*

Language, then, is a system of *signs.* How does Saussure define a sign? His famous diagrams make it clear enough, up to a point. We have above the line a concept and below the line a sound image. In other words, I think of something and that thinking of something corresponds to, is inseparable

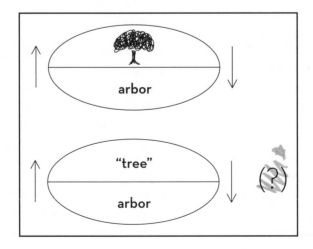

from, a sound image that I have ready to hand for it. This relation can be understood as thinking, for instance, of the concept "tree"—in quotation marks to indicate that it's not supposed to be a sound image—and recognizing that the sound image correlative to the concept tree is necessarily *arbor* if I speak Latin. Or, more problematically as we shall see, I can think of something like this drawing of a tree for which the sound image below the line—I still speak Latin—is *arbor*. I am not likely to get back to this soon, but in the question mark next to the second diagram we can find the secret of deconstruction. I hope that will keep you alert and on tenterhooks!

Saussure conceives of this mutuality above and below the line (indicated by the up and down arrows) as an *arbitrary* relationship between the concept and the sound image. The concept he calls a "signified" and the sound image he calls a "signifier." A sign, in other words, is made up of the two sides, as it were, of a thought moment: a relationship between that which is signified and that which signifies it. But the one is not prior to or independent of the other. We have to think of them together. Their relationship is necessary, established by convention, but also arbitrary. The signifier for the signified "tree" could in theory and just as easily be any other Latin word or a word that is not in Latin because there is no *natural* relation between signifier and signified. The way we put signs together is to take these pairings, these binary relationships between a concept and a sound image, and adjust them in an unfolding sequence. That's how we speak sentences.

Saussure's insistence that a signifier refers to a *concept* and not—by a very strong and necessary implication—to a *thing* is not in itself new. The claim that a word signifies an idea and not an object is already fully developed in John Locke's *Essay on Human Understanding* and has been more or less commonly accepted since then. In verbal language, we say, and by implication in all languages despite intermittent illusions, there is no such thing as a *natural sign*, some imitative quality in the signifier, that is, that "hooks on" to a signified in the world; there are only arbitrary signs. This is a hard lesson, but it is not a new one. What *is* new in Saussure, what *is* foundational in his version of semiotics as a science, resides in another principle that he goes on to establish concerning the sign. The way in which we know one sign from another, hence understand what any given sign means, is *differential*, a concept that entails coming to recognize that the way in which we "recognize" objects is not positive but negative. Much of what remains will elaborate on this concept.

This then is a first walk through some essential ideas, leaving much still to be clarified. I want to go back now to the distinction between language and speech and refer you to the first passage for this lecture in your appendix. Like the Russian formalists, Saussure is chiefly concerned with establishing the semiological project as a science. Also like the Russian formalists—and in a way like the New Critics, too—talking about their "academic" contemporaries, Saussure is vexed by the messiness and lack of system in the current study of linguistics. This is what he says in this first passage:

> If we study speech from several viewpoints simultaneously, the object of linguistics appears to us as a confused mass of heterogeneous and unrelated things.

The horizontal axis of the coordinates in the diagram below is "speech." If I'm a linguist, I study as many speeches as I can empirically, and if I do so, all sorts of confused criteria jostle disturbingly for attention when I try to organize my material. Saussure continues:

> [This] procedure opens the door to several sciences–psychology, anthropology, normative grammar, philology, etc.–which are distinct from linguistics, but which claim speech, in view of the faulty method of linguistics, as one of their objects.
>   As I see it, there is only one solution to all the foregoing difficulties: *from the very outset we must put both feet on the ground*

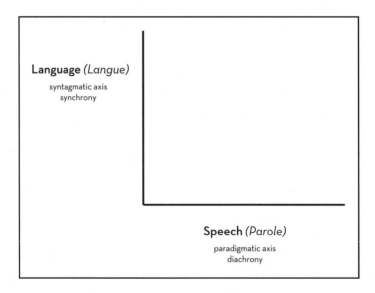

Language *(Langue)*
syntagmatic axis
synchrony

Speech *(Parole)*
paradigmatic axis
diachrony

of language and use language as the norm of all the other manifes-
tations of speech.

We put both feet on the ground of language, in contrast with speech, so that we can make it intelligible as a system of relations among signs. Speech is too protean, actualized in too many contexts, to be approached within the delimited field that a scientific object needs to inhabit. Language, on the other hand, can propose itself as such a field, organized around Saussure's two guiding concepts: the arbitrariness of signs and the negative identity of signs in relation to other signs.

In order to understand why and how signs are negatively differential, we should pause over the various ways in which we can think of signs in language—our scientific object—all of which have to do with the way a given sign might be chosen for a place in a spoken sentence. Take the word "ship." As a signifier, "ship" is very closely related in sound to certain other signifiers. We won't specify them for fear of a Freudian slip ("boat" may be replacing "ship" for this very reason), but what I have left unspoken amounts already to one cluster. Signs contiguous in sound constitute one associational network of clustered signs in language, but there are also *synonyms* for "ship": "bark," "boat," "bateau," "sailboat," "skiff," *Schiff* (note that these last two signifiers belong also in the sound cluster). Synonyms, too, exist in a cluster: words that don't sound at all the same for the most part but are still contiguous. Furthermore, "ship" also has antonyms, hence enters into a relationship with "train," "car," "truck," and "mule"—alternative modes of transportation. In all of these ways and many others, "ship" is clustered to make it available for choice from among other candidates to advance a meaning that we try to unfold when we speak.

In this manner, each sign harbored by language sits in a set of clusters that overlaps with the cluster-set of many other signs but is ultimately unique to itself (no other sign belongs in exactly that set of clusters), waiting to be slotted into some vacancy in an unfolding utterance. By the way, I have grossly oversimplified in indicating casually that the basic unit of language is the "word." That's not at all necessarily the case. Linguists can work at different levels of abstraction with language. Sometimes the basic unit is the phrase or the sentence, but at other times the basic unit is the phoneme— the indivisible sound unit—or if one's studying language as a system of writing, it might be the syllable. Again in the study of writing it could be the letter, understood as a graphic element. The multiple ways in which one can choose a basic or constituent unit for study in linguistics requires a special term to cover any and all constituent units: the tagmeme. Thus the differential association of signs in a system, no matter which constituent unit is chosen to constitute a sign in a given system, is tagmemic. The relationality of signs in any system, then, we call syntagmatic; in acknowledgment of this system-term, the vertical axis of our diagram is called the syntagmatic axis.

The negatively differential nature of signs hinges on their arbitrariness. That's why Saussure, like the Russian formalists, is on his guard against onomatopoeia. An onomatopoetic word looks and sounds like a natural sign, but Saussure is at pains to show that onomatopoeia is always subject to transient accidents of etymology or vagaries of dialect, never intrinsic to or constitutive of the signifier-signified relation, which is always without exception arbitrary. The bark of a dog, for example, sounds different in every human language (bow-wow, vaow-vaow), a fact that can only be explained as the positioning of such sounds in relation to other sounds in a given language, not as a mimetic imperative that's built into signifiers. One might speculate that in English "vow" is commandeered for getting married and in German "bow" (Bau) is reserved for building.

The clustering of signifiers in language streamlines the choices made in speech, limiting the number of signifiers available from slot to slot along the "paradigmatic axis" of our diagram, the axis on which speech goes forward. E. E. Cummings boldly challenged this principle, attracting the attention of a linguist named Dell Hymes. Cummings wrote sentences like "He danced his did," where "did" is obviously not a word you would have supposed to be in any way involved in a relevant associational cluster.[1] "He danced his did": that seems in every sense a misfire, as one school of thinking about language would call it, and Cummings with such "deviations" (as the linguists call them) seems to be thumbing his nose at semiotics. Yet a certain amount of ingenuity is all that's required to notice that the "d" sound or "duh" reiterates the "duh" sound in "danced," and that in fact there are all sorts of combinatory pressures guiding Cummings to choose "did" as opposed to some other seemingly irrelevant word.

If on one side of the border, as Saussure puts it, we look at a cow and say "Ochs" (or "Kuh"), and if on the other side of the border we look at a cow and say "boeuf," and if we cross a considerable body of water, look at a cow, and say "cow," plainly any natural relationship between the *thing* and the sign just doesn't exist. Signs are arbitrary, then, and they're also differential. I have to be able to distinguish among all the signs I use in any communicative sequence. How do I do it? By *choosing signs that are not other signs*. I don't know any constitutive unit *positively*; I don't point to it and say that, in and of itself, it is sign x, even though it feels as though that is what I am doing. I know it *negatively. I know it only because it is not everything else*. Its direct relationship with the sign that's most closely adjacent to it owing either to similarity or dissimilarity can never be a relationship of identity. It's not that other sign, and certainly not any other sign. This is clearly true—confining ourselves here to spoken language—even and especially of homonyms. "Here" and "hear" can be known only by their context, and we cannot pretend for a moment to know them positively by their sound.

I'm about to give an example that should clarify what I mean by negative recognition, but first a couple of passages in Saussure that reiterate the point. First (845):

> Language is a system of interdependent terms in which the value of each term results solely from the simultaneous presence of the others.

I can't know it except by the way in which it differs from everything that surrounds it. He goes on to say (847):

> [A] segment of language can never in the final analysis be based on anything except its noncoincidence with the rest. *Arbitrary* and *differential* are two correlative qualities.

And then again (846): "[C]oncepts are purely differential and defined not by their positive content but negatively by their relations with other terms of the system." Again, as I've acknowledged, this is hard to accept intuitively. I look at something and tell myself that "I know what it is," forgetting that I know what it is only because of a context in which it is not the things that surround it—and it is not, furthermore, any of the absent things the presence of which would alter the landscape of those surrounding things.

Here, then, is an example of a sign that moves around among various semiotic systems and can be known only negatively. It's a unit of language, but it also belongs to other sign systems. My example is the red light. Regarding a stoplight, which is probably the simplest semiotic system that we have—three variables, red, yellow, and green—we have two ways of thinking about the red light. If on the one hand we think that our knowledge is positive, we say red just means stop. If all we had to work with were this semiotic system alone, it would be hard to put up resistance to positive thinking, because we'd quickly add that "yellow" means "pause" and "green" means "go." Everybody knows these things, and I'm certainly not thinking, when I approach an intersection where the light is red, "Oh, not yellow, not green." My mind just doesn't work that way. I seem so far then to have made good the positive claim that a red light just means stop. But suppose the red light appeared on or as the nose of a reindeer. In that case, the red light would be a beacon that means "forward," "go," "follow me," "damn the torpedoes." And we race off in response to the red light, which clearly means "go."

During the Cultural Revolution in China, Madame Mao disapproved of the fact that red lights meant "stop" because red is, of course, the color of progress. She wanted to change the system, but fortunately, it was considered unwise to redefine the colors. Their meaning in fact depended not on the intrinsic value of any color but on the difference between the colors that was a universally accepted convention. As long as red means not-green-go, not-yellow-pause, everything's fine. To make it mean anything else ("go," for example) requires that it appear negatively in a completely different, nonexistent system.

Now for yet other red lights: a red light over a street door means "go in," "come in," existing as it does in a semiotic, that is, negative, relationship with a white light over the neighboring street door, which is probably kept on at night to keep burglars away, hence means "stop." The red light is intelligible only, in other words, within the "binary" (we'll come back to that) of that particular semiotic system. Over an auditorium door, the red light doesn't mean "come in," it means "go out," "exit."

I suppose there are red lights that mean neither "stop" nor "go," but let's confine ourselves still to the red lights that indicate locomotion or its binary opposite, stasis. On a light-up valentine, the red light means "don't stop." Interestingly here, it has the function of negating its own meaning in another semiotic system, and of course naughtily reinforcing its meaning in yet another. On an ambulance or a police car—admittedly, many of these lights are blue these days but let's suppose, tradition prevailing, that they were still red—the red light means "get out of the way" or "stop." It probably bears a distant relation to the semiotics of the stoplight, putting into your head the notion of "don't go." It's a notion that's complicated in this case by the equally imperative notion "get out of the way," which means going, but going in a different direction. Many drivers are paralyzed by this perplexity, which shows that ambulance lights belong to a somewhat inefficient semiotic system.

Then finally we should consider the red light on a Christmas tree. At first we are perhaps relieved to think, that has *no* meaning at all. Obviously it's no use talking about the negative relationship between a red light and a green light and a yellow, white, or blue one, we want to say, because they all have the same value. They're all bright and festive and that's all there is to it. So here there's a red light that doesn't seem arbitrary and differential with respect to lights of other colors. Well, that's because this red light is not at the level of the basic constituent units in this particular semiotic system. It is not in itself a sign at all. "Bright lights" is the relevant constituent unit, and the variety of the colors within this unit is neutralized by their common signification—particularly on a tree or festooning another object that cultural circumstance accords a similar value. Once you get that, once you get the value, "Christmas tree," as opposed to "red lights," "red lights" being perhaps a part of some Christmas trees, then you see that you're back in a very obvious semiotic system: we know a Christmas tree negatively as not-menorah, not-Kwanzaa candles, not the bah-humbug absence of all festive decoration. The case is perhaps still not closed, though. We still know what a Christmas tree is even if we don't celebrate Christmas, even if we put out Kwanzaa candles instead; hence we say that this knowledge can't be "culturally determined." But we're mistaken to think that this sense of free, spontaneous understanding proves that as a sign the tree is neither arbitrary nor differential, because it's very possible to imagine a circumstance in which someone, a visitor from Mars, wouldn't know what it was, forcing us despite its familiarity to imagine the semiotic environment in which we understand it.

One more word about the red lights on a tree and then I'll liberate you from this example. We say there's no difference on a Christmas tree between red, yellow, green, blue, and so on, but of course that's true only within the system that we might call "winter solstice decoration." The color spectrum after all is *also* a semiotic system, and in that system of course we know red differentially in relation to shades of purple in one direction and shades of orange in the other, or, if the system is distilled to primary colors, in relation to blue or yellow. In every case, even though in one sense we can say we know red in contradistinction to all the not-red signs in the system to which it belongs, we should here look more closely to observe a principle that's readily apparent in a system of colors but easy to lose track of in more multifaceted systems: we know a red light first and foremost in its opposition to the sign that is most closely interdependent with it (a white light on a dark city street, a brown fuzzy nose on a reindeer, and so on). When we think abstractly about a traffic light, for example, we can agree that red is primarily not-green, only secondarily not-yellow. The relation of red and green, in other words, a relation of mutual negation, is *binary*. But when I approach a yellow light at an intersection, then the operative binary for red, felt as the threat of danger or police arrest, is not-yellow. Binaries move around freely within a given system, in other words, but under analysis some particular binary can always be isolated as the primary motivating factor in sign selection. The differential matrix in which signs appear is always complex, but within this matrix binary relations are the basic indivisible moments of differentiation. The multiple "this-is-not-those," in other words, is the sum of relevant binaries, each of which is a "this-is-not-that."

Much of the time in a course like this what we seem to be saying is that we can't know anything. But that's really never the case. What we're talking about at this moment in particular is how we *do* know things. If we take semiotics seriously, it gives us a rather sophisticated means of understanding precisely how we know things, but insists at the same time that we know things because of their conventional nature. Interesting to ask in this regard why, then, we do *not* know, or recognize, things whenever that may occur. Note that we still know them as not-other-things; it's not as though they're in an undifferentiated blur. The systematicity or situatedness of their identity is still clear, in other words, yet the nature of their identity still eludes us. Think here of the Christmas tree puzzling a visitor from Mars. The visitor sees clearly that it's a sign but still can't figure out what system of signs it belongs to. That's the key: when we fail to identify a sign, it's not because we don't recognize and process it as a (differential and arbitrary) sign but because we can't identify the semiotic system in which the sign can become intelligible. This in turn suggests our higher-order failure to grasp the system of systems, as one might say, in which any given system, a gross constituent unit among other system-units, can become intelligible.

A lot of huffing and puffing merely to say "we don't recognize the context"? Perhaps; but putting the matter in semiotic terms can at least allow us to meet the Saussurian claim to have founded a science half-way. "Context" can take us a long way intuitively, and can even authorize fields of research, but it pushes us in too many directions, like the study of "speech" according to Saussure, and doesn't allow us—in his unlovely metaphor—to put both feet on anything in particular.

The intelligibility of sign systems, then, is their shared conventionality. That's why it's impossible for any individual to come along and make the red traffic light the symbol for "go." The ecological movement has made it equally difficult for any individual to make the green light the symbol for "stop." These remarks direct us to a further point that needs to be established. As Saussure insists in discussing "diachronic change" in the history of language, we cannot impose our individual will on signs, which change through glacial alterations of usage, not by fiat. A seeming exception is the fact that sometimes apparently individuals have successfully exerted influence and prestige to substitute new signs for old. Jesse Jackson almost single-handedly convinced us that we should use the expression "African American" even though it's cumbersome and polysyllabic. That seems to exemplify somebody taking language by the scruff of the neck and changing it. The semiotician's answer to this, though, is that it never could have happened simply as an imposition of will. It had to be acquiesced in. You need the community that makes use of linguistic conventions to acquiesce in a change of use. Remember, language exists *synchronically*: it exists only in a moment of simultaneity. We study language diachronically—that is to say, we study its history, its unfolding in time. Now according to the semioticians, this unfolding is studied—and here's another link with the Russian formalists—not as the way language is changed from without, "modification" in Tynianov's parlance, but rather as a sequence of synchronic cross-sections. At each cross-section, people are either willing to use a certain sign in a certain way or they're not. That's the crucial thing: if they're not willing, the innovative use of the sign doesn't take hold, which confirms the idea that nothing in language can be changed by individual fiat.

Despite this last-minute preview, synchrony and diachrony remain to be explained. We're going to keep using the coordinates on our diagram, along which the perpendiculars synchrony and diachrony are parallel, for example, to *langue* and *parole*, to the syntagmatic and the paradigmatic, even to metaphor and metonymy. We need to understand why so much that's on the vertical axis is in virtual space while most of what's on the horizontal axis unfolds in real time. All that's to come.

CHAPTER 9

Linguistics and Literature

Readings:

Lévi-Strauss, Claude. "The Structural Study of Myth." In *The Critical Tradition*, pp. 860–868.

Jakobson, Roman. "Linguistics and Poetics." In *The Critical Tradition*, pp. 871–874.

Jakobson, Roman. "Two Types of Aphasia and Two Types of Language Disturbance." In Roman Jakobson and Morris Halle, *Fundamentals of Language* (The Hague: Mouton, 1956), pp. 69–96.

In preparation for a discussion of structuralism, I need to provide a fuller account of synchrony and diachrony, the binary pair with which we ended the last lecture. This pair, which maps onto the coordinates of our diagram as a vertical and a horizontal axis, corresponds with a feature of the Russian formalists' thinking about literary historiography. You may remember from your reading that the formalists understood the "function" of a device in a literary text to have two facets. There is the *syn-function*, which is the relationship between that device and all of the other devices in a given text; but the same device has also an *auto-function*, which is the way in which the device persists and recurs throughout the history of literature, sometimes as the dominant, sometimes latent or recessive, but continuously present as a variable in relation to other variables. Syn-functionally, terza rima helps organize *The Divine Comedy* and resurfaces by way of allusion to a prophetic tradition in Shelley's "Ode to the West Wind" and *The Triumph of Life*. Auto-functionally, terza rima is always either latent or present as a stanzaic option in the history of poetry.

In Saussurian linguistics, the relationship between synchrony and diachrony is largely parallel to that of syn-function and auto-function in Russian formalism. To consider language as a system is to consider it at a given moment *synchronically*. You tend not to think of language as a system if your focus is the way it develops and changes through time. Jakobson, you will notice, seems to introduce an element of time into the synchronic analysis of a semiotic system by saying that you've got to take into account both archaic and innovative features, but keep in mind that in a synchronic cross-section such features are simply flagged as archaic or innovative with respect to the norm of any historical moment (which looks both forward and backward without being itself temporal), not with respect to temporal change.

Yet it is also true that a system in one historical moment is not the same as that system in the previous, the next, or in any other historical moment. Systems change through time. A semiotic system, language (*langue*), the history of literature, the history of poetics—whatever it might be—changes through time, and when you reflect on that change through time you think of it *diachronically*.

Saussure argues that the relationship among the parts of something viewed synchronically—a semiotic system, let's say—are not *necessary* in the sense that—because the sign, the constituent unit of the system, is arbitrary—they might be any number of other relationships. But if you study a semiotic system such as language diachronically, change *is* necessary in the sense that *that* change and not some other change has perforce taken place for some reason and not for any other. Yet diachronic change, though necessary, is not *regular*; it doesn't introduce itself with respect to the structure of synchronic system but rather because some aspect of language use has altered for any number of reasons that don't lend themselves to generalization. When people start saying "exuberant" instead of "gay," or "sinuous" instead of "plastic," these modifications reflect various pressures on the system from without that don't have to do with the system as a structure. This argument, by the way, poses a challenge to certain ideas in traditional linguistics such as the one you probably all know, "the Great Vowel Shift," which is sometimes considered a systemic change. A structuralist's view of language entails arguing, however, that the Great Vowel Shift, when every vowel sound in English went up a notch in pitch at some mysterious change-over moment in the fifteenth century, has only the appearance of regularity but is actually a diachronic phenomenon, perhaps having to do with the geographic movement of dialects, that should not be considered regular. So synchronic data is regular but not necessary; diachronic data is necessary but not regular.

Matters are complicated somewhat on those occasions in your reading when theorists are talking about the way a system of language or other semiotic system is inferred from existing data, for example, the way we infer language, *langue*, from speech, *parole*. (I'm actually concealing from you the fact that Saussure brings in a third term, *langage*, to indicate the cumulative record of all speeches. We'll stick to the *langue-parole* relation.) *Langue* as we have said is a virtual entity frozen in time. As I'll explain more fully below, Lévi-Strauss says the field of a sign system can be traversed in "revertible time," meaning you can move backward and forward within it without altering its synchronic character. By contrast, *parole* unfolds in nonrevertible time, or real time, in that the beginning of any uttered sentence (in speech or in a completed text) perforce comes before the end and unfolds, signifier by signifier, in time. One doesn't ordinarily think of speech as diachronic, but strictly speaking that is what it is. When one changes a sentence in the course of speaking or writing, sometimes going back to restate something in what looks like revertible time (linguists call such changes "recursive"), this change is necessary (it happens) but not regular (it happens for a-systemic reasons) and builds toward an endpoint in real time experienced by an auditor or reader, hence diachronically. Even the person who revises goes back in the sentence but always forward in real time.

We can turn now to structuralism. When this movement arrived from France on the shores of the United States in the early and mid-1960s, many people awoke from their dogmatic slumbers and realized almost overnight that they were or wanted to be theorists. This happened to me when I was a graduate student at Harvard, where absolutely nobody else was paying any attention to structuralism. At Yale, Johns Hopkins, and Cornell, people were then taking notice, but at Harvard I was initiated into structuralism by a brilliant undergraduate, Charles Sabel (now a social science and law professor at Columbia), who was I think the only person in Cambridge who knew anything about it.

Structuralism inaugurated all the trends that made literary theory a flourishing growth industry until the late 1980s, including French psychoanalysis as the Americans got to know Lacan and the French Marxism of Louis Althusser and others. Yet the amazing thing about it is that as an undisputed contribution to literary theory, structuralism lasted only two years! At a famous Johns Hopkins conference in 1966, several years before I met Charles Sabel, Jacques Derrida, whose contribution to that conference we'll be reading next, appeared at least to have turned structuralism on its ear, and theory in the United States took up "deconstruction." Nevertheless, to say that structuralism really only lasted two years is scarcely fair. The lasting effect of structuralism as it's indebted to semiotics is something one still feels and senses throughout literary theory. The are many lasting contributions, not all of them between 1964, when the first structuralist texts were translated in this country, and 1966, when the conference in Baltimore took place. There's a wonderful book called *On Racine* by Roland Barthes. There is an essay on Baudelaire, "Les Chats," or "The Cats," written conjointly by Lévi-Strauss and Jakobson. The anthropologist Edmund Leach wrote a structuralist analysis of Genesis in the Bible. Indeed, it's no accident that he wrote about Genesis, as I will indicate later on. There is also important work by the linguists Nikolai Trubetzkoy, Julien Greimas, Louis Hjelmslev, and Emile Benveniste.

Probably the most lasting and rich contributions of the structuralists were in the field that we know as "narratology." We'll be passing some narrative theories in quick review when we read Peter Brooks's text in conjunction with Freud, but for now I'll just mention the key text in narratology by Roland Barthes: a long essay called "The Structural Analysis of Narrative" in which he approaches a James Bond novel as a system of binary pairs; important books by Tzvetan Todorov, crucial among them *The Grammar of "The Decameron"*; and a series of books called *Figures* by Gérard Genette, whom you will find quoted repeatedly in the work of Paul de Man that you'll be reading soon. All of this work and a great deal else in the theory of narrative is directly indebted to or is an aspect of structuralist thought.

I promised that I would describe the relationship between formalism and semiotics as it clarifies itself in the work of writers like Claude Lévi-Strauss and, in particular, Roman Jakobson. As you can see from reading Jakobson—the one figure who was involved in both movements— structuralism takes from formalism the idea of "function." From formalism, too, structuralism derives the relationship between syn-function and auto-function, which become synchrony and diachrony. From semiotics on the other hand comes the concept of knowledge as negative differentiation: in Lévi-Strauss's analysis of the Oedipus myth, for example, the notion that there is no true or originary "version," no seminal account of the myth of which everything else is a derivative or variant, is inspired by the moment of negation in semiotics. This sense of the object of study as a composite, a synchronic system that is not to be identified with one particular *parole* but emerges from studying the common features of objects of a certain kind is the essential premise that characterizes the work of structuralism.

Perhaps the best way to grasp this essential gesture of structuralism can be found in an aphorism by Roland Barthes in "The Structuralist Activity" (871): "Structural man takes the real, decomposes it, then recomposes it." This is the moment in which you can see the radical difference between what structuralism is doing and what formalism is doing. Formalism doesn't decompose its object in order to recompose it. It just breaks its object down into its respective devices, showing them functionally in relationship with each other. This sort of analysis considers the way the object is "put together"—but there's no question of deducing this structure from anything other than that object: Gogol's "Overcoat," Cervantes' *Don Quixote*, Sterne's *Tristam Shandy*. For formalism, data does accumulate and one can generalize, for example, about the works of Dostoyevsky; but there's no question of recomposing a virtual object, such as "the novel," out of one's observations of individual texts.

By contrast, as Barthes says, "Structural man takes the real, decomposes it, then recomposes it." What he means is that you bring together variants or versions, you create a body of data, not necessarily all the data but a representative amount of the data relevant to any given idea or concept, and then you ask—and this is where Lévi-Strauss introduces the idea of gross constituent units—whether the data can be arranged in a significant pattern, or "structure." What emerges from such a reconfiguration of constituent features is a virtual object recomposing the "real" one(s): in the case of the excerpt you have read from Lévi-Strauss's *Structural Anthropology*, the virtual object might be called the underlying meaning of the Oedipus myth. Thus structuralism takes things apart, like formalism, not however just for the sake of seeing how they work, as when taking apart the parts of an engine, but rather in order to lend the parts to an analysis that reveals a new virtual object.

So let's take a look at the Lévi-Strauss chart, if you want to call it that, of the Oedipus myth (864) and just say a word or two about it. He considers a lot of versions. Let's not trouble ourselves with how many. He doesn't have nearly as many versions by the way as he would have if he were studying a

overdetermination of blood relations	underdetermination of blood relations	denial of autochthony	confirmation of autochthony
Cadmus seeks his sister Europa, ravished by Zeus			
		Cadmus kills the dragon	
	The Spartoi kill one another		
			Laudacos = lame? Laius = left-sided?
	Oedipus kills his father, Laius		
		Oedipus kills The Sphinx	
			Oedipus = swollen foot
Oedipus marries his mother, Jocasta			
	Eteocles kills his brother, Polyneices		
Antigone buries her brother, Polyneices, despite prohibition			

North American Indian myth or the sorts of myths that he did study in a variety of versions during his field work as an anthropologist, but he has some. One of them is Freud's version, one is Sophocles's, and there are others. He notes that there are recurrent features (events, symbols, lexical patterns, ritual practices) in these versions and that they fall into discrete categories. They can be placed in columns indicating a common theme; and these columns in turn can be cross-sectioned in horizontal rows that show how the columns interrelate. For example, there's a cluster of events, happenstances, and accidents of naming that falls into a column called "overdetermination of blood relations." Thus when Antigone tries to bury her brother and risks everything in the attempt, going to extremes that seem excessive, that's an overdetermination of blood relations. Yet at the same time, there's a series of actions in the myth—reaching back into Oedipus's ancestry and forward through the history of his offspring—that have to do with the undervaluation of blood relations. People don't seem to care as much about blood relations as they should (ignorance being no excuse in tragedy), and bad things happen, as when Oedipus kills his father and sleeps with his mother.

Then there's a column reflecting—in all the versions—a strange preoccupation with that which is born from the earth: the teeth of monsters that are scattered on the ground and spring forth as the alphabet in the story of Cadmos, and the variety of ways in which heroes have to confront monsters as Oedipus confronts the Sphinx. All of these monsters seem not to be born from parents—from two beings—but to have emerged rather from the earth of which they are fierce guardians. They are chthonic, or "autochthonous," as Lévi-Strauss puts it, meaning they are self-born from the earth.

There seems to be a strange preoccupation with autochthony in this myth, yet this preoccupation is offset (but also of course reinforced) by the fierce resistance to it, as though the crucial thing were to insist on the binary parental relationship that produces us, to be reassured in our humanity by the idea that one of us is born from two. There are ways, however, in which the myth evokes autochthony in precisely the opposite way. Lambda, the letter that begins so many of the names of the figures in Oedipus's genealogy—Labdacus, Laius, and others—in character form (λ) looks like a limping person. Oedipus means "swell foot," "one who limps." What emerges in the fourth column is the idea that there are signs of autochthony not just in monsters but within our own makeup. The reason we limp is that we have a foot of clay, that something of the earth from which we were born sticks to us, and this is a recurrent intuition in the unfolding of the Oedipus myth. Notice that this is one of those occasions on which the myth explodes into other cultures. Adam, whose name means "red clay," is created from the red clay that has been taken from the earth.

So there you have your four columns: overvaluation of blood relations, undervaluation of blood relations, denial of autochthony, and persistence of autochthony. I'm going to leave it at that for now, but we'll return to these columns to consider the curious issue of two versus one in relation to the problem of human origin, and at that point we'll see to our astonishment—or at least to mine!—that Lévi-Strauss's analysis turns out to be nothing other than an allegory of the structuralist activity itself. Of course the seeming inevitability with which not just meaning but meaning pointedly of a particular kind emerges from the games the magician plays with his little note cards may have something to do with the apparent circularity of decomposing in order to recompose, creating a virtual systemic object. Notice that I have made the vertical axis along which this object appears a dotted line. You cannot be blamed for thinking those four columns subject to some measure of prearrangement.

Not that there isn't a surprising amount of force in Lévi-Strauss's conclusions. You can confirm them in fact by thinking of things he leaves out that would slip easily into the structure he has given us. Jocasta hangs herself, but he doesn't mention that. It's not in any of the four columns, yet obviously it has something to do—you can take your choice—with either the over-determination or underdetermination of blood relations. She feels guilty because she committed incest, hence she underrated blood relations before and overrates them now. Oedipus at his birth is hamstrung and exposed on Mount Cithaeron. Lévi-Strauss doesn't mention that either, but obviously that's why Oedipus limps like the letter lambda. Plainly his hamstringing at birth and discovery on the mountain as though he had been born there must have something to do with the persistence of autochthony. Finally, at the end of *Oedipus at Colonus*, Oedipus is swallowed up by the earth when he dies. Dust thou art, to dust thou shalt return. The equivalent of this in the Oedipus myth is "where I came from is where I will go." So the chart works not just for what Lévi-Strauss sees fit to mention but for what we can think of ourselves. That should put us on our guard against assuming that his arrangement of his note cards is just an arbitrary exercise.

As I turn to Jakobson, it would be a fair objection on your part to re-mark that despite all this emphasis I've been throwing on "decomposing in order to recompose," you don't see that going on in "Linguistics and Poetics." You may feel that Jakobson is just making a formalist argument. He breaks any speech act into six functions. But Jakobson has a decidedly new contri-bution to make to the notion of the poetic function, which the formalists would call "literariness." I'll just quote the key passage here for the first time and hope to explain it in the long run as a structuralist idea dependent on semiotics. It's a mouthful (858): "The poetic function projects the prin-ciple of equivalence from the axis of selection into the axis of combination." What, then, is "the principle of equivalence"? It can be understood as what Jakobson in "Two Types of Aphasia" calls "metaphor."[1] You'll remember that in discussing semiotics I talked about how signs cluster in the vertical axis on our diagram. The word "ship" is similar to some words in sound and meaning and sharply dissimilar to others in sound and meaning, but has no particularly close relation to yet other words, such as "grassy," for in-stance. Certain signs, that is, cluster with certain other signs in the queue to be selected (this is the "axis of selection," remember) on the basis of strong similarity or dissimilarity. Those ways of clustering, so that one sign could substitute for another metaphorically or propose itself as the binary oppo-site of another, are what Jakobson calls "the principle of equivalence."

If that sounds too vague, maybe it's better not to use the language of difference or similarity at all, but to insist on near-identity or opposition:

signs that are virtually synonymous, and signs that are antonymic or brought
into proximity by some other form of mutual opposition. Obviously, though,
the principle of equivalence is somewhat elastic, just as versification is elastic. Slant rhyme can substitute for full rhyme. These relationships stretch
in various ways, then, but the principle of equivalence remains the way in
which signs understood as phonemes, lexemes, or tagmemes cluster in proximity to each other. The readiness with which we select signs of that kind
from *langue* and combine them in the production of *parole* along "the axis
of combination" is what a person attending to the poetic function looks for.
If the spoken or written utterance seems to involve a predominance of
equivalences of various kinds, then this utterance, which is unfolding on
the axis of combination, results from having projected that principle of
equivalence—call it metaphor, call it a principle of similarity or dissimilarity—
from the axis of selection: from that perhaps virtual axis along which language is a system (note again the dotted line) to the actual axis of combination,
that real axis—"real" because nobody doubts the existence of speech—along
which language is not a system but a combination of signs augmented
through time.

Thus the poetic function, or projection of the principle of equivalence
onto the axis of combination, imposes metaphoric tendencies on a combinatory process that would otherwise be *metonymic*. Metonymy in this
vocabulary, as we'll see also when we read de Man, has two different but

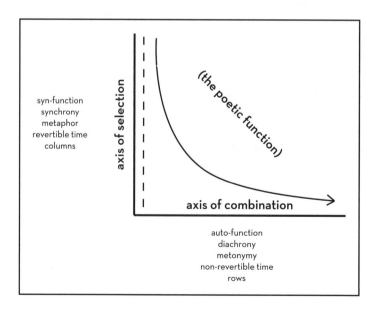

related senses. In one sense, if I put together a declarative sentence, what I'm doing is putting words next to each other because they are a smooth fit grammatically and syntactically but without special attention to parallels in meaning or repetition in sound. There's also the rhetorical device—with which you're probably familiar—whereby obliquely related but not synonymous or metaphoric words substitute for each other. Metonymy is a broadly connected group of signs, if you will, that go appropriately next to each other according to the rules of grammar and syntax and according to the rules of logic, but also in keeping with the premise of the rhetorical device. If I choose "hut" instead of "house" for my sentence—I'm using an example actually taken from Jakobson's "Aphasia" essay—saying something like "The hut is small," there is a metonymic relationship implied with houses, shacks, mansions, and other sorts of edifice, but which can only really be resolved, perhaps, by the combinatory logic of the sentence that moves me to say, almost redundantly, "The hut is small." So for ordinary utterances in which the poetic function is not the dominant, combinatory processes—borrowing the rhetorical term "metonymy" as the substitution of one sign for a nonequivalent but adjacent sign—are basically metonymic.

Now let's look at Jakobson's six functions taken all together. I think these observations are by no means difficult, yet I also find Jakobson's analysis of the six functions to be airtight and exhaustive. There isn't much else to say about an utterance. Obviously in different registers there are lots of things to say, but in the spirit of Jakobsonian analysis there's no possible complaint you can make about this—except possibly one, to which I'll return.

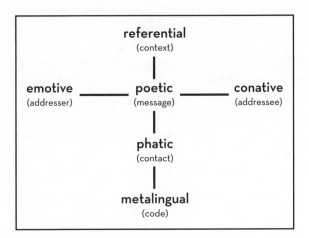

For a proof text, I've been at some pains to find the most uninteresting possible expression in order to show that any utterance whatsoever must entail these six functions. My proof text—try to contain your excitement—is "It is raining." You see on the diagram that we have a "set" to the addresser that is emotive, a set to the addressee that is conative (an attempt to command or convince), a set to the context that is referential, a set to the contact that is phatic (testing, one, two, three), a set to the code that is metalingual (a mare is a female horse), and a set to the message itself that is poetic.

So let's say I am an addresser who is a romantic lyricist. I say—probably ill-advisedly if I'm a poet—"It is raining." What do I mean? Well, probably either "I'm singing in the rain" or "It's raining in my heart." In other words, I'm expressing something emotional in saying "It is raining," fulfilling the sense of the expression in what Jakobson calls the emotive function.

Now someone is being addressed. The thrust of the message is toward the addressee. A small child is going out the door without her coat on, and her mother or father says, "It is raining," which means "Put your coat on." They don't necessarily say, "Put your coat on." They say, "It is raining," and that fulfills the sense of the expression in the conative function.

There's a real-world context for any utterance. This much I suppose none of us would think to disagree with. I'm a meteorologist. I look at my charts and announce confidently through the microphone, "It is raining." Everybody takes me seriously. The referential function of "It is raining" is supposed to convey information. If the referential function predominates in the utterance when spoken by an authority, I believe that it is raining. I don't expect the weatherman to be telling me covertly that he's happy or unhappy when he says "It is raining." All I expect—hence all I hear—is a fact about the weather.

Now "the set to the contact": Jakobson gives you wonderful examples from Dorothy Parker's representation of a date: Well, here we are, yeah, here we are, yeah, we sure are here, and so on; in other words, you're in a state of abject and acute nervousness filling the air with words because you're on a date and you can't think of anything to say. So you say, "It is raining," and of course your interlocutor says, "Yeah, it's raining," and you say, "It's raining hard," and she says, "Well, yeah. Maybe it'll stop soon." So the conversation stumbles along, and that's the "phatic" function, checking to make sure the contact is working: can you hear me? You don't care at all whether it's raining; you just want to make sure the circuitry is working. If I'm a physicist out on a date with another physicist and I say, "E equals MC-squared," I'm not declaring or announcing that "E equals MC-squared," which would scarcely be necessary; I'm filling the air with words. This is the set to the contact, and any message in the right speaking situation has that function, just as any message in the right speaking situation has any of the other five functions.

The set to the code is when we're not sure that we share the meaning of words with another person on a given occasion, so we back away from simply saying things to make sure that what we're saying is clearly defined. I say, "There's a mare in the field." Somebody says, "What is a mare?" "Well, it's a female horse." As a definition, that is the metalingual function. But our proof text is "It is raining." This is where it really gets interesting. What on earth is this "it" that is either the definition of "is raining" or the source of the rain? Other languages have this same weird phenomenon: "Il pleut," "Es regnet." What is "il"? What is "es"? What is "it"? Is it God? Is it Jupiter Pluvius? Is it the cloud canopy? Maybe it is the cloud canopy, yet we feel that that's not what's meant by "it." "It" is a kind of grammatical and syntactical anomaly that is difficult even for linguists to analyze and to explain; so when I try to get away wth saying "It is raining," if I am talking to a literalist I can expect the metalingual function to come running up and bite me in the shin.

Unlike the metalingual function, the poetic function of "It is raining" is unfortunately not very interesting. That's the one drawback of this example. But there's still something to say: "ih-ih" and the double "ih" in *raining*, the monosyllables reinforcing quick declaration followed by a sense of duration that one may have when looking out the window: "It is rainnnnnnning," with the prolongation of the word conveying a kind of semantic value. To make the poetic function to be the dominant—even with all those *i*'s— would be taxing for anyone who wanted it to be, as I suggested when I said a romantic lyricist wouldn't be very smart if he or she said, "It is raining." But I repeat: *any* function in any utterance *could* be the dominant if the right situation were found for it.

This may suffice as an analysis of the sixfold structure of an utterance in Jakobson. When the poetic function dominates, giving rise to the poetics within the linguistics of Jakobson's title, it reflects a metaphoric as opposed to a metonymic structure insofar as we observe some kind of pressure from the axis of selection, with its principle of equivalence, bringing itself to bear on the way in which the combination takes place. What could be more prosaic than "It is raining"? Yet all of a sudden you notice that string of *i*'s, the repetition of like monosyllables, and perhaps other things. The way even the most banal utterance is combined can lend itself to the observation of self-reference in the combination (the "set to the message"). As Jakobson points out, we say "innocent bystander" and not "unconcerned witness" because the former is a double dactyl; but if we said "unconcerned spectator," we might suddenly find ourselves wondering why all such faces in the crowd are double dactyls. Language has an uncanny way of going poetic on us when speech makes use of it.

You may still object that I haven't shown how Jakobson "decomposes in order to recompose." Well, apart from urging you to read his essay with Lévi-Strauss on Baudelaire's "Les chats" (in which a sonnet is reconstructed as a deep sound-based thematics having little or nothing to do with the unfolding of the poem's argument from line to line), I think I can say that what's recomposed in Jakobson is a phantom axis of selection hovering above and within the axis of combination. Everywhere along a composed line combining signifiers, which one can think of as a *row*, especially where the poetic function is the dominant, one senses above and below each new signifier the virtual *column* consisting of all the metaphorically related signifiers that were not selected but could have been. And in "Two Types of Aphasia: Metaphor and Metonymy," the aphasic disorder at the metaphoric pole makes the axis of combination a kind of frequently incoherent duplicate of the axis of selection. This is indeed a neurophysiological derangement, yet it is also, as Jakobson frequently reminds us, a tendency that one finds in poets.

Now I've actually reached the point at which I could raise an objection, a niggling objection in itself that Jakobson actually attempts to counter but that does bring to mind a more general question. Let me call your attention to one problem in what seems to me otherwise to be a truly remarkable exercise of thought in sorting out the six functions. Jakobson pauses over the relationship between the poetic function and the metalingual function, between the set to the message and the set to the code:

> It may be objected [Yes, here we are objecting] that metalanguage also makes a sequential use of equivalent units when combining synonymic expressions into an equational sentence: $A = A$ (*"Mare is the female of the horse"*). Poetry and metalanguage, however, are in diametrical opposition to each other: in metalanguage the sequence is used to build an equation [in other words, to prove that one term can be understood in terms of other terms], whereas in poetry the equation is used to build a sequence.

Now in one sense this is true, obviously. That is, I know when I'm speaking metalanguage and when I'm speaking poetry. Maybe you know it, too, but what Jakobson has actually done is exposed a structuralist nerve, because he has appealed to intention: he has said the metalingual expression has one intention and the poetic expression has another intention. If this is the case, utterances have a *genesis*; they have an origin in an intending consciousness, just as in traditions that are not structuralist, traditions indeed opposed to structuralism, things have origins in prior causes and not in the negative relationships between two things—binary pairs. In other words, if structuralism is in itself a critique of genesis, as is the case with Edmund Leach's analysis of the biblical text Genesis, as is the case certainly with Lévi-Strauss's understanding of the Oedipus myth, *born from two and not from one*—if structuralism then is a critique of genesis, what happens when you have to make a distinction between two entities in your system, the poetic function and the metalingual function, *in terms of their genesis*—that is, of the intention that stands behind them?

As I said, the example seems trivial because we're all more than prepared to agree with Jakobson that we know the difference when we see it between the metalingual and the poetic functions, but he's not actually saying we know the difference when we see it. Maybe it would have been safer if he had just said anybody can see what's metalingual and what's poetic. But what he says instead is that the metalingual is intended to do one thing, to make a sequence equational, and the poetic is intended to do another thing, to make it an equation sequential. If I were a talking horse writing a valentine to my sweetheart, I might very well rhapsodize, "Mare is the female of the horse": dactyl-trochee-anapest, embracing the "female" with opposed feet, with an Oedipal suggestion thrown in by way of the homonym for "mère," two for one.

Once we see the problem, however, we may have a comparable doubt about all six functions. I stand here in front of you and say, "It is raining." How do you know what I intend? Whether I'm nervous and just being phatic; whether I am unhappy or happy; whether I think you're crazy because it is, in fact, raining outside and I don't see any coats; or whether I am actually a meteorologist masquerading as an English professor? You have to infer an intention. If you do so in order to make these distinctions, how can the structuralist insistence on structural determination of knowledge (which is negative) rather than genetic determination of knowledge (which is positive) be preserved intact? I leave you with this rhetorical question to explore on your own.

The critique of Lévi-Strauss I will defer until the next lecture because you'll find that the essay by Derrida that you're reading, "Structure, Sign, and Play in the Language of the Human Sciences," is largely about Lévi-Strauss, so it will make a natural segue to deconstruction first to return to certain aspects of Lévi-Strauss's argument.

CHAPTER 10

Deconstruction I

Jacques Derrida

Reading:

Derrida, Jacques. "Structure, Sign, and Play in the Discourse of the Human Sciences" and "Différance." In *The Critical Tradition*, pp. 915–925, 932–939.

In this lecture we confront one of the most formidable and influential figures in our reading. In the years preceding and since his recent death (2004), Jacques Derrida has enjoyed a second vogue on the strength of having turned to ethical and political issues. He never repudiated his earlier thinking or his notoriously involuted style, but he adapted these signatures to the interests of progressive humanists. Together with the Italian philosopher Giorgio Agamben in particular, late Derrida is associated with what's called "the ethical turn" in theoretical approaches to literature and other matters that is very much of the current moment. Hence owing to his latest books, Derrida's reputation, endangered when deconstruction came under more or less theoretical attack during the late 1980s within the academy (no longer just in the broadsides of the public press), is very high again today. The materials that we are reading for this lecture date back much earlier, however, and belong to an earlier sphere of influence.

The essay "Structure, Sign and Play in the Language of the Human Sciences" was delivered during a conference about "the sciences of man" at Johns Hopkins University in 1966. The event was intended as a kind of coronation of Claude Lévi-Strauss, whose work, understood as a "science," had burst upon the American scene only a few years earlier. Lévi-Strauss was there. He gave a talk, he was in the audience; but Derrida's talk was widely viewed, not least by Lévi-Strauss, to be a dethroning rather than a coronation. Lévi-Strauss, who died in 2009 at the age of 101, expressed great bitterness in his old age about the displacement of his own work by what happened subsequently.

It is easy to blame Derrida's lecture (I am not aware that Lévi-Strauss ever did), but one of the million complications in thinking about this lecture and about Derrida's work in general—and, for that matter, about deconstruction—is deciding how absolute its departure from the work of structuralism really is. There is a self-consciousness, even irony, in thinking about his own approach to structure that we find frequently in Lévi-Strauss and that Derrida freely acknowledges in his essay. Again and again Derrida quotes Lévi-Strauss in confirmation of his own arguments, only then to point out that there is something in what Lévi-Strauss is saying even at his most circumspect that hasn't quite been thought through, or at least not thought through elsewhere in his oeuvre. "Structure, Sign, and Play" is not anything like a wholesale repudiation or even a very devastating critique of Lévi-Strauss. Derrida, I think, supposes that he is acknowledging the degree to which he stands as a thinker on the shoulders of Lévi-Strauss.

In any case, however, this extraordinary crossroads event for people thinking about theory in the United States did effect an almost overnight revolution away from structuralism toward deconstruction, a revolution that remained—amid widespread, diverse, and well-publicized hostility—the reigning paradigm in theory throughout the 1970s and the early 1980s. Derrida, one of the two key figures during this period, was for many years an annual visitor at Yale for part of the spring term. The notion that there was what one critic then called a "hermeneutical mafia" at Yale arose largely from the presence of Derrida together with Paul de Man, J. Hillis Miller, and—more loosely connected with them—Geoffrey Hartman and Harold Bloom.[1]

That group comprised the so-called Yale school. It generated extraordinary influence in some circles, while at the same time drawing down upon itself an outpouring of unprecedented anger. This had to do with what is still sometimes called "the crisis in the humanities." State legislators and boards of trustees believe today more than ever that deconstruction has never gone away and that the humanities should no longer be funded because the apostles of poststructuralism have destroyed the foundational values of Western civilization. That together with panic about the competitiveness of American science and the undoubted need to restock the lagging American workplace with scientists has brought on severe hard times for the humanities in the universities, not to mention in secondary education.

So you have read all of one essay and part of another, "Différance," and you've found Derrida very difficult. Indeed, in addition to finding him very difficult, you've probably wondered irritably why he has to write like that. You can see that he's a challenging thinker but suspect that he's making himself more difficult than he needs to be. You wonder in particular why he doesn't just say one thing at a time. You may even acknowledge that it's all deliberate on his part, that as a thought process deconstruction is a kind of evasive dance whereby one refuses to settle for distinct positions, for any sort of conclusion that could be governed—this is what "Structure, Sign, and Play" is all about—by a blanket term, by what Derrida often calls a "transcendental signified." But still you frown at the style.

Yes, Derrida's prose style, a crablike, sideways movement away from the normal course of argumentation, is meant to avoid seeming to derive itself from some definite guiding concept—necessarily so, because deconstruction is precisely the dismantling of the grounds whereby we suppose our thinking can be derived from one or another definite concept. He also refuses to allow that a writing style might be shaped to fit a particular genre. One of the key distinctions between Derrida and de Man is that Derrida is not a *literary* theorist. Although he very often discusses texts that we call "literary," his view of writing (*écriture*) entails the insistence that we can't reliably discriminate among genres. In other words, genre is as unsuited to be a transcendental signified as any other blanket term. For this reason Derrida is one of the people who persuade us that there's no such thing as, or at least no clear demarcation among, literature, legal texts, theological texts, philosophical texts, and scientific texts. There is only "text," and to think about the field of texts is to think about something that is full of *difference* (not to mention the neologism *différance*, to which we shall return)—too much difference too constantly in play to be subject to the simplifications of category.

I've been talking so far about difficulty and confusion, but in view of the fact that we're all in a state of high tension about this—I'm in a state of tension, too, because I'm the one who has to risk betrayal of Derrida's manner by trying to make it clear—let me remind us that before today we've already been "doing deconstruction," and that much of what's problematic

in reading Derrida has *already been explained.* Let's begin with a kind of warm-up sheet that we can anchor in these little drawings I've made. I trust that when you look at these drawings you will recognize the vertical axis. (When we arrive at feminist theory, we'll encounter a rather different graphic for the vertical axis—which of course I won't presume to draw.)

The Eiffel Tower offers a wonderful way of showing the degree to which the vertical axis is *virtual.* If you ever saw a dotted line standing upright, it's the Eiffel Tower. There's nothing in it. It's transparent. Yet if you're in the viewing station at the top of the Eiffel Tower, suddenly all of Paris is organized at your feet. It's a splendid axis of combination that you're gazing down upon, Notre Dame, the Opéra, the Arc de Triomphe, and the rest as the Tower exercises its power of selection. The landmarks of Paris, its key signs, lie at the feet of the Tower in a certain order: they would be combined in a different order from the vantage point of a different axis of selection. According to Roland Barthes in an essay called "The Eiffel Tower":

> [Guy de] Maupassant often ate at the restaurant in the tower even
> though he didn't particularly like the food. "It's the only place,"
> he said, "where I don't have to see it."[2]

The point appears to be—in the words of Saussure once again—that if we "put both feet squarely on the ground" of the Eiffel Tower, we're liberated from the idea that it's really a governing presence. If we're actually there, we no longer have to worry about the way it organizes everything around it into a rigorous unfolding pattern. After all, there's a very real sense in which we infer the Eiffel Tower from its surroundings. It was built in the nineteenth century. It by no means *causes* the skyline of Paris. It's something that comes in belatedly just as *langue* comes in belatedly in relation to *parole*. The Eiffel Tower is a virtuality that organizes things, as one might say, arbitrarily.

As a reflection on these same ideas, there is a poem by Wallace Stevens. I am sure you recognize my drawing as the earthenware jar in Stevens's "Anecdote of the Jar." Stevens says the jar "made the slovenly wilderness / Surround [the] hill" on which it stands. Hence the jar "took dominion everywhere," like "the dominant" in a literary text. It is the "center," as Derrida puts it, of the system or structure that it creates, yet it is not actually part of the structure, it is outside the structure, a creator withdrawn from its creation: "It did not give of bird or bush, / Like nothing else in Tennessee." The jar is arbitrarily placed in the middle of the free play of the natural world, a free play that is full of reproductive exuberance, full of a joyous excess that is part of what Derrida suggests in emphasizing what's "left over": the surplus usage of the sign, the *supplementarity* of the sign. There's an orgasmic element, too, when Derrida writes of "the seminal adventure of the trace" toward the end of his essay. In any case, the jar just stands arbitrarily in the middle of that sprawl, organizing everything without participating in the *nature*, the reproductivity, of anything. It is, in other words, a Derridean center that is outside the structure: "a center which is not a center." More of that in a minute.

Now the Twin Towers. I started using this example long before 2001, but what they suggested even then was what today we realize in grief: the ephemerality of the vertical axis. The Twin Towers had the same function in New York that the Eiffel Tower has in Paris. The restaurant, called "Windows on the World" (as though it were not part of the world), afforded an incomparable view of the city, with everything organized at its feet. A very fine essay about the Twin Towers—again, long before 2001—by Michel de Certeau makes this argument in sustained form.[3]

These, then, are real-world examples of the uneasy sense we may have that to infer a spatial moment from which we then say the irreducibly temporal nature of experience is *derived*—to infer a moment isolated from the continuum of this experience as a necessary *cause* of it—is always problematic. To realize the virtuality of an organizing idea is to recognize its arbitrariness even as we also recognize that without it there is no basis for organized thought. In a very important sense we must recognize that when we engage in thinking, we can't do without a transcendental signified, hence must put it, as Derrida would say, "under erasure," even while conceding its necessity. Derrida never really claims that you can do without it. If you want to get a sense of structure, you've got to work with some inference of this sort; Derrida admits that he himself can scarcely write without the governing concept of the "sign," but it had better be in quotes because its very existence is always questionable, and it must not be promoted to the status of creative origin. All of this we learned at the outset from Marx on the commodity fetish, and we have reminded ourselves of it ever since when we represented the vertical axis of semiotics and structuralism as a dotted line. "Structure, Sign, and Play" is in one sense simply an insistence on this dotted line.

There are other ways, too, in which we've already hinted at what you've been reading today. Consider the two passages (921) in which Derrida quotes Lévi-Strauss on the nature of myth. Once having quoted these passages in turn, I'll return to Lévi-Strauss's analysis of the Oedipus myth and show how it is that Derrida both benefits from what Lévi-Strauss has said and is enabled at the same time to criticize Lévi-Strauss's position. First:

> "In opposition to epistemic discourse [the kind of discourse that has some principle or transcendental signified or blanket term as its basis—in other words, something that in a given moment makes it possible for all knowledge to flow from it], structural discourse on myths—*mythological* discourse—must itself be *mythomorphic*. It must have the form of that of which it speaks."

Derrida then says:

> This is what Lévi-Strauss [himself] says in [the following passage taken from one of Lévi-Strauss's most famous books] *The Raw and the Cooked*. I just want to quote the end of that passage now: "In wanting to imitate the spontaneous movement of mythical thought, my enterprise, itself too brief and too long, has yet to yield to its demands and respect its rhythm. Thus is this book on myths itself and in its own way a myth."

Here, then, is a moment when Lévi-Strauss is admitting—even proud of—something about his own work that he is *not* admitting in his analysis of the Oedipus myth in the essay from *Structural Anthropology*. What Lévi-Strauss is saying in *The Raw and the Cooked* is that his approach to myth is itself only a version of the myth. That is, it participates in the mythic way of thinking about things. It uses what in the *Structural Anthropology* essay he calls "mythemes" or "gross constituent units" of thought. It deploys and manipulates those gross constituent units of thought in the ways that we reviewed, but notice what Lévi-Strauss is saying in that essay *as opposed to* the passage Derrida has just quoted. Lévi-Strauss says there, in effect, that the form of the myth he gives us in his columns and rows is scientific, not mythic. One of the versions he makes use of to arrive at this "scientific" conclusion is what he calls Freud's version of the Oedipus myth. Freud, Sophocles, all of the other versions he has at his disposal have equal merit as versions, but none of them provide the deep structural explanation or meaning of the myth. The meaning of the myth is discoverable only in the science here presented.

Well, Freud, too, thought he was a scientist, and his reading of the myth was also supposed to be scientific. And what was Freud's reading of the myth about? You guessed it, *two or one!*—in other words, it was about incest, the meeting point of the overdetermination of blood relations and the underdetermination of blood relations. In short, Lévi-Strauss's conclusions are already anticipated in Freud. Furthermore, what do we find Lévi-Strauss doing on this occasion? He's denying the influence of Freud—it's my myth, not his myth—which is precisely what happens in Freud's primal horde. In repudiating the father, Lévi-Strauss falls into the very mythic pattern that Freud had been the first to analyze. The moments for which Derrida is criticizing Lévi-Strauss are those moments in which Lévi-Strauss has unguardedly said that his work is scientific, which is also to say, as we'll see, that in Derrida's terms it has a "center." But there are lots of occasions, too—and Derrida also scrupulously quotes Lévi-Strauss to *this* effect—when Lévi-Strauss concedes that his viewpoint disappears unstably into the thing viewed.

Now because we've anticipated this as well, let's look at a passage where Derrida is talking not about Lévi-Strauss but about Saussure (917). Here he revisits Saussure's foundational definition of the sign, and he is troubled by the alleged relationship between the concept and the sound image—the signified and the signifier—that is the basis of the science of Saussure: the arbitrary and differential pairing of signified and signifier that is the ground on which Saussure puts both feet. Concerning this pairing, Derrida says:

> [T]he signification "sign" has always been comprehended and determined, in its sense as sign-of, signifier referring to a signified, signifier different from its signified. If one erases the radical difference between signifier and signified, it is the word signifier itself which ought to be abandoned as a metaphysical concept.

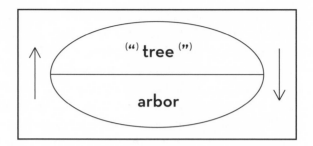

Here's where I come back to that diagram I already qualified with a question mark when I was talking about Saussure. Suppose I think of the relationship between "signified" and "signifier" not as the relationship between a represented thing and a word but as the relationship between two *terms*— because, after all, one way of indicating the concept "tree" is to write the word "tree" and put quotation marks around it. If I take away the quotation marks, all I have is the word with no indication that it's a concept. Notice that this is now a relationship that Jakobson would call "metalingual." What it suggests is that "tree" is another *word* for "arbor." In other words, it's a relationship not between a signified and a signifier but between a *signifier* and a signifier, so that the binarism of the relationship is broken down and we begin to understand the combinatory structure of speech or writing as just one signifier leading to another signifier: Derrida said above that we might as well jettison the word "signifier," but he might as easily have said that about the word "signified." When I "think" a signifier ("tree," no doubt inspired by a previous signifier, such as "elm"), it triggers by association a subsequent signifier (*arbor*), which triggers another, which triggers another. That's what gives us, in the language of deconstruction, "the chain," the signifying chain: not an organizational pattern but an ever self-replicating and self-extending movement, irreducibly linear and pushing ahead through a sequence of temporally spaced associations. Derrida and his followers call this "the chain of the signifier."

When you demystify the relationship between a concept/signified and a sound image/signifier, you also demystify the relationship between a *set* of associations, which exist in virtual space, and the way in which association actually takes place, which is necessarily in time. In other words, if one signifier leads to another in a chain, then that is the dimension in which the associations described by Saussure occur. They do not occur in a systemic space but in unfolding time. We find ourselves caught up in a stream of signification. All the possibilities existed before we came along; hence our associative process is moved, as down a stream, by—well, by something. When we take up "supplementarity" and *différance*, we can think of this movement more precisely.

There's yet another way Derrida's essay from the very outset confirms a point we've been making, in this case about the crisis of structuralism being the need to deny the provenance of *genesis* or cause. In structuralism, if something emerges, it emerges from *between* two things. It's not *this* and it's not *that*, or it "emerges" as that which is not this, not that. It doesn't derive from an antecedent single cause as an effect. It emerges as a difference within a field. That's what Derrida is indicating with extraordinary intensity of complication in the first paragraph of "Structure, Sign, and Play" (915):

> Perhaps something has occurred in the history of the concept of structure that could be called an "event" [*évènement*, something that comes forth, something that is there now and wasn't there before].

In those first words, Derrida proleptically announces the most problematic issue for structuralism. When structuralism considers that yesterday things were different from the way they are today, it has to say: yesterday there was a certain synchronic cross-section of data, and today there's a slightly different synchronic cross-section of data. But structuralism in its synchronic register is unable and furthermore *unwilling* to say anything about how yesterday's data turned into today's data—in other words, to say anything about *change*. It sees successive cross-sections, and it calls that "history." Not "one thing leads to another" but, in Arnold Toynbee's dismissive remark about his rivals' approaches to history, "one damned thing after another."

Derrida deliberately struggles with this premise in his first paragraph:

> an "event," if this loaded word did not entail a meaning which it is precisely the function of structural—or structuralist—thought to reduce or to suspect. But let me use the term "event" anyway, employing it with caution and as if in quotation marks. In this sense, this event will have the exterior form of a *rupture* [the event as lava from a volcano] and a *redoubling* [something that has always already happened before].

As Bob Dylan would say, something has happened, but it's not something new, it replicates, Mr. Jones, what you never knew, yet was always there. The event emerges but at the same time presses on us its having already been there, always already been there. That, Derrida implies, is what structuralism is forced to conclude about the nature of an event. And yet, he persists, wasn't this event, the event of structuralism itself, after all, *new*? And if so, engendered by what?

"Structure, Sign, and Play" is a critique of "structurality." It's not by any means just a critique of structuralism. It quizzes anything that has a "center." I look at a structure and I say it has a center. I mean a blanket term, a guiding concept, a transcendental signified, something that engenders the structure. Derrida says that this center is also what allows for limited free play within the structure. A structure has boundaries; it may be amoeboid, but it still has boundaries, and boundaries always limit the free play within the structure. In the phenomenological tradition, this limited free play is called the "intentionality" of the structure. Kant, you remember, calls it "purposiveness": the way the object is organized according to an internal dynamic.

But to speak of intentionality as a center is not at all the same thing as to speak of an intending person, author, being, or idea that brought it into existence as a center, because those origins are extraneous to the structure itself: genesis, a cause. But how do we get from an intending author to the intentionality of structure and back? A center is "both a center and not a center," as Derrida maddeningly tells us. (By the way, the genetic double helix, which both produces us and is carried within us, is a good example of a center that is not a center in this parlance.) A center is typically conceived as that which organizes a structure yet isn't really qualified to organize anything because it's not *in* the structure; it's not participatory but outside the structure, something that imposes itself from without like a cookie cutter.

After these first remarks about the "center," Derrida describes the history of metaphysics as a history of successive appeals to a center: to some genetic impulse from which everything derives. The list is very cunningly put together (916). It's not necessarily chronological, but it does give you a sense of successive concepts of first causes. I'll just take up the list toward the end: "transcendentality, consciousness, or conscience, God, man, and so forth." Notice that though the list isn't strictly chronological, man nevertheless does succeed God. Derrida is thinking about the development of Western culture. In the Middle Ages and to some extent in the early modern period, we lived in a theocentric world. Insofar as he understood himself as "man" at all, man understood himself as a product of divine creativity, as one entity among others that participate in and benefit from the divine presence. The ensuing rise of the Enlightenment is also the rise of anthro-pocentrism, and by the time the Enlightenment is in full cry, you get every-body from Voltaire to Blake to Marx to Nietzsche saying not that God invented man, but that man invented God. Man has become the transcen-dental signified. Everything derives now in this historical moment from hu-man consciousness, and all concepts of whatever kind can be understood in that light.

But then, having said "man," Derrida adds, enigmatically, "and so forth." Something comes after man, who exists as a center only at a certain historical moment. The argument Derrida is making about the emergence of the "event" is that a new transcendental signified has actually substituted itself for man. With the advent of structuralism, the world is no longer an-thropocentric, it's *linguistic*. The latest emergence, the rupture, the event that makes a difference, is the emergence of language understood as a sys-tem of signs (*ibid.*):

> The moment [of emergence, the event] was that in which lan-guage invaded the universal problematic [in other words, the moment in which language displaced the previous transcenden-tal signified, which was man]; that in which, in the absence of a center or origin, everything became discourse—provided we can agree on this word—that is to say, when everything became a system where the central signified, the original or transcen-dental signified, is never absolutely present outside a system of differences.

The new origin, then, language in the discourse of structuralism, consists in the denial of origins. Derrida is making a claim for language while *erasing* it. He's painfully aware that language is in one sense just the new God, the new Man. (Language produced me just as I produced God.) Many critiques of deconstruction take the form of saying that in the absence of other agen-cies, it authorizes language, gives it agency, even consciousness, as though it were God or man. You can see that Derrida anticipates this critique and views it as an inescapable double bind.

Yet the "event" of structuralist language did occur in a new and com-paratively clear-sighted way, Derrida says in its defense, because hitherto there had been a problem with each successive account of origins in meta-physics. We were always saying God is immanent in all things, human consciousness pervades everything that it encounters—in short, we spoke of something that is part of a structure yet is also outside of it. God creates the world and then, as Milton says, "uncircumscrib'd withdraw[s]." God is not there, becomes the *Dieu caché*, absent from the world yet also the structure of the world. The same thing can be said of man. Human thought brings the sense of what the world is into being, then stands aside as an observer.

Language doesn't do that, Derrida says, language is different because it makes no sense to talk about it as standing outside of its frame of reference. Having acknowledged that, the "event" is structuralist language, he then develops this argument as his essential critique of structuralism. Language is not *other* than speech (or rather "writing," for reasons we'll get to), it is perpetually manifest in speech (writing) and only there. Just as the difference between signified and signifier must be put under erasure, so too must be the distinction between *langue* and *parole* (*écriture*). If it is not a virtual system of signs, however, what then *is* "language"? Deconstruction questions the distinction between language and thought in questioning the distinction between signifier and signified, so language is not quite Saussurian, even though, as Derrida says, it's difficult to discuss it without a Saussurian vocabulary.

Another problem, likewise related to the critique of Saussure, is the premise that the thinking that's inward (Saussure calls it "psychological") is something unmediated that can be *voiced* and indeed should be voiced, reserving for writing the representation of that voicing. Note that Saussure calls the utterance of a concept a "sound image." According to Derrida, in the Saussurian tradition the unmediated presence of language is presumed to be sound, "voice" instead of script, speech instead of writing. He claims that this "privileging of voice as full presence" is a hidden bias in the whole history of metaphysics. Why, after all, should we think of language as a producer of speech, of that which is voiced? Why do we think of voice—as in the divine *logos*, the Word: "in the beginning was the Word"—as a fully present simultaneity that reflects the essence of language as well as its manifestation in speech?

Writing, Derrida argues, is very little different from voice. Voice, too, is articulated combinatorially in time. Voice is a noise *inscribed on the ear.* This is a metaphor for speech that Derrida frequently uses: a writing on the ear. The distinction that Saussure wants to make, which Derrida takes to be "metaphysical," between something primary, something immediate and underivative—voice—and something merely reproductive of voice—namely, writing—needs to be questioned. Derrida does so in one of his most influential early books, *Of Grammatology.*

Speech and writing for Derrida are binary correlates of each other, but Derrida argues beyond this contention, if only to offset opposed prejudices, that writing can be understood as primary. To follow that argument, we need to say something about a number of key terms that Derrida uses to sustain his criticism of traditional ideas about language. The first is the notion of supplementarity. A supplement, he points out, is something that either completes something that isn't complete or adds to something that is already complete. For example, I take vitamin C. I also drink a lot of orange juice, so I've got plenty of vitamin C, and if I take a vitamin C pill I am supplementing something that's already complete; if I don't drink any orange juice, then my pill supplements what's not complete, but either way we always call it a supplement. It's very difficult even to keep in mind the conceptual difference between these two sorts of supplement.

Now a sign as traditionally viewed is self-sufficient, self-contained. Saussure made it a scientific object by saying that it's both arbitrary and differential; but a sign understood under the critique of deconstruction is something that is perpetually proliferating signification, something that doesn't stand still, and something that can't be viewed as self-sufficient or independent in its nature. It bleeds or spills into successive signs in such a way that it perpetually leaves what Derrida calls "traces." As we examine the unfolding of a speech act, we see how successive signs are contaminated, influenced, by the signs that precede them. Supplementarity is a way of understanding the simultaneous self-sufficiency and self-overflow of signs in the chain of signification.

Différance is in part a synonym for supplementarity, but it is also a way of talking about the difference between voice and writing. There *is* a difference between voice and writing even though they have so much in common. As I've said, voice and writing are not a stable binary. (There are no stable binaries in Derrida.) The difference between voice and writing is that writing can give us many indications of difference that voice can't give us. Part of the interest of misspelling *différence*, as Derrida insists on doing, is that if we think of language merely as voiced, we can't at all easily tell the difference between *différance* and *différence*. *Différance*, in other words, with its substitution of the *a*—and remember the riff in the essay "Différance" on "a" as a pyramid, as alpha, as origin, and as killing the king because the king, remember, is the transcendental signified: "God, man and so forth"— the importance of the *a* in *différance* is something that we can pick up only if we orient language toward writing, because in speech these modes of difference don't register.

Différence (with an *e*) is simply the Saussurian linguistic system, a system of differences understood as a simultaneity: available to us as a smorgasbord from which we pick and choose. (Yet even the word "difference" stands in subtle contrast with the more schematic notion of "opposition.") *Différance* by contrast introduces the temporal idea of *deferral* and reminds us that difference—that is to say, our understanding of difference, our means of negotiating difference—is not something that's actually done in space; it's done in time. When I perceive a difference, I perceive it temporally. I no longer see the relation among signs as an issue of simultaneity. I want to see it as a spatial relation in order to pin it down scientifically, but in my actual stream of consciousness I grasp difference temporally. *I defer difference.* Time is the medium in which signs bleed into each other, supplement each other, and to enter this medium I need the concept of *différance*.

There a couple of things I want to say in the next lecture about the characteristic moves of Derridean thought. I will also try to say something more about the troublesome keywords I have just introduced and their relation to Derrida's understanding of language. Then on to de Man.

CHAPTER 11

Deconstruction II

Paul de Man

Readings:

De Man, Paul. "Semiology and Rhetoric." In *The Critical Tradition*, pp. 882–892.

Additional passages.

I'm going to forego what for me would have been fun, though perhaps not for you: an explication of the astonishing passage that concludes Derrida's "Structure, Sign, and Play" (926), but I'll quote it so you can think some more about it, considering how it picks up earlier motifs, returns the essay to its beginning, and reflects on its own metaphors:

> Here there is a sort of question, call it historical, of which we are only glimpsing today, the *conception, the formation, the gestation, the labor.* I employ these words, I admit, with a glance toward the business of childbearing—but also with a glance toward those who, in a company from which I do not exclude myself, turn their eyes away in the face of the as yet unnamable, which is proclaiming itself and which can do so, as is necessary whenever a birth is in the offing, only under the species of the non-species in the formless, mute, infant, and terrifying form of monstrosity.

Well, there is a sentence for you, and perhaps a title for a commentary: "The Monstrosity of Deconstruction."

I want to go back briefly to the relationship between Derrida and Lévi-Strauss. I suggested in the last lecture that while in some ways "Structure, Sign, and Play" is a critique of Lévi-Strauss, to a remarkable degree, confessed or unconfessed, it repeats his thinking. There is the moment when he quotes from Lévi-Strauss's "Introduction" to the work of Marcel Mauss on the subject of the birth, event, or emergence of language. What he quotes would seem, on the face of it, to have just the sort of reservation and hesitation about the emergence or birth of language that Derrida himself has. Lévi-Strauss writes, quoted by Derrida:

> "Whatever may have been the moment and the circumstances of its appearance in the scale of animal life, language could only have been born in one fell swoop. Things could not have set about signifying progressively. Following a transformation the study of which is not the concern of the social sciences but rather of biology and psychology, a crossing over came about from a stage where nothing had a meaning to another where everything possessed it."

With a big bang, all of a sudden you had language. There in place was a semiotic system, whereas before—yesterday or a minute ago—there was no language at all. There's no suggestion that suddenly someone looked at something and assigned it a meaning, then looked at something else and assigned it a meaning, and in the long run, lo and behold, there was language. (If you hear echoes of Mel Brooks and Carl Reiner's "2000 Year Old Man" in this, that's no accident.) The reason this reconstruction makes no sense is that bringing into existence the very thought of meaning, Lévi-Strauss wants to argue, instantly confers meaning on everything. There is no gradual emergence of language; there is a rupture.

Derrida is interested in this argument because he recognizes its affinity with his own hesitation in talking about events, births, emergence, and so on. At the same time, he points out by way of criticism that to suppose that yesterday there was no language, there were just things as they are without meaning, and that today there is language—that things have meaning because that semiotic system we call language is in place—means that culture must come after nature. On this view, as soon as culture emerges—as Lévi-Strauss argues poignantly in a book called *Tristes Tropiques*, we begin to feel overwhelming nostalgia for the immediacy of nature, which is distanced and corrupted by culture. Derrida points out, however, that this nostalgia brings into existence what we are nostalgic for. There is no nature unless there is culture to give it meaning, part of which is regret for its disappearance. The nostalgia or regret of the ethnographer who says that because of the obtrusive research of ethnocentric Europeans in the field there is no longer a savage mind is of the same kind. "The Savage Mind" (an expression that provides the title of one of Lévi-Strauss's most ambitious books) is a concept that the ethnocentric observer brings into being.

But Derrida could have found his critique already expressed in Lévi-Strauss. *The Raw and the Cooked* itself stages this critique in its very title. Raw? If Adam sits in the garden and eats a carrot, would he call it raw? Certainly not, because the concept "raw" is meaningless except in contrast with "cooked." Raw as opposed to what? Adam would say. "Cooked" brings "raw" into being in exactly the way culture brings nature into being.

This basic move in theory, which we've seen before and will see many more times, looks like an inversion of priority in a binary pair, but it's not so much that as a reminder that they cannot exist apart from each other. In other words, criticizing the imputed emergence of one state of things from another state of things is basically saying—I'm sorry to be so reductive about it but I really can't see the distortion in saying this—that we can't know whether the chicken or the egg came first but we do know you can't have the one without the other.

This is perhaps the essential move of deconstruction, but anyone who studies philosophy as well as literary theory will find it familiar, from Hegel right on through to the postdeconstructive thinkers we encounter in the rest of our reading—preeminent among them the gender theorist Judith Butler, who argues, for example, that the "heterosexual" is inconceivable without the established framework of the "homosexual." The absolute interdependency of these concepts is central to Butler's view of gender.

Just a bit more, then, in this regard, concerning Derrida's distinction between writing (*écriture*) and speech. This distinction is not meant counterintuitively to suggest that writing precedes speech. Derrida insists only that we must not suppose writing to have come into being belatedly in order to reproduce, imitate, or transcribe speech. Writing and speech are interdependent phenomena. Last time we spoke about *différance*. We said that the difference between *différence* with an *e* and *différance* with an *a* can't be voiced. It's a difference, or *différance*, that comes into being precisely in writing, and it's only in writing that we suddenly grasp the twofold nature of *différance* as difference and deferral. I'd like to pause—this will be my segue to de Man—over an interesting example in French that we don't have in English but is, I think, so instructive that it's worth bringing in: *est/et*. For one thing, the written *s* in *est*, the *s* that means "signification," we might say, is dropped out of this word when you *say* it, *est* (eh), the word for *is*. "Eh," then, is also the pronunciation of *et*, the word for *and*. These two words precisely express in French what Derrida is trying to describe as the double meaning of "supplementarity." *Is* in the sense of the metaphor—"This is that, A is B"—is a supplement that adds to a whole. It's a means of completing a whole through the declaration that A, which awaits fulfillment through comparison, is also, among other things, B.

But *is* has another sense that is not a rhetorical sense. Even though metaphorically A is B, we know perfectly well that A is not B. How can A be B? A is only A. In fact, it's even a question whether A is A, but it's certainly not B. In the grammatical sense, the mystification of the metaphor doesn't enter in. In the grammatical sense, this word is the means or principal of predication whereby we say one thing is another thing: a mare is a female horse, for example. Notice that the relationship between the rhetorical *is* and the grammatical *is* is basically the relationship between what Jakobson calls the "poetic function" and the "metalingual function." As you'll see in de Man, there is an irreducible tension between the rhetorical sense of this word, which claims metaphoricity, and the grammatical sense of this word, which makes no such claim but is simply the establishment of predication in a sentence.

Now the overlap of *est* and *et*, which latter is implied in the grammatical sense of *est*, reinforces the idea of the supplement, not as the completion of something that requires a supplement to be complete—the fulfillment of meaning in a metaphor—but rather in the sense of adding on to something that's already complete. The appositional addition of meaning in the expression *and* or *et* is also very much like what Jakobson calls "metonymy": the adding on of things that are contiguous, making no claim to be metaphorical, as in grammatical predication. So the tension that arises simply by looking at these two similarly voiced words gives us an emblem of what Derrida calls "supplementarity" and what de Man calls the irreducible conflict between rhetoric and grammar. This conflict will be the focus of what we have to say about de Man in this lecture.

Now in the last lecture I mentioned the presence of Derrida and de Man together at Yale, together with J. Hillis Miller and scholars who were linked with them—Geoffrey Hartman and Harold Bloom—in a period of flourishing in the 1970s and early 1980s, elsewhere called "the Yale school," subject to much admiration in the academy and much vilification both within and outside the academy. This was a moment in which academic thinking about literature had a strong influence on topics much broader than literature. The paradigms of deconstruction infiltrated every nonscientific discipline, including fields as unlikely as law and architecture.

In the 1980s, Miller went to UC Irvine and Derrida followed him there. In 1983, Paul de Man died, and the movement began to give way to other interests and trends both at Yale—where Bloom and Hartman developed new interests—and elsewhere. (I should mention, though, that deconstruction, or "rhetorical reading" as de Man called it, is practiced with integrity and skill by a considerable number of scholars, many of them de Man's students and students of his students, to this day.) And then, shortly after his death there came a shocking revelation about de Man—mentioned by our editor in the italicized preface to "Semiology and Rhetoric"—that was horrible in itself and made it impossible ever to read de Man in quite the same way again—but that was also, I have to say, precisely what the enemies of deconstruction were waiting for. This was the fact that in his youth, de Man, still living in Belgium, the nephew of a distinguished socialist politician, wrote for a Nazi-sponsored Belgian newspaper a series of cultural articles that were anti-Semitic in tendency, several of them openly anti-Semitic. Racially and culturally Eurocentric, they argued for the exclusion of Jews from the intellectual life of Europe. These papers were gathered and published as "Paul de Man's wartime journalism," and there was a tremendous furor about them, similar to the outcry against revelations, which had never been completely repressed but grew in magnitude as more and more was known about them, concerning Heidegger's association with the Nazi government. In the late 1980s, there was a furious public dispute among both those who had actually read de Man and those who hadn't. Some were opposed to his work, finding the cancer of Nazism in deconstruction itself, and some scrambled to save his work from wholesale indictment and preserve the legacy of deconstruction.

All of this is a matter of record, and even though I am one of those who strongly oppose the contaminated-through-and-through thesis, decency requires that we pause to weigh the somewhat narrower question to what extent his work can be seen to excuse his concealment of the past. In the book *Allegories of Reading*, where you'll find also a version of "Semiology and Rhetoric," one of de Man's essays that those who had actually read de Man pointed to most accusingly is called "The Purloined Ribbon." It concerns the passage in Rousseau's *Confessions* where Rousseau describes having stolen a ribbon in order to give it to a serving maid to whom he felt attracted and then, when asked who had done it, having blurted out her name, Marion. De Man says this really wasn't an accusation—in fact, this is just a meaningless word blurted out—and that in any case there is no possibility really of confession, no authentic subjectivity that can, as it were in its own voice, affirm or deny guilt or responsibility. The public, which had no evidence of anti-Semitism in de Man's later life to point to, was inclined to focus instead on his concealment of the past, his refusal to confess, and singled out "The Purloined Ribbon" as a kind of allegory in self-defense, an allegorical reading with a personal application in a book called *Allegories of Reading.*

As with Heidegger, in any case, it has been very difficult to read de Man in the same way we did as a result of what we now know. Let me just say also, though, that there is no cryptically encoded rightism—anti-Semitic or otherwise—either in de Man or in deconstruction. There are two possible ways of reacting to what deconstruction calls "undecidability," which is certainly a form of skepticism. The hostile response is to claim that undecidability opens a void in the intellect and in conscience, a void into which fanaticism and tyranny can rush. Many entertain this view. The positive reaction to undecidability—far more reasonable in my view when we consider that fanaticism everywhere in the world arises from unquestioning belief, not from doubt–takes this form: undecidability is a perpetually vigilant scrutiny of all opinion as such, precisely in order to withstand and to resist those most egregious and incorrigible opinions of all: the opinions of fanaticism and tyranny. This isn't the first time in this course that I've paused at a crossroads where you can't possibly take both paths but where it is difficult to make up one's mind. More than one can say or care to admit, it may ultimately be a matter of temperament which path one chooses to take. Yet I do think that the choice of a path in this case is easier than the choice of a path in hermeneutics.

While we're on the subject of deconstruction in general and before we get into de Man, let me just add that there is one other way, if I may, *not* to criticize deconstruction. It's always supposed popularly that deconstruction denies the existence of any reality outside a text. In *Of Grammatology,* Derrida notoriously said "there is nothing outside the text." What he meant by that is that there's nothing *but* text. The entire tissue, structure, and nature of our lives—including history, which we can only know as a text, including the text of memory—is readable as and only as a text. He didn't mean at all that "the" text, some text, contains everything that matters and that nothing else exists. It is widely believed, though, that that is what he did mean. De Man, in a passage included in your appendix, returns to the attack against this popular supposition:

> In genuine semiology as well as in other linguistically oriented theories, the referential function of language [notice the allusion to Jakobson here] is not being denied–far from it; [In other words, it's not a question of the idealist denial of reality refuted by Dr. Johnson when he kicked a stone and leaped away in terrible pain saying, "I refute it thus." Nobody denies the existence of that hard thing we call a stone. Reality is simply given, whatever it may be, and the referential function is perpetually trying to evoke that reality.] what is in question is its authority for natural or phenomenal cognition. . . . [That is to say, can we know what things are—not *that* things are but *what* things are—using the instrument of language? De Man goes on to say very challengingly:] What we call ideology is precisely the confusion of linguistic with natural reality, of reference with phenomenalism. [In other words, ideology is nothing other than the belief that language, my language—what I say and what I think in language— speaks true.]

Deconstruction never says that what's out there doesn't exist. But what's out there does present itself to reflection, Derrida says, as a text. All that means is that it remains to be deciphered.

The essays collected in de Man's first book, *Blindness and Insight*, were mainly influenced by French existentialism, in particular Jean-Paul Sartre's *Being and Nothingness*. The argument of *Blindness and Insight*, while already both skeptical and dialectical in anticipation of the later work, for the most part precedes de Man's later preoccupations with linguistics and what he sees as the unsignifying materiality of language as such, the same language in which OPOJAZ in 1914 discovered the nonreferential nature of sound. The texts in that first book, in particular the essay called "Criticism and Crisis"—containing a passage that I quote in the appendix—can best be read as existentialist; but soon de Man absorbed the influence of Saussure in linguistics and structuralism, and his vocabulary henceforth took on the coloring of that tradition. The vocabulary that we wrestle with in today's essay, for instance, derives from Jakobson's discussion of the relationship between metaphor and metonymy, as we'll see.

In the meantime, it's probably on this occasion, once we see that they share the influence of Saussurian thinking, that we should say a little bit about the similarities and differences between Derrida and de Man. In common, they take for granted that it is very difficult to think about beginnings, but that at the same time, one has to have some way, some quasi-structuralist way, of realizing that before a certain synchronic moment there was a different synchronic moment. Thus in a quote found in the appendix, to which I'll return in the end, we find de Man saying, "Literary theory can be said to come into being when . . ."—that is de Man's version of Derrida's "event," and it is every bit as fraught with complication. He agrees that the coming into being of language differs qualitatively from the emergence of prior head signifiers ("God, man, and so forth"). What both Derrida and de Man say about the difference between the emergence of language and all those prior emergences is that language does not purport to stand outside of itself. Language is perpetually caught up within its own systematic nature, a center that is *not* outside the structure as well as in it, as all the other "events" were.

They agree also on the interdetermination of binary relations. De Man, for example, says (891–892):

> It is easy enough to see that this apparent glorification of the critic-philosopher in the name of truth is in fact a glorification of the poet as the primary source of this truth.

Now he does not mean—as Freud meant in saying the poets came before him and knew everything he knows before he knew it—that poets' ideas preceded critic-philosophers' ideas. What he means is what he says in the following clauses:

> [I]f truth is the recognition of the systematic character of a certain kind of error, then it would be fully dependent on the prior existence of this error.

In other words, truth arises out of error. Error is not a deviance from truth. Error is not a poetic elaboration on things that undermines the integrity of the truth identified by philosophers, as Plato claims. On the contrary, philosophy is what comes into being as the full acknowledgment of a preexisting error. That is the way de Man wants to think about the relationship precisely between literature and other forms of speech. Literature propounds error, and the critic-philosopher then recognizes the truth—the irreducible necessity—of that error.

De Man's treatment of the interdeterminate truth-error binary brings me to his divergence from Derrida. As I said, Derrida sees all utterance as a continuous tissue of discourse, or discursivity. We are awash in discourse. Yes, we can provisionally or heuristically speak of one form of discourse as opposed to another—literature, law, theology, science, and so on—but such distinctions are all easily undermined and demystified. De Man does not agree. De Man thinks, on the contrary, that there is such a thing as "literariness." He follows Jakobson much more consistently in this regard than Derrida does. Again and again, in what amounts to a "defense of poetry," de Man insists on the difference between literature and other forms of discourse.

Here is a passage (883) in which de Man sounds very much like a Russian formalist talking about the characteristic of literature that is lacking in other forms of discourse. He says:

> [L]iterature cannot merely be received as a definite unit of referential meaning that can be decoded without leaving a residue. The code is unusually conspicuous, complex, and enigmatic; it attracts an inordinate amount of attention to itself, and this attention has to acquire the rigor of a method. The structural moment of concentration on the code for its own sake cannot be avoided, and literature necessarily breeds its own formalism.

It is when we consider the implications of this difference from other forms of discourse, however, that de Man sounds less like a formalist. The "residue" of literature, its "literariness" or "set to the message," is in his view the disclosure of the necessary error that other forms of discourse, supposing themselves to refer to things, remain unaware of. Literature knows itself to be fictive. It is not based on something but is made up. (It may help you to remember our account of what Sidney says in the *Apologie for Poesie* here.) Criticism, which is "about" literature (de Man's criticism, for example), perforce refers to, as a truth, the error or failure of reference that inevitably appears in the residue, the literariness, of literature. That is why criticism and all other forms of referential discourse perpetually forget the error of their ways.

De Man writes accordingly (in a passage included in your appendix): "the statement about language [by criticism], that sign and meaning can never coincide, is what is precisely taken for granted in the kind of language we call literary. Literature, unlike everyday language, begins on the far side of this knowledge; it is the only form of knowledge free from the fallacy of unmediated expression"—free from the fallacy that when I say "It is raining" as a meteorologist, I must be saying something true. When literature says "It is raining," it is not looking out of the window. The *author* may have been looking out of the window, but a text can't do that. It makes up weather. "All of us," de Man continues, "know this, although we know it in the misleading way of a wishful assertion of the opposite. Yet the truth emerges in the foreknowledge we possess of the true nature of literature when we refer to it as *fiction*."

This is why, in a passage taken from an interview with Stefano Rosso, de Man is willing to venture on a categorical distinction between his own work and that of his close friend Jacques Derrida. He says:

> I have a tendency to put upon texts [and he means literary texts] an inherent authority, which is stronger, I think, than Derrida is willing to put on them. . . . In a complicated way, I would hold to the statement that "the text deconstructs itself [in other words, literature is the perpetual denial of its referentiality], is self-deconstructive," rather than being deconstructed by a philosophical intervention [Derrida bringing his delicate sledgehammer down on every conceivable form of utterance is a "philosophical intervention"] from outside the text.

Historically, "Semiology and Rhetoric" comes near the end of the investment in deconstruction that "Structure, Sign, and Play" inaugurates. De Man's essay, published in *Allegories of Reading*, dates from the early 1980s in its presented form, having appeared in a different form and with a slightly different concluding argument in 1979. Even before the death of de Man and the revelations about his past, there were a lot of people shaking their fists and saying, "What about history? What about reality?" I've already suggested that this response can be and often has been a naive misunderstanding, but it was still very much in the air and actually determined the future course of literary theory, even the "ethical turn" within deconstruction itself. De Man says, in this atmosphere of response (883):

We speak as if, with the problems of literary form resolved once and forever and with techniques of structural analysis refined to near-perfection, we could now move "beyond formalism" toward the questions that really interest us and reap, at last, the fruits of the aesthetic concentration on techniques that prepared us for this decisive step.

From his viewpoint clearly he's saying that if we make this move, if we move beyond formalism, we will have forgotten the cardinal rule of the Russian formalists: namely, that there's no distinction between form and content, that we in effect cannot move beyond formalism no matter how much we may wish to do so. That's the argument he develops in this essay. The task of the essay is to deny the supposed mutual reinforcement and complementarity of rhetoric and grammar even in rigorous rhetorical analysis like that of Gérard Genette, Todorov, Barthes, and others, all of whom have "regressed from the rigor of Jakobson." De Man argues on the contrary that in any text, rhetoric and grammar are inescapably at odds.

This argument, I think, has something to do with an essay by Derrida called "The Supplement of Copula," which I was alluding to earlier in discussing the misfit between "is" as a metaphor (rhetoric) and "is" as a predication (grammar). The former asserts identity while the latter indicates either transitive agency between a subject and a predicate (the boy is batting the ball) or the intransitive connection between a subject and its attribute (the boy is agile).

In pursuit of this distinction, de Man begins with a popular sitcom of the time, "All in the Family." As de Man explains, Archie Bunker becomes exasperated when his wife Edith begins to tell him what the difference actually is between bowling shoes laced over and bowling shoes laced under in response to Archie's rhetorical question, "What's the difference?" Of course, the meaning of the *rhetorical* question was "I don't care what the difference is." But Edith, a reader of sublime simplicity, as de Man says, misinterprets the rhetorical question as a *grammatical* question: "What *is* the difference? I'm curious to know." Archie can't stand this because to him it's perfectly clear that a rhetorical question is a rhetorical question.

That too, though, is sublimely simple. De Man's point is that without appealing to intention a question is both rhetorical and grammatical—and that inevitably the two questions lurking within the one will have conflicting answers. He complicates without changing the argument by turning then to

Yeats's poem, "Among Schoolchildren," which concludes, you remember: "How can we tell the dancer from the dance?" Another twofold question. The rhetorical question completes the usual reading of the poem. The answer to the rhetorical question is that we cannot tell the difference between the dancer and the dance because they are unified in a synthetic, symbolic moment that constitutes the work of art. (Note that rhetorical questions in general imply some metaphorical identity—"what's the difference?"—which is what makes them rhetorical.) All the preceding metaphors in this reading of the poem lead up to this triumphant sense of symbolic unity as the essence of the work of art—a unity that entails among other things the unity of author and text, agent and action, the unity of all of those dualities that much literary theory deconstructs.

But suppose this were a grammatical question, de Man asks, a question posed out of sincere, if simple, curiosity? The answer to that question seems painfully obvious. Here is the dancer and here is the dance that is performed and clearly they're not the same thing. Then de Man, who had written a doctoral dissertation on Yeats, adduces an impressive array of examples from other Yeats poems showing that Yeats clearly grasps the irreducibility of grammatical difference. On this evidence de Man argues that there is a measure of irony in the poem that saves it from the symbolizing mystifications it appears to indulge in. But he's not claiming, as he is at pains to point out, that his explication is the true one. He claims only that it is available and can be adduced from what we call "evidence" in the same way that the symbolic interpretation, based on the rhetorical question, is available and can be adduced from evidence. These two readings, then, can't be reconciled, yet neither can be ruled out.

In a sentence built around or implying the copula "is"—in all sentences, that is—metaphor and predication are always going to be at odds. A metaphor is what we call a poetic lie. Everybody knows A is not B. A predication, on the other hand, usually goes forward in the service of referentiality. It's a truth claim of some kind. But if rhetoricity and grammaticality coexist in all sentences, the truth claim and the lie are perpetually at odds with each other, they belie each other. Of course, we know perfectly well what Edith intends and what Archie Bunker intends, so *we* don't confuse the meaning of what they're saying. But Archie's question does harbor two meanings, and Edith helps clarify them by managing to confuse them.

But, de Man continues in a magnificent flight, suppose Archie Bunker were *Arche* (Greek for "origin") *De*bunker? Suppose Archie Bunker were Jacques Derrida and put the question "What is the *différance*?" That would be an entirely different matter, wouldn't it, because you would have absolutely no idea whether the question was rhetorical or grammatical. In that case, it wouldn't be possible to invoke an intention because the whole complication introduced by Derrida is precisely to raise the question about not being able to voice the *différance* between *différence* (metaphor) and *différance* (metonymy) and not knowing therefore whether Archie is right or whether Edith is right.

De Man's reading of Marcel's allegory of reading in Proust I can only skim in the space remaining. Remember to begin with that de Man sets up his climactic discussion of this passage at the beginning of the essay by talking about the grandmother who's always driving Marcel out into the garden because she can't stand the interiority of his reading. In the long run, de Man then discusses Marcel's description of how he brought the outside inside, perpetually conscious while reading in his cool, darkened room of everything that was going on in the sun-drenched garden, so that ultimately, in the charmed moment of his reading, there was no difference between inside and outside. Thus a *rhetorical* understanding of the relationship between inside and outside, a metaphor conflating the two, has been accomplished. Yet grammatical analysis shows that the whole structure of the passage is additive, a complication and elaboration of the imagery with no implication of identity. This more temporal unfolding de Man calls metonymic.

We should concede in passing that a perhaps needless confusion arises in making a rhetorical device, metonymy, synonymous with *grammar* on the axis of combination. But as I said earlier, this slippage of rhetoric into grammar is already authorized by Jakobson, and once we encounter "the rhetoricization of grammar" in this reading of Proust we may feel the need to acquiesce in the confusion. In the meantime, lest we rest content feeling that the structure of the passage is grammatical after all, we must remember that the whole description is spoken by a *voice*, the overarching sameness of tone and attitude that unifies everything after all. "This is what I call," says de Man, "the rhetoricization of grammar." But he is not finished! That voice is not that of the author. The speaker is Marcel performing his metaphoric magic, but we know there is an *author*, Proust, painstakingly putting this description together in the most laborious, calculating way, building one image on another in a sequence that's grammatical (metonymic), not rhetorical. We have arrived, without thinking for a moment by this time that we could remain there, at the "grammaticization of rhetoric." The interior is cool and dark, the exterior is hot and bright, both are silent; but they merge in the audible confluence of Marcel's word *torrent* (as of cool water) with its near-homonym *torride*. The interior is metaphorical, the exterior is grammatical; sometimes they merge, sometimes draw apart—but always undecidably.

One last criticism of deconstruction to fend off: "it makes literature meaningless." De Man often says, and I hope these illustrations show, that rhetorical reading is not a denial of meaning but an acknowledgment that meaning always exists in excess, seminally, supplementarily. You can never have enough of it.

Author (Reader) and Psyche

CHAPTER 12

Freud and Fiction

Readings:

Brooks, Peter. "Freud's Masterplot." In *The Critical Tradition*, pp. 882–892.

Freud, Sigmund. "The Dream-Work." In *The Critical Tradition*, pp. 500–508.

In this lecture we mark a transition. We have completed our survey of theory that makes form and language its focus. We move now to an emphasis on the psychological profile of literature, and from there to the social and cultural determinants of literature.

So far we have reviewed ways of arguing that thought and speech are brought into being by language and are inseparable from their linguistic milieu. Our transition from language-determined ideas about speech, discourse, and literature to the psychological determination of discourse will be a smooth one, though, because Peter Brooks and Jacques Lacan, two of the theorists we'll consider who borrow from Freud and view their projects in psychoanalytic terms, are nevertheless still using what is now for us an extremely familiar vocabulary. They maintain that consciousness in its relation to the unconscious is best viewed in the context of the formalist and semiotic traditions we have been studying. Lacan famously said, as you'll hear again soon, "The unconscious is structured like a language," and Brooks plainly does agree. Apart from his reliance on the texts of Freud, especially *Beyond the Pleasure Principle*, a context I'll be attempting to sketch in, you'll find Brooks writing on what for you is now familiar ground. He was at Yale, by the way, during the heyday of the Yale school and long thereafter. Although he was a respected, somewhat younger member of the circle I mentioned last time, I did not mention him then because his work is grounded in structuralism and psychoanalysis (like Lacan's in that regard) and withstands the influence of deconstruction. When we get to Lacan, whose *manner* is much closer to Derrida's than to Brooks's, I'll try to show just wherein structuralist psychoanalysis differs from deconstruction.

Brooks begins the excerpt you have read from *Reading for the Plot* by borrowing the Russian formalist distinction between "plot" and "story" in an effort to explain what narrative fiction is. I had better let you know finally, overcoming my embarrassment about using words I can't even pronounce, that the Russian words for these concepts, plot and story, are *sjužet* and *fabula*, respectively, because those are the terms Brooks uses. They're a little counterintuitive, it seems to me, because if you try to find cognates for them in English you'd think that *sjužet* would be "subject matter," something much closer to what the formalists translated into English mean by "story," and you'd think that *fabula* might well be something like "plot" or "fiction." But it's just the opposite. *Sjužet* is the plot, the way a story is constructed, and the *fabula* is the subject matter or material out of which the *sjužet* is made.

In addition, concerning the relationship between plot and story, Brooks uses terms that are familiar after our reading of Jakobson and de Man: "metaphor" and "metonymy." There's a tacit agreement among modern literary theorists to reduce all the many tropes of classical rhetoric to just these two terms. When it's necessary, they add a few (there are four in Kenneth Burke's appendix to *The Grammar of Motives*, six in Harold Bloom, and de Man himself turns also to allegory, irony, and prosopopoeia), but the essential bifurcation in classical rhetoric, as literary theory sees it, is the distinction between metaphor, which unifies, synthesizes, and brings together, and metonymy, which makes one sign contiguous with another but makes no claim to unify or establish identity.

What, then, does Peter Brooks take from Freud? He is a distinguished Freudian scholar who has a deep interest in every aspect of Freud, but for our purposes let us say that what he takes in particular from Freud is the structuring of desire in the unconscious and the nature of that structuring: the idea, insofar as we can imagine Freud anticipating Lacan (Lacan himself certainly claimed that Freud anticipated him), that the unconscious is structured like a language but, as it were, a *volitional* language. In turning to the psyche, we are back in the realm of intention, needless to say, only now we encounter something like unconscious intention. Brooks wants to map this broad idea onto the construction of fictional plots.

Aristotle tells us that a plot has a beginning, a middle, and an end. We are likely to think that the most self-evident concept ever posited by a philosopher, yet we must accord a degree of acumen even to Aristotle on plot. Well, of course, we grumble, it has to have a beginning, and we assume that unless we're desperately keeping things going like Scheherazade, it has to have an end. Yet we might well ask ourselves, why does it have a middle? What is the function of the middle with respect to the beginning and the end? And not just any middle: Why does Aristotle say, as Brooks quotes him, that a plot should have "a certain magnitude"? Why shouldn't it be shorter or longer? What in particular does the middle have to do with revealing to us the necessary connectedness of the beginning with the end? The beginning, after all, is not just an arbitrary starting point (it has antecedents that could have been a beginning) but a moment or event that precipitates a certain logic, a moment that is resolved in turn tragically, comically, or noncommittally by the end *after* the middle has done its work. How especially does the middle become a field in which this logic is tested and explored? Brooks believes that he can understand these questions in psychoanalytic terms.

Brooks also borrows from Freud the methodological idea that one can think about plot structure in terms of the distinction Freud makes in *The Interpretation of Dreams* (1905) between *condensation* and *displacement*. Condensation takes the essential symbols of the dream and distills them into an overdetermined unity so that if one studies the dream work, one can see the underlying wish or desire expressed in the dream manifest itself in a particular symbolic unity or nexus. In displacement, certain elements of desire in the dream, probably the most severely repressed, are not expressed in condensed symbols but rather are displaced onto seemingly irrelevant ideas, images, or activities that the interpreter needs to decode. Displacement is a delay or detour of interpretive understanding, and condensation, on the other hand, is a distillation perhaps so extremely compressed that it too challenges understanding. These operations work simultaneously. The dream work simultaneously condenses and displaces what it is at once concealing and struggling to make manifest as its object of desire.

The first person to notice that there might be a fruitful theoretical connection between Freud's condensation and displacement and Jakobson's metaphor and metonymy was Jacques Lacan, whom Brooks quotes to this effect. The premise is that desire in everyday discourse, in our conversation but also in our account of our dreams and in the rest of what we tell our analyst, expresses itself through the medium of these two aspects of the dream work understood as tropes. Condensation works metaphorically and displacement works metonymically. Metonymy is the delay or perpetual *différance* of signification. Metaphor is the gathering up in a crystalline moment of the desire that's attempting to articulate itself along a plot line. In fiction, as Brooks argues, we observe that these two rhetorical tendencies coexist. You can perhaps feel an implied tension with de Man's "Semiology and Rhetoric" in the background here: metaphor and metonymy may or may not work in harmony, may or may not conduce to an ultimate unity, depending whom you read. Be that as it may, though, they nevertheless do coexist in such a way that we can observe the resemblance between the development of a fictional narrative and the development of dreams.

If this sort of thing is what interests Brooks in Freud, we should recognize immediately that he is not anything like what we may be tempted to caricature as a traditional psychoanalytic critic. He doesn't go around looking for Oedipus complexes and phallic symbols. He doesn't pause, at least for long, when somebody lights a cigar or wears a necktie. He says as much at the end of your excerpt (1171);

> [T]here can be psychoanalytic criticism of the text itself [what he's doing, that is] that does not become—as has usually been the case—a study of the psychogenesis of the text (the author's unconscious), the dynamics of literary response (the reader's unconscious), or the occult motivations of the characters (postulating an "unconscious" for them).

In other words, Brooks is not interested in developing a psychoanalytic theory of the author, of the reader, or of character. I said we were back in the realm of intention during this phase of the syllabus, and we are; but it's a carefully confined sort of intention, perhaps not immune to criticism: it's the agency of language itself, or of the text.

Brooks in this passage is not condescending toward traditional Freudian criticism, or certainly not all of it; he is just announcing a different purpose. Although we don't linger over traditional Freudian criticism in this course, it can indeed be extremely interesting: just for example, Freud's disciple Ernest Jones wrote an influential study of Shakespeare's *Hamlet* in which he showed that Hamlet has an Oedipus complex. You can't respond honestly to the play without seeing that there's a good deal in what Jones is saying; in fact, famously in the history of the staging and filming of Shakespeare, Sir Laurence Olivier played the role of Hamlet under the influence of Ernest Jones. His Hamlet makes it painfully clear in his relations with Gertrude that he had an Oedipus complex. Again, there are actual works of literature written directly under the influence of Freud. In D. H. Lawrence's *Sons and Lovers*, the central character, Paul Morel, is crippled by an Oedipus complex that he can't master. Moving closer to the present, an important figure in literary theory whom we'll be studying later, Harold Bloom, develops in a series of books, beginning with *The Anxiety of Influence*, a theory of the author that views the relationship between belated poets and their precursors as a rivalry between sons and fathers. I myself have invoked this pattern of thought in arguing that Lévi-Strauss's version of the Oedipus myth betrays his Oedipus complex in relation to Freud. Plainly, Freudian criticism with these sorts of preoccupations is widespread, continues sometimes to appear, and cannot simply be discounted as an influence upon the theory of literature.

But as I've said, the odd thing in Brooks's work, or maybe not so odd, is that although the novelistic text is not there to tell us something about its author or its characters or our own secret selves, it seems in itself nevertheless to be alive like an author or a character. A plot unfolds to articulate desire, indeed some particular desire, yet it's not the author's desire, it's a form of desire, broadly characteristic of the unconscious, that plays itself out in the mechanics of plot. Despite this abstraction from any individual profile, Brooks does say that he has a certain desire in mind. Let us hesitantly call it a universal desire. The function of the text's structure is to fulfill this desire for what Freud in his analytic work frequently calls reduced excitation: this desire can be associated sexually with the pleasure principle or otherwise with the death wish that Freud explores in *Beyond the Pleasure Principle*, where the reduction of excitation would consist in achieving death, or closure, in the right way. Through these two forms of desiring reduced excitation that can only be achieved in having passed through excitation— and it remains to see whether, or to what extent, these two forms can coexist— Brooks interprets the delay, the arabesque, the postponement of the end that the "middle" of a plot orchestrates.

Obviously, then, neither dreams nor stories simply blurt out the fulfillment of this desire; they also delay it by sustaining the excitation that prompts the desire. I'm sure we have all had the experience of waking up and thinking that we have been stuck in the same dream loop all night long, typically on the threshold of some signal event. Many of our dreams are neither pleasurable nor frightening but exhibit the tedium of a treadmill, even though some sort of excitement seems to lurk around the edge of them as a possibility. The superiority of fiction to the dream work may be that its art, its structure, protracts delay to a pleasurable degree but not unduly beyond that degree.

Not only do the middles of fiction involve these techniques of delay, such as repetition, they also have a curious tendency to revisit unpleasurable things. Yes, everything we love to read is a "page turner," but that doesn't mean we're having "fun" in any conventional sense. Mayhem, catastrophe, and grief lurk around every corner, even in comic fiction. It's all distinctly unpleasurable. I should admit that this aspect of reading fiction has grown on *me* so much in recent years—it affects my ability to watch film even more—that I am losing my taste even for crime fiction, which in former days I read constantly. But most readers, and the affective strategies of most plots, just don't have my problem. Most readers engage in a psychological balancing act. They wince away from the bad news even as they eagerly turn the page.

One reason why plots revisit the agonies of life, especially in the monuments of nineteenth-century realism that particularly interest Brooks, is that the characters keep compulsively making bad object choices. They fall in love with the wrong person. They're mired in sticky situations that they can't get out of because they're not mature enough, they haven't thought things through, or because—as in Hardy—fate looms over the possibility of making a better choice. However the case may be, the experiences that flesh out the middles even of the greatest and the most exciting fiction do have a tendency to be unpleasurable. What can this possibly have to do with the pleasure principle that presumably fuels desire?

That's the question that Freud asked himself in Brooks's proof text, *Beyond the Pleasure Principle* (1919), a text that begins with a consideration of trauma victims. Freud's pamphlet was written at the end of the First World War, and its concern for trauma victims was shared by other writers in Europe. Almost contemporary with *Beyond the Pleasure Principle*, there are novels written in England that reflect the findings of institutional psychologists about trauma victims. Virginia Woolf treats the suicidal returned soldier Septimus Smith in *Mrs. Dalloway* as a traumatized war victim, and Rebecca West wrote a novel called *The Return of the Soldier*, the protagonist of which returns to his estate having lost his memory. Freud's *Beyond the Pleasure Principle* contributes to this postwar theme. Brooks likes to refer to the text of *Beyond the Pleasure Principle* as itself a "master plot" with a fictive ambiance. Perhaps Derrida's breakdown of the relation between literature and other genres is implied here—just as *The Phenomenology of Mind* and *Capital* have been called great novels of culture—but that is not Brooks's main point. He finds in Freud's pamphlet a special relation to the plot structures he has in mind and at the same time an explanation for those structures. It is a center that is both inside and outside of its structure.

Freud begins, quite obviously without yet knowing what his end will be, by remarking that the trauma victims he has treated seem, when recounting their dreams or exhibiting neurotically repetitive behavior (you know, returning the ash tray to some precise spot again and again), compulsively to repeat the traumatic event that brought them to him in the first place. They don't shy away from it. They don't in any strict sense repress it but keep circling back, ordinarily however displacing the event itself in some metonymic way. So the question was—a disturbing question that challenged what had hitherto been a cornerstone of psychoanalysis—how could such behavior possibly accord with the "wish fulfillment," driven by the pleasure principle, that Freud had always considered the sole motivating force of the unconscious? Implicit in Freud's previous assumption was what we would now call the sociobiological premise that the protraction of life is meant to ensure sexual reproduction; and that the displacement or inhibition of the sex drive—call it the life-instinct—takes the form in the ego of the desire to succeed, to improve oneself, to mature emotionally and intellectually. All of this we can associate with the pleasure principle. But how does the compulsion to return to a traumatic event in any way correspond to the workings of the pleasure principle?

Then he remembers an example from his own home life: his infant grandson, little Hans, standing in his crib throwing a spool tied to a string out of the crib saying, "*Fort!*," meaning "away, not here," then reeling it back in and saying, "*Da!*," meaning "here it is again": "*Fort! Da!*" Why on earth is little Hans doing this? Well, Freud pretty quickly figures out that little Hans is expressing his frustration about the way his mother keeps leaving the room. The accomplishment of his game, then, is that he's figured out how to keep her on a string. Sure, she goes away—I have to understand this: I know my mother goes away—but guess what? I can reel her back in and there she is again. This is the "mastery" of a traumatic event, as Freud puts it and as Brooks follows him in arguing, that we can acquire through the repetition of the event. Yet it can't just be the achievement of mastery alone that's involved, because the return to the trauma is so clearly only half the point. It is almost as though that, too, were a pleasure.

If we think of it as an effort of mastery, the compulsion to repeat takes the form, Freud argues, of mastering in advance through rehearsal, as it were, the inevitability of death. The trauma of death that awaits has been heralded by the traumatic events in one's life, the near escapes. Freud mentions the frequency of train accidents in such patients' cases. He comes to see the compulsion to repeat as a *repeating forward* of an event that is itself unnarratable, at least to ourselves: the event of death, which ultimately looms.

But then Freud starts to wonder how it could be that a living organism would behave this way, when everything seems to point toward the will to grow, reproduce, and stay alive. Why this almost eager anticipation of death? He notices (controversially, by the way, but it helps his argument along) that in the behavior of certain organisms, even molecular ones, there's an inclination to return to a simpler and earlier state of organic existence, to that which existed prior to our emergence into life. The relationship between the beginning and the end that I have been intimating, in other words, is the common denominator of death. As organisms we begin inanimate and end inanimate, hence there must be in us a desire to return to the beginning. "The aim of all life," Freud then says, "is death."

We should now allow Brooks to comment on that extraordinary assertion (1166) so that we can move closer to an application of these ideas to the structure of a fictional plot:

> We need at present to follow Freud into his closer inquiry concerning the relation between the compulsion to repeat and the instinctual. The answer lies in "a universal attribute of instinct and perhaps of organic life in general," that *"an instinct is an urge inherent in organic life to restore an earlier state of things."*

Building on this idea, Brooks continues (1169): "This function [of the drives] is concerned with the most universal endeavor of all living substance— namely, to return to the quiescence of the inorganic world." "Peace at last," as it were—and indeed one bump on the road of Freud's speculation is the nagging question whether the death wish is not itself pleasurable, possibly a kind of masochism. It still wouldn't be the same as the pleasure principle because its underlying motive wouldn't be life-sustaining, but the sense of contradiction that so troubles Freud would be somewhat lessened.

But there's more, and this is why novels are long: not *too* long, but not too short—of a certain magnitude, as Aristotle said. There is more because the organism doesn't just want to die as soon as possible. The organism is not suicidal. That's the mistake we probably make when we first try to understand what Freud means by "the death wish." The organism *wants rather to die on its own terms*, at the right time and in the right way, which is why it has an elaborate mechanism of defenses—"the outer cortex," as Freud is always calling it—that attempt to withstand and to keep at arm's length the possibility of trauma. Trauma victims blame themselves for not having been vigilant enough to ward off the blow. The mastery hoped for in the compulsion to repeat is the building up of defenses to prevent its recurrence.

So the organism only wishes to die on its own terms. If you are reminded here of the passage by Tynianov in which he makes the distinction between evolution and modification in literary history, I think the parallel would be legitimate. What the organism in Freud wants to do is *evolve* toward its dissolution, not to be modified: not to be interfered with by anything from external trauma to internal disease. It wants to live a rich and full life, of a certain magnitude, but with a view to achieving the ultimate desired end, which is to return to an inorganic state on its own terms. If a story then were *modified*, there would be no plot, or not enough plot. There might be a beginning, but then you would have a sudden cutting off that prevents the arabesque of the plot from evolving to a proper end.

Now what Brooks argues following Freud is that as the emplotting process goes forward, the pleasure principle and the death wish cooperate (1166–1167):

> Hence Freud is able to proffer, with a certain bravado, the formulation: "*the aim of all life is death.*" We are given an evolutionary image of the organism in which the tension created by external influences has forced living substance to "diverge ever more widely from its original course of life and to make ever more complicated *détours* before reaching its aim of death." In this view, the self-preservative instincts function to assure that the organism shall follow its own path to death, to ward off any ways of returning to the inorganic which are not imminent to the organism itself. In other words, "the organism wishes to die only in its own fashion." It must struggle against events (dangers) which would help to achieve its goal too rapidly—by a kind of short-circuit.

Brooks then says further along (1169):

[W]e could say that the repetition compulsion and the death instinct serve the pleasure principle; in a larger sense [though], the
pleasure principle, keeping watch on the invasion of stimuli from
without and especially from within, seeking their discharge,
serves the death instinct, making sure that the organism is per-
mitted to return to quiescence.

In this way, these apparently conflicting drives coexist and in some measure cooperate to develop the good life and the good plot.

As I've intimated already, an imperiling objection to this theory, one
that Freud acknowledges, is that it's awfully hard to keep death and sex
separate in the functioning system we call human. The reduction of excitation is obviously what the pleasure principle is all about. The purpose of sex
is to reduce excitation, to annul desire. The purpose of death, Freud finds
himself saying in 1919, is to do the same thing. So how can we tell one from
the other? There's a rich vein of literary history that insists on their near
connection. We all know what "to die" means in early modern erotic poems.
We all know about "Liebestod" in "Tristan and Isolde," with other moments
of death in literature that are sexually charged. There is a manifest and knowing confusion of the two in literature—Freud always says that the poets
preceded him in everything—that poses a problem. One countervailing
thought, as I've said, would be that the compulsion to repeat nasty episodes,
to revisit trauma, might be a form of masochism, pleasurable after all and
obviating the need for a theory of the death drive. Freud admits that it's
hard to make the distinction, though he thinks he has clinical evidence that
warrants it. Masochism, he would say, has its etiology in unusual developments at the Oedipal stage, whereas the death instinct, as a compulsion to
repeat, builds up defenses against the arbitrary threat of trauma in order to
secure an independent ending.

Turning, then, to the plot of fiction according to Brooks (here following Lacan and the theorist of fiction, D. A. Miller): desire emerges or begins
as the "narratable," that which contains within it the seeds of a plot. What
then might the *un*narratable be? The unnarratable is the ongoing immersion
in life—Lacan calls it "the real," Žižek calls it "the blot"—that prevents a
sense of order or structure. Anything is unnarratable if we don't have a sense
of a beginning, a middle, and an end to provide it as a context. The narratable, in other words, must lend itself to a structure. So the narratable begin-

ning, which is meditated on by Sartre's Roquentin in *La Nausée* and quoted to that effect by Brooks (cf. 1163)—the narratable begins in a moment of entry into a pattern of desire that can launch a plot.

When the narratable becomes a plot, the identity of this desire emerges through metaphor, which unifies or "binds" the plot and governs the coherence of its parts. Narrative theory nearly always remarks with satisfaction that there's no such thing in fiction as irrelevant detail. Nothing, we are told, is there by accident. This feeling about the inescapable rightness of detail (a prominent interpretive emphasis when the New Criticism eventually imported "close reading" from poetry to fiction in books by Mark Schorer, Reuben Brower, and David Lodge) is represented by Brooks as the metaphoric pressure brought to bear on plotting in the course of composition. Everything is arranged with a motive, namely, the underlying desire that's driving the plot forward.

To some extent by contrast, however, metonymy functions as the principle of delay, the detour, the arabesque, the refusal of closure: making bad object choices and other unfortunate outcomes, the return of the unpleasurable, all the things that happen in the excursive wandering of "middles" in literary plots. It's not that these elements are incoherent, at odds with metaphorization; the plot, after all, binds material together, and both metaphor *and* metonymy are arguably forms of binding. Brooks says (1166): "To speak of "binding" in a literary text is thus to speak of any of the formalizations (which, like binding, may be painful, retarding) that force us to recognize sameness within difference, or the very emergence of a *sjužet* from the material of *fabula*."

Now I want to turn to *Tony* (have you missed him?) to show how reading for the plot can take place. I should mention first, though, that the choice of reading matter for this lecture is not just a way into questions of psychoanalysis as they bear on literature and literary theory, but also a gesture toward something that those of you whose favorite reading is novels may wish we had a little more of: narrative theory or "narratology." I refer you to the opening pages of the Brooks excerpt, where he passes in review some of the most important work in narrative theory, work that I mentioned when discussing structuralism. Roland Barthes, Tzvetan Todorov, and Gérard Genette are the figures Brooks singles out within that tradition.

Anyway, *Tony the Tow Truck*. In the context of *Beyond the Pleasure Principle*, we could retitle this story *The Bumpy Road to Maturity*. It certainly has the qualities of a picaresque fiction. It's on the road. The linearity of its plot, its events laid out metonymically like beads on a string as in picaresque

(Cervantes compares the members of a chain gang Quixote encounters to beads on a string), lends the feeling of picaresque to the narrative. Let's quickly reread it, this time as prose, not broken up by line:

> I am Tony the Tow Truck. I live in a little yellow garage. I help cars that are stuck. I tow them to my garage. I like my job. One day I am stuck. Who will help Tony the Tow Truck? "I cannot help you," says Neato the Car. "I don't want to get dirty." "I cannot help you," says Speedy the Car. "I am too busy." I am very sad. Then a little car pulls up. It is my friend, Bumpy. Bumpy gives me a push. He pushes and pushes [by the way, this text, I think, is very close to its surface a kind of anal-phase parable. In that parable, the hero is not Tony in fact but a character with whom you are familiar if you're familiar with *South Park*, and that character is, of course, the one who says, "He pushes and pushes"] and I am on my way." [In any case, that is part of the narrative, and then:] "Thank you, Bumpy," I call back. "You're welcome," says Bumpy. Now that's what I call a friend.

I've said that this plot is picaresque. Its linear repetitions are the delay that pries apart an origin and an end. In the past, we've spoken of this feature as the triadic form of the folk tale that Brooks also mentions; but it is also, in its dilation of the middle between the beginning and end, a way of putting pressure on the relation between beginning and end. Tony comes from a little yellow garage, and we can't help wondering—though this may be part of the unnarratable—whether he is going back there. We know he's "on his way," but we don't know whether he's on his way back to the little yellow garage or whether—as being "stuck," having broken down, would suggest—he's on his way to the junkyard.

In either case, no matter which the outcome—little yellow garage or junkyard—he's going to get there on his own terms, but *not* as a me-first narcissist who begins every sentence in the first part of the story with the word "I," because it's not enough just to be an autonomous hero. (Freud says, by the way, that being a superhero is what's unhealthy about daydreams.) On your journey, as in folklore, you need a helper. Part of the arabesque of fiction is its introduction of an ancillary hero. Constructively encountering another mind like the helper's prevents the narcissism, even in a nice guy like Tony, that is manifest in the "I," "I," "I" at the beginning of the story.

Eventually the "I" appears only when embedded in a line, an identity among others rather than an inaugural ego that drives the story like a truck.

The arabesque of the plot is a matter of encountering bad object choices and rejecting them: neatness, busyness—choices which, by the way, offer temptations. We all want to be neat and busy, don't we? But the mutuality of regard that this story wants to recommend as life—as life properly lived to its end—is not an attribute of neatness and busyness. Closure comes with a mature object choice that's a gentle push forward of the plot, but we don't quite know toward what. We have to assume, though, that it's a push toward a state in which the little yellow garage and the unmentionable junkyard (it's not unnarratable) are one and the same thing.

We've pointed out many elements of metonymy, but there's one that functions at the level of theme. This is a story about cars and other mechanical objects. Some move and some are stationary—remember the frowning and smiling houses in the background— but they're all mechanical objects. They're not organic. This is a world viewed metonymically as that which lacks organicity, which is only contiguous to the human values it inculcates. Yet at the same time the story is thematically metaphoric, asserting the common humanity of us all: "That's what I call a friend." The whole point of so many animal stories and other stories like this one—its prototype *The Little Engine That Could*, for example—is to humanize the world, to make the whole world friendly and inviting to a child. Metaphorically, Tony is not a tow truck but a human being, and he realizes his humanity in recognizing the need for a friend, something Neato and Speedy fail to do, so they remain cars. The unity of the story, in contrast with its metonymic displacements through the mechanistic, is the triumphant humanization of the mechanistic and the fact that as we read the story, we feel that we are not in mechanical company but in human company. Neat and Speedy move on, Tony is still there, and Bumpy has his back. Having emerged from his garage door into the world, Tony is delayed, detoured, then pulls ahead to the end.

Next we turn to the formidable task of understanding Lacan.

CHAPTER 13

Jacques Lacan in Theory

Reading:

Lacan, Jacques. "The Agency of the Letter in the Unconscious." In *The Critical Tradition*, pp. 1129–1148.

There is an obvious link between the work we reviewed of Peter Brooks and this particular essay of Lacan, "The Agency of the Letter in the Unconscious," that I'd like to begin by emphasizing. It concerns the part of Lacan's argument that is probably most accessible to you after your tour through structuralism and offers perhaps the best means of understanding the relevance of Lacan for literary theory.

Brooks treated the arabesque toward completion in fictional narrative as the sustaining of desire through a series of *détours*, inadequate or improper endpoints risked and avoided, resulting in a continuation of desire until a proper ending is reached—an ending that corresponds to what Freud posited as the desire of the organism to die in its own way and not according to the modification or pressure of something from without. This sequence of *détours* in the elaboration of a narrative plot Brooks called metonymy, which by this time we should recognize as what happens in the sequencing of signs along the axis of combination as described by Jakobson. But Brooks remarks also that at the same time there is a *binding* of this sequence of signs—of events in the case of a plot. There is an effect of unity, and this effect he calls "metaphor." Something like what Jakobson calls the "poetic function" has been superimposed on the metonymic axis of combination in such a way that the feeling of unity, the sense of the recurrence of identity in the signs used, is an impression we carry away with us but can also confirm exegetically. Metaphor unifies the plot even through the zigs and zags of its delay. The delay of fulfillment is most obvious, of course, in a marriage plot and most immediately intelligible there—but there are many sorts of plot, all of which elaborate a form of desire.

I pause in this way to review Brooks because I think you can see—whatever frustration you may be feeling with Lacan—that the same basic contrast shapes Lacan's approach to the unconscious. The deferral of fulfillment for Lacan, in his case potentially an endless deferral, is central as well to his thinking. Like Brooks, Lacan harkens back to the connection made by Freud and as it were completed by Jakobson between condensation and metaphor and displacement and metonymy. The deferral of desire's object, and for Lacan the impossibility of ever realizing one's desire for a certain kind of "other" that I'm going to be trying to identify during the course of this lecture, is understood as metonymy, just as Brooks, again, understands the movement of metonymy as a plot-sustaining *détour* or deferral of the end.

Lacan views metaphor, on the other hand, as what he calls at one point "the quilting" of the metonymic chain, the *point de capiton* or "quilting button" that suddenly holds together a sequence of disparate signifiers in such a way that a substitution of signs rather than a displacement of signs can be accomplished. We'll come back to this later when attempting to grasp what Lacan says about the line from Victor Hugo's poem "Boaz Asleep": "His sheaves were neither miserly nor spiteful." In the meantime, what makes Lacan's reading of desire different from Brooks's, and indeed what makes his reading of desire different from that of anyone else who thinks of these structuralist issues in psychoanalytic terms, is that Lacan really doesn't believe in a suitable ending. He doesn't think we can ever have what we desire. He has no doubt that we can have what we *need*, and for our part we need to keep in mind this fundamental distinction between having what we desire and having what we need. The distinction is often put—and when you read Slavoj Žižek soon you'll find much made of this—as the distinction between the "big Other," which one can never appropriate as an object of desire because it is perpetually and always elusive, and the "*objet petit à*," the little object at hand, which is not really an object of desire at all but is available to satisfy need. Sociobiologically, you can get what you need. Psychoanalytically, you cannot get what you desire.

Now the obvious gloss here is the Rolling Stones. If Lacan had been the Rolling Stones, he'd have slightly rewritten the famous refrain by saying, "You can't ever get what you want, but sometimes if you try"—and you've got to try. Even for what you need, you've got to try, you can't just sit there—"Sometimes if you try you'll get what you need." Lacan speaks of the impossibility of realizing an object of desire, because the metonymic structure of desire follows what he calls "an asymptotic course," "asymptotic" meaning the line that curves toward the line it wants to meet but never reaches it, with the punning sense of concealing the symptom. The only thing that can reveal the symptom is those moments of quilting, the moments at the *point de capiton* when metaphor, as Lacan says on two different occasions in your essay, reveals the symptom. So this is what happens when you can't ever get what you want. I doubt that Mick Jagger made a close study of Lacan in order to make that important distinction, but it's still one that you might want to salt away the next time you feel confused about the distinction between desire and need.

It'd be great if we could just stop there, but we do have to get a little closer to the text and try to figure out why in these terms given to us by Lacan, terms both structuralist and psychoanalytic, the concepts we've introduced thus far ramify—not to say explode—in so many directions. I should first say a couple of things in passing, though.

First, the enormously allusive, diffuse, and appositional style of Lacan, which maddeningly takes so many things for granted as common knowledge, perhaps reminds you of Derrida; and Lacan's opening gambit about lingering somewhere between what was spoken and what is written may suggest that we're back with Derrida's complication of the relation between writing and speech, as in a way we are. Certainly they both cultivated difficulty, and for much the same reason. Both felt that the linearity and clear organization of normative prose were at odds with their projects, which were, in common, the representation of the multilayered and labyrinthine way in which language subverts the communicative ambitions of speech. "I like the way in to be difficult," intones Lacan near the beginning of his essay, and all you survivors of Derrida's opening paragraph in "Structure, Sign, and Play" know that he would not disagree. Beginnings and origins are suspect for both and need to be subverted.

Yet there is an important difference between these two titans of French theory, one that I can only touch on here. In his "Seminar on 'The Purloined Letter,'" Lacan had argued that the disappearance of the letter from under the nose of everyone but Dupin corresponds to the concealment of a symptom by the unconscious, but that what stands revealed in the end, like the letter itself and the implications of its contents, is something like a truth. Derrida's response to this was an essay called "The Purveyor of Truth," meaning Lacan, which not unsurprisingly deconstructs the conditions of what truth might mean in Poe and Lacan alike. Without doing justice to either argument, we can see clearly here the difference between deconstruction and structuralist psychoanalysis.

For students of the humanities, there is more than one Jacques Lacan. There is a Lacan for literary studies who is very well represented by the text we have before us, even though some of his most important ideas are only hinted at here. For example, we hear nothing here about his triadic distinction among the Real, the Imaginary, and the Symbolic. This is something we can't really explore with only this text before us, although it might be fair to remark cautiously, in a vein that we'll in fact circle back to, that the imaginary is metonymic and the symbolic is metaphoric. There is only the slightest hint at the very end of the essay of the distinction I have just made between the "big Other" and the "*objet petit à*." We'll have lots of time to think about that because it's central to the essay of Žižek; but again, for literary studies when focused on the structuralist legacy in Lacan, this is an exemplary selection. But there's also a perhaps more current Lacan, one better known even now to some of you in film studies and women's studies. This is the Lacan of "the gaze," the complicated dialectic of "the gaze," which does very much involve negotiating the distinctions among the real, the imaginary, and the symbolic. As I say, this Lacan we shall only be able to approach obliquely, owing to the selectivity of what I've given you to read.

The other thing I should say in passing will I hope explain the quite curious tone of the assigned essay. You'll notice that Lacan is fairly bristling with hostility and condescension, spoiling for a fight. Of all the swelled heads on our list of reading, his is by far the biggest. We just have to get used to it and come to realize that Lacan's condescension isn't mainly directed toward the stupidity of his auditors and readers. It's aimed more particularly at what he takes to be the distortion of Freud's legacy by his psychoanalytic contemporaries in the International Psychoanalytic Association, many members of which were the so-called American ego psychologists.

An ego psychologist is somebody who begins as Lacan does with Freud's famous agenda for the analytic procedure, "Wo es war soll ich sein": "Where it was, there I should be." In other words, out of the raw materials of the id—"it," "*es*"—in the unconscious, the ego or *ich* should arise as the capacity of human consciousness to grow into its maturity through the sublimation of libidinal drives. In other words, the relationship between instinctual drives and the proper inhibitions of human or adult consciousness according to the ego psychologists can and should be a progressive one; and the purpose of psychoanalysis, the purpose of bringing people beyond their entrapment in the various infantile stages or in some form of neurosis, is to shore up the emergence and strengthening of the ego. Lacan hates this idea, because the proclaimed emergence of a stable and mature ego is presupposed by the idea that there is such a thing as stable human subjectivity: in other words, that there is such a thing as autonomous consciousness, under the authority of which our communicative and linguistic and other semiotic systems develop.

Lacan takes a completely different view of consciousness. The source of his most intense hostility throughout this essay, expressed as contempt, concerns the question of whether there is for each of us a stable and, by implication, unique subjectivity. The point of Lacan's skepticism in these matters is not that we don't differ from each other. We can scarcely suppose ourselves to *be* each other, or to participate in some universal continuum of subliminal thought (which was something like Jung's idea). As ethicists we in fact complain of our isolation from each other. But for Lacan the relationship between interior symptomology and the apparent externality of the language that inscribes itself upon it constitutes the central enigma that defeats any facile conclusions about what "I" suppose myself to be in relation to what "it" determines me to be. In this essay you will find, as a kind of turn in his argument, that Lacan does entertain a limited sense of psychic individuation, at least as a possibility: nothing that can by any means authorize notions of autonomous subjectivity or free will, but a sense that, owing simply to the semiotic complexity of the unconscious, each of us, as it were, inhabits a somewhat different form of that complexity. He scoffs, though, at the idea that a "subject" thus brought into being could ever emerge from analysis or simply through maturation with a stable, coherent, well-organized sense of self and identity.

Let's start, then, with the one piece of serious clinical work that Lacan ever did, the concept of the "mirror stage," first put forward in the 1930s as a hypothesis about infants' responses to their reflections and abstracted increasingly for the rest of his career into a permanent facet of psychic functioning. Lacan's psychoanalytic philosophy is largely speculative, as he very much preferred it to be. He worked in depth with philosophical and literary materials and was never glued to the analyst's chair. He was impatient with his analysands and took a heretical interest in analytic procedures that were either shortcuts, on the one hand, or, on the other hand, "interminable"—as described in Freud's late essay, "Analysis Terminable and Interminable." But the mirror stage is a clinical concept, one that actually does generate much of the system of ideas that Lacan expands in speculative directions.

The mirror stage, clinically speaking, is the moment when a baby who no longer feels at one with the breast of the mother, hence has become aware of some difference between self and otherness, views itself in the mirror. At six to eighteen months, it is acutely aware that it lacks control and coordination in its own body, yet what it sees when it hoists itself up, holding itself erect with its hands on the mirror, is a picture of unfragmented wholeness. There has been controversy from the time this phenomenon was first studied about when and whether infants actually *recognize* themselves when they look in the mirror, but arguably this criticism misses at least part of the point. For Lacan, especially as he thought about the matter over the ensuing decades, the point of interest was the frustrating contrast, however vaguely intimated, between the infant's sense of its own body and the gloriously upright image it gazes upon.

There may be an exultant moment in which the baby thinks it's so handsome (supposing it to have recognized itself) that it must be the object of the mother's desire. That may or may not be the case, but what we may suppose to follow upon this exultant moment seems more plausible. The rather wonderful epigraph from Leonardo da Vinci with which Lacan begins "The Agency of the Letter in the Unconscious" is all about this. In imagining the subject position of another—a subject that requires predication— the baby *falls into language*, and in that moment it no longer sees itself as the ideal *I*—"das Ideal-Ich" in Freud's language. It knows that the upright verticality it has witnessed belongs to another; the image in the mirror stands before it as a signifier, as what it is not, and the infant still in swaddling clothes (*infans*: "'for those who bind you will not understand your language nor will you understand them'") awakens to the recognition that it doesn't even have its own name, let alone an identity. It has "the name of the father," the signifier of and as another, but it doesn't have the phallus of the father, or rather it is not the phallus *as* the father, and it begins to recognize competition in desire. But the father, which is at the same time the *name* of the father, the unpossessed signifier bespeaking language, is only symbolically the father. In Lacan the object of desire can be just absolutely *anything* depending on the unraveling of the metonymic sequence that desire follows; but this point of departure is, after all, the Oedipal phase, so the entry point of the child into the language that harbors his destiny is called *le nom du père.*

It is a necessary lack, in Lacan's revision of Freud, that perpetually motivates desire. Yet this lack is not at all physical. It's *not* the penis! It is, on the contrary, something that is by nature symbolic, something that is an ego ideal (that figure of perfection in the mirror) yet no longer *oneself* and never again to be discoverable in one's self-observation. This lack henceforth takes a bewildering variety of—let's just say—"phallogocentric" forms. In film criticism, some of you may know the Lacanian essay by Laura Mulvey in which the female object of the spectator's desire or gaze, dressed in a sheath dress, is actually just like that baby, just like anything else that's upright. This "phallus" is what I have been calling the vertical axis and characterizing as virtual, my dotted line suggesting that it only hypothetically exists. Except, that is, insofar as it is itself "literally," as Lacan puts it, the "letter" that governs the psychic life, seated in or insisting upon itself as an agent in the unconscious.

In any case, to address a question that you remember Derrida addressed with great circumspection in "Structure, Sign, and Play": how is it that *language* comes to play such a determinate role? What is it about language that introduces this problematic that's beyond repair? Lacan begins the essay with a declaration about the Freudian unconscious, taken, he claims, from the part of *The Interpretation of Dreams* where Freud speaks, as we know, of the relationship between condensation and displacement in the dream work. Lacan says, "The unconscious is structured like a language." That's the single expression that people take away from Lacan, I think rightly so, because it is foundational for what we need to understand if we're to get along with him.

"The unconscious is structured *like* a language." He doesn't say, "The unconscious *is* a language," by the way, and he doesn't say that he means the unconscious is structured exclusively like human language. He means, to put it as precisely as possible, that the unconscious is structured like a semiotic system. He also draws from Freud's *Interpretation of Dreams* the idea that the way the dream works resembles a *rebus*—one of those puzzles in which you can find a hidden sentence if you figure out how to put together drawings, numbers, and syllables—in other words, a sequence of signs taken from different semiotic systems that can be decoded as human language. "I 'heart' New York," "4u, 'deer,'" and so on.

If it is structured like a language, this means the unconscious cannot any longer be considered the speechless, undifferentiated seat of the instincts.

Here there is an enormous gulf between Lacan and most other practitioners of psychoanalysis. The unconscious does not precede—being more primitive—those derivative forms of articulation that we're accustomed to call "language." In resembling a language, then, *it*—the id, *es*—must itself be the signifier, the "letter," that is the obscure object of desire, ever barred from consciousness. This is not at all to say that the unconscious works in the service of thought. Like many others in our reading, Lacan denies that language is a medium functioning as the facilitator or clothing of thought. Rather, language constitutes thought; it brings thought into being and is really inseparable from thought.

You can probably recognize here the conflict not just with other forms of psychoanalysis but with a whole philosophical tradition. If you are a materialist—a Marxist, for example—and believe that things come first and consciousness comes second to refer to them and react to them—that consciousness, ideology, or call it what you will, is determined by existing material circumstances—you can't very well think that existing material circumstances are produced by language. If by the same token you're a positivist, if you believe that ideas about things are expressed by language, which exists for that purpose, then you are likewise giving priority to things and the reference to them that is the province of thought. Lacan actually attacks both the Marxist tradition in a rather brilliant sideways blow (cf. 1130) and the positivists (1132). If it were just a question of Marx versus Hegel, as Marx himself wanted to stage the quarrel, Lacan's insistence on the priority of language, according language certain powers and energies that may remind one of *Geist*, certainly does make him, very broadly considered, a Hegelian.

So what is *it*, id, or *es*? What is this thing, the id, which is normally associated with "the instinctual drives," the unmediated, unruly energy of desire? Well, Lacan says it is nothing other than the signifier (1130): "[H]ow are we to take take this 'letter' here? Quite simply, literally." The primordial basis of consciousness is the letter. Remember Lévi-Strauss saying in the text quoted by Derrida that language doesn't come into being just a little bit at a time. One day there is no language, and the next day there is language: suddenly there is a way of conferring meaning on things, best understood in semiotic terms as differentiation among arbitrary signs. Language brings with it the arbitrary nature of the sign and the differential relations among signs that are featured in the work of Saussure. So it is for Lacan. The letter is not that which comes into being to express things, not a policeman hired by the ego to discipline and civilize the id, but rather the id itself. That is merely to say, it is the beginning. "In the beginning was the word," the letter, which disseminates consciousness through the signifying system that it makes available.

I actually hope that in saying these things you'll find me rather dully repeating myself. This is the part of Lacan that repeats, albeit strangely at times, a good deal of what you must be getting used to by now. Lacan activates a structuralist model to show how the unconscious dictates signification. He accepts Jakobson's distinction between metaphor and metonymy and sees the cooperative building-up of metaphor and metonymy in the discourse of the unconscious and in the psychopathology of everyday life and of the aphasias in much the way that Jakobson does. Remember Jakobson associates metaphor and metonymy not just with "poetry" and "prose," respectively, but also with mental disorders. In its extreme forms, metaphor and metonymy in linguistic practice take the form of two fundamental aphasias or word processing disorders, as Lacan, too, points out.

Of course, Lacan draws likewise on Saussure, but as your editor rightly points out in a footnote, the algorithm Lacan uses for Saussure's diagram of the sign is quite revisionary. Saussure's "signified/signifier" becomes Lacan's "S/s." In Lacan we have the big looming signifier over the timid little signified, because the signified scarcely participates in the metonymic discourse of the imaginary. After all, you can never cross the bar to get to it, or if the signifier does "slide under" the bar, it displaces the signified with itself. In Saussure the bar binds the two parts of the sign together; in Lacan the bar is the abyss between them, the bar between them. Saussure's diagram has in common with Lacan's so-called algorithm *only* in fact the bar itself: the fact that the relationship between signifier and signified, or signified and signifier, is an arbitrary one that can't be crossed by evoking anything natural in the nature of the signified that calls forth the signifier. There they agree, but as to what produces what, they appear to be divided. Saussure implies that in an indissoluble linkage the question is meaningless, whereas Lacan seems to insist that the big S is what generates the little s—is that from which any possibility of grasping a signified arises.

Let's exemplify this difference by going back to what I said about the red light over a door when introducing semiotics, because in this case, too, I think, we'll have continuity. The red light over a door is a signifier that has to do with desire. This we take for granted. The red light in other contexts has nothing to do with desire, but the signifier "red light over a door" caters to desire. But desire for what? Well of course we think we know, but then look at the signifier. It is over the door as though the door were a bar to what's behind it. Is the door the signified? Hardly. But if it is not, nothing else being visible, how then can the signifier lock itself into place, in the mutuality of binarism, with a signified? What's desired is behind the door, concealed by a thickening opacity of the bar—always supposing, after all, given the difference between desire and need, that what's desired is even there. You don't desire the door, any more than the boy and the girl in Lacan's anecdote desire the doors on which *hommes* and *femmes* are written. The little girl says, "We've arrived at Gentlemen," and the little boy says, "We've arrived at Ladies." Well, that seems to be quite healthy! We're on our way to something like hetero-normative desire. But where can we say the objects of these desires are located?

The only attraction behind these doors is the chance to restore your personal comfort. And were the visible signified to remain in question, we cannot even say, as we could say provisionally in the case of the door under the red light, that the doors are themselves the bar over the signified—covertly signifiers, not signifieds, in the signifying chain. To complicate the matter further, in Lacan's anecdote there are the railroad tracks, which for him constitute a truer bar. The little boy and girl sit there primly, facing each other, the bar of a taboo between them, quite knowingly ironic about the absurdity of the effort made by *hommes* and *femmes* to signify anything whatsoever. Their own chain of signification or axis of combination rolls past *hommes* and *femmes* into the night. This boy and girl are wonderful characters right out of Nabokov's *Ada*, where the incest taboo is violated. I don't know whether any of you know that novel, but the boy, Van Veen, is a charmingly obnoxious little genius, like Lacan, and his sister Ada is even worse. "Idiot" is a term of endearment favored both by Ada and by Lacan's little girl (*idiotes* in Greek means undifferentiated). Lacan's little boy and girl are barred because, with a bored knowingness, they find themselves on track toward something like the hetero-normative expression of desire. It's not an expression of desire at all. It's an expression of need because they are barred from representing the object of desire indicated by the signifier.

Desire, then, is the endless deferral of that which cannot be signified in the metonymic movement of discourse, of dreaming, or of the way in which the unconscious functions. Lacan is very ingenious, I think, in convincingly showing us how it is that we get from one signifier to another: in other words, how what he calls the chain of the signifier works. You have a series of concentric rings, but each ring is made up of a lot of little concentric

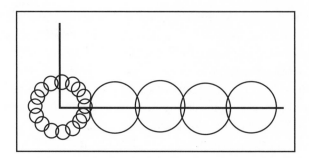

rings that hook on to surrounding rings in variable ways. This image very nicely rediagrams Saussure's sense of the associative structure of the vertical axis: of the synchronic moment of language within which some signifiers naturally cluster with other signifiers, not just with one group but many groups with different properties. But they don't at all naturally cluster with just any or all signifiers; hence you get associative clusters on the axis of selection, and they are indicated by these chains within chains.

Now every once in a while the possibility of *metaphor* arises. It's a moment to be celebrated in Lacan because, as he says, it's "poetic," and it is also, as he says, a manifestation, the only possible manifestation, of the *symptom*. A symptom calls itself to our attention as an awareness of lacking the object of desire that is expressed openly, not endlessly displaced in the babble of metonymy. One can see it. One can't grasp it, but one can see it as that which has been displaced by the very act of signification. Metaphor appears at these *points de capiton*. The stuffing of a quilt is the discourse of metonymy (in Shakespeare's time, quilt stuffing was called "bombast"), and the *points de capiton* hold it in place.

Lacan gives several examples of poetic metaphor. I shall focus on the Hugo because it's more compact than the Valéry. I am delighted that Lacan uses the word "sparks." You remember that when I was talking about Wolfgang Iser, I spoke of the need to gap a sparkplug, to have a certain distance between two points in order for the spark to happen. If it's too close, you just short out, but if it's too distant nothing happens either. The spark Lacan identifies is the relationship between Boaz and his sheaves in "his sheaves were neither miserly nor spiteful"; the sheaves themselves, which give of themselves freely, are certainly not miserly or spiteful for that reason—hence you would think that metonymically, by dint of their association with Boaz, Boaz must be like that, too.

His munificent crop is neither miserly nor spiteful, and yet, as Lacan points out, miserliness and spitefulness come back in that word "his": if he is a possessor of the sheaf, Boaz is subject to the spirit of capitalism or Darwinian competition that entail both the thrift and competitive envy or spite that appeared to have been banished from the sentence. Metaphorically speaking, Boaz is substituted for by the expression "his sheaves." The possessive means, on the basis of what Jakobson would call dissimilarity within the principle of equivalence, that Boaz is the opposite of the things that he's loosely said to be metonymically; yet at the same time within the metaphor, the phallic sheaves themselves are precisely what he has been in the Oedipal phase or primal horde, precisely what he would be if objectified by a baby looking at him. I often think that Keats's "Ruth amid the alien corn," suppliant at the feet of Boaz as in Poussin's "Autumn," is just such a baby.

Here I think you can see Lacan's sense of the relation between metaphor or metonymy hovering between that of Jakobson or Brooks and that of de Man, because there seems to be an underlying irreducible tension between the two readings of the line. It seems to say all at once, and undecidably, that Boaz was generous and free of spite and that he was just necessarily miserly and spiteful because he was a property owner. But this is not to deny that Jakobson is the primary and central influence on Lacan's way of thinking about the axis of combination. The appearance of metaphor on the axis of combination, the way in which we can identify quilting buttons along its surface, is nothing other than what Jakobson said and meant when he said that the poetic function is the transference of the principle of equivalence from the axis of selection to the axis of combination.

To sum up, Lacan says language is a rebus, and he says the movement of the signifier in whatever semiotic register, the movement of desire, is the articulation of a lack. The impossibility of attaching the signifier to any signified (if it "slides under the bar" it displaces the signified in doing so) is the impossibility of realizing an object of desire.

The most obvious consequence of theorizing the primacy of "the letter," and this isn't the first or last time we will have encountered this implication in various vocabularies and contexts, is the realization that "language thinks me." For example: "I think where I am not, therefore I am where I do not think" (1142). That which constitutes my thought is not present to me. It is *it*, the letter. I am not present to myself because what is present is the way my self comes into being through discourse, which nevertheless cannot identify me. It cannot identify me either as subject or—in a phase of narcissism, supposing I could somehow reimagine myself in the mirror phase—as an object of desire.

There's more to say about desire and need as the distinction appears in texts that we encounter. As we think about it, it's not that we're not happy with the things that we merely need. Obviously we are, yet we recognize in our lives as reflected in the magical world of film—the world of illusion promoted by film and also fiction—that the distinction with its attendant pathos has been prominent for hundreds of years. The essay by Žižek called "Courtly Love" and based on one of Lacan's published "Seminars" features readings of a series of films in which barriers prevent consummation with the Big Other yet turn out to mask an actual avoidance of the possibility.

CHAPTER 14

Influence

Readings:

Eliot, T. S. "Tradition and the Individual Talent." In *The Critical Tradition*, pp. 537–541.

Bloom, Harold. "A Meditation upon Priority." In *The Critical Tradition*, pp. 1156–1160.

Those of you who are chiefly familiar with *How to Read a Poem*, the books on religion, and *Shakespeare and the Invention of the Human* may be surprised to find Harold Bloom on a literary theory syllabus; but the great outpouring of work that began with *The Anxiety of Influence, A Map of Misreading, Poetry and Repression*, and many other books in the 1970s put Bloom in the very midst of the theoretical controversies then swirling. He was associated with the so-called Yale school, and although even at the time he expressed disaffection with many aspects of his colleagues' work, he was willing to edit and also to contribute to a volume that was called *Deconstruction and Criticism*.

Even in reading what you have before you, you can see how relatively little Bloom has to do with deconstruction, although perhaps broadly speaking one can think of the defensive struggle between poets as *negation*, hence as another contribution to the anti-positivist thrust of most literary theory. Since the period of *The Anxiety of Influence*, although he has never openly renounced his theory of influence, he has stopped reading poems through the machinery of "the six revisionary ratios." I'm not going to insist that you understand these, yet I do think it exciting to appreciate the dynamic of clinamen, tessera, kenosis, askesis, demonization, and apophrades—to become acclimatized to these ideas and actually to use them as a machinery for practical criticism. I'll have more to say about at least some of the revisionary ratios later.

I would say that Bloom's most important contribution to literary theory is the sets of ideas that make him an important literary historiographer. Together with figures like Tynianov and Jakobson earlier in our reading and Hans Robert Jauss and Fredric Jameson later, Bloom offers a challenging theory of literary history. This hasn't often been remarked upon. As a matter of fact, the common attitude toward Bloom, especially in retrospect since the 1980s, takes for granted that he's hopelessly ahistorical, caring nothing about history or about the way in which the real world impinges on literature. To a considerable extent, this judgment is fair, and Bloom proclaims it proudly as a virtue; but what's interesting in Bloom as a theorist— as in Tynianov—is his view of *literary* history, not history. (It should be said that the historical knowledge on display when Bloom works on a nonliterary topic is broad and detailed.) He offers a powerful argument about the logic of succession among poems in a tradition, an argument that as interpreters I think we ignore at our peril. The argument is psychoanalytic in structure, though it is much oversimplified, like Brooks's argument, by anyone who thinks it is merely biographical. Bloom focuses on the psyche of "poets as poets," distinguishing this focus sharply from any consideration of "poets as men."

In the tripartition of our reading, we first considered logological genesis, the production of literature by language. We are now reviewing concepts of psychological genesis, the production of literature by the human psyche. We will turn soon to sociopolitical genesis, the production of literature by social, economic, and political and historical factors. Well and good, but you may have noticed how much trouble we've had moving to "psychological" genesis. We keep saying we've arrived there, and I'm already starting to say we're about to leave, yet we actually continue to be working with linguistic models, as I'm sure you've noticed. We've had Lacan telling us the unconscious resembles a language, that it's structured like a language, and Brooks telling us that it's the verbal structure arising out of the relationship between metaphor and metonymy that constitutes a narrative text. We're still waiting for somebody to say something about the psychological genesis of the text.

Well, Bloom brings us closer, though it remains to be seen how close. When he speaks of "the poet in the poet," he is concerned with describing what he calls an "agon," a psychological struggle between the belated poet and the precursor poet that takes place at a presumably instinctual layer of the psyche. Yet even Bloom, of course, is finally talking about the relation of text to text, having no other source of evidence for the dynamic he describes as psychological. He describes relations that he prefers to consider thematically but that must perforce arise from verbal cues. The search for verbal influence he always professes contempt for, calling it "moldy fig philology." But I think that as you study the examples of literary influence in *The Anxiety of Influence, A Map of Misreading,* and their successors, you will see that there remains a dependence on verbal echo, which the strong version of his theory resists as best it can but does nevertheless require. I want to move into a general exploration of the topic of influence by talking, in fact, about how slippery the distinction is between an idea of influence that is, let's say, psychological or world-based and an idea of influence that is word-based.

There's a long tradition of the confusion between psychological and the linguistic factors in discussing influence, a confusion that runs deepest within the very traditional concept of imitation. Plato and Aristotle agree that poetry is imitation. It is, both of them say, an "imitation of nature." Plato thinks it's done badly, Aristotle thinks it's done well, but both agree that poetry is an imitation of nature. Eventually this idea of *mimesis,* the imitation of nature, was transformed. During the Silver Age of Roman literature, a high-water mark of elegance in the Latin language, rhetorical theorists like Quintilian, Cicero, and others no longer discuss *mimesis* but instead focus their attention—in Latin, of course—on *imitatio,* which is only seemingly the same idea. It's no longer a question of the imitation of nature but rather of the imitation of literary models: *imitatio* is the imitation of language, a topic that enables Silver Age and Alexandrian critics to establish canons by thinking about the relationship between particular poets and the tradition of literary expression from which they emerge. *Imitatio,* then, was a language-based theory of influence arising out of a nature-based theory of influence. This took place as literary traditions elongated themselves and originary models like Homer and Aeschylus (of whom one could say that they had nothing to imitate except nature) were succeeded by intermediary authors, highly "literary" in their attitude toward the past, like Virgil and Seneca.

During the course of Alexander's Pope's "Essay on Criticism," the relation of Virgil to the imitation of nature is touched upon. Homer, the argument goes, imitated nature directly, if only because there were no literary models to imitate. Virgil began by supposing that he could just write his own national epic, imitating nature, but then he started looking at Homer. At first he felt terrible because Homer seemed to have said it all. After *The Iliad* and *The Odyssey*, there seemed to be nothing left to say. Well, the solution to this problem for Virgil was that if he couldn't imitate nature because Homer had done that, he could still imitate Homer:

> But when t' examine ev'ry part he came [every part of Homer's compositions, together with every part of his own composition as he undertook to write his own epic]
> Nature and Homer were, he found, the same.

So here you have emerging the idea that to imitate nature and to imitate art—to imitate people and historical events and to imitate language—is part and parcel of the same process. To do one, you necessarily have to do the other. That's what I mean in remarking that we're still struggling to get away from the linguistic origins and move on to the psychological origins of literature. Even in the most traditional accounts of how influence works, like Pope's, we still find it very difficult to distinguish between nature and art. When Samuel Johnson, fifty years after Pope, pronounces that "Nothing can please many, or please long, but just representations of general nature," he is poised between the idea that art represents the world and the idea that art represents agreed-upon norms for imitating the world that withstand the test of time.

If we turn, then, to the two texts that you've read for this lecture, both of which are theories of influence, you can see that T. S. Eliot, too, is somewhat unclear about the relationship of these two sorts of imitation. For Eliot the individual talent that confronts tradition has to cope with what he calls "the mind of Europe" (539). I'll read a fairly extensive passage that provides one of the most accessible summaries of what Eliot has to say:

> [The poet] must be quite aware of the obvious fact that art never improves, but that the material of art is never quite the same. He must be aware that the mind of Europe—the mind of his own country—a mind which he learns in time to be much more important than his own private mind . . .

Let me just stop there and say that this seems as much *unlike* Bloom as it can possibly be because Bloom, the Romantic, celebrates the individual mind, or in any case honors the struggle of the individual mind to distinguish itself from all of those minds jostling for attention that precede it. This sort of struggle *seems* to be absent from Eliot. Eliot seems to insist on self-effacement, the recognition that the mind of Europe is more important than one's own mind, and that if one is to contribute anything as an individual talent to tradition, that contribution has to be grounded in the acutely sensitive awareness of everything that one is not, and not capable of being, oneself.

To continue the passage:

> [The mind of Europe is] a mind which changes, and that this change is a development which abandons nothing en route, which does not superannuate either Shakespeare, or Homer, or the rock drawing of the Magdalenian draftsmen. That this development, refinement perhaps, complication certainly, is not, from the point of view of the artist, any improvement.

The individual talent must enter into a vast matrix of literary, philosophical, and other sorts of expression that changes and yet never really transforms itself and certainly can't be understood as a grand march or progress toward some great goal, because nothing is ever lost and nothing radically innovative can ever be introduced.

I hope you see in this passage a good deal that we've passed through already: Gadamer's sense of tradition as something that requires the awareness of continuity, the willingness to meet the past halfway, finding a merger of horizons in which the past and the present can speak in an authentic way to each other; or the Russian formalist idea that the dominant and the recessive elements of any literary text are always present at any time but change places with each other in successive texts. In short, according to historical theories of this kind, the whole gamut of literary possibility is always already present, and one's own entry into this vast sea of expressive possibility can never display the sort of original genius that the Romantic tradition looks for. From this traditionalist perspective of Eliot we would imagine that Bloom must diverge sharply.

I want to argue, on the contrary, that actually there is a tremendous amount of continuity between Eliot and Bloom, and that in order to deny this influence Bloom is a strong misreader of his precursor. I don't want to develop this argument in full detail for fear of being considered obsessive, but I'd like to make a few points about it, because these points will exemplify the argument of *The Anxiety of Influence* itself as effectively as anything else I could say. Bloom has always denied the influence of "Tradition in the Individual Talent." He does acknowledge influences: Emerson, Nietzsche, Freud, the great Romantic poets, and more recently Shakespeare. But it seems to me that at least in skeletal form, in suggestion, Bloom is all there already in Eliot's "Tradition and the Individual Talent."

Just for example, Bloom is at pains to show the way in which the new *reconstitutes* the old. The precursor text for "Tintern Abbey," he says, is "Lycidas." Perhaps there are other poems that may have influenced "Tintern Abbey," such as Coleridge's "Frost at Midnight," but the poem with which "Tintern Abbey" struggles is "Lycidas," and Bloom is able to show how Wordsworth revisits and revises the subject matter of elegy as Milton had definitively presented it. But the point here is that once the belated text is written by a strong poet, we can never read the precursor text the same way again. Wordsworth's strong misreading of the precursor text is so powerful, in other words, that it becomes our own strong misreading. We just can't think about "Lycidas" in the same way on this view after we've read "Tintern Abbey." We now find Wordsworth's reflection on a former quality in himself that he has lost already to be present in Milton, with the deceased Edward King now standing proxy for a crisis in Milton's own poetic vocation.

If this seems implausible, you may at least see the point by considering an example or two. The most obvious, though far from the most Bloomian, is the Borges story called "Pierre Menard, Author of *Don Quixote*." This is an anecdote about a Frenchman at the end (as I recall) of the nineteenth century writing a novel in Spanish that turns out to be, word for word, Cervantes's *Don Quixote*. Only it's not Cervantes's *Don Quixote*; it's Pierre Menard's *Don Quixote*. Think how different it is. This is a Frenchman writing in Spanish not so long ago. That's pretty impressive, much more impressive, you might say, than Cervantes merely writing in his own language and his own time, and as a virtuoso performance Menard's novel introduces a completely different historical perspective on the Quixote story. Whereas Cervantes thinks he's being ironic about his own historical moment— chronicling the death of chivalry and so on—think how ironic one can be about that historical moment when writing several centuries later, with everything that one knows now a sort of layering of second thoughts. How can we ever read Cervantes's *Don Quixote* in the same way? It seems naive. Yet with the benefit of the belated text we are now enabled to recognize that

Cervantes has *already performed* Pierre Menard's feat: superimposing one historical perspective on another (his own on Quixote's), and "writing," as a Spaniard, words translated from the Arabic by a Moor, Cide Hamete Benengeli.

Think of Joyce's *Ulysses*. We all know that *Ulysses*, like the first half of Virgil's *Aeneid*, is based on *The Odyssey* and that it recycles the episodes of *The Odyssey*; but it seems to be looking at *The Odyssey* through the wrong end of a telescope. It's dragging the heroic outlook of the poem down into an unheroic account of everyday life in recent society. Precisely in following *The Odyssey*, Joyce debunks the heroic scale of *The Odyssey*. With this perspective, it's hard to read *The Odyssey* in the same way again after we've read *Ulysses*. Yet *The Odyssey* offers its countercommentary on everything that's sordid and mean in *Ulysses*, and, more importantly, the protean, time-serving survival instincts of Odysseus, modeling for the future the seagoing Mediterranean merchant, furnish in advance the outlines of Leopold Bloom's character.

Now it has to be said, and Harold Bloom would certainly say this himself, that *Ulysses* is not a strong misreading of *The Odyssey* because it's perfectly conscious of what it's doing. It's a deliberate misreading that has other virtues. Neither of the examples I have given are psychologically agonistic. *Ulysses* is not an exemplar of strong misreading, then, but what it does have in common with Bloom's theory and also with Eliot's idea about the relationship between the individual talent and tradition is that it reconstitutes tradition. It doesn't just innovate. It makes us see tradition itself in a different way. Eliot says (538):

> The existing monuments form an ideal order among themselves which is modified by the introduction of the new (the really new) work of art among them. The existing order is complete before the new work arrives; for order to persist after the supervention of novelty, the whole existing order must be, if ever so slightly, altered.

We can't quite see it the same way again. So it's a dynamic, mutual relationship that exists between tradition and the individual talent *or* between the strong precursor and the belated poet that seems to be in play.

In Bloom, the belated poet's strong misreading of the precursor, denying that the precursor already said what's being said now, asserts the egoistic priority of the belated poet: I'm doing something new, I'm going where no one has ever gone before. I'm innovating so powerfully that I doubt whether there actually was anybody before I came along. This Oedipal overgoing of the father is the strength of the belated poet. Yet as we have seen, the strong precursor turns out already to have said everything the belated poet says. Bloom's theory emphasizes a rhetoric of literal *originality*, in the sense of being first, while acknowledging that earlier poets have always already said everything. It was Milton's Satan, not the great Romantics, who said that he knows no time when he was not as now. Thus Bloom's literary historiography places a premium on innovation and on conservation, or tradition, at one and the same time. Unlike Gadamer leaning toward the conservative or traditional, and Iser or the Russian Formalists, who lean toward the innovative, Bloom simultaneously countenances the idea of tradition as unchanging—such is the logic of "always already said"—and also the idea of tradition as what is constantly being remade or at least rethought. That, I have to tell you, is very similar to what T. S. Eliot had said already.

We come, then, to the famous aphorism of Eliot (539): "Someone said: 'The dead writers are remote from us because we know so much more than they did.' Precisely, and they are that which we know." Rather good, I think, and something that Bloom, in his own way, might very well say. The past is what we know, but if we're strong, we're not aware of knowing it. In other words, I write the past when I write my belated poem, but I think I'm doing something different. In the first revisionary ratio, *clinamen*, I am swerving from the past: I swerve out and down, I find my own space like a Lucretian atom. Lucretius says that all the atoms would fall in the same place if they didn't swerve, and that describes the belated poet's sense of what he's doing in relation to the precursor. He's actually falling in the same place, but the strength of that swerve, the rhetorical gesture of the swerve, is so powerful that we do feel that we have been transported. Once again we feel both the innovation and the necessary conservatism, or preservational aspect, of the new poet's composition.

Surely, however, nothing could be less Bloomian than Eliot's emphasis on the poet's impersonality, on the wish to escape personality (541): "But, of course, only those who have personality and emotions know what it means to want to escape from these things." To enter the world of art is to abandon the sense that what's important is one's personal psychological agony (or at least to hope to do so: Eliot's poet only *wants* to escape from personality), to immerse oneself as a poet and creator, if one can still retain this term, in that which is infinitely more vast than one is oneself.

Well, that doesn't sound very Bloomian, but look at Bloom's fifth revisionary ratio, askesis (1150). He's talking about what the belated poet does in order to find space for himself, to make himself different from other people. You'd think the answer would be to make yourself bigger than anybody. Wallace Stevens has a wonderful poem called "Rabbit as King of the Ghosts," in which the rabbit swells, or thinks it swells, until it is so big that it takes up all space. I always think of that rabbit as Bloom's belated poet, but with askesis something very different happens, though perhaps to this same end.

About halfway through the definition of askesis, Bloom says, "[The poet] yields up part of his own human and imaginative endowment." In other words, he curtails himself; he makes himself less than he might have been—in order, to be sure, to be more than he has been. He yields up part of his own human and imaginative endowment so as to separate himself from others, including the precursor. Thus in askesis—and also in kenosis, by the way—there is a self-shrinking or self-effacement on the part of these particular moves of strong misreading with respect to the precursor. It's not, in other words, just a question of the rabbit as king of the ghosts. It's not a question of a massive ego swelling to the point where it fills all space. It is more complicated than that, and in being more complicated it is frankly more Eliot-like.

The masculine pronoun, by the way, is something that Bloom has never apologized for. What he would say, or what an apologist who speaks the language of gender would say (we'll be coming back to gender, of course), is that a poet is gendered masculine but that any woman can be a poet. Bloom does think of Emily Dickinson, for example, as a strong poet. The masculine gendering of the theory is modeled on the idea of Oedipal conflict, a father-son rivalry that Freud himself is always likewise being criticized for.

Turning now to Bloom directly, no longer so much in comparison with others: his career has always involved a sense of struggle in the relationship among poets. In his earliest work—Shelley's Mythmaking, Blake's Apocalypse, and The Visionary Company—the idea of struggle was embodied in what Bloom called Protestantism. He saw the tradition that interested him arising in relation to the Reformation, that time when, as I said in my thumbnail history of hermeneutics, people began to feel something personal in their connection to the Bible and to God. This was the time also when human individuality came to matter—the time associated by many others with the emergence of the bourgeoisie. In that moment, the idea of Protestantism— purely in the sense, as a character in Lawrence Durrell says, "that I protest"— creates an atmosphere in which each poet feels independent of previous literary models. The word "Protestant" gives way in early Bloom to the word "revisionary," the word he uses primarily in *The Visionary Company*. With the aid of Freud, revisionism gives way in turn to "misreading."

Surprisingly enough, the notion of Oedipal struggle among authors is not new to Bloom, as we can observe in reviewing a few passages taken from the whole span of the history of criticism. The first two are by Longinus, probably a second-century tutor of a Roman youth, whose *On the Sublime* I quote:

> As if instinctively [this is in the moment of the sublime] our soul is uplifted by the true sublime. [Thus far that's what you would expect anybody to say.] It takes a proud flight and is filled with joy and vaunting [and this is where the surprise comes] *as though it had itself produced what it has heard* [italics mine].

A possession *by* the other takes place, as an external voice transports us, yet this is experienced psychologically as possession *of* the other. In my fantasy, it's my own speech. A child watches a ball game, somebody hits a home run, and the child in his exultation starts swinging an imaginary bat as though he had hit it himself. He *is* the hero. Longinus says it's the same with literary sublimity, exerting thereby a strong influence on Bloom.

I think that what Longinus says in the next passage is actually quite true: Plato is constantly abusing Homer, yet nothing can be easier than to show how the great Homeric actions and even tropes help shape Platonic thought. It's a fascinating topic, and Longinus, it seems to me, is exactly right about it: "There would not have been so fine a bloom of perfection on Plato's philosophical doctrines unless he had with all his heart and mind struggled with Homer for primacy." Longinus even thinks in Bloomian terms of wanting to be first even though in some part of your mind you know you're second. Plato struggles for primacy, "showing perhaps too much love of contention and breaking a lance with [Homer], as it were, but deriving some profit from the contest nonetheless; for as Hesiod says, 'This strife is good for mortals.'"

The more commonplace example, taken from a famous essay by Sainte-Beuve called "What Is a Classic?," is again proto-Bloomian. There's a tradition of essays called "What Is a Classic?" Eliot wrote a great one in 1944, and they're all important contributions to the theory of influence. Sainte-Beuve writes:

> Goethe spoke the truth when he remarked that Byron, great by
> the flow and source of poetry, feared that Shakespeare was
> more powerful than himself [it's true, Byron was always abusing
> Shakespeare] in the creation and realization of his characters. He
> would have liked to deny it. The elevation so free from [this is
> Goethe talking] egoism irritated him. He felt when near it that
> he could never display himself at ease. He never denied Pope be-
> cause he did not fear him. He knew that Pope was [and you know
> how short Pope was] only a low wall by his side.

In other words, Byron chose as his literary model somebody he supposed
inferior to himself, at least in creative energy ("the little Queen Anne's man,"
he called him), while constantly denying a very powerful influence, quarrel-
ing constantly with Shakespeare, bardolatry, and the overrating of *Hamlet*.
He chose a weak precursor instead of a strong precursor.

What complicates Bloom's argument, apart from the vocabulary and
the philosophical range of his thought, is the issue I began with: the traditional idea of influence as an art-nature problem, of which Bloom is very
much aware. In one sense, the crisis of influence concerns one's orientation
to nature, and in another sense, apparently the more prominent sense in
Bloom, the crisis concerns one's orientation to other texts. But notice that
Bloom really doesn't want to say at all times that it's just about texts (1157):
"Freud's disciple, Otto Rank, show[s] a greater awareness of the artist's fight
against art, and of the relation of this struggle to the artist's antithetical
battle against nature." In other words, nature is death. Nature is that into
which the author will fall back in the form of death should he fail to sustain
himself in the triumph of his assertion of priority and superiority to the
life cycle in nature.

Bloom wants to insist that in part what the belated poet struggles for
is immortality. Part of what it means to come first and to know nothing
that was there before you is to suppose that you are also going to be last,
that you're going to be immortal, that you don't belong in an ordinary trajectory of life. You are a force, genius, or power that transcends history. Here
we find the poets' "lie against time," as Bloom calls it, holding off death
while insisting, too, that one is touched neither by priority nor even genesis.

To illustrate this very quickly, let's turn to Wordsworth, the key strong
misreader and belated poet with respect to Milton, who writes in a promis-
sory poem that we now call "The Prospectus to 'The Recluse'" that he is not

interested in writing *Paradise Lost*. *Paradise Lost* for him is just archaic, a thing of the past. He claims indifference to the things Milton cares about: "All strength–all terror, single or in bands,/ That ever was put forth in personal form,/ Jehovah– with his thunder, and the choir/ Of shouting angels, and the imperial thrones–/ I pass them unalarmed." *Paradise Lost,* that's just playing with toy soldiers. It's nothing compared with what Wordsworth himself is going to do: "Not chaos,/ Not the darkest pit of lowest Erebus,/ Nor aught of blinder vacancy, scooped out/ By help of dreams–can breed such fear and awe/ As fall upon us often when we look/ Into our minds, into the mind of man–/ My haunt, and the main region of my song." God, heaven, hell, war, myth, archaic heroism—all these give way to the true and only subject, "the mind of man," which doesn't entail the risk of falling back into the hungry generations of nature because it is not my mind, it's *the* mind, immune to time in my voice.

Ah, but look at tatty old, archaic *Paradise Lost*: here are three proclamations by Satan. Following Blake and Shelley, who had made the same claim, Bloom says it's not so much Milton who is Wordsworth's strong precursor, it's Satan: "The mind is its own place and in itself/ Can make a heaven of hell, a hell of heaven." Apparently, Satan is writing "The Prospectus to 'The Recluse,'" because that's Wordsworth's claim. "We know no time," Satan tells the fallen legions, "when we were not as now." That's what the belated poet always strives to say. And finally, "Myself am hell." That's rather an uncomfortable thing to say, but still, it's the rabbit as king of the ghosts talking: "my haunt and the main region of my song," it is the mind that is all things.

Wordsworth, then, has strongly misread *Paradise Lost* in order to think he's doing something completely new, while revealing that the strong precursor poet has always already written anything that the successor poet can write. The dynamic interplay between conservation and innovation is present in any moment that reflects the anxiety of influence.

High time we returned to *Tony the Tow Truck*. For Lacan, *Tony the Tow Truck* represents consciousness settling for the *objet peti tà*, little Bumpy the Car, an imperfect being but a helpful one and a friend—"that's what I call a friend"—whereas the objects of desire, Neato and Speedy, well, those are bad cars. As Brooks would say, these objects of desire are improper object choices on the face of it. That's what an American ego psychologist would say, too, but Neato and Speedy are, in a more Buñuelesque way of putting it, *obscure* objects of desire as they motor on down the road, simply unavailable to Tony as object choices at all. So Neato and Speedy are the big Other, and Bumpy is the *object petit à*.

For Harold Bloom, *Tony the Tow Truck* is a strong misreading of *The Little Engine That Could*. This is clearest in that Bumpy, not Tony, plays the role of the hero of *The Little Engine That Could*. The misreading of the belated text involves making Tony the hero in need of Bumpy's help. In folkloric terms, Bumpy becomes the helper and not the hero, but we can see nonetheless that the essential narrative model—the model of the weak doing with perseverance and energy what the strong fail to do—reflects on the strong and the weak. We can't ever read the character Tony in quite the same way again after the appearance of Bumpy, yet Bumpy is nothing other than the hero of *The Little Engine That Could*, a subject position that has been appropriated by Tony in this text. So the relationship is again an agonistic one involving the transposition of heroism from one character focus to another while at the same time—as anybody can recognize who has read both stories to their kids—simply rewriting the story in a way that *The Little Engine That Could* completely anticipates.

We shall return now to more Lacanian pastures when we study Deleuze and Guattari and especially Slavoj Žižek in the next lecture.

CHAPTER 15

The Postmodern Psyche

Readings:

Deleuze, Gilles, and Félix Guattari. "Introduction: Rhizome." In *A Thousand Plateaus: Capitalism and Schizophrenia.* Minneapolis: University of Minnesota Press, 1987.

Žižek, Slavoj. "Courtly Love." In *The Critical Tradition*, pp. 1181–1197.

In this lecture, we're still focused on individual consciousness, even though the authors you read are known for their political engagements. We shall still be considering the psychological genesis of the text or film as the site, or model, for the symbolic patterning of a text, undoubtedly in the case of Žižek, to some extent also in that of Deleuze. This is actually our farewell to the psychological emphasis, and it is so arranged—with the consequence of separating Žižek from Lacan—because today's authors make sure we understand that there are political stakes in art and interpretation.

In his brilliant reading of *The Crying Game*, for example, Žižek argues that the final twist of plot isn't just an individual's abdication from responsibility for the Irish Republican cause. The soldier has not merely walked away from his role in revolutionary activity; he has discovered in his private life—in the erotic dimension of his consciousness—the need for revolution from within. He has necessarily disrupted his own thinking in ways equally radical to and closely parallel to the disruption of thinking that's required to support the Republican movement in Ireland. Thus the ultimately tragic encounter with the Big Other is inseparable from the political implications of the protagonist's behavior.

Perhaps one should be given pause, at least momentarily, by this claim. As your editor points out in his italicized preface, there are temptations entailed for the individual in this fascination with an obscure or even perhaps transcendent object of desire, but there are temptations also for the social psyche. It would be discouraging, arguably, though perhaps not unrealistic, if a political ideal were considered precisely what one cannot have. There is also in Žižek's work a rather surprising friendliness toward religion. After all, faith, or the struggle for faith, certainly counts as an effort to enter into a meaningful relationship with what one desires yet cannot meet face to face. But what remains problematic is Žižek's recognition that in both religion and politics there is excitement but also potential danger in becoming fascinated by a big idea. There are moments when he confesses to a measure of instability in his own political thinking, even though he is by and large on the left and heavily influenced by Marx. He sees clearly, however, that any form of progressive collectivity, including fascism, brings with it the charisma of a forbidden wish. Žižek is aware, in short, that the train of thought he borrows from Lacan brings with it a vertigo of dangerous possibilities in the political arena. (I'll be coming back to Hitchcock's *Vertigo* eventually.)

There is also an emphatic political dimension in Deleuze. (For the most part, I shall be saying "Deleuze" rather than "Deleuze and Guattari"— Félix Guattari was his frequent collaborator—just as I said "Wimsatt" rather than "Wimsatt and Beardsley.") You are reading the first chapter of his book, *A Thousand Plateaus,* in which he proposes a kind of thought experiment, a recommendation to the reader that is echoed by the organization of the chapter itself. Deleuze indicates the need to perform in thought what you might call a revolution from within, but the implications for politics, as in Žižek, are somewhat ambiguous. That is to say, the "rhizomatic" mode of thinking—we'll come back to that—which is radically decentering and thereby lends itself to pluralistic, progressively democratic causes, may lend itself likewise not so much perhaps to fascism or communism as to libertarianism at the far side of democracy.

Deleuze is indeed careful to point out that rhizomatic thinking takes place both for the *best* and *worst.* Rats are rhizomes. Crabgrass is a rhizome. In other words, everything that organizes itself dispersively without a taproot is rhizomatic, no matter what. On the whole, though, as I'll try to

explain more carefully later, rhizomatic thinking is for the good in Deleuze's view. In any case, however, both Žižek and Deleuze are introducing
new possibilities of thought—very different possibilities—and are candid
enough to admit that they don't quite know where these possibilities are taking them. Beyond implying a measure of liberation, they don't say what the
implications or consequences of successfully entering their thought worlds
might be.

I'm about to suggest what the connection is in theory between these
two very free spirits, not to say loose cannons, but for the moment I need to
stress the enormous differences between them. Deleuze's thought experiment departs from the tree or "arboresque" model of thinking (interesting,
perhaps, that he must strain to avoid the root sense of "radical" among his
metaphors); while Žižek, focused at times on what is left over when the semiotics of desire and need is exhausted, wants to develop his curious notion of the *blot*—the element in narrative discourse that can't be interpreted,
can't be said to have meaning. Hard to find any common ground there.
(I partly invoke Brooks in putting Žižek's project this way—with Brooks's
intermediary link to Lacan, D. A. Miller on "the narratable"—but for Žižek,
Lacan on "the real" stands in the background.) There are points of divergence
here, then; one is tempted to say points of incommensurability. But notice
that both of these projects are striving to approximate a reality beyond a
certain tedium or predictability that infects normal modes of signification:
the arboresque, which is not unrelated to the "transcendental signified" in
Derrida, or the combinatory logics of the imaginary, lost in a thicket of
cliché and received ideas, and even the symbolic in Lacan. In common,
Deleuze and Žižek are proposing latter-day forms of defamiliarization.

As you read the rather bouncy and frantic prose of both these texts,
you can see that they also share a mood, a stance or orientation toward
critical and theoretical precedents. They seem to be of the same moment.
You could even imagine these two texts being written—if it was just a question of their style—by the same person. Well, perhaps not quite; yet the
kind of high-energy, too-caffeinated feeling that you get from the prose of
both may cause you to wonder just what historical moment this rambunc-
tiousness belongs to.

You may be ready to tell me what moment it belongs to: yes, "postmodernism." Deleuze and Žižek are exemplars of what is by far the most
slippery concept to which cultural history been exposed in the last twenty
or thirty years. If one likes it, one wants to say it's flexible; if one doesn't like

it, one wants to say it's murky. We can bring both essays into focus as we pause over "postmodernism."

Probably we can agree quickly about what postmodernism is in artistic expression. Especially in the visual arts, but I think as reflected in certain trends in fiction, drama, and poetry as well, postmodernism is an eclectic orientation to the past. In a limited sense, it's a return to the past, an opening up of textual possibility to traditions and historical moments of expression that modernism, with its emphasis on autonomous forms, had supposed obsolete and set aside. In architecture, many examples of eclectic poaching on the past are quite extraordinary, but many are quite hideous. There was a point fifteen or twenty years ago when every strip mall was renovated. Until then they had been long flat boxes, but then in the name of the postmodern, the renovators came along and put little gables on the boxes, intrinsically ugly and out of scale—but what's worse, old news overnight. The most awful things were done with suburban ranch houses, all in the name of a blind, bland return to tradition, especially to ransack and travesty Palladian neoclassicism.

But the postmodern has done its work differently in other fields, such as painting. Since the advent of postmodernism, the New York scene hasn't consisted in single dominant schools of abstract painting superseding each other. The postmodern in the art world is not at all a wholesale return to earlier movements such as realism, although they're accommodated; it's a mixture of everything, including the cutting-edge concept, performance, and digital art (the "Duchampian") that questions easel art, the flat picture plane, and so on. Artists have always been obsessed with their place in art history, but what we have seen under the banner of the postmodern is not just groups of artists wanting to place themselves with respect to this or that moment of art history. There's an anarchic independence in thinking about what art is that has gone global and informs such important work in the philosophy of art as that of Arthur Danto.

In philosophy, postmodernism reflects doubt not just about the grounds of knowledge, as in, say, Richard Rorty—the widespread sorts of doubt that we have been discussing more or less continuously in this course—but doubt in particular about the relationship between or among *parts* and *wholes*. Can I be sure that my leg is part of my body when at the same time it is a whole of which my foot is a part? How is it that I know in any stable way what a part or a whole is, or what therefore a *field of inquiry* is (here especially I hope you're reminded of Deleuze)? To take a more interesting

example—this is from Wittgenstein's *Philosophical Investigations*—
consider the French flag, which is called the tricolor. It's made up of three
color stripes: blue, white, and red. As a composite, they have symbolic value.
Yet blue, white, and red aren't confined to their symbiosis on this piece of
cloth, viewed as a whole. The little stripe of white is *part* of whiteness, the
concept of white. And if you look at the tricolor without knowing what it is,
how can you say in any case that the white is part of a whole? You could say
that the white is an autonomous entity that somebody happens to have
sewn together with the blue entity and the red entity. We have to wonder
how we know what an entity *is*.

Philosophical thinking is dominated by metaphors of vision. We assume that we have a clear sense of reality because we can see it. But *how* do
we see it? The focusing capacities of the eye, resulting in the arbitrariness
with which "things" (presumed to be independent entities) come in and out
of clear outline, is worth remembering. If you look too closely at something, a face, for example, all you can see is dots, follicles in nature or pixels
on-screen, a retinal Mark Tobey painting; if you are too far away ("too far
away to discriminate," as we say), all you can see is a blur, or Žižek's "blot." If
you look at something and close your eyes, that too becomes a retinal Mark
Tobey painting. If you're in a jet looking down, what you see certainly looks
like it has form and structure, but it's a completely different form and structure from what you're seeing if you're standing on the ground, even if you're
on a flat plain and can see almost as much looking out to the horizon as you
could see from the jet. It's not at all just a question of "perspective," of looking
at "the same thing from more than one angle." Your vision is constituting
entirely different "things."

I continue this long digression in hopes that it's not really a digression
but a way of accounting for today's reading. Part-whole confusions also
beset the history of science. During the golden age of the linear accelerator,
the relationship between subatomic particles reversed itself: the particle that
was thought to be the fundamental unit turned out *to have within it*, revealed by bombardment in the accelerator, *a fundamental unit of which it
was a part*!

The difficulty that we have deciding what a whole is has consequences.
When we think of a whole, we infer unity. If then we have trouble identifying wholes, might we not be on the wrong track in considering the nature
of things to be unified, interfused yet firmly articulated structure? Deleuze
for one wants nothing to do with unity. The whole function of his thought
experiment is the decentering of things such that one can no longer talk

about unities or wholes or isolated entities. It's the being together, merging together, flying apart, reuniting, and kinesis or movement of entities, if they can even be called entities, that Deleuze wants to emphasize.

Another aspect of the postmodern is what the postmodern philosopher Jean-François Lyotard, in particular, has called "the inhuman," or the dehumanization of the human.[1] This is a weird term to choose, I think from one viewpoint an unfortunate one, because Lyotard's drift is not at all anti-humanistic. Although it does keep in focus the historical atrocities of dehumanization (and this is, after all, why the term is chosen), "the inhuman" is really a new way of appreciating the human. Deleuze, you'll notice—not just in this excerpt but everywhere in his work, which is why he has so little to say about it here that's explanatory—talks about "bodies without organs." That may have brought you up short. What it suggests is that we are, as Deleuze would put it, machinic rather than organic. If the problem with centered thought is that it approaches everything as arboresque, as a rooted tree, that problem has to some extent to do with the fact that we consider a tree to have human organs for parts. The roots and branches are muscles and circulation; the leaves are capillaries; the blossoms are genitals; the crown or canopy of leaves is the mind of the tree reaching up to the sky, the mentality of the tree. By the same token, if we think of our own bodies as arboreal, we think of certain parts of those bodies as cognitive, other parts as having agency, as doing things. If that's the case, then we think of a centered and ultimately genital or genetic understanding of the body as being *productive*.

Deleuze wants to think of the body as interactive. The body in Deleuze is everywhere and nowhere, unsituated among other fluidities, sensitive and functionally interactive at all points with a far-reaching environment. In order for this to happen, the interface with other things of the body without organs has to be active without manipulative will, and also without cognitive intention, such as "I think, therefore I am, myself and not another, and the world is what I think it to be." In short, the dehumanization of the postmodern results not in denying the importance of the human but in rethinking the human among other bodies and things.

Plainly, this emphasis stresses a dissolve into otherness, a continuity between subject and object in which the difference, ultimately, between what is inside me, what is authentic or integral to my being me, and what's outside me become completely permeable and interchangeable. The late nineteenth-century author and aesthetic philosopher Walter Pater, in the conclusion to a book called *The Renaissance*, anticipated much of what Deleuze has to say. Pater said in effect that we are too much used to thinking that we're in here, that everything else is out there, and that, somehow or another, our perspective on everything out there is a saving isolation that enables our power of objectivity. Then Pater says, in paraphrase, that we actually subsist in a biochemical interchange with what's outside of us, permeable to the molecularity of things. What is inside us is also what "rusts iron and ripens corn," in his words.

Deleuze and Guattari have their own excited, jumpy way of putting these things, but you can see that it's not really new to say that we exaggerate the objectifying isolation of consciousness from its surroundings. It is the two-way permeability of inside and outside that this kind of rhizomic, decentered thinking is meant to focus on. Now if we go back to our vertical and horizontal coordinates, we could say that Deleuze, like so many others we've read, is interested in rendering virtual, or possibly even eliminating, the vertical axis: rendering virtual or putting under erasure that center or head or crown of the tree, the arboresque, which constitutes everything that unfolds on the horizontal axis—whether it be language or the unconscious structured like a language.

But what now remains of the horizontal axis? Here is where Deleuze differs from deconstruction, for which speech and especially writing are exclusively linguistic. I'm going to compare him in this one respect, and only in this respect, with Lacan. You remember that in Lacan's "Agency of the Letter" essay, he doesn't *just* talk about the axis of combination as a series of concentric circles, each of which is made up of little concentric circles. He also compares the combinatory powers of the imaginary in language, or of desire, with a musical staff. The organization of signs, in their contiguity with each other, can be either melodic or harmonic, notated both horizontally and vertically *along* the horizontal axis.

To express this multilayeredness along the axis of combination, Deleuze and Guattari introduce the concept of "plateau." The book in which your excerpt appears is called *A Thousand Plateaus*. Ultimately, the plateau is even more important to them than the rhizome, but when they introduce the concept of plateau they're likewise—as with the rhizome—drawing attention away from a single governing concept to many simultaneous concepts. The plateaus are not, however, simply multiple meanings or sign systems within language. Deleuze and Guattari emphasize "multiplicity of coding," thinking that does not just take place in language but careens among the verbal, the pictorial, the musical, the filmic, and yet other codes. Here, too, there is a link with Lacan—and with Freud in Lacan's opinion. Freud having said the dream work is like a rebus, Lacan makes Freud's observation his model for the semiotics of speech. That sounds a lot like Deleuze's "multiplicity of coding."

Deleuze's relationship with all the figures we have been reading is rather problematic, really, but it is especially so with the proponents of psychoanalysis. The book preceding *A Thousand Plateaus* was called *Anti-Oedipus*, a continuous attack on Freud "the General." As you can guess, Deleuze rejects the Oedipus complex not so much because it's flawed in itself (there are plenty of others to do that), but because it's an arboresque organizational principle. Deleuze sets out to show how limiting and unfortunate for the legacy of psychoanalysis focusing on a particular issue has been. You would think, then, that Deleuze would feel a lot closer to the polyvalent Lacan, but here is what he says about Lacan (34): "[I]t is not surprising that psychoanalysis tied its fate to that of linguistics." It's impossible to say on the face of it—probably not by accident—whether Deleuze alludes here to Freud or Lacan if he takes seriously Lacan's implication that the unconscious is structured like a language because Freud says it is in *The Interpretation of Dreams*. But I think Deleuze is just avoiding a fight. All agree that Lacan's focus on linguistics is a massive (some would say unjustified) revision of scattered observations by Freud, and it seems clear to me that Deleuze's target really is Lacan.

Additionally, the target beyond psychoanalysis is linguistics itself. Deleuze wants to conceptualize language in a way that no linguistics has successfully accommodated as far as he's concerned. He keeps talking about Noam Chomsky, who is arguably the villain of this essay, just as Freud was the villain of the previous book. Deleuze's hostility to Chomsky's notion that the mind is hardwired for a universal, arboresque "deep structure" common to all languages is not hard to understand. But I still think that making Chomsky stand proxy for the whole field is just a way to avoid talking about Saussure and angering all those structuralists, including Lacan. In Deleuzean terms, after all, the problem with Saussure, too, is that his focus on the binary, on the arbitrary nature of the sign, is likewise arboresque, at odds with Deleuze's interest in the seepage of signs into each other and into other codes.

How then do we know a rhizome when we see it? Whatever frustrations Deleuze's essay puts in your path, I suspect that in the long run you're pretty clear on what a rhizome is. If you have any doubt, just think about the flu. Deleuze calls it "rhizomatic flu." It's something we get from other people, and because we all come down with it around midterm period, the circulation of this disease is rhizomatic: we are vulnerable, it finds its way to us. It parallels the relationship between the wasp and the orchid. The wasp, like the virus, flits about from blossom to blossom, descends, and spreads pollen. By contrast with the flu, there is hereditary disease—that which lurks in us because we're hardwired for it genetically. This form of disease Deleuze associates with the arboresque. It comes from an origin, a root cause. The give and take of tensions within rhizomatic colonies—the rats tumbling over each other, the maze of the burrow, the spreading of crabgrass—all of this is random and unpredictable. It is free play but not governed by a center, hence not structural.

Again, the value system surrounding these metaphors is not fixed. It's not quite "arboresque bad, rhizomatic good." He's coming pretty close to that, but he acknowledges the perils of the rhizomatic, as I've said. As to the arboresque, he rescues it in some degree by distinguishing, in speaking of books, between kinds of roots. One is what he calls the "root book," the traditional book that announces a theme and develops it systematically, with due attention to a logical sequence of subtopics. Then there is what he calls the "fascicle book," with complicated offshoots of roots that still trace back to a taproot. This is what he associates with modernism. The fascicle book is like Joyce's *Ulysses,* containing everything including the kitchen sink. It looks as though it were totally rhizomatic, but it is brought into coherence by a single focusing authorial consciousness (think of de Man's "rhetoricization of grammar"), hence remains a fascicle book, more commendable than a root book but not quite a breakthrough. And now, by proclamation, *A Thousand Plateaus* is going to be a rhizomatic book. It's collaborative, it rejects sequencing for layering, it cheerfully says everything at once, scrambling unpredictably and seemingly at random from metaphor to metaphor—not in order to evoke one root idea or hobby horse but to imitate the permutation of permutation itself. You can decide whether they succeed.

Žižek, then, can help us understand Lacan, and he also allows us to revisit Peter Brooks. Although the examples of the way the conflictedness of desire in narrative works for Žižek in your essay, "Courtly Love," are excellent and I think largely self-explanatory, the best example of all is actually in a book by Žižek called *Everything You Wanted to Know about Lacan (but Were Afraid to Ask Hitchcock).* In that book, a lot of attention is paid to *Vertigo.* Just think about *Vertigo* as an instance of the kind of plot Žižek is talking about, with one variant. It could be considered a pathological study of *not* settling for the *objet petit à.* Scottie's friend who is in love with him, the artist Midge, is continuously available, yet he is oblivious to her attractions, indifferent to need, throughout his obsessive pursuit of the enigmatic

Madeleine/Carlotta/Judy. The object of his desire is not just distant (he wants to make love with her but finds a million excuses not to), she is also obscure, the final discovery of her identity destroying both her and her allure for Scottie all at once. Preceding the catastrophe are the painful scenes in which he fetishistically remakes Judy into an exact replica of Madeleine, unable to possess her until every hair of the Other is in place. At just the moment when this is accomplished, the Other herself is exposed as inauthentic, herself a replica of what was perfect because nonexistent, and Scottie's courtly love disintegrates altogether.

It's useful, perhaps, to think about the relationship between the elusiveness of desire in Žižek and the dilation of plot in Peter Brooks. Brooks describes the way middles in plots protract themselves through episodes, all of which manifest some sort of imbalance in need of corrective repetition. Because the characteristic plot of realist fiction is the marriage plot, many of these *détours* have to do with inappropriate object choice. But such wrong turns, as in the case of *The Crying Game* in Žižek, may also, and perhaps at the same time, involve inappropriate political object choices. Consider the plot of Henry James's *Princess Casamassima* in that regard. Poor Hyacinth Robinson strikes out on both counts in parallel ways. He ends up on the wrong side in politics, confusing socialism with anarchism like a character out of Conrad, and on the wrong side of love, the mercuric Christina Light being a decidedly inaccessible Big Other, as she had been, too, for the eponymous Roderick Hudson in James's first novel. (That Christina Light persists as a princess, a fairy-tale outcome linked to a woman whose given name even promises religious enlightenment despite the real-world expectations of James's fiction—as a princess she is not sacred illumination but a big house, *casamassima*—secures her a place in Žižek's "courtly love" tradition.)

In any case, for Brooks the navigation of a plot toward a suitable end reaches equilibrium through the reduction of excitation, possibly even in the form of death. One thinks again of the Miltonic catharsis, "calm of mind, all passion spent." Žižek is more postmodern. Following Lacan, he sees the object of desire as asymptotic, as being ultimately and always inaccessible; or if it *becomes* accessible—or one might say almost accessible—this gives rise to as many problems as it seems to eliminate (1193):

[P]erhaps, in courtly love itself, the long-awaited moment of highest fulfillment, when the Lady renders *Gnada*, mercy, to her servant is not the Lady's surrender, her consent to the sexual act, nor some mysterious rite of initiation, but simply a sign of love on the part of the Lady, the "miracle" that the Object answered, stretching its hand out towards the supplicant.

The object, in other words, has become subject. In this moment of exchange, mutuality of recognition, or becoming human on the part of the lady—whom Žižek has associated with the dominatrix in a sadistic relationship—in this moment of becoming human and of offering love, the object becomes more accessible. There is now the chance of surrender, yet as she becomes more accessible, the energy of desire is threatened with dissolution. In other words, closure in Žižek is a threat to the energy of desire,

Hans Holbein the Younger, *The Ambassadors* (1533).

not the fulfillment of it. Desire inheres in language, according to Žižek; it is the characteristic movement of language, and it is threatened by fulfillment. The lady says, "Sure, why not? Don't mind if I do," and her "servant" is thrown off his game completely, refusing the act he has so long represented to himself as the answer to his dreams, because *in fulfillment there's nothing more to desire.* Desire becomes need, merely a matter of gratification and no longer a question of sustaining that which makes us human: the endless propulsion, or agency, of the letter.

But what about the real, the unnarratable? Consider Hans Holbein's *The Ambassadors.* There are the two diplomats with a table between them. They are negotiating probably over one of Henry VIII's marriages, and as a crossing between politics and love that is perhaps not insignificant. The painting then concerns an object of desire, and that object is absent, implied at most. In the foreground, there is this *thing.* It angles toward us like a shadow, but it is not a shadow, a mirror or negative reflection, of anything in the painting. If you look at it from the side, it begins to resemble a skull. Indeed, there's something approaching a consensus among scholars that it may be a weirdly distorted shadow or representation of a skull. What the skull is doing there in such oblique perspective is hard to say, though perhaps not impossible to say. This is the age of the memento mori, which Holbein distorts almost beyond recognition to remind us that we do not always remember death yet death still follows us around like the imaginary stretcher in an ad for pills that lower cholesterol. Psychoanalytically, and as an axiom in the theory of narrative we have been studying, we find ourselves observing a model of the death wish and the pleasure principle as mutual presences. The shadow of death is also the shadow of the phallus, which surely this blot resembles as well. It is, after all, a marriage negotiation. So certainly there are things we can say. But still, this blot must always be a breach of decorum. Insofar as it is the shadow of our own death, which is unnarratable, as it is, too, for the ambassadors, for Henry, and for his latest fiancée, the skull or whatever it is obtrudes in untimely fashion, at an oblique angle, in the very midst of the plot of life. We can interpret it in the register of the symbolic (the phallus, the "letter"), or the imaginary (the skull as conventional memory aid). Insofar as it cannot be interpreted, though, insofar as it obtrudes on any and all conventions of representation, it is the *real*, that which has no meaning until we give it one.

Both in the book on Hitchcock, where he finds something like this in just about every film Hitchcock ever made, and also in Holbein's painting, Žižek calls this "the blot." In fiction, we would call it irrelevant detail. We feel that we can find a formal role, a function, for absolutely everything in fiction. The weather, the flowers on the table, the dust in the road: we can place these formally, but there may be something in fiction that is simply an unaccountable presence, and that's the blot for Žižek.

A word now about desire in language: there's a part of Žižek's essay that you may have found digressive. He's suddenly talking about J. L. Austin's ordinary language philosophy, together with the linguist Oswald Ducrot's idea of predication. But what's relevant for Žižek is the element of performance one finds in any utterance according to Austin, and the dominance of an entire sentence by predication according to Ducrot. Performance in Austin and predication in Ducrot take over the field of language even though they were supposed to cover only a part of it. Austin began by distinguishing between performatives and constatives; but in the long run, the argument of *How to Do Things with Words* suggests that there are only performatives, as statements of any kind harbor elements of performance. Ducrot similarly ascribes to the predicate an energetic agency that simply takes over the grammatical subject and constitutes a kind of performance within the sentence—where performance in both cases means "desire," a staging of the self in the act of speaking with respect to some wish. When I promise to do something, I enact the desire to fulfill the promise. When I predicate something, I enact the desire that that something be the case—rather than false—through my own instrumentality. These arguments then illustrate what Žižek means in insisting on the inescapability of desire in language, and the way desire permeates everything we can say to each other and certainly permeates the plot—or, as they say in film studies, the "diegesis"—of the film examples that Žižek gives us.

We have perhaps grown skeptical about whether we can ever turn a new page in our reading (dwat that pesky langwidge), but next time we'll try again.

The Social Context

CHAPTER 16

The Social Permeability of Reader and Text

Readings:

Jauss, Hans Robert. "Literary History as a Challenge to Literary Theory." In *The Critical Tradition*, pp. 981–988.

Bakhtin, Mikhail. "Heteroglossia in the Novel." In *The Critical Tradition*, pp. 588–593.

As we turn now to theories that are concerned chiefly with the social context and milieu of literature, we begin with a pairing that's perhaps as odd as that of Deleuze and Žižek: Mikhail Bakhtin and Hans Robert Jauss. The most egregious difference between your authors for today is that Bakhtin's primary concern is with the life world that produces a text, and Jauss's primary concern is with the life world, or perhaps better succession of life worlds, in which a text is received. I think you can tell from reading both excerpts, however, and will find in the materials ahead in our reading, that once you factor in a social setting the production and reception of literature are not as easy to tell apart as you might have supposed. In all discourse exchanges, such as conversation, we recognize that the listener is also a speaker and the reader an author. In theories of literary influence like Bloom's, the author simply *is* the reader, and in a sense I think this is true of Jauss as well; but in broader senses, too, we'll come to see that the production and consumption of literature are difficult to separate as topics. In literary history, the author is a reader who stands in relation to the past; and the reader in turn, who plays a role circulating texts for the future, is perhaps even in concrete terms a writer. He or she expresses opinions, circulates values, keeps texts on the best seller list, and perhaps contributes to their lasting reputation.

Although Jauss does not say this, I've always felt that of necessity his reader is almost as much a writer as Bloom's is. Any reader responsible for the continued presence, or influence, of a text through literary history must in some sense have expressed an opinion. Silent participation in the nineteenth-century lending libraries or even purchases at the bookseller's are going to be ephemeral: the fate of a book is dictated by reviews, buzz, word of mouth. Our blogs, online reader feedback, book clubs, and discussion groups make this truer today than ever before. The reader as tastemaker is also a writer. Perhaps to belabor a point that has not been acknowledged: if Bloom's theory of strong misreading as a principle of literary historiography can be understood as a relationship between writers as readers and readers as writers, there is a sense in which for Jauss, too, the reader is a writer and the writer is a reader. Both of them, Bloom as well as Jauss, have made plausible contributions to literary historiography.

Let us return, though, to remembering that this lecture marks a moment of transition in our reading. There may be times, again, when we wonder whether we're really moving ahead or whether we do perhaps need to acknowledge that "formalism," for all its alleged and apparent indifference to history and the world, was after all talking about "life" all along. Shklovsky hoped that literariness would defamiliarize not just language but historical and social reality. Richards said that poetry is capable of saving us. Cleanth Brooks said that one of the uses of poetry was to make us better citizens. For Jakobson there is no utterance that lacks a referential function. Derrida speaks of the mystery of the "event," de Man of Proustian atmospheres. So how can we agree upon at least a provisional difference between what went before and what we'll read now? We shall say, not sure whether the distinction will hold up but still with the sense that we need one, that hitherto the text has constituted a world but that henceforth the world lives in the text. The text is no longer a microcosm but a medium through which the real world passes. It is as much as ever a distorting medium, but it is no longer a separable entity with a discrete ontological status (note that this follows equally from Derrida's premise that there is nothing outside the text, properly understood); the text is an object in the world, produced, sustained, and undone by social forces.

So far we have been thinking of language as a semiotic code, while suspecting that this code may be only a virtual one. We have been emphasizing the degree to which we are passive in relation to, even "spoken by" this language. In other words, it has been a constant in our thinking about these matters that language speaks through us; yet we have exercised so far a curious reticence about any sense we may have that this language is not *just* a code, not just something that exists virtually at any given historical moment, but is in fact a code made up of *other people's language*: it is language not just in the abstract but in circulation. This makes it perhaps less a *langue*, in Saussure's sense, and closer to what he called *langage*, the sum of all speeches in circulation. Lacan, too, sees language as inherited, to be sure, the language "of the father" that we speak no matter how much we wish we didn't; but clearly that way of putting it is a psychoanalytic distillation of a far more diffuse and multifaceted inheritance.

So we are thinking of language still, and of the distinction we have learned to make between language and speech, but now it's not a language abstracted from reality; it's a language that *circulates* within reality as an instrument of social exchange. Language is now and henceforth in our reading a social institution. In literary theory, this new, institutional sense of language retains the same determinate relationship with individual speech that we have observed in linguistic and psychoanalytic formalism, but we now begin to understand the claim that language speaks to us in a new way. My voice—and the word "voice" is obviously under heavy pressure here, even though nobody ever quite says it goes away—my voice is permeated by all the sedimentations, registers, levels, and orientations of language in the world that surrounds me. Insofar as my speech retains agency, it is in the sense that I *take* language from other people. When I lecture ad-lib from a few notes, the social circulation of language is even more pronounced in what I say than it might be otherwise. When you listen to me blather on without a script, you're hearing the internet, you're hearing newspaper headlines, you're hearing slang. You're hearing the expression "you're hearing," a rhythmically repeated phrase in the cadence you'll recognize from pulpit and political oratory, a kind of seesaw or rocking-horse effect that I'd probably try to get rid of if I were writing. As we'll learn, writing is indeed an effort to take possession of language, to make it do one's bidding, but writing too never stops being voiced in the language of others.

What's "out there" gets to the point where it's in here, and the next thing you know, it becomes part of the ongoing patter of an individual, the grain as it were of even the most idiosyncratic speech. I suppose the extent to which this might be the case, where it is absolutely so or only one factor in the makeup of individual speech, is always subject to debate. Soon we'll take up a couple of examples. But in any case, you can see that without the *structure* of the relationship between language and speech having changed—and in fact it won't really change as we continue along—the *substance* of this relationship and the way we talk about it is very much changed when we think of language as a social network rather than a virtual system.

In order to see more concretely how this change appears in the work of the two authors we read for this lecture, I want to quote from a couple of passages. The first is from Bakhtin, whose roots are in Russian formalism. The passage concerns the relationship between what he takes to be a formalist understanding of double-voicedness and "genuine heteroglossia." A conventional sense of double-voicedness is reflected in the notion of irony as not meaning what one says in a way that in most cases speaker and hearer can agree upon. But Bakhtin wants to call a different phenomenon to our attention:

> Rhetoric is often limited to purely verbal victories over the word, over ideological authority. [These are the ways we can subvert received ideas that exert tyrannical authority over thought by submitting them to figures of rhetoric such as irony.] When this happens rhetoric degenerates into formalistic verbal play but, we repeat, when discourse is torn from reality it is fatal for the word itself as well. Words grow sickly, lose semantic depth and flexibility, the capacity to expand and renew their meanings in new living contexts. [Something bad happens and we say "great!" We have done this for several generations and the expression doesn't have much oomph any more.] They essentially die as discourse, for the signifying word lives beyond itself; that is, it lives by directing its purposiveness outward. Double-voicedness, which is merely verbal, is not structured on authentic heteroglossia but on a mere diversity of voices.

It is a diversity of voices, that is, probably no more than two, manipulated by an individual. In other words, double-voicedness doesn't take into account the way in which there are complex overlays among the possibilities and registers of meaning, depending on diverse speaking communities coming together to forge any aspect of discourse and forcing us to think about the life world of an utterance in order to understand its play of voice.

We can point to a comparable response to formalism on the part of Hans Robert Jauss. Like Bakhtin, Jauss is strongly influenced by the Russian formalists. This influence is not enunciated fully in the text that you have but rather in Jauss's best known essay, the pamphlet-length "Literary History as a Provocation to Literary Theory." In his theory of the relationship between the text and the life world, Jauss stitches together aspects of Russian formalist historiography, particularly that of Jakobson and Tynianov, with a Marxist approach to the marketing, reception, and consumption of literary production. These two sets of ideas function side by side in Jauss's thesis about literary reception, to which we'll return at the end of the lecture.

The second passage, in which Jauss attempts to distance himself somewhat from both of these influences, goes as follows:

> Early Marxist and formalist methods in common conceive the literary fact within the closed circle of an aesthetics of production and representation. In doing so, they deprive literature of a dimension that inalienably belongs to its aesthetic character as well as to its social function, the dimension of its reception and influence.

In other words, the way in which a text makes its way forward in time, the way it changes in the eyes of readers and grows or diminishes as time passes—this is a social process, but its dynamics and contours can be charted only as a matter of successively collective aesthetic and interpretive judgments. What takes place in the social medium or network—the process of "reception"—is a matter of evaluation and interpretation, as we'll see.

As we try to get closer to the connection between thinking of this kind and the formalist tradition, consider where Bakhtin discusses (cf. 589) literary "parody," here in the narrow sense of a spoof of some well-known literary model or text. He implies that the theory of parody understood in a broader sense belongs primarily to Russian formalist literary historiography, where the innovative principle that distinguishes a new text from an old one is just called parody. To pause over "parody," then: if we conceive of it only in the narrow sense, we cannot have a sufficient grasp of the complexity with which the dialogic or the heteroglossal modulates, ripples, and makes complicated the surface of literary discourse. Parody narrowly conceived once again leaves us confined to a binarism: the previous text was such and such, the successive text plays off that previous text in a way that we can call parodic but that remains a binary interaction. It's one text in relation to another and leaves out the flooding of multiple voices that pervades successive texts.

Implicit in this revision is the refusal to allow a separate track, isolated from social history, for literary history. Bakhtin insists that literary and social voices are inseparable. Jauss makes the same refusal. In a passage quoted below, you will find him directly responding to that passage at the end of Tynianov's essay, "On Literary Evolution," which we have discussed before. You remember Tynianov makes the distinction between evolution—the way a sequence of texts mutates, as one might say, the way successive texts (again) parody or alter what preceded them—and modification, which is the outside influence on texts by nonliterary factors that still bring about textual change. Tynianov says that it's important both for the study of history and also for the study of literary history that the two be kept clearly distinct from each other.

Jauss's response to that claim is perhaps more rhetorical than substantive, but it nevertheless once again does mark the shift toward conceiving of language as social that I've been wanting to begin by emphasizing. Jauss says:

> The connection between literary evolution and social change [that is to say, those features in society that would and do modify texts] does not vanish from the face of the earth through its mere negation. The new literary work is received and judged against the background of the everyday experience of life.

Note that this is a fairly elementary misreading of Tynianov, who thinks the way works replace each other within their history and the way they're judged in relation to the everyday are very different matters. But it may still be fair to argue that Tynianov's distinction is fragile and certainly difficult to maintain when studying literary reception, especially if one takes authorial attitudes as well as textual relations into account. An author in creating a new work reshapes many things in a prior work besides its literary conventions—reshapes its opinions, for example. Also, there is no easy or even possible way to distinguish between formal innovations and those sorts of innovation that are produced by essentially social pressures. The avoidance of metaphor in socialist realism only *looks* like a formal choice. Aesthetic and social factors seep into one another in exactly the same way that all the registers and sedimentations of human voices interact and seep into one another in Bakhtin's heteroglossia.

These, then, are Bakhtin's and Jauss's shared revisions of formalist ideas that have played a prominent part in most, if not all, of the literary theory that we have studied until now. I'd like to discuss Bakhtin for a while now before turning back to Jauss. Heteroglossia, or diversity of speech as Bakhtin calls it sometimes, is what he singles out to be "the ground of style" (592). It is the diversity of speech and not the unity of a normative shared language or that which is distinctive in an author that is the ground of style. When I speak to you, I'm not speaking in an official voice. I am not speaking the King's English. In fact, on this view there's really no such thing as the King's English, no such isolated, distilled entity that one can point to. Some hermetically sealed environments, like that of an inward-looking aristocracy at one extreme and perhaps some isolated settings at the opposite end of the social spectrum, are what Bakhtin would call "monoglossal." (Bakhtin probably would not agree that the language of any underclass is monoglossal because he takes all such speech environments to be in a ferment of protest and resistance.) But the language of most of us is the language of many others.

If this is true, how is a distinctive style generated? We speak of a style as though it were purely a question of an authorial signature: "Oh, I would recognize that style anywhere." Coleridge said of a few lines of Wordsworth that if he had come across those lines in the desert, he'd have cried out "Wordsworth!" And certainly it is true that we do recognize a style—the style of Jane Austen, for example. I suppose arguably you could think that the first sentence of *Pride and Prejudice* is the style of Dr. Johnson, but most people would recognize it as the style of Jane Austen. At the same time nevertheless, as we'll see in a minute, it is a style made up of many voices that are very difficult finally to factor out and distinguish from each other.

The idea of a style as a composite of speech sedimentations would seem to put the notion of an authorial voice in jeopardy. That might lead us to ask in turn whether agreeing that the sociolect speaks through the idiolect, that the language of everyone is, in fact, the language that speaks my speech—whether agreeing to this once again brings us face to face with that dreary topic, the death of the author. I don't think so, not quite anyway, and certainly not in Bakhtin, who gives us a rather bracing sense of the importance of the author (593):

It is as if the author has no language of his own, but does possess his own style, his own organic and unitary law governing the way he plays with languages [so style is perhaps one's particular way of mediating and allocating the diversity of voice that impinges on what one's saying] and the way his own real semantic and expressive intentions are refracted within them. [And here Bakhtin saves or preserves the author by invoking the principle of unifying intention and the way we can recognize it in the discourse of any given novel.] Of course this play with languages (and frequently the complete absence of a direct discourse of his own) in no sense degrades the general, deep-seated intentionality, the overarching ideological conceptualization of the work as a whole.

So this is not, though it may seem to be in certain respects, a question of the death of the author as provoked by, let's say, Foucault or Barthes at the start of our reading. Everything that we've been saying so far about plurivocality can be seen at work in a vast array of novels. The novel is the privileged genre for Bakhtin. I think somewhat oversimplifying in this regard, he reads the history of the novel, its emergence and flowering, against the backdrop of genres he considers to be monoglossal: the epic, which simply speaks the unitary voice of an aristocratic tradition; the lyric, which simply speaks the unitary voice of the isolated romantic solipsist. Over against that, you get the polyglossal, the rich multiplicity of voice in the novel. As I say, I think that the generic contrast is somewhat oversimplified because nothing is easier and more eye-opening than to read both epic and lyric as manifestations of heteroglossia. Just think of *The Iliad.* If you really believe that it's monoglossal, what are you going to do with the speeches of the malcontent Thersites? You could say they're an exception proving a hegemonic rule, but the fact remains, they're not the voice of the peevishly godlike Achilles, which in turn after all is not the voice of the stuffy official Agamemnon, the ideological relativist Sarpedon, or the wily Odysseus.

Despite this caveat, however, I think the basic idea of heteroglossia both rich and important. Let's try it out with the first sentence of *Pride and Prejudice,* which I'm sure most of you know: "It is a truth universally acknowledged that a single man in possession of a good fortune must be in want of a wife." Generally speaking, this is an example of the precarious balance between what Bakhtin calls "common language"—"It is a truth universally acknowledged" because everybody speaks of it—and something like authorial reflection—what Bakhtin elsewhere calls "internally persuasive discourse."

In traditional parlance, this would be considered a speech that manifests irony, the rhetoric of irony against which Bakhtin sets himself in the first passage on your sheet. We easily conclude that Jane Austen doesn't believe what she says. It's drawing-room wisdom, and everything in her sentence points to the ways in which it's obviously wrong, even while it's being called a truth: "universally" means the thousand silly people or so who matter, not the thousands who neither acknowledge nor care about any such thing. Then, of course, the idea that "a single man in possession of a good fortune," or indeed otherwise, has nothing to do but to be "in want of a wife" is on the face of it exaggerated. Hence we conclude that Austen is being ironic at the expense of drawing room chatter.

But now we start to complicate these confirmations of a simple irony at work. Bear in mind that the plot of the novel *confirms* the "truth" of its first sentence, *even though* it is a truth that we seem not to be intended to endorse. Darcy and Bingley, both of them "in possession of a good fortune," do turn out to have been in want of a wife and procure one by the end of the novel. Then, of course, there is this word "want." What it means depends on who's speaking it. We've been thinking a lot about want lately because we have just gone through our psychoanalytic phase. What exactly does this single man really want? There's a subtle pun in the word "want," which means both "to desire" and "to lack." If I lack something, after all, I don't necessarily desire it, I just don't happen to have it. On the other hand, if I want something, true enough, I can also be said to desire it. Well, which is it? Is it a lack that social pressure of some sort is calculated to fill ("high time he was married, odd that he isn't considering how rich he is"), or is it desire? If it's desire, then possessing a good fortune is scarcely what accounts for the want. There are elements of a romance plot in this novel—not quite the same as a marriage plot—that raise precisely that question. Desire ignores mere bank accounts, though it likes royalty. Luxury, convenience, social acceptability, comfort: all of those things have to do with fortune, but desire we suppose to be of a somewhat different nature. The complication of the sentence has to do actually with the way the meanings of these words as they are used socially circulate through the sentence and make us see that our confident inference about Austen's ironic distance from the drawing room is qualified by all sorts of tempered allegiances, borne out as I've said by her plot. We need Bakhtin's help to see that the ascription of irony is too blunt an instrument for reading Austen.

It is also important to grasp Bakhtin's idea of common language. This is not a concept that is supposed to have one particular value attached to it.

"Common language" is a little like a rhizome; it could be good, it could be bad. It *could* be (I allude here to Bakhtin's book on "carnival") a Rabelaisian, carnivalesque, subversive, energetic body of voices from below overturning the apple carts of authority and the fixed ways of a moribund social order. It could be that, but at the same time it could itself be authoritative, reactionary, mindless. Common language could call forth that depressing universality of appeal that seems to authorize unreflected, knee-jerk responses to what one observes and thinks about, for example, on the campaign trail. Common language covers this whole range.

The important thing about it is that it's out there and that it circulates and exists in relation to what Bakhtin calls "internally persuasive discourse"—in other words, the way in which the filtering together of these various sorts of language result in something like what we feel to be *authentic*. We sense a power of reflection, a posing of relations among the various strata of language, such that they can speak persuasively, not necessarily in a way that we agree with but in a way that we recognize to constitute that coherent consciousness that we still do call "the author"—and to which we ascribe, in some sense, authority. In the peculiar self-mocking relationship between the first sentence of *Pride and Prejudice*—every word of which is "common language"—and the plot of *Pride and Prejudice* as a whole, we feel something like the internal persuasiveness, the coherence of the discourse.

To sum up these remarks on Bakhtin, I want to quote from the other long excerpt that you have in your anthology, which I would encourage you to read. It's called "Discourse in the Novel," and I just want to quote this part of it (580): "The ideological becoming of a human being . . . is the process of selectively assimilating the words of others." The achieved coherence of anyone's mind results from selecting out of the words of others something like an autonomous world view. The novel, with its emphasis on education and development, is the social text *par excellence* for Bakhtin, and its "internally persuasive discourse," achieved through the complex juxtaposition of common languages as demonstrated in Bakhtin's examination of Dickens's satiric style, is the site on which the selection of other people's languages becomes a recognizable voice.

Hans Robert Jauss takes us back, by way of Iser, to Gadamer. You've noticed, I'm sure, that Jauss's talk about horizons of expectation and the disruption of expectation has a great deal to do with Iser's account of the role of the reader in filling imaginative gaps that are left in the text, gaps caused by departures from conventional expectations that need to be negotiated. What Jauss has to say about horizons of expectation is a way of thinking through the conditions in which Gadamer's "merger of horizons" is possible. But for Jauss it's not just one reader's horizon and the horizon of the text that need to meet halfway in mutual illumination. Such mergers take place or fail to do so along a succession of horizons that change as modes of aesthetic and interpretive response to texts are mediated by historical circumstances.

It's not just that the text once had a certain identity that readers now conceive differently, hence need to reconsider from their own horizon. It's rather a matter of deciding what has happened, studying changes in the way the text has been received between that other time and one's own. The text has had a life. It has passed through life changes, and these life changes have to be understood at each successive stage in terms of the three moments of hermeneutic grasp as described by Gadamer in the historical section of *Truth and Method*. The eighteenth-century distinction between *intelligere*, *explicare*, and *applicare*—understanding, interpretation, and application— that Jauss talks about at the beginning of his essay exists to distinguish the three moments of hermeneutic understanding for any reader or reading public at any moment in the history of the reception of a text.

Jauss makes a considerable point of distinguishing between the aesthetic response to the text and a subsequent, reflectively interpretive response to the text. This may seem a little confusing because he does admit with Heidegger and others, as we've indicated ourselves in the past, that you can't just have a spontaneous response to anything without reflection. There's always a sense in which you already know what it is, which is to say a sense in which you've already interpreted it. Yet Jauss does make a considerable point of distinguishing between these two moments—the aesthetic, which he associates with understanding, and the interpretive, which he associates with *explicare* in the hermeneutic tradition. We need to understand what he means by "the aesthetic." A text enters historical circulation and remains before the gaze of successive audiences in history because it has been admired aesthetically. Aesthetics is the nourishment that keeps the text alive through history. People continue to say that they like it. If they don't say they like it, there will never be a question of interpreting it or transmitting it historically, because it's going to disappear. As Dr. Johnson said, "That book is good in vain which the reader throws away." In other words, from the standpoint of interpretation, a book may have been good, just incontestably good—but if it didn't please, if it didn't give pleasure, if it didn't attach itself to a reading public aesthetically by means of pleasing, none of what would have followed could ever take place.

With this understanding of how readers and reading publics behave within a given horizon, the historical study of reception (what Jauss and his colleagues at the University of Konstanz, including Iser, called "reception history") is what shows us the degree to which any particular moment of aesthetic and interpretive reception is mediated by what has gone before it and what comes after. In other words, a text gradually changes as a result of its *reception*, and if we don't study reception, we are left naively supposing that time has passed and that interpretation of a past text has become difficult but that the difficulty has nothing to do with historical change itself. The fact is, there has been an unfolding process of successive interpretations whereby a text has gone through sea changes: it has become less popular, more popular, more richly interpreted, and less richly interpreted, but tends to keep eddying out from what it was sensed to be originally, to the point where all sorts of accretive implications and sources of pleasure may become available to us, though perhaps also lost. A recently emergent field in English called "Medievalisms" studies successive ideas of the medieval over the centuries, including the Pardoner's new life in queer studies, the Wife of Bath's new life as a feminist, the vicissitudes of the Clerk's reputation (is he a sage or a sponger?) as the social cachet of advanced humanistic studies waxes and wanes, and of course the increasingly "dialogic" emphasis on the carnivalesque ways in which the Miller's story rebuts the Knight's story. Reception history considers such changes wherever they appear—perhaps the commonest instance of which (nearly everyone is aware of it) being the correlation of attitudes toward Shakespeare's Henry V with bellicose and pacifist national moods.

Perhaps more influential today than "reception history" is the concept of the "public sphere" introduced by another student of Gadamer, Jürgen Habermas, who studied this new milieu for the circulation and reception of ideas as a feature of the Enlightenment in the eighteenth century, but whose concept has been rather broadly adapted to the study of media shifts, especially the rise of print culture. Although many of Jauss's examples of reception history focus on anomalies within a single horizon (as in his illuminating contrast between the reception of Flaubert's *Madame Bovary* and the reception of Ernest-Aimé Feydeau's *Fanny* in "Literary History as a Provocation to Literary Theory"), I assign him in preference here as a contributor to the theory of literary history. Another and closely related field, often combined with audience studies, is "media history," especially the history of the book in literary scholarship, which takes the material object circulated (manuscript, book, viral blog) as its point of departure for understanding reading audiences.

The history of reception, then, studies two things: first, changing horizons of expectation whereby a reader in a given moment has to come to terms with conventions and their breach in any given text, discriminating between what's new and what's merely culinary—horizons that don't just change once in the here and now but have changed successively through time. This consideration is largely aesthetic. Reception history also involves changing semantic possibilities or, if you will, changing possibilities for and of significance: why does the text matter to a reading public at given times? This consideration is largely interpretive.

Just to take examples of how alertness to the historical moment of reception might work in the here and now, there was recently a Broadway revival of *Damn Yankees*, an old musical about a baseball player who sells his soul to beat the Yankees, produced at a time when the Yankees were considered an invincible machine. One can't help but think now that the revival of interest in *Damn Yankees*, at a time when the Yankees no longer have the reputation of invincibility, has something to do with the steroid scandals and the way so many athletes do sell their souls in order to win and to have good careers. It is in this atmosphere of social and cultural censure that we're suddenly interested in *Damn Yankees* again. *Tony the Tow Truck* appeared in the early 1980s, prosperous times when the vices of affluence needed a dressing down. Perhaps there will be a revival of *Tony the Tow Truck* because now, in the economic downturn, obviously to be rich or glamorous like Neato or selfishly busy like Speedy seems obsolete, more or less irrelevant and beside the point, and what really matters is little guys helping each other. Should this revival occur, *Tony* will be heard by every toddler, give pleasure to parents, and find itself interpreted (with applications: *applicare*) by English professors. It will survive to live another day historically, fulfilling the three moments of reception specified by Jauss.

CHAPTER 17

The Frankfurt School of Critical Theory

Readings:

Benjamin, Walter. "The Work of Art in the Age of Mechanical Reproduction." In *The Critical Tradition*, pp. 1233–1248.

Horkheimer, Max, and Theodor Adorno. "The Culture Industry." In *The Critical Tradition*, pp. 1255–1262.

Passages from Adorno.

As we move into social perspectives on literature and art, you may ask yourself, "Why Marx? Why so much Marx? Why is it Marx who seems to stand behind the idea that the social criticism of art is the best and most relevant way to approach this subject matter?" Well, it's because whatever the outcome of Marxist thought may have proven to be or yet prove to be historically, it remains nevertheless the most devastating critique we have of social delusion as it both inspires and conditions works of art historically. When we turn to Fredric Jameson in the next lecture, and already in considering Walter Benjamin now, we'll see that Marxist thought reveals what stands behind our conception of reality and our understanding of our place in the world in the form of a "political unconscious." We have first considered a linguistic unconscious, or in any case linguistic preconditioning, then a psychoanalytic unconscious; and now, following the title of Jameson's book from which we'll read an excerpt for the next lecture, we arrive at a political unconscious.

There *are* other ways of approaching the social criticism of literature and art. On the conservative front, there is an extraordinary book by Leo Strauss on Aristophanes, together with his influential readings of the traditional texts of political philosophy, beginning with *The Republic* and laying strong emphasis on Socrates's critique of poetry. And there is, as well, a very strong *liberal* tradition of criticism, particularly in the journalism of the public sphere. Perhaps the most notable proponent of a liberal criticism of art undertaken from a social point of view was Lionel Trilling, especially in the essays collected in *The Liberal Imagination.* So there are and have been socially oriented approaches to literature from other points along the political spectrum, but by far the most pervasive mode of social critique in literary theory remains the Marxist one. As we go on trying to keep at least one eye on literature, our concern will remain primarily with Marxist aesthetics.

In the meantime, what do we need to know about Marx? I hope I can take for granted in a course of this kind that most of you have some familiarity with the history of ideas and with Western culture, hence have some notion of Marx comparable to what you know about Freud (two of Foucault's "founders of discursivity"). Of special importance to us, hence worth a pause, is the slippery notion of "ideology."

In the writings of Marx and Engels and all the Marxist writing that has succeeded them, ideology is a concept about which there has never been wholehearted agreement. The disagreement concerning ideology in this tradition chiefly concerns whether it ought properly to be ascribed to conscious as well as to unconscious preconceptions about the world. If I know to the very core of my being that the moon is made of green cheese—I am fully conscious of this opinion, can reason fluently about it, and can prove it as indubitably as Quixote can prove a windmill is a giant—the question arises whether this knowledge of mine can be demystified as ideology. Just so, a belated aristocrat is prepared to defend the idea that hierarchy and privilege are beneficial to society, perfectly conscious that this is an unpopular, more or less disgraced idea, but committed to it nonetheless and prepared to cite learned authorities in its defense. We again face the question, "Is this still ideology?"

Particularly in the writings of Engels, indeed perhaps more than in the writings of Marx, the answer by and large is yes, it is still ideology. We can define ideology as the belief, whether conscious or unconscious, that holding a point of view is knowing the truth. Ideology dictates that the way things appear from the materially and economically grounded standpoint of my own consciousness is not just the way they appear to me but the way they actually are. Now according to Marx, this is a mode of belief that in successive historical periods has characterized each dominant class in turn. With the rise of capitalism and its evolution into what's called late capitalism, this mode of belief is what's called "bourgeois ideology." In the bourgeois mind, the ideas that have enabled middle-class life to flourish—the work ethic, the idea of family, certain codes of moral behavior—are the best ideas for all classes in all circumstances at all historical times. Thus does ideology suppose that the ideas and foundations of behavior suited to one set of material conditions are suited to all.

We began the course with the quotation from Marx's *Capital* on commodity fetishism. There Marx shows how it is just spontaneously supposed, without reflection, that the labor value of something that's produced—the value that can accrue to it because of the amount of labor that has gone into it and the accordant amount of practical use that can be derived from it—is superseded by a value that's thought to be inherent in the product itself as though it were itself the agent of its being. This transvaluation applies as well to art, and it's something to which Benjamin alludes when he characterizes the commodification of art as its "aura." If we forget that art is *produced*—that a certain quantum of labor has gone into its production—and if we then simply address ourselves to the work of art with rapt contemplative absorption as though it had objective value—the glow of its authenticity—apart from having been produced, then what we're doing is "commodifying" the work of art. From Benjamin's point of view, in other words, to be seduced by the aura of the work of art is to experience the work ideologically as a commodity.

To return, then, to the whole question of the aesthetic objectives of Marxist criticism: one needs to sort through a varied tradition, as befits a "founded" discursivity; but there are basically four Marxist options for determining what the aesthetics of art ought actually to be. Factors to be taken into account from every standpoint are, how should art reflect society? How should it constitute a critique of society? How should it predict an ideal, emergent, utopian society? All of these questions are questions of aesthetics because the way art does express the social—as opposed to a political treatise, say—is necessarily aesthetic. Social expression is mediated by form, genre, style—all understood as modes of production that are conditioned by material factors.

The aesthetics of Marx and Engels themselves—our first option—was realist, but their realism was dispassionately analytic and quite sophisticated. When aspiring writers, already caught up in the idea that they ought to be writing for the advancement of the proletariat, would write to Engels— I'm thinking of Ferdinand Lassalle, Minna Kautsky, and others—sending him manuscripts of their "socialist realist" novels, Engels disapproved and responded that there was no obligation to glorify the proletariat, no need to project the future in this way. What his correspondents should attempt to do, he said, is to see the social dynamic as it exists in the present moment—to understand the world realistically but not tendentiously. Engels's literary hero was Balzac, a royalist reactionary who nevertheless successfully evoked society in all of its manifold complexities, especially its class structure, and whom Engels considered the best model for realist writing.

This aesthetic prevailed widely in Marxism through its early energetic years, including the early years of the Russian Revolution. In 1927, the year of Eikhenbaum's "Theory of the Formal Method," of Heidegger's *Being and Time*, and of Benjamin's visit to Moscow, the literary philosopher Georg Lukács wrote a book called *The Historical Novel*. Lukács had been a Hegelian and had written a brilliant metaphysical meditation called *The Theory of the Novel* (1920) before he turned to Marxist thought. *The Historical Novel* reads as though it were taken from Engels's letters. It's partly an attack on what Lukács took to be the narcissistic inwardness of high modernism, particularly Joyce and Proust, but its thesis is also argued along the lines chosen by Engels to recommend Balzac in his letters to disciples. Lukács champions the novels of Sir Walter Scott, a political reactionary like Balzac, whose grand dialectical balances between Highland and Lowland, feudal and mercantile, Scotland and England, the old social order and the new Lukács took to be perfect instances of seeing class relations as they really are.

But more or less at the time of *The Historical Novel*, alongside the rise of Stalin, the ideas of all those people who used to write to Engels—Kautsky, Lassalle—began to prevail in Soviet thought. A literary critic named Andrei Zhdanov articulated a doctrine of socialist realism that was showcased in the writings of Maxim Gorky and espoused as official doctrine at the International Soviet Writer's Conference in 1934. That was the second aesthetic option. You probably know the joke: boy meets tractor, boy loses tractor, boy goes to the city to find tractor, takes tractor back to the countryside and lives with it happily ever after. This fundamental plot, obviously a variant on the marriage plot but engaged also in what Benjamin would call "mechanical reproduction," prevailed in Soviet writing, with formal as well as ideological deviations subject to censorship, until the Iron Curtain fell in 1989.

So those are the forms of realism that are most often identified with Marxist criticism and literary production. Yet probably the most dynamic criticism since Lukács in the twentieth century has recognized that realism is a rhetoric, an ideology in itself, that has been appropriated by the bourgeoisie. Who else "tells it like it is"? Who else keeps reminding you about "the real world"? Who else proclaims around the dinner table that he or she is a "realist"? Just as it commandeers everything else for itself, the middle class has appropriated the idea of realism and made it banal, aesthetically outmoded. Hence, as we shall explain over time, the third and fourth options turn away from realism toward formalism and utopian romance, respectively.

Walter Benjamin espouses neither of these possibilities, yet he too is acutely conscious of the limits of realism, which he grants to be a late capitalist form of commodifying the aura, a last gasp of bourgeois art and appreciation. Benjamin does not however advocate a departure from the real (which is why I don't describe his as a fifth option); he urges immersion in it. For him the banality of realism needs to be counteracted with a *participatory* aesthetic: the fragmentary perceptions and the distracted attention span of daily life are part of this, yet there is no question of turning away from the real. The participatory artist and audience are, on the contrary, communal workers engaged with the very mode of production that ushers the work of art into the real world. We'll develop these topics when we turn to Benjamin's "Work of Art" essay.

Perhaps the most unusual aesthetic move for a Marxist critic is the one that you will find in Adorno (the third option). Theodor Adorno was devoted to precisely what Lukács had attacked in *The Historical Novel*, namely, the high modernist aesthetic. He admired Beckett in literature, Schönberg, Berg, and Webern in music. (Adorno was by training a musicologist and devoted much of his writing career to essays and treatises on music and the history of music.) These modernists were heroes in Adorno's pantheon, provoking the question of how artists who have nothing striking to say about social relations, who are largely preoccupied with the medium they work in, and who seem to be indifferent to the whole course of history (apart from the history of their medium) can be the aesthetic benchmarks of a Marxist critic. The answer to this question is worked out in "On the Fetish-Character in Music and the Regression of Listening," from which I've given you two excerpts in the appendix. I want to pause over them because I think Adorno's essay incisively distinguishes between the totality, or wholeness, that's offered by artistic form and the mere totalization or totalitarianism that's imposed by modern hegemonic forms of government—whether obviously totalitarian or insidiously totalitarian, like the "culture industry" to which he devotes the essay that you've read.

So this is what Adorno says in these two passages. He's describing the way people who enjoy, or think they enjoy, music under the sway of the culture industry are completely victimized by coloratura local effects, what you might call—this is a conductor whom Adorno hated—the Toscanini effect: the highlighting of a particular moment in a composition, riding it into the ground at the expense of the whole, and all the virtuoso turns that show off what Adorno elsewhere calls "lip-smacking euphony"; in other words, cultivating the perfection of local sound at the expense of comprehending the total composition. So he says in the first passage:

> The delight in the moment and the gay façade become an excuse for absolving the listener from the thought of the whole, whose claim is comprised in proper listening. The listener is converted, along his line of least resistance [because after all, it's so beautiful to listen to], into the acquiescent purchaser. No longer do the partial moments serve as a critique of the whole [as they sometimes do in Modernism. Dissonance, in other words, is in and of itself a critique of that overarching harmony that we associate with wholeness. So there's a real sense in which the parts can be understood as a critique of the whole without challenging or breaking down the whole.]; instead, they suspend *the critique which the successful esthetic totality exerts against the flawed one of society.* [italics mine]

In other words, nothing can criticize the inauthenticity of the bad totalities of society except the authenticity of genuinely achieved wholeness in a work of art. The difference between these senses of the whole is precisely the zone of critique that might—just might—awaken the victim of the culture industry from the slumbers of happy conformism and acquiescence.

Now the second passage, just to reinforce this:

> Great Modernist composers like Berg, Schönberg and Webern are called individualists [by other Marxist critics, by people who don't like what Lukács would call "fetishization of form,"

reification of form at the expense of social reference and expression], and yet their work is nothing but a single dialogue with the powers that destroy individuality—powers whose "formless shadows" fall gigantically on their music. In music, too, collective powers are liquidating an individuality past saving, but against them only individuals are capable of consciously representing the aims of collectivity.

The totality—the achieved, successful, authentic totality—of the work of art models the utopian totality of a collective state in ways that none of the false totalities of current states can even approximate. In other words, there is an implicit progressive politics, Adorno argues, in pure form. The achievement of pure form, which is, after all, a collection of parts, models the achievement of a collective society.

This is a fascinating turn of thought. It's somewhat quixotic because it's hard to imagine a practical result. Imagine somebody listening to Schönberg and saying, "Gosh, maybe I should become a communist." But it is still a challenging dialectical reversal (Adorno is perhaps the most subtle dialectician since Hegel) of what Marxist thought supposes to be the mainstream aesthetic of Western civilization: the fetishization of wholeness. Think of the New Criticism laying stress on the unity of the poem, on the discrete ontological object as a unified whole. This is *the* commonplace typically attacked by commonplace Marxist criticism, and it's quite wonderful that Adorno sees the discrete ontological object not as a model of narcissistic individuality but of collectivity.

The last aesthetic option for Marxism, in part the subject of the next lecture, is another surprising one. It goes back to a three-volume work by Ernst Bloch called *The Principle of Hope* (1938–1947) in which Bloch essentially argues—in this respect largely anticipating Adorno—that in the late capitalist world as we inhabit it there is no longer any hope available. This dark outlook Bloch counters with the idea that especially in folk art, folkways, oral culture, and popular culture—that is, in the expressions of longing one finds in the work of the dispossessed and the oppressed—there is a kind of utopianism, a *romance*, and a sense not so much of wishing for something past, even though it seems to take the form of nostalgia, but rather of projecting a possibility on the future that is simply unavailable in the real world.

The best example I can think of is "The Big Rock Candy Mountain," sung by people on chain gangs about liquor running down the sides of mountains in rivulets and everything else just as they wish it to be. Bloch's idea is picked up and taken very seriously by Fredric Jameson, not so much in the excerpt from *The Political Unconscious* that you'll be reading but in an earlier part of that introductory chapter in which he discusses the important role of *romance* in replacing the bankrupt aesthetic of realism, expressing in a seemingly hopeless world the hopes of the oppressed and the dispossessed.

Today, however, we zero in on the participatory aesthetic of Benjamin and the modernist totality of Adorno. You can see the way they conflict with each other. Adorno's "Fetish Character" essay (1938) was actually a response, in friendly disagreement, to Benjamin's "Work of Art" essay; but "The Culture Industry," too, is in its way a response. Adorno was a close friend of Benjamin's and exchanged letters with him disputing the claims of the "Work of Art" essay—letters that were republished in the *New Left Review* of 1973 and are well worth reading for anyone who wishes to pursue the interesting implications of their disagreement.

Adorno and Benjamin were members together of the Frankfurt Institute for Social Research, or "Frankfurt School," which—before its members fled the Nazis, many emigrating to the United States—produced volumes of important dialectical thought combining the insights of Marx and Freud and focused on the roots of totalitarianism (as in Adorno's essays, "The Authoritarian Personality" and "Anti-Semitism and Fascist Propaganda"). The best known of these works is *The Dialectic of Enlightenment,* written with Max Horkheimer, from which your excerpt is taken. In this country during the 1960s and 1970s the best-known work emanating from this circle was Herbert Marcuse's *Eros and Civilization.* In addition to Horkheimer, Friedrich Pollak and Siegfried Kracauer (whose theory of the "mass ornament" explores the cultural fetish, as does Adorno) published important work of relevance to our subject. A younger member of this school whom I mentioned in the last lecture, and who is the most prominent of them all today, is Jürgen Habermas, whose viewpoint, however, is closer to liberal humanism than to the ultimately nonrevolutionary dialectical materialism of his mentors and colleagues.

Benjamin was only for a brief period in the 1930s a committed Marxist critic. He had hitherto been much more interested in Kabbalistic literature and in the Hegelian tradition of philosophy, and even in the 1930s he was famously torn between two possibilities. After his Moscow visit, he had become interested in what was still a vibrant or in any case strikingly different culture in the Soviet world. Thanks to the intercession of the charismatic Asja Lacis, he had also formed a close friendship with the Marxist playwright

Bertolt Brecht, whose influence can be felt in the "Work of Art" essay. But another very close and equally influential friend was the Jewish theologian Gershom Scholem, a Zionist who emigrated to Jerusalem and wanted Benjamin to join him studying the Kabbalah there. From Scholem, from his own eclectic learning, and perhaps distantly from Bloch, Benjamin absorbed the idea of a "messianic" presence, discernable within history, that may have the power to redeem history—an idea worked out epigrammatically and brilliantly in his last work, "Theses on the Philosophy of History." (While attempting to emigrate to the United States in 1940, Benjamin committed suicide when the government in Spain decided to send everyone in his refugee camp back to Vichy France.)

The "Work of Art" essay is Benjamin's best-known piece of sustained Marxist thinking, but a shorter essay of 1936 called "The Author as Producer" is also of interest. Here Benjamin takes up an issue he mentions in passing in "The Work of Art" essay: his observation that in Russia everybody is judged not just for being able to do a job but for being able to talk about doing the job, to write a brochure or a letter to the paper about it, to *participate*; to be engaged not just in the labor force but also in reflections on the labor force, enabling everyone who is a producer to be an author as well. To become involved in this way is what Benjamin recommends, largely by implication, in the "Work of Art" essay—insofar, that is, as he can be said to recommend anything.

No one reading "The Work of Art in the Age of Mechanical Reproduction" can fail to notice that Benjamin evinces strong nostalgia for the "aura," the very attribute of art that progressive art with its invasive apparatus is meant to jettison. It's not an easy thing for Benjamin to say we have to tear down the aura and replace it with hands-on involvement, liberatory as that may be, in mechanical reproduction. He had a particular weakness for the soft-focus portraits of such Victorian photographers as Julia Margaret Cameron, which are an almost decadent effort to cultivate the auratic.

And who could blame him? When I was a student in the 1960s I worked on and off in an art supply and picture framing store on the Berkeley campus. All the students needed pictures for their rooms, so we had huge stacks of Van Gogh's *Sunflowers* and Matisse's *Dancers* and a few other surefire hits, all of them eighteen-by-twenty-four, which we called "brushstroke prints." They were mounted on cardboard, and a huge stamping machine of some kind had come down on top of them, embossing the prints with the appearance of brushstrokes. If you squinted at the beginning of a semester you could see the stacks of prints diminishing in height, as in time-lapse photography. When the stacks were gone you knew for a fact that hundreds of students' rooms were festooned with Van Gogh's *Sunflowers* and Matisse's *Dancers*. Was *this* the fruit of mechanical reproduction? What value could anyone find in this phenomenon as an aesthetic?

Yes, it takes the work of art out of the museum. Nobody has to pay to wait in a long line and get a peep at the *Mona Lisa* around somebody's enormous hat. But how can the substitution of those little brushstroke prints for a decent acquaintance with art history be considered progressive? These may seem like challenges to Benjamin's thesis, but it has really been the point of my anecdote that Benjamin is not unaware of them. He knows very well that the greatest threat to the aesthetic he propounds is that it can easily be hijacked by capitalism and probably will be. I'm getting ahead of myself, because that's precisely what Adorno retorts in opposing his argument and I do wish to turn to that, but I shall return for now to Benjamin.

Benjamin lived in Paris after 1933, and Adorno had gone to the United States, which he hated. Adorno's gloomy view of the world in books of the American period like *Minima Moralia* is not so much the result of his experience of the weak forms of democracy in the Weimar Republic, ominous as those experiences were; not even so much the rise of Nazism because he had never doubted that would happen; the deepest gloom he felt as a social observer resulted from his exposure to American culture. He found our popular culture unbearable. He couldn't stand "jazz." Remember this was not yet the age of bebop, and I've always felt that maybe if Adorno had hung around a little longer he could have been reconciled to what was no longer the jazz of the aptly named conductor Paul *White*man; but even that is doubtful. Adorno disliked the movies, too, to an extent that put him at odds with the cineaste Benjamin, who agreed with him in any case about "Hollywood." The "Work of Art" essay had celebrated the progressive potential of film; the "Fetish Character" essay responds with a few sideswipes at film but renders its critique of Benjamin oblique by focusing on the degradation of music. Still, one knows what Adorno thought. I just saw a film called "Broadway Melody of 1940" with Fred Astaire and Eleanor Powell tap dancing. Astaire and his sidekick, George Murphy, are snatched out of obscurity to be the dance partners of Eleanor Powell. It's a perfect Samuel Smiles success story, replete with catchy tunes and the need for nobly bourgeois self-sacrifice on the part of both male leads. This film, which was quite enjoyable, was made to incur the wrath of Adorno.

Adorno anticipated that whole trend in the sociology of the 1950s and 1960s that was obsessed with American conformism. He ascribes the eclipse of the individual to the oppressive thumb of the culture industry, which scrutinizes for market value our very eccentricities, our very quirks and little originalities. A market is found for the darndest things kids say, and soon every madcap personality is a simulacrum of all the others. For Adorno there is no sideways escape from the surveillance and dominance of the culture industry. Against all that, Adorno quixotically ranges the forces of artistic totality—as long as it is not contaminated by the bravura elements of performance. He felt, for example, that musical compositions should be suspended in the mind, like a chess match in the mind of a grandmaster; and that, when they are performed at all for nonregressive listeners, they should be played colorlessly on ordinary-sounding instruments.

"The Work of Art in the Age of Mechanical Reproduction" is influenced, as I've suggested, by the promise of Russian art before 1934: the films of Dziga Vertov in particular, where passersby and persons performing tasks are the content of successive scenes, and by other examples that cast the spectator as a participant. In such contexts, Benjamin can unequivocally affirm the removal of the pedestal from beneath the work of art. We no longer clasp our hands in rapturous adoration but become engaged with works of art; we become part of them.

In this essay, participation takes place primarily through the intrusion of the representational apparatus into the represented field. What Benjamin means by this complicated idea is that the spectator sees the object, sees whatever the field in question is, from the standpoint of the mode of production—that is to say, the spectator participates by joining the *process* of production. Most obviously this means that when I watch a film, I see the film—necessarily of course—from the standpoint of the camera eye; my eye, in other words, joins that of the camera. In his prewar *Berlin Stories*, Christopher Isherwood entitled one story "I Am a Camera." I have often thought there's some sort of bond between Isherwood's notion of being a camera and the way in which this notion appears—by a happy coincidence, no doubt—in the work of the Berlin native, Benjamin.

What is the consequence of sharing the camera's eye? For one thing, the spectator by this means becomes a *critic*. Benjamin keeps comparing the eye of the camera with a "test." He even compares it with a vocational aptitude test. It's as though what would count as an audition on the stage— appearing before the director, reciting certain lines of the script—were substituted for by the perpetual auditioning of the film actor before the camera. The camera records what the film actor is doing and has the option of throwing out what isn't any good later on. Thus the actor in front of the camera is constantly being tested and auditioned in just the way that you might be tested or auditioned if you took a vocational aptitude test for a job.

If the spectator then takes the camera's eye position, she herself becomes a critic, like a sports fan. Benjamin takes the sports fan analogy from Brecht. He doesn't pretend for a moment that to become a critic of this kind is to become a good critic; not at all. Without intending disparagement of film, Benjamin agrees with people who say more disdainfully than he that we go to the movies when we're tired and just want to be entertained. In fact, he argues, we are characteristically *distracted*. We are critics, then, hence active participants, yet at the same time we are critics in a state of distraction. The German word is *Zerstreuung*. We are *zerstreut*, not quite paying attention even while we are seeing things from the camera-eye point of view.

I'll come back to distraction in a minute, but first, to see things from the camera-eye point of view is a position of privilege because it exposes aspects of reality that we wouldn't otherwise notice: slow motion, unusual angles, and so on. Benjamin remarks upon these effects (1235): "photographic reproduction, with the aid of certain processes, such as enlargement or slow motion, can capture images which escape natural vision"; then later he gives these effects a name (1245): "The camera introduces us to unconscious optics just as does psychoanalysis to unconscious impulses." In exposing an optical unconscious, the camera demystifies our ideology by reminding us that things as we see them aren't necessarily the way things are. It's not that we trade illusion for reality by this means. The camera, too, may have its bias. Slow motion is an obvious bias, speed-up is an obvious bias; but we are made to realize that the speed at which we see things is a bias, too. The psychoanalytic unconscious doesn't tell the truth either. Dreams don't expose a reality in contrast with the mystified world surveyed by consciousness. The dream poses a challenge to consciousness from the world evoked in the unconscious; it doesn't pose the question of what's real and what isn't real. Well, it's the same with the camera's-eye point of view, with the added complication that we don't experience it in a very sophisticated way.

Remember, the spectator is distracted—*zerstreut*. Well, what then? The point is this: there is a dialectic between distraction and *shock* that is crucial, Benjamin thinks, for any progressive aesthetic revelation. Perhaps the best analogy is Saul on the road to Damascus. You know how the story goes: Saul is trotting along on his horse and not paying a lot of attention. He's distracted, and all of a sudden he falls off his horse. That's a shock, a shock dependent on a prior distraction, such a shock indeed that Saul is converted to Christianity. He stands up, brushes himself off, and his name is Paul. Distraction is the atmosphere or medium in which the shock of revelation can take place, and that's why it's a good thing—though horrifying for Adorno to contemplate—for the spectator-critic to be swallowing popcorn inattentively.

We may be the sorts of people who actually pay a lot of attention at the cinema, hence can't be shocked. Benjamin convincingly shows, though, that there's one art form that all of us receive most of the time in a state of distraction. We receive architecture simply by passing through it. I work in the Yale Center for British Art every day, hence I've long since ceased to pay any attention to the British Art Center as a building. I "receive" one of Louis Kahn's two greatest buildings, in other words, in a state of distraction, but that doesn't mean it's not part of my aesthetic experience. What it shows is that the aesthetic and the ways in which we process the forms of the world can be assimilated in more than one state of attention. It is in one's bones, in a certain sense, to appreciate architecture as shelter; yet at the same time, unless we are tourists gaping at the Taj Mahal—and Benjamin does take this into account—unless we are in that particular mode, we receive the forms of our dwellings in a state of what you might call constructive distraction—all of which contributes to Benjamin's aesthetic of participation.

We turn next to Jameson, whose early studies of Frankfurt School thought, especially that of Adorno, will be found in a book called *Marxism and Form*.

CHAPTER 18

The Political Unconscious

Readings:

Jameson, Fredric. "The Political Unconscious." In *The Critical Tradition*, pp. 1291–1306.

Passages from Jameson and Marx.

Last time I reviewed four possible options for an aesthetics of Marxist approaches to literature and art. I paused over realism, both objective realism as it accorded with the tastes and historical agendas of Engels and Lukács, and also tendentious realism as it pervaded the Soviet world, especially after 1934, with the participatory aesthetic of Walter Benjamin in 1936–1937 considered as a way of lending theoretical interest to tendentious realism. I then mentioned two ways of turning away from realism once it has become a cornerstone of bourgeois ideology. The first of these is the high modernist aesthetic of the "whole" embraced particularly by Adorno, and the second is the turn to romance in the line of thought that descends from Ernst Bloch to the key figure for today, Fredric Jameson. (Please note the spelling of his first name, which even prose published by Jameson's acolytes manages to get wrong most of the time.)

Jameson's argument favoring romance appears earlier in the introductory chapter of *The Political Unconscious* under the heading "Magical Narratives." Very much in keeping with the thinking of Northrop Frye about the role of romance in society—in Frye's case the religious role of romance in society—Jameson proposes that an aesthetic of the romance that entails folklore, the folktale, the fairy tale, and various forms of folk expression as a magical resolution of conflicts that can't otherwise be resolved is the most constructive means of combating the seemingly insuperable contradictions of class conflict in late capitalism—for example, the ease with which the political right can persuade the labor force to vote against its own economic interests by appealing to an out-of-sync superstructure of cultural and religious values. The long passage I quote below from "Magical Narratives" is meant to promote the romance aesthetic and also to mount a critique of what the consequences would be for progressive thought if one clung to a realist aesthetic. Jameson writes:

> Let Scott, Balzac, and Dreiser serve as the [and remember that Balzac is the favorite author of Engels; Scott is the favorite author of Lukács in 1927; and the American novelist Theodore Dreiser from the so-called naturalist movement is an appropriate figure to add to this list] non-chronological markers of the emergence of realism in its modern form; these first great realisms are characterized by a fundamental and exhilarating heterogeneity in their raw materials, and by a corresponding versatility in their narrative apparatus. In such moments, a generic confinement to the existent [the only thing you have to do if you're a realist is talk about things as they are] has a paradoxically liberating effect on the registers of the text and releases a set of heterogeneous historical perspectives—the past for Scott, the future for Balzac, the process of commodification for Dreiser— normally felt to be inconsistent with a focus on the historical present. Indeed, this multiple temporality tends to be sealed off and recontained again in "high" realism and naturalism [in other words, it starts getting too easy, and the formulas of representing and evoking the real begin to harden into mannerism], where a perfected narrative apparatus (in particular the three-fold imperatives of authorial depersonalization [i.e., the speaking voice in *style indirect libre*], unity of point of view, and restriction to scenic representation) begin to confer on the "realistic" option the appearance of an asphyxiating self-imposed penance. It is in the context of this gradual reification in late capitalism that the

romance once again comes to be felt as the place of narrative heterogeneity and freedom from the reality principle.

In a way, this last is a jab at Freud's enshrinement of the reality principle as the goal of constructive therapy; but at the same time, Jameson is acknowledging that Freud participates in a growing despair over the unexamined moral imperative that the bourgeois hero confront an increasingly grim reality face to face, like a gunslinger. When reality becomes a straightjacket, the big rock candy mountain can no longer beckon.

Before we venture very far upon an analysis of Jameson's three horizons or concentric circles of interpretation from other points of view, I thought it would be interesting, as a warm-up, to find his *romance* aesthetic at all three levels. We're talking, of course, about the "political," the "social," and the "historical": the *political,* which is the chronicle-like record of successive happenings in a fictive context, constructed as a plot by some individual voice; the *social,* which is the conflict—or awareness of its being a conflict—between what Jameson calls "ideologemes" or ways of thinking about the world as expressed by disparate and conflicting classes; and finally the *historical*, which Jameson calls "necessity." At the end of the chapter, he says that history is "what hurts," but in terms of literary analysis, as we'll see, "history" is a matter of understanding the overlapping succession of modes of production, with corresponding superstructures lagging behind (as they do today, again, for proletarian reactionaries), as it all unfolds in historical time. We'll have more to say about "modes of production," by the way, but our basic three horizons, then—where I am now going to single out the romance aesthetic—are what Jameson calls the political, the social, and the historical.

It's important that Jameson does sometimes call them *concentric* circles, because you have to understand that as you advance hermeneutically through the three horizons or stages of analysis, you're not leaving anything behind. The political is contained within the social, and the social is contained within the historical. Everything the reader passes through is meant to be rethought, reconsidered—Jameson sometimes says "rewritten"— from the standpoint of each more inclusive horizon.

What, then, is the *political* moment of the creative act? Well, it's what Jameson, borrowing from Kenneth Burke, calls "the symbolic act." As an individual writer, I undertake to resolve a contradiction symbolically— contradiction here entailing the perspective of any class as it exists in conflict both with its own needs and desires and with other classes. The symbolic act at the political level is designed to resolve a contradiction in fiction that has no resolution in the real world. In other words, it's a fantasy, a fairy tale about the princess and the pauper. It is an arbitrary happy ending tacked onto a situation for which in reality there can be no happy ending. In short, it is a romance revision of the world.

"Slumdog Millionaire" is an interesting example. It's an auteur film made by Danny Boyle, an individual act in other words that magically resolves a contradiction through the whole Bollywood apparatus that it brings to bear on it. Contradictions are rife between Hindu and Muslim, between indigenous slum life and globalization, between castes, and none of those contradictions can be resolved realistically. But a symbolic fiat can do the trick: you hit the Lotto. Against all odds you win a prize that makes you a millionaire. Who wants to be a millionaire? Well, we all want to be millionaires, but only one of us, magically, through a series of completely implausible happenstances, is able to become one—and get the girl in the bargain.

But notice this: it's not that it *can't* happen. People do hit the Lotto. People do win the $64,000 question or whatever it may be. The point to be kept in mind, however, is—and I think this is finally the ironic point of that extravagant communal dance in the railroad station at the end of the film— that even were a gambling miracle to happen in reality, it wouldn't resolve any contradictions. *Your* life would change, perhaps even scripted to perfection (the money *and* the girl); but the whole world is not going to fall into line with your dream come true, dancing behind you; and being surrounded by unhappy realities, some of them predatory, is bound to impair your fairy-tale life to come. It can be tragic to hit the Lotto, as many sad reports confirm. In any case, we have thus isolated the romance element at the political level of interpretation as understood by Jameson.

The second level, the social, brings to the surface the element of subversion that's entailed in this same fairy-tale resolution of a conflict that can't otherwise be resolved. There are all sorts of other factors to consider at the second level, but remember that at this point I'm discovering the romance aesthetic in all three levels before turning to other factors. At the second level, Jameson acknowledges Bloch (1297):

> Thus, for instance, Bloch's reading of the fairy tale, with its magical wish-fulfillments and its Utopian fantasies of plenty and the *pays de Cocagne* ["The Big Rock Candy Mountain" *is* an American *pays de Cocagne*, by the way], restores the dialogical and

antagonistic content of this "form" by exhibiting it as a systematic deconstruction and undermining of the hegemonic aristocratic form of the epic.

In other words, the fairy tale is not just a symbolic fantasy, it is a social gesture. It thumbs its nose at hegemonic forces. It is an act of antagonism arising precisely from its recognition of the impossibility of resolution or reconciliation. At the second level, the social level, in which the ideological voices of various classes and perspective are openly in conflict, you don't get even a knowingly arbitrary resolution. What you get is subversion and reaction, a tension of voices that is not meant to resolve anything but is meant, rather, to lay bare the conflicts.

Through this voicing of subversion, however, there emerges a carnivalesque uprising from below that Jameson also associates with romance: it is a letting off of steam, entertaining the possibility of utopia, that takes place on that day when someone is called the Lord of Misrule; the entire social order for that one day is inverted; the low are elevated to positions of authority and for that one day receive the keys to the city. On this day, a carnival or Guy Fawkes day, conflict is expressed but not resolved because everybody knows that tomorrow it's going to be the same-old same-old, the occasion having been orchestrated by the ruling class as a safety valve. But the romance element is still there, the folk expression of a wish, a wish similar to what's expressed at the first political level but now expressed no longer individually but collectively. At this level, we could reconsider the Bollywood dance finale of "Slumdog Millionaire" not as an improbable "falling into place behind" an individual fortune but as a collective expression of ironic bitterness about problems that suggest nothing better than absurd solutions.

The third level, the historical level, exposes for any time frame a dominant mode of production in relation to others. A mode of production is a system of manufacture (of ideas as well as goods) generated by an overarching social or economic arrangement. Jameson lists them in his text. We'll come back to the list and think about some of its terms. Jameson gives an excellent example of overlapping modes of production: in the latter part of the eighteenth century, the Enlightenment came to be the dominant form of expression for an emergent, quite well-educated capitalist bourgeoisie. The values that drove the development of industrialization and capital circulated in reaction against feudal and aristocratic ideals that were more ritually encoded, less "realistic" and more quixotic, less concerned with getting things done in the world. The Enlightenment is understood as an expression of an emerging new mode of production: capitalism as it succeeds feudalism.

But Jameson points out—and here's where romance comes in—that alongside the Enlightenment, there are two modes of resistance or contestation. On the one hand, there is Romanticism, which can be read in this context (and often is) as an atavistic throwback to aristocratic and feudal idealism, an effort to recode in an age of Enlightenment the idealism of the age of romance, chivalric and otherwise, that had come to seem outmoded. Romanticism, then, on this view is a reactionary mode of production overlapping with or expressing itself through the dominant one. At the same time, however, there is *folk* resistance to the increasing mechanization of the Enlightenment. Against the doctrines of Political Economy, against the rise of social engineering and the various forms of social organization associated with utilitarianism, there is popular backlash that can be politically and socially disruptive: "frame-breaking," interference with labor activity, protest against factory work standards. This ferment of activity is also atavistic, like Romanticism (and the two forms of resistance come together in the life and poems of John Clare), because it insists on earlier forms of agricultural and industrial production (the cottage industry, for example). Here too, then, in the forms of Romanticism and popular resistance to industrialization, the Enlightenment coexists with overlapping modes of production that express romance longings. The tension among modes of production, which is the focus of analysis at the third, historical level, once again reveals utopian nostalgia as a principle of hope.

So much, then, for Jameson's more or less explicit aesthetic. We turn now to the question, what is the *interpretative* payoff of undertaking literary analysis at these three levels? Jameson argues that each of these three tiers or concentric circles of analysis is meant to lay bare an element of the "political unconscious." As in deconstruction, as in Freud, such a focus exposes or reveals something that is antithetical to ordinary consciousness, something that undermines our conventional understanding of things, beneath which there are laws and causes and dynamics at work that we need to understand. In this case, however, the unconscious in question is neither linguistic nor psychological. Alongside these other determinations and underlying them as their "material base," in Marxist terms, there is the political unconscious. We do what we do, rather than doing other things, for political reasons of which we may not be fully aware, or aware at all; hence the need to infer a political unconscious.

With respect to the three levels, then: at the "political" level, what element of the political unconscious is revealed by the individual symbolic act? Jameson gives a wonderful example taken from structuralism, on which you can see that he leans very heavily for his understanding of the way narrative form itself expresses unconscious wishes. He asks us to consider Caduveo face painting. Lévi-Strauss asks, both in *The Savage Mind* and in *Tristes Tropiques*, how we can account for the somehow excessive complexity of this painting. Why the curious tension in the marks on the faces between the vertical and the horizontal? Why is there a feeling of tension, of aesthetic beauty but also of tension and complication, in the horizontal lines especially?

So Jameson's argument—which I think he enunciates more unequivocally than Lévi-Strauss, though Lévi-Strauss does say much the same thing, contrasting Caduveo face painting with that of neighboring tribes like the Bororo—is that the Caduveo are a hierarchical society in which there are open and obvious forms of inequality that one must perforce be aware of as a member of the tribe, but that neighboring tribes (and this is something that probably the tribe itself can observe) work out a way of seeming to *resolve* the contradictions inherent in hierarchy by the exchange of moieties: the kinship gifts, wedding gifts, and so on that Lévi-Strauss discusses. This exchange of moieties seems to impose on these social orders in real life, in real terms, a way of making society seem more equal than perhaps it is. Yes, it's still hierarchical, but at the same time wealth is distributed and each person has some means of asserting dignity and self-worth.

The Caduveo have no such arrangements to fall back on. Lévi-Strauss and Jameson remark that the Caduveo never worked out a system of gift exchange, so they're stuck with a simple form of hierarchical organization. Face painting, then, according to Lévi-Strauss followed by Jameson, is the Caduveo way of symbolically resolving the problem by introducing horizontal marks—expressing at the artistic level (to which such expression must be confined) the ways in which other tribes have successfully offset hierarchy by distributing wealth and prestige more equally. The symbolic act that other tribes were able to accomplish in real life, in real terms, the Caduveo accomplish individually, with each individual woman painting her face as a symbolic act, one that we can take to express the political unconscious—because this is not a motive, we suppose, of which any individual is aware. That, then, is the way in which the political unconscious, as Jameson describes it, is brought out at the first, political, level of understanding as an individual symbolic act.

At the second level, the social—in which the text, as Jameson says, rewrites itself not as an individual act but as a heteroglossal expression of voices very much in the spirit of Bakhtin—at this level the political unconscious must be understood as an interplay of "ideologemes," a term Jameson coins again in relation to structuralism, on analogy with Lévi-Strauss's "mythemes," or gross constituent units of myth. In other words, perhaps unbeknownst to themselves, people reflexively express not just "themselves" but views and opinions that reflect their economic and social class. It follows from their situation in life that they will hold certain views, speaking as mouthpieces for ideologemes that Jameson considers to be at least in part unconscious. One doesn't know, in other words, that the opinions one so fervently expresses and so devoutly believes in are opinions conditioned by the social circumstances in which one finds oneself. Literature, then, becomes a drama of ideologemes, a representation of unresolved conflict that manifests itself in the variety of situated voices that are brought together.

You can see that this is the point at which Jameson's work is closest to Bakhtin's and most clearly reflects some of the preoccupations of Bakhtin as we have encountered them already. Jameson gives a good example of the way this conflict works, explaining that part of the mystery of these clashes is that they always present themselves *within* a shared code. Jameson here discusses the violent religious controversies of the seventeenth century in England between Cavalier and Roundhead, with all the controversies surrounding the interregnum of Cromwell, the restoration of Charles II, and the tremendous ferment—largely religious—taking place during that period; but for any Marxist—and Christopher Hill is the leading historian who has made this period most clearly intelligible in these terms—this conflict has an underlying political unconscious: its ultimate motives are an assertion of rights and an expression of class views. Again, the dialogue of class struggle is one in which two opposing discourses fight it out within the overarching unity of a shared code. Thus, for instance, the shared master code of religion becomes in 1640s England the place in which the dominant formulations of a hegemonic theology are reappropriated and polemically modified. The Church of England stands for—and this is the word that was then used—"establishment," political as well as religious. Roundhead points of view, various forms of Puritanism, and other forms of religious rebellion, are antiestablishment, yet they are all coded within the discourse of the Christian religion. They have to fight it out on a common battlefield.

Closer to our own time, consider the battle fought in the 1960s and 1970s within the common code of ethical discourse. Think, for example, of the sexual revolution. Again there is a common ground, a shared sense of the centrality of sexual conduct to human life; and what gets reflected in the conflict of generations on this topic is an inversion of values, not a new set of values exactly but a simple transvaluation of the values that exist. Everything that one faction considers bad, another faction transvalues and considers good. The very thing against which one is warned is the thing that one rushes to embrace. So once again you can observe an unresolved clash that arises from and participates in a common code. That's the way *social* antagonism expresses itself at the second level.

At the third level, we witness the tension among modes of production jockeying for position historically. As Jameson puts it, the danger of thinking about modes of production as a succession of hegemonies is that each mode of production in turn might seem like a synchronic moment frozen in time. If you're in capitalism, you may be lulled into thinking that no other mode of production exists, and likewise if you're in "patriarchy," to cite one of the terms on Jameson's list of successive modes of production. Yet as Jameson points out, the tension between corporate hierarchy and patriarchal hierarchy—the tension that has often driven a wedge in polemic between Marxist and feminist points of view—is a reflection of the coexistence of modes of production from different eras: one contemporary, one supposedly a thing of the past, yet persisting and still overlapping, in the form of "the glass ceiling," with a mode of production that is contemporary.

All that is simply part of the historical record, but when in literary analysis we begin to think of the third level in more formal terms—and I'll be taking as an example Shelley's famous poem, "Ode to the West Wind"—we can see the very choice of verse form as an instance of what Jameson calls "the ideology of form" expressing the conflict of modes of production. Shelley's "Ode to the West Wind" has five strophes, each exactly the same in form. Each is simultaneously a sonnet and—in the first twelve lines before the concluding couplet—a succession of terza rima stanzas. Now these two forms, synthesized as a single strophe, are coded in entirely different ways, each with its own ideology. Terza rima is coded "prophecy" because it is in the tradition of Dante. It's the verse form in which *The Divine Comedy* is written, a three-part unit that carries the poem toward the resolution of all contradiction through the divine Trinity in the third canto, *The Paradiso*. (Note the relevance of the folkloric triad.) Thus terza rima expresses for Shelley the hope that the west wind will be through him the trumpet of a political prophecy. If winter's here, can spring be far behind? Revolution is in the offing, everything's going to be great.

But at the same time, the poem is shot through with a kind of pessimism—or, if you will, realism: an awareness that this notion of prophecy is rather far-fetched. Why should the wind do Shelley's bidding? The wind is just wind. It's not inspiration. Therefore, the very strophe that is written *until almost the end* in terza rima is written at the same time as a sonnet of fourteen lines. The first stanza in particular is coded not just as a sonnet but as an allusion specifically to one sonnet, Shakespeare's seventy-third, which begins, "That time of year in me thou mayest behold." I'm getting old, I don't have any hair left, I'm just a bare ruined choir where late sweet birds sang, and there's nothing to be done about it. At the end of the poem, the embers of the speaker's fire are about to be snuffed out. In other words, winter's here and no spring is coming. There is no prophetic possibility, only the trajectory of a spent life. These facts of life, as the sonnet form codes it, are realities in politics as well that idealism—that Romanticism as Jameson describes it elsewhere—cannot override.

So what you get in Shelley's verse form is a tension between ideas, the prophetic idea at home in a feudal and theocentric world in conflict with the tough-minded realism of a mercantile class whose heyday is the Enlightenment (Shakespeare is often thought of as a proto-Enlightenment figure), which is also a tension between forms, terza rima and the sonnet. Thus "the ideology of form" reflects conflicting *modes of production*, feudal and Enlightenment, respectively. They reflect attitudes that one can associate with those modes of production. Shelley was an incredibly self-conscious poet, much admired by Marx and his circle, so perhaps we had better not speak of a political unconscious in his case, but just say that in his poem a political "quasi-consciousness" can be observed expressing itself at Jameson's third level of analysis.

In formal terms, we can think of the essential critical task at the first or political level as thematization: what theme is the plot structure of an individual symbolic act trying to express? What contradiction is being resolved in this symbolic act? At the second level, the formal principle that we bring into play is the Bakhtinian idea of heteroglossia: the clash of voices and the transformation of voice from the individual to the social. At the third level, we find what Jameson calls "a repertoire of devices," on which I have reflected in the example from Shelley.

Let me just add another example, also taken from Romanticism, in keeping with Jameson's reminder that the overlap of modes of production is particularly interesting in the age of Enlightenment. Romanticism inherits the long tradition of the formal Pindaric ode. Wordsworth is still making use of that tradition in writing his "Intimations of Immortality," but in the meantime he and Coleridge have developed a new kind of ode, if you will, which is called the "conversation poem": Coleridge's "Frost at Midnight" and "This Lime-Tree Bower My Prison" together with Wordsworth's "Tintern Abbey" (which he compares with an ode in a note to the poem) are notable examples of the conversation poem.

We can easily see the difference between these types of ode as a conflict of modes of production. The formal ode, derived ultimately from Pindar celebrating the Olympic victories of aristocratic patrons in Greece, is coded once again as feudal-aristocratic, whereas the conversation poem belongs very much, as the descriptive term suggests, to the emergent public sphere. In mode though not in setting (that in itself is of interest, as we'll see), this is the atmosphere of the coffeehouse, where people address each other and exchange views. These are poems addressing an individual person; they turn to that person at a certain point, sometimes even soliciting an opinion. Hence the very transition from the formal ode to the conversation poem is itself intelligible as a transition between—or what Jameson calls "a cultural revolution" brought about by a seismic shift in—modes of production. Yet the conversation poem is still betwixt and between: it is a monologue, its interlocutor remaining silent and only to be inferred as a presence in atmospheres of romantic solitude and inwardness. The conversation poem does not reflect the triumph of a particular mode of production—the public sphere—that we find in the lively give and take of opinion in, say, Diderot's *Rameau's Nephew*.

These then are some ways to put Jameson's three levels to work. Jameson himself reminds us of the dangers. If we settle into thinking of a narrative as a symbolic act, we are much too prone either to forget that it's based on reality by emphasizing the structuralist subtext or else to forget that form is involved at all by emphasizing the social contradiction that's being resolved. As Jameson says, these two dangers at the first level are the danger of structuralism and the danger of vulgar materialism, respectively. The point in analyzing the symbolic act, on the contrary, is to sustain a balance or a synthesis between formal and social elements within the text. At the second level, the problem is that if we start thinking in terms of irreconcilable class conflict, our analysis can become static, as though class perspectives didn't shift, as though one perspective might not succeed another as the hegemonic: in other words, as though change didn't take place and class conflict were a mere fact of life. The boss is always going to speak demeaningly of the worker, and the worker is always going to laugh at the boss behind his back. That's just the way it is.

Finally, at the third level, there is the danger of thinking in terms of impasse—late capitalism, for example, as an impasse that simply can't be surmounted. Think of Adorno's incredible gloom about the culture industry. There isn't much hope in Adorno, is there? And you could, after all, argue that Jameson himself is maybe a tad melodramatic about history as necessity, history as "what hurts," hence subject to this sense of impasse himself. This is why I quote for you, as Marxist critics themselves so often do, the ringing reminder of Marx in his Eleventh Thesis on Feuerbach: "The philosophers have only interpreted the world in various ways. The point, however, is to change it."

Let's revisit *Tony* briefly. A reified realist approach to *Tony*, the kind that Jameson criticizes in the long passage I quoted at the outset, would point out that nothing happens to Neato and Speedy. They are manifest villains, yet nothing can happen to them. They simply have their place in the social order: one of them is a fastidious aristocrat or snob who doesn't want to get dirty; the other is completely committed to productivity and the time clock and the work ethic, a bourgeois Speedy. There they are, reflecting conflicting modes of production, with nothing to be done about it. They're not nice to Tony, but there is no recrimination against them apart from our indignant disapproval as readers.

But then at the first level, if we understand the resolved plot as a symbolic act, the resolution of what would otherwise be a hopeless conflict comes about through friendship—the friendship of Bumpy and Tony. It's perfectly okay if I'm just a working guy because I've got my buddies. We drink beer, we have a good time, life is great. It doesn't matter that the class structure leaves insults in its wake. I'm happy, Tony says in effect. "I like my job." That claim in itself, of course, is a resolution in advance of any conflicts that the story might otherwise reveal.

At the second level, you get the discourse of ideologemes. "I can't help you," says Neato the car. "I don't want to get dirty." "I can't help you," says Speedy the car. "I am too busy." "I can help you," says Bumpy; but notice that these responses are all made within a single, shared code, as the parallelism of the utterances indicates. Within a single code, these ideologemes, which can't be resolved, struggle for authority.

Finally, then, as to modes of production at the third level: the very existence of Neato and Speedy in the same story suggests that there is a tension between the feudal and the bourgeois, but it's not a tension that works itself out in any way dynamically. The important thing to notice here, it seems to me, is the conflict between *pulling and pushing*. Tony is a mode of production, a tow truck. It's quite interesting—and I've said this before—that something that pulls needs to be pushed. It must be educational for Tony. Bumpy, like the Little Engine That Could, is a throwback to an earlier, less energized and powerful, less mechanically efficient mode of production. He has to push. Think of the way walls were put up in the past: a prefabricated wall before the invention of the crane and the pulley had to be pushed up by a bunch of people. Pushing was the focus of construction labor before the kind of technology arose that made it possible to pull something. After that, you have a crane, you let the hook down and just pull the wall up into place. Here then, as we watch Tony being helped forward by a throwback, we find the overlap of older and newer modes of production at Jameson's third or historical level of analysis.

We'll come back to *Tony* in the next lecture when we discuss the New Historicism and seize the chance at that point to see whether we can map Benjamin and Adorno onto *Tony* as well.

CHAPTER 19

The New Historicism

Readings:

Greenblatt, Stephen. "The Power of Forms." In *The Critical Tradition*, pp. 1443–1445.

McGann, Jerome J. "Keats and Historical Method." In *The Beauty of Inflections: Literary Investigations in Historical Method and Theory*. New York: Oxford University Press, 1988.

In this lecture, we turn to a way of doing literary criticism that swept the academy, beginning in the late 1970s, through the 1980s and into the 1990s, that is called the New Historicism. It began, or at least had its first intellectual center, at the University of California at Berkeley under the auspices of Stephen Greenblatt. Greenblatt and others (Thomas Lacqueur, Svetlana Alpers, Howard Bloch) founded a journal, still one of the most important and influential journals in the field of literary study, called *Representations*, which has always been a headquarters for New Historicist thought. The new attitude taken by this group toward historical ("old historicist") methods took for its earliest focus of attention the early modern period, otherwise known as the "Renaissance."

The New Historicism is itself, in effect, responsible for the replacement of the term "Renaissance" with the term "early modern." There has, in fact, been a lot of field or period renaming in recent years, substituting time spans for alleged intellectual characteristics ("long eighteenth century" for "neoclassicism," "late eighteenth and early nineteenth century" for "Romanticism"), with the intention of reminding scholars that periods are full of ferment and diversity that offset this or that dominant intellectual trend. These changes have all followed from historicist, if not always strictly New Historicist, inclinations.

The method of the New Historicism quickly extended to other fields, to some fields perhaps even to this day more than to others. I say "to this day" because the New Historicism is very much with us today. The premises of the movement are still in evidence, although in focus, subject matter, and also in the lowered decibel level of its rhetoric it has lost some of its edgy profile. In any case, it might be worth a lecture that I'm not going to give to explain why certain fields seem to lend themselves more readily to New Historicist approaches than others, but by this time all have had their share of attention. I think it's fair to say, though, that in addition to the early modern period, the three fields that have been influenced the most by the New Historicism are the eighteenth century, British Romanticism (forgive the outmoded nomenclature), and Americanist studies from the late colonial through the republican period. This last era—featuring the emergence of print culture, a lively public sphere engaged in the discussion of newspapers and feuilletons—has been studied with galvanizing results from New Historicist points of view, updated by way of media history. When we discuss Jerome McGann's essay, I'll say something about how McGann in particular has influenced Romantic studies.

What probably accounts for the remarkable popularity and influence of the New Historicism in the period roughly from the late 1970s through the early 1990s was the increasingly politicized sensibility of academic thought. The New Historicism was a response to pressures from without and to related pressures from within. History was increasingly "what hurt," in Jameson's expression, and in that atmosphere within the academy there was an increasing and loudly proclaimed sense of ethical failure in the isolation of literary texts from historical currents by literary study as it was allegedly practiced in certain forms. Beginning with the New Criticism through the period of deconstruction and the recondite discourse of Lacan and others in psychoanalysis, there was a feeling widespread among younger scholars in particular, in view of pressing social concerns—post-Vietnam, sensitive identity concerns, concerns about the distribution of power and global capital—a feeling amounting to what one can only call a guilt complex in academic literary scholarship that a change of direction was required; and that wave of guilt resulted in the "return to history." It was felt that an ethical tipping point had been arrived at and that the modes of analysis that had been flourishing needed to be superseded by those in which history and the political implications of what one was doing became prominent and central.

I have to say that in debates of this kind there's always a lot of hot air, perhaps on both sides. In many ways, as I've tried to indicate from time to time, it's just not the case that the so-called isolated approaches really were isolated. Deconstruction in its second generation wrote perpetually about ethics and history and tried to orient its techniques to possible ways of approaching history, just to give one example. The New Historicism for its part evinced a preoccupation with issues of form and textual detail that certainly followed from the disciplines that preceded them, not always, I think, with sufficient acknowledgement. As is true also of a good many other approaches that we're about to investigate, approaches driven by social identities in particular, to a large degree the New Historicism appropriated the *language* of the theoretical avant-garde (or, to speak more broadly, the language of theory-speak inherited from the enemy as a cloak of respectability) and also took over some useful structuralist ideas: for example, the binary relationship between self and other and among social groups. In short, it was in a polemical atmosphere and at a moment of widespread self-doubt in the academic literary profession that the New Historicism came into its own.

The procedure of New Historical analysis fell into a pattern, a quickly recognizable and very engaging one, which is wonderfully exemplified in the brief introduction by Greenblatt that I have asked you to read. The pattern begins with an anecdote that's often rather far afield, at least apparently far afield, from the literary issues that are eventually turned to in the argument of a given essay. For example: a flour-covered miller was walking down the road, thinking about nothing in particular, when he encountered some functionary on the local power grid, call him—probably a him—a bailiff. From this encounter certain legal issues are raised, and the next thing you know we're talking about *King Lear*. This rather marvelous, oblique way into literary topics was owing to the brilliance in handling it of Greenblatt, in particular, together with Louis Montrose and many others, including historians by training like Carlo Ginzberg and Natalie Zemon Davis. This technique became a hallmark of the New Historicism, so vulnerable to parody indeed that it has been abandoned for the most part, which is rather a pity.

Parodied or not, though, this sort of anecdotal entrée shows you something important about how New Historicist thinking works. Foucault is really their founder of discursivity. I won't say as much about this today as I
might feel obliged to say if I weren't soon to return to Foucault in the context
of gender studies, when we take up Foucault and Judith Butler together—
but I will say briefly that Foucault's writing, especially his later writing,
concerns the circulation through social orders of what he calls "power."
Following Foucault, the New Historicism is interested in the distribution of
power. The study of history is undertaken by this school of thought in part
to reveal systems of power.

It is important to understand, however, that even and especially in
Foucault, power is not just the power of vested authorities, of state-sanctioned
violence, or of tyranny from above. Although it *can* be those things and frequently is, power in Foucault is much more pervasively and also insidiously
the way in which *knowledge* circulates in a culture: the way what we think
that it is appropriate to think—acceptable thinking—is distributed by
largely unseen forces in a social network or system. This sort of power differs from ideology, we can say, because whereas ideology is the reflexive expression of social and economic interest, power is the conformance or
conformism of thought to perceived, though not necessarily coercive, social
pressures. Power in Foucault is *knowledge*, or to put it another way, it is the
reason why certain forms of knowledge come to prevail—"knowledge," by
the way, being not necessarily the knowledge of something that's true. Here
I get to quote my favorite motto of all, courtesy of the American humorist
Josh Billings, a contemporary of Will Rogers: "The trouble with most folks
isn't so much their ignorance, it's knowin' so many things that ain't so."
Foucault and his followers the New Historicists are the scientists of this
down-home truth.

Hence the interest of those preliminary anecdotes. Start as far afield as
you possibly can from what you will finally be talking about, which is probably some textual or thematic issue in Shakespeare or Spenser or the Elizabethan masque. Start as far afield as you possibly can from that, precisely in
order to show the pervasiveness of some habit of thought or legal idea, the
pervasiveness of some social constraint or limitation on freedom, that reveals Foucauldian power to be a grid or system, an insidious and ubiquitous
mode of circulating knowledge. All of this is implicit, sometimes explicit, in
New Historicist approaches to literary and cultural studies.

Foucault on power, then, is the crucial antecedent. Under Foucault's
influence, literature as a supposed specific kind of utterance tends to collapse

back into the broader or more general notion of "discourse," because it's by means of discourse in general that power circulates knowledge. Here, though, it's proper to say that the New Historicism modifies Foucault, because the literary training of which I have spoken, even when it's being shrugged off, fosters an attention to expressive detail that accounts not only for form but for genre—with the understanding, however, in common with sophisticated Marxist criticism, that form and genre are themselves effects of power. Despite the fact that the New Historicism wants to return us to the real world, it must acknowledge that that return is language-bound. It is by means of language that the real world shapes itself. That's why the New Historicist lays so much emphasis on the idea that the relationship between literature and history is *reciprocal*.

Yes, history conditions what literature can say in a given epoch. History is an important way of understanding the valency of certain kinds of utterance at certain times. As what Greenblatt calls the "old historicism" had always argued, history is the background of discourse or literature. But the New Historicism wants to emphasize something quite different. Literature itself has historical agency, the discursive power to influence history reciprocally. This is the point of Greenblatt's opening anecdote. "I am Richard II, know you not that?" says Queen Elizabeth when, at the time of the threatened Essex Uprising, she gets wind of the fact that Shakespeare's *Richard II* is being performed, as she believes, in the public streets and in private houses. Wherever there is sedition, she thinks, wherever there are people who want to overthrow her and replace her with the faction of the Earl of Essex, *Richard II* is being performed. This is terrifying to Queen Elizabeth because, as a supporter of the theatre and no enemy to Shakespeare, she knows that *Richard II* is about a king who has many virtues but also a weakness of temperament—the kind of weakness that makes him sit upon the ground and tell sad tales about the death of kings—a king whose throne is usurped by the future Henry IV, replacing an old dynasty with a new one. Hence Queen Elizabeth has to assume that her enemies are staging this play to compare her with Richard II in preparation for deposing her and probably executing her in the bargain for the usual reasons of state. Naturally she's worried, and what she's worried by is a *play*.

So *literature* hurts, too! Literature has a discursive agency that influences the course of history. Literature is even more dangerous when it is "out there," because the playhouse, Greenblatt argues, was thought to have a mediatory effect that defused or at least reduced the possibilities of sedition. One views literary representation in the playhouse—or receives any sort of literature within preestablished boundaries—with a measure of objectivity, perhaps, that is absent altogether when interested parties take up the same text and stage it for the purpose of fomenting rebellion. Literature, in short, influences the course of history as much as history influences literature.

It is in this respect, Greenblatt argues effectively, that the New Historicism differs from the old historicism. In addition to this difference, it is necessary to see that the old historicism distorts its subject, playing into the hands of modern regimes of truth (as Foucault sometimes calls power) by laying claim to a false objectivity. John Dover Wilson, a highly respected traditional Shakespeare scholar, is the case in point Greenblatt chooses in order to characterize the old historicism. The view I'm about to quote ironically paraphrases that of John Dover Wilson, pointing toward a former consensus about the relationship between literature and history (1443):

> Modern historical scholarship [meaning old historicism] has assured Elizabeth that she had nothing to worry about: *Richard II* is not at all subversive but rather a hymn to Tudor order. The play, far from encouraging thoughts of rebellion, regards the deposition of the legitimate king as a "sacrilegious" act that drags the country down into "the abyss of chaos"; "that Shakespeare and his audience regarded Bolingbroke as a usurper," declares J. Dover Wilson, "is incontestable." But in 1601 neither Queen Elizabeth nor the Earl of Essex were so sure.

Greenblatt wins. It's the genius of Greenblatt to choose examples that are so telling and so incontrovertible. We know Queen Elizabeth was scared on this occasion, which makes it merely obvious that John Dover Wilson was wrong to suppose that *Richard II* was no threat to her. It's not at all a point to be made in rebuttal that Wilson was right about the general attitude toward *Richard II*. Certainly he was right, certainly Bolingbroke *was* considered a usurper, and certainly it was thought tragic that Richard was deposed. But that doesn't mean the text can't be hijacked and made subversive, which is what Elizabeth believed to have happened even if the threat was less severe than she supposed it to be. Uneasy sits the crown, and literature doesn't help.

Wilson doesn't acknowledge this because his view of the relationship between history and literature is only that history influences literature, not the other way around. The old historicism points to a broad political or ideological consensus at that time about the legitimacy of monarchy, the divine right of kings, authorized succession under the sanction of the Church of

England, and all the rest of it—all of which was in fact loosening its ideological stranglehold when these history plays were being written—as a background to the reception of such plays, as though all they could *do* was reflect a consensus. This despite the fact that anyone could take the plots and reverse their values, posing real threats to established power.

As I suggested above, another way in which the old historicism and the New Historicism differ is that the old historicists never acknowledged the role of the historian's subjective views. History was "not thought," says Greenblatt, "to be the product of the historian's interpretation" (1444). Notice that at this point we're back with Gadamer. Remember that this was Gadamer's accusation against historicism (what Greenblatt calls the old historicism): its belief that we can bracket out our own historical horizon, eliminating all of our own historical prejudices in order to understand the past objectively—"as it really was," as an influential historiographer of a century before, Leopold von Ranke, had put it.

Greenblatt, too, says it's naive to suppose that one has no vested interest in one's subject. The reminder that John Dover Wilson delivered himself of these opinions about *Richard II* before a group of German scholars in 1939 is wonderfully placed in Greenblatt's argument. Hitler is not only about to be, but really already is, the Bolingbroke of Germany, succeeding upon less poisonous regimes that had all of Richard's temperamental weaknesses. We assume John Dover Wilson wanted his audience to conclude, in response to his version of Shakespeare, that they have a weak democracy, but still a democracy that they must not lose. That horse already having escaped from the barn, he can speak thus reassuringly with no motive more than to confirm his belief that legitimacy was secure in Elizabethan England.

The New Historicist by contrast is fully cognizant of the subjective investment that leads to a choice of research. Greenblatt's personal interest, for reasons best known to him, was the circulation of power as knowledge, viewed as a contest of strategies between vested authority and voices of dissidence. The world as the New Historicism sees it is essentially a dynamic skirmish about power, a struggle for expression between networks of vested authority and subversion—which in circulation is also a kind of power. One place to look for subversion is within the very texts that ceremoniously shore up authority. The Elizabethan masque, for example, which stages the relation of court to courtier, to visitor, and to hanger-on in carefully orchestrated ways, is a means—because it's polyglossal—of containing within its structure the elements of subversion.

It's not clear to me whether Jerome McGann has ever thought of himself as a New Historicist. He has been so designated by others, but I think there is one rather important difference in emphasis, at least between what he's doing and what Greenblatt and his colleagues do in studying the early modern period. McGann doesn't put as much emphasis as they do on the reciprocity of history and literature. He is interested in the presence of historical, social, and also personal circumstances in the very grain of the texts we read, or rather the texts we are directed to read by scholarly selectivity. His attention in the essay you have read is devoted chiefly to textual scholarship, to the way the makers of scholarly editions and editors who select materials for classroom anthologies shape our understanding of an author's work. He himself is the editor of the new standard works of Byron, he has performed a comparable service for Swinburne, and he has been an influential spokesperson for a strong point of view within the recondite debates surrounding textual scholarship: Should textual scholarship publish a text that amalgamates a variety of available manuscripts and printed texts? Should the text it produces be the last and best thoughts of the author?—that's an oversimplification of the position that McGann takes in this essay—or should it be the author's first burst of inspiration? This last position seems dubious, perhaps, but all the critics who prefer the earliest versions of Wordsworth's *Prelude*, for example (I include myself), would side with it at least on that occasion. In sum, we should understand McGann's essay on Keats and the historical method to be a contribution to textual criticism, published in a book called *The Beauty of Inflections* that's largely concerned with such matters.

The primary influence on McGann, then, is not so much Foucault as it is Bakhtin, whom he acknowledges as the member of a school:

> What follows is a summary and extrapolation of certain key ideas set forth by the so-called Bakhtin School of criticism, a small group of Marxist critics from the Soviet Union who made an early attack upon formalist approaches to poetry. The Bakhtin School's socio-historical method approaches all language utterances—including poems—as phenomena marked with their concrete origins and history.

In their diversity, these phenomena are invoked to undermine standard notions of romanticism. If one listens to history with the attunement of

Bakhtin, on McGann's view, one realizes that the voice of the romantic solitary individual is not really that voice at all but a polyglossal infusion of various perspectives.

McGann's most influential contribution to the return to history that marked the 1970s and 1980s was a short book called *The Romantic Ideology*, which is an attack on widely received ideas about the British romantic poets—those of M. H. Abrams and the Yale school, for example—but is really at bottom an attack on romanticism itself, the trouble with modern critics being, as McGann puts it, that they are "still in romanticism." *The Romantic Ideology* is an amalgam of two titles. One is the important early critique of romanticism by the German poet and sometime romantic Heinrich Heine called *Die romantische Schule*, or *The Romantic School*, in which the subjectivity, even solipsism, and the isolation from social concern and from unfolding historical processes of the romantic poets is emphasized and criticized. That's where the word "Romantic" comes from in McGann's title. The other title it draws on is Marx's pamphlet *The German Ideology*, which is about many things but in particular about coffeehouse intellectuals who consider themselves progressive but who think with Hegel that thought produces material circumstances rather than the other way around: people, in short, who are idealists and therefore, under this indictment, likewise romantic. The so-called Yale school is still under attack in McGann's Keats essay.. Paul de Man, together with Geoffrey Hartman's well-known essay on Keats's "To Autumn," are singled out for particular scorn, on the grounds that our reading of romanticism, if we are politically engaged and invested in the world as a social community, must necessarily be an anti-romantic critique.

I have explained that McGann is engaged primarily in talking about issues of textual scholarship in this particular essay. He defends Keats's last deliberate choices, and to this end he argues that the 1820 *Indicator* text of "La Belle Dame Sans Merci" is Keats's last deliberate choice, or in any case his best choice, not the posthumous 1848 text published by Monckton Milnes. McGann's general pronouncements about the historicity of texts, about the saturation of texts by the circumstances of their production and by social pressures, are bracing and worthwhile. The idea that a text just falls from a tree—if anybody ever had that idea—is plainly not a tenable one, and the opposite idea that a text emerges from a complex matrix of social and historical circumstances is certainly a good one. Whether McGann is right about "romanticism" is a more complex question. Certainly no good critic could ever happily read these poets if the stereotypes about them were valid, and McGann himself is on the fence about whether they are. The Keats essay is on the whole meant to rescue Keats from such stereotypes. The trouble is, and this is perhaps not surprising if one takes Greenblatt's candor about the subjectivity of honest historical criticism seriously, that everything McGann says about the texts he has extracted for attention in this essay is quite consistently vulnerable to counter-argument.

Take, for example, "La Belle Dame Sans Merci." In the first place, who *says* we only read the 1848 text? A scholarly edition—and McGann's main object of attack is Jack Stillinger's scholarly edition of Keats—gives you a variorum apparatus. Sure, a typical edition gives you a particular text in bold print, but it gives you the variant text in a footnote, sometimes even on a facing page. It doesn't conceal the variant text from you. Everybody knows the 1820 *Indicator* text. "What can ail thee, wretched wight?" is at least as familiar to me, as a romanticist, as "What can ail thee, knight at arms?"—which is how the 1848 text begins; and frankly, how many people who aren't romanticists think a great deal about either text?

The romanticists are not in any way hornswoggled by this alleged historical conspiracy against the 1820 *Indicator* text, and people who aren't romanticists don't care. McGann's argument is that the 1820 version is better because it's a poem about an ordinary guy (a "wight") and a girl who meet up and have sex and it doesn't turn out so well. In other words, it's about the real world. It's not a *romance*; whereas "What can ail thee, knight at arms?" in the 1848 version—and all of its other variants, the "kisses four" and so on—is an unself-conscious romance fantasy subscribing to medieval ideas about women, simultaneously putting them on a pedestal and fearing them because they might take the sap out of deserving young gentlemen. Why did the bad ideology of the 1848 version prevail? Because Charles Brown, who saved that version, behaved despicably toward women and didn't like Fanny Brawne, and because Monckton Milnes, the actual editor of the 1848 edition, was a collector of erotica.

Apart from that, who's to say the 1848 text wasn't Keats's last thought? He was already ill when the *Indicator* text was published in 1820. He was close to the end of his ability to think clearly about his own work and to worry very much about how or whether it was published; and at the same time we don't know when Brown received *his* version of the text. We can't suppose Brown just sat down and rewrote it, and if he didn't rewrite it, then Keats must have given it to him in the 1848 form. Who's to say that wasn't his last thought, if not his best? After all, the title, taken from a medieval ballad by Alain Chartier, "La Belle Dame Sans Merci," bears out the "What can ail thee, knight at arms?" version. It's about a Morgan Le Fay. For better or worse, whatever we think of it ideologically, if the title is right, the poem is about the kind of woman who is evoked in the 1848 version, not the less colorful one in the 1820 version.

So the 1848 version is simply more consistent with the title one finds in both versions, though the title is certainly less knowingly ironic in the 1848. The additional point to be made is that while there are all sorts of things to say about the scrupulous intelligence of Keats (nothing to do with "romantic" in other words if romantic means stupid), there is in fact no reason to admire his recorded opinions about women. McGann wants to infuse Keats's text with a pleasing political correctness. From our own historical horizon—which Greenblatt for his part emphasizes as part of any historian's agenda—we don't want Keats to have thought in that demeaning way about women. But his letters and his other poems suggest that he did. Therefore, you might feel free to conclude, the 1848 text is the one he intended and preferred. Or rather, since both texts do exist and offer different sorts of interest, let's just have both of them, which the various editions after all do give us.

The same variety of objections can be made to McGann's readings of the other poems he singles out. They are ingenious arguments, and certainly provoke reflection, but they are not as conclusive as McGann wants them to be. They argue for victory. All historicist criticism is tendentious, as Greenblatt fully acknowledges, producing and reproducing texts as much as it is produced by them, and his own criticism clears the air in being openly so.

Let me turn quickly to review *Tony* from Bakhtin to the New Historicism, gliding over *Tony* according to Jameson, because we did that at the end of the last lecture. Starting then with Bakhtin, you can see that the first part of *Tony the Tow Truck* is completely saturated with the first person singular: I do this, I do that, I like my job, I am stuck—I, I, I, I. Then as you read along, you see that the "I" disappears, or if it still appears, it's in the middle of a line, cozily surrounded by other sounds, rather than at the beginning. The emphasis on the self—me first, however charming I may be—is gradually subsumed by the sociality of the story as it unfolds. I am no longer "I" defined as a romantic individual. I am "I" defined as a friend and defining a friend, even "calling" a friend (now that's what I call a friend): a person whose relation with otherness is what constitutes his identity. In that mutuality of friendship, the first-person singular disappears. What is spoken in *Tony the Tow Truck*, in other words, is not in the long run the voice of individual subjectivity but the voice of social togetherness. Yet this altered voice is pitched polyglossally against voices that don't alter. The fastidious voice and the workaholic voice share an impermeable egoism, the first-person singular always singularly first.

According to Jauss, the important thing about *Tony the Tow Truck* is that it is not the same story as *The Little Engine That Could*. In each generation of reception, the aesthetic standards that prevail at a given time are reconsidered and rethought, reshuffled. A new aesthetic horizon emerges, and texts are constituted in a different way, much also as the Russian formalists had said, only with the sense in Jauss of determinate historical issues behind literary change. *The Little Engine That Could* concerns the inversion of power between the little guy and the big guy, so that the little guy helps the big guy in a definite reversal of roles, demonstrating, with the prophet Isaiah in the Bible, that the valleys have been raised and the mountains made low. That's not the way *Tony the Tow Truck* works. The little guy himself needs help. He needs the help of another little guy. There is a reciprocity that is not dialectical between little and big but a mutual reinforcement of little by little, and that is the change in horizon that one can witness between *The Little Engine That Could* and *Tony the Tow Truck*. Watty Piper's *Little Engine*, itself drawing on a story of 1910 but quickly canonical in its new form, appeared in 1930, the depths of the Depression. Winds of Marxist doctrine circled the world, and revolution was in the air. *Tony*, by contrast, reflects the impasse of late capitalism, so hard to imagine surmounting even for Jameson. Little guys and big guys are like ships in the night, and little guys help each other because nobody else will.

In Benjamin, the important thing is the idea that *the narrator is the apparatus*. We see things, in other words, from the point of view of the apparatus. Just as the filmgoer sees things from the point of view of the camera, so we see *Tony the Tow Truck* from the point of view of the tow truck. And what happens? Just as the camera-eye point of view leaves that which is seen, as Benjamin puts it, "equipment-free," so, oddly enough, if we see things from the standpoint of equipment, we are pointed toward the moral of the story: in other words, toward the *humanity* of the story, with its moral that instrumentalization, the reduction of others to mere equipment, is a bad thing. What we see, in other words, surrounded by all of this equipment, is nothing other than the equipment-free, purely humanized aspect of reality. The humanization of a mechanized world, through our identification with it, is what takes place in *Tony the Tow Truck*. So *Tony the Tow Truck* works in a way that is consistent with Benjamin's theory of mechanical reproduction. For Adorno, however, the acquiescence of the apparatus of mechanical reproduction in its abject service role, *towing* again and again and again, in the inequity of class relations, rejected as always by Neato and Speedy, proves that the apparatus Benjamin's theory supposes to be independent of the machinations of the culture industry can be and inevitably will be suborned by the culture industry for its own purposes.

The old historicist reading of *Tony* reconfirms a status quo in which virtue is clear, vice is clear, both are uncontested, and nothing changes—in other words, a status quo that reflects a timeless social dynamic. The New Historicist approach might stop short with this reading as well, as it certainly seems inescapable. But let me just conclude by suggesting that if literature influences history, *Tony the Tow Truck* might well explain why today we're promoting fuel-efficient cars. *Tony* is an attack on the gas guzzler, the SUV and the minivan—remember the car that says "I am too busy" may be a soccer mom. If we get rid of the Humvee, if we downsize and streamline the available models to a more human scale, maybe it's because of Tony and his friend Bumpy. Here, then, is yet another text influencing history as much as we have shown it to be influenced by history.

One thing that needs to be said about *Tony the Tow Truck* is that there are no women in it, at least not on the street, and that is the issue that we'll be taking up next.

CHAPTER 20

The Classical Feminist Tradition

Readings:

Woolf, Virginia. "Austen-Brontë-Eliot" and "The Androgynous Vision." In *The Critical Tradition*, pp. 602–610.

Showalter, Elaine. "Toward a Feminist Poetics." In *The Critical Tradition: Classic Texts and Contemporary Trends*, ed. David H. Richter (2nd ed.: Boston: Bedford, 1998), pp. 1375–1386.

Quite a bit of this lecture consists in preliminaries, yet like the rhetorical device called "prolepsis" in literary texts, they are preliminaries that cover for the first time topics to be revisited later.

First, let it be said that in entering upon the phase of this course that concerns particular human identities as theoretical focal points, we shall find ourselves engaged with critical approaches that are, in practical terms, remarkably rich and productive. It is simply amazing how, as Jonathan Culler once put it, "reading as a woman," or reading as an African American, or reading in any other "subject position" transforms everything. The practical payoff of identity criticism is more than considerable.

As we saw last time, Stephen Greenblatt's anecdote begins with Queen Elizabeth saying, "I am Richard II, know you not that?" Greenblatt wasn't at the time concerned to read a pronouncement of that sort from the standpoint of feminist criticism, or indeed from the standpoint of gender theory, to which we'll be turning on a later occasion; but still, it's quite an amazing thing for Queen Elizabeth to say, isn't it? It shows how remarkable it is that she, a woman, would find herself fearing not only the kind of suffering and peril that her own sex has traditionally endured but fearing in addition the suffering and peril that one would experience in a masculine role. Her claim is complicated yet more because she knows full well that despite the rarity of a woman "being" Richard II, it's not unheard of. Elizabeth herself has made a Richard II of Mary Queen of Scots. She has imprisoned and beheaded Mary, just as she fears the Earl of Essex will imprison and behead her. So this remark—"I am Richard II, know you not that?"—comes to life in a completely different way from its life in a New Historicist anecdote when we think about it as a question of a gendered experience.

At the end of the last lecture, by way of further preliminary, I told a little fib. I said that there were no women in *Tony the Tow Truck*, and of course in looking only at the prose there are no women. There are just male cars talking. However, if to the prose text you add the illustrations that I've told you about, you can see that there are characters other than the cars. There are frowns and smiles on the faces of the houses. It's not just the cars that are happy about what's going on when Bumpy finally comes along and pushes Tony, it's also the houses in the background, which until now have been expressing disapproval at the selfishness of Neato and Speedy. When Bumpy helps Tony, the houses beam their approval that the morally correct thing is being done.

But they have not been able to perform as moral agents themselves. They are helplessly fixed in place as sites of domesticity. In the Victorian period—and I do think *Tony the Tow Truck* in this regard hearkens back to the Victorian period—there was a poet named Coventry Patmore, not really a bad poet, who became notorious in the feminist tradition for having written a long poem in which he describes woman as "the angel in the house." You're probably familiar with that expression. It's an idea that's embodied also in a monumental book of some thirty-five years ago by Ann Douglas called *The Feminization of American Culture*. This book argues that in nineteenth-century America, moral, aesthetic, and cultural values passed into the hands of women (and clergymen) in the drawing room and at the tea table, dictating to the *agents* of society—all of whom were male—what a proper decorum in the conduct of affairs ought to be. In other words, the role of the angel in the house was not just to cook the meals and take care of the kids, although that has always been a big part of it. The role of the angel in the house is also to adjudicate the moral aspect of life at the domestic level and beyond, and that's exactly what these houses are doing, obviously inspirited by angels that make them smile and frown. So after all, there are women in *Tony the Tow Truck*.

The transition to an identity focus is not exactly a crossroads in our reading. It's not like moving from language to the psyche to the social, because obviously we're still very much in the social. In fact, it's not as though we haven't hitherto encountered the notion of social perspective. Obviously we have in all sorts of ways; but particularly in the work of Bakhtin or Jameson, we're introduced to the way class conflict is expressed in literary form dialogically and needs to be read with notions of identity in mind—in this case class identity—if the literary text is to be understood.

But herein lurks a problem. I have pointed out certain moments in our reading in which one arrives at a crossroads and simply cannot take both paths. What complicates considerations of identity at the theoretical level, though not at all necessarily at the practical level, is that such crossroads moments are inescapable. As we turn our attention to identity, we begin to feel an increased *competitiveness* among admirably progressive perspectives. I'm going to be pointing this out from time to time in the sequence of discussions that we now undertake, but from the very beginning there is a source of competition that remains problematic to this day: the relationship between the Marxist perspective, with its focus on class, and other sorts of identity focus, including the feminist one. What is the underlying determination of identity and consciousness? Is it class *or* gender, just for example? This is not a new topic that we stumble upon today as a result of some belated sophistication we have achieved. Listen to Virginia Woolf in *A Room of One's Own* (600):

> For genius like Shakespeare's is not born among labouring, uneducated, servile people. It was not born in England among the Saxons and the Britons. It is not born today among the working classes. How, then, could it have been born among women whose work began, according to Professor Trevelyan, almost before they were out of the nursery, who were forced to it by their parents and held to it by all the power of law and custom? Yet genius of a sort must have existed among women as it must have existed among the working classes.

Notice that in the face of the problem she has uncovered Woolf is pulling her punches here. She is not saying class has priority over gender or gender has priority over class, even as she admits that they could be rival modes of explanation when we consider the history of the oppression of women or the history of the limits on the forms of women's expression. Things were different for aristocratic women like Mary Cavendish or Katherine Phillips (the "matchless Orinda") than they were for Woolf's "Judith Shakespeare"—though not *wholly* different. The title of *A Room of One's Own* calls our attention to a problem that touches at least in part on class, surprisingly, perhaps, if we think of this pamphlet solely as an early feminist salvo. Even more clearly class-oriented is the title of Woolf's later pamphlet about the possible scope of activity for women in progressive social movements, *Three Guineas*. These titles are grounded in material circumstances. Woolf stands before her audience of Oxbridge women and says she has just one thing to say: if you expect to get anything done in the way of writing or any other activity that frees itself from patriarchal prohibition, you really need to have 500 pounds a year and a room of your own.

In fact, as you read through the six chapters of *A Room of One's Own*, you find that after the wide array of impressionistic insight that enriches each chapter, Woolf is always pulled back to this one particular. If you're not Jane Austen, if you're not a genius sitting in the family parlor whisking your novel-in-progress under a piece of needlework every time a servant or relative comes into the room, then you simply must have 500 pounds and a room of your own. I think one could show that even in *A Room of One's Own*—which is, if not the greatest, certainly the most eloquent feminist treatise on the conditions of women's writing ever written—there is a measure of priority given to the perspective of class. Gender will continue to be conditioned by the effects of money and power if something isn't done to redistribute money and power.

These sorts of tension continue to haunt not just feminist criticism but other forms of criticism grounded in identity to this day. Conferences featuring identity perspectives typically develop into debates on precisely this issue. The cleverest debaters at such conferences are the ones who get in the last word and say that everyone present has been naive to suppose that the announced identity topic of the conference is the basic issue. It's not always the Marxist card that's played in this setting, although it frequently is. You can nearly always count on a last word of this kind that sends everybody off to wonder whether they were supposed to have been thinking about women—for example—or about something else. As I hope to have made clear by the end of the lecture, "classical feminist criticism" needs to be supplemented, perhaps in the Derridean sense, by other emphases, one of which is the consideration of class mentioned here and one of which is gender theory. At the end of the lecture, I'll begin explaining what this latter supplement might entail, and then come back to it when we discuss Judith Butler and Michel Foucault a few lectures from now.

A Room of One's Own is an amazing tour de force. It's one of my favorite books. I read it like a novel, and in many ways it is a novel. Woolf scholars like to call it a "novel-essay." Yet to make this uncontroversial claim about it may already raise a question. If Charlotte Brontë is to be called to account for tendentiousness, for complaining openly of perceived oppression, and if Charlotte Brontë's tendentiousness gets in the way of the full expression of her novel; if, that is, as Virginia Woolf rightly remarks, we wonder why Grace Pool suddenly appears after Jane's diatribe about wishing that she could travel and that her horizons were broader, and we realize that Grace Pool is out of place because Jane's complaint has made a rift in the narrative fabric: if this criticism of Charlotte Brontë is fair, then it could also be turned against the interspersing of narrative and protest in A Room of One's Own itself—though undoubtedly Woolf is more deft at blending narrative and protest with the solvent of irony than Brontë was.

This could only strike you forcefully if you read the whole of A Room of One's Own, all six chapters, which I urge you to do because it's so much fun. The speaker says, "call me anybody you like," not unlike Melville's speaker saying, "Call me Ishmael." Call me Mary Beton, Mary Seton, Mary Carmichael. It doesn't really matter, but I've had certain adventures and you the reader or listener may suppose that they are fictitious. The narrative shelters itself quite by design in the world of fiction.

It really isn't true, as she tells us in the first chapter, that she, Mary Beton, has been sitting by the river wondering what on earth she's going to tell these young ladies about women and fiction when finally she gets a little idea. It's like pulling a fish out of the river, and the fish starts swimming around in her head. She becomes quite excited and she walks off across the grass. At that point a beadle rises up, a formidable person wearing college gowns and pointing at the gravel path where she, as an unauthorized woman, should be walking, as the grass is intended only for the men affiliated with the university. She goes to the library in this preoccupied state, only to be told by an elderly gentleman that since she's a woman she needs a letter of introduction to get in. And so her fictitious day of thinking about what on earth she should say to these young women about women and fiction begins, unpleasantly for her character, as a presented fiction by a woman about a woman treated unfairly.

It continues with a very pleasant lunch. She's been invited to the campus as a distinguished writer. It's okay to be a woman who is a novelist as long as you don't rock the boat too much. In that capacity and no doubt as an acquaintance of someone present, she has been invited to such a lunch, which is very pleasant because it's paid for by men in an atmosphere that is designed for men. Then she goes to visit a woman friend who is teaching at the fictitious women's college. She has dinner with the friend in that college's dining hall, the dinner is inferior and plain, and then they go to the friend's rooms and start talking about the conditions under which this college was built. A group of women in the nineteenth century did all they could do to raise 30,000 pounds, no frills, thank you very much. None of them had any money, there have been no major donations, so the grass never gets cut and the brick is plain and unadorned.

The next day the protagonist goes to the main reading room of the British Library in London (where women are allowed) because she decides she really must find out what people think of women. She doesn't know what a woman is even though she's been asked to discuss women, she confesses with malicious humility, so she'd better consult the experts. She finds out that hundreds and hundreds of men have written books about women: on the inferiority of women, the moral sensitivity of women, the lack of physical strength of women, on and on and on. She lists them as items in the library catalogue. It's an occasion for delicious satire, hilarious yet still tendentious. She wouldn't let Charlotte Brontë get away with that, one feels. Charlotte Brontë has to suspend her anger, Virginia Woolf wants to say, if she's going to get the whole of what's on her mind expressed. Well, Virginia Woolf doesn't sound very angry, she knows better than to sound angry; yet we know she is venting her anger in comic effects, as well she might.

The rest of *A Room of One's Own* takes place in the speaker's study, the room of her own, where she pulls books off the shelf more or less in chronological order. For the earliest periods in literary history, she looks on the shelf where the women writers ought to be and there aren't any; then later, yes, there are women writers, quite a few novelists. More recently yet, women writers get a little more scope for their activity, yet still struggle for shelf space with objectionable male writers.

That's the structure of *A Room of One's Own* overall, which I give you as a plot summary in hopes that you'll read it for yourselves. There were precedents for the kind of writing that hovers between fiction, literary commentary, and social criticism. Oscar Wilde's *Portrait of Mr. W. H.* offers one precedent in particular. That's a speculative, novella-like reflection on Shakespeare's sonnets, but it, too, is literature that's about literature. As you can imagine, what Woolf says about Charlotte Brontë has been controversial in subsequent feminist criticism. There are a number of ways in which feminist critics feel that Virginia Woolf is misguided or needs to be supplemented, and this is one of them. By and large, feminist critics feel that Charlotte Brontë, or any other writer, has the right to be tendentious; and they see in Woolf's reaction to Brontë her unthinking acceptance of the modernist—and male-driven—aesthetic of autonomous unity (still unquestioned, as we've seen, in the New Criticism). We'll have more to say about Virginia Woolf's criterion of androgyny, which in part calls for the avoidance of thinking like either sex. Most feminist criticism in the meantime has argued that androgyny isn't the ideal toward which women's prose ought to be aspiring, however much it may realize the ideal of elegance, urbanity, and highly wrought polish, and takes Virginia Woolf to task therefore for having signaled her allegiance with aestheticism in criticizing Charlotte Brontë.

Although it is certainly possible to criticize *A Room of One's Own* on such grounds, one should recognize at the same time how completely Virginia Woolf's arguments anticipate the subsequent history of feminist criticism. I just want to point out a few of the ways in which they do. As Elaine Showalter points out, the first phase of modern feminist criticism primarily paid attention to men's treatment of women in fiction. Mary Ellmann's *Thinking about Women* (1968) and Kate Millett's *Sexual Politics* (1970) are both books that focused on sexist male novelists whose demeaning treatment of women needed to be recorded. This criticism was superseded in Showalter's account by what she prefers, "gynocriticism" or "the gynocritics." Gynocriticism is not so much concerned with men's treatment of women in fiction as with the place of women as writers in literary history and as characters—regardless of whether they are characters in men's or women's novels or treated simply in their own right—in the history of fiction. Gynocriticism turns the emphasis of feminist criticism in the late 1960s and early 1970s from the history of oppression by men to the history, reconstruction, and amplification of what is known about a female tradition.

This succession of interests reflected in modern feminist criticism is already fully present in Woolf. She, too, wants to talk about the possibilities for women writers, about how women writers can and must feel that they're not alone. At the same time, however, she frames this emphasis on the woman's perspective with her grim satire on men demeaning women and keeping them in their place—men like the ones who wrote books about women, as she pretends to have discovered in the British Library. All of this corresponds to that first phase of modern feminist criticism that Showalter identifies with Ellmann and Millett. You can see the capaciousness of Woolf's approach in her ability to bridge both sorts of modern tradition, not chronologically as Showalter presents them but as a kind of simultaneity in which the emphasis on men's marginalization of women and the emphasis on women's consciousness and traditions can be set forth at the same time and seen in certain ways as giving rise to each other.

Also as it happens in reference to *Jane Eyre*, this time in oblique reference to that novel, there is Virginia Woolf's anticipation of the fascinating book by Sandra Gilbert and Susan Gubar called *The Madwoman in the Attic*. Bertha, the madwoman in the attic of *Jane Eyre*, is made available for feminist criticism after Gilbert and Gubar as its madwoman thesis: the idea that because women could not openly express themselves creatively as writers or as artists in other media, they were forced to channel their creativity into subversive, devious, and perhaps psychologically self-destructive forms, as exemplified in Charlotte Perkins Gilman's *The Yellow Wallpaper*. You find Woolf already touching on this madwoman theme (600):

> When, however, one reads of a witch being ducked, of a woman possessed by devils, of a wise woman selling herbs, [and then of course she adds] and even of a very remarkable man who had a mother . . .

In such cases, in other words, one strongly suspects that there is a person whose creativity has been oppressed and unfortunately channeled in unsocial or antisocial directions. Woolf's invention, "Shakespeare's sister," buried ignominiously at a crossroads, is her full-dress case in point. Showalter's gynocritical perspective, which expects scholars to become familiar with the history of women as well as the history of women's writing, must likewise entail the recognition of such forms of repression as witchcraft, madness, and herbalism.

Also very much on the mind of Woolf already is the essential task of gynocriticism: to insist that one *needs* a tradition, that one of the great difficulties and shortcomings facing the woman writer is that, yes, there are a few greats—the ones who are always named, Austen, the Brontës, George Eliot—but there is no sense of an ongoing, developing tradition within which one could write companionably. Woolf talks about "the man's sentence" (606), the difficulty of not having even a language of one's own, let alone a room. "Perhaps the first thing she would find, setting pen to paper, was that there was no common sentence ready for her use." All the models of novelistic prose are gendered male, because the atmosphere of writing— and this is a point that we'll be getting to soon—the very *fact* of writing, poking a pen about, has a male aura attached to it:

> That is a man's sentence [she has just quoted a long sentence]; behind it one can see Johnson, Gibbon and the rest. It was a sentence that was unsuited for a woman's use. Charlotte Brontë, with all her splendid gift for prose, stumbled and fell with that clumsy weapon in her hands. George Eliot committed atrocities with it that beggar description. Jane Austen looked at it and laughed at it and devised a perfectly natural, shapely sentence proper for her own use and never departed from it. Thus, with less genius for writing than Charlotte Brontë, she got infinitely more said. (606)

By the way, this claim is disputable. Surely it's possible to understand Jane Austen's prose style as emerging from that of Samuel Johnson and perhaps Samuel Richardson. Still, Woolf's point is that Austen was able to shake herself free from the problem of wanting to say something but finding that one doesn't have one's own language for saying it. One wants to write as a woman, to say the things that a woman wants to say, but all one has for the purpose is a man's sentence. That's Woolf's point, and of course it has many and long ramifications.

I'm holding at bay the criticism of Woolf's remarks about "women's" and "men's" writing that has been leveled at them by feminist criticism and gender theory roughly since 1980, but in the meantime the ramifications I mentioned are interestingly reinforced by the theoretically very sophisticated wing of feminist criticism that we call "French feminism." Some of you may know the work of Luce Irigaray and Hélène Cixous. Writers of this kind insist that there *is* such a thing as women's language. Women write not just with their heads and their phalluses but with their whole bodies. They don't write carefully constructed periodic sentences, but linear, paratactic, impressionist, digressive, ad hoc sentences: sentences without ego—as lack of structure on this account more or less corresponds to being without ego. We'll come back to this in Showalter, but in the meantime French feminism was willing to settle upon and promote an idea of women's writing and—implicit behind this idea—an idea of what a *woman* is that runs into a different kind of trouble. The identification of women with a certain kind of sentence is at the same time their banishment from other kinds.

Why *can't* a woman write a good periodic sentence? After all, that's the kind of sentence that Jane Austen did, in fact, write. Why can't a woman, if she is really free to be whatever she wants to be, write a sentence that isn't necessarily of this gendered sort that the French call *écriture feminine*? Why does women's writing, in other words, have to be *women's* writing?

You could say it is a possible critique of French feminism that Virginia Woolf anticipates when she embarks on her perhaps equally perilous idea of androgyny. The kind of mind that is both male and female and writes in a way that's fully self-expressive precisely in the moment when one no longer thinks of being male or female—this advanced mind no longer writes a man's sentence or a woman's sentence. Although it could be argued that Woolf's concept of "androgyny" rejects French feminism in advance, and suggests also that there need not exist, in spirit or practice, some essential entity to be identified as "woman," at the same time we should recognize an ambivalence on Virginia Woolf's part about the distinct identity of the sexes. There is a forgivable inconsistency, the effect of differing rhetorical occasions, between her ideal of androgynous writing as untethered expression and her insistence that Jane Austen expressed herself fully because she shrugged off the tyranny of the man's sentence and wrote like herself. We can't know for sure whether Woolf thinks there is something identifiable as "women's writing" or whether for that matter there is something identifiable as woman.

Showalter discusses three phases in the history of the women's novel. First there is the "feminine," the phase in which women try to write as though they were men (or at least appear to do so), by deferring to male values as much as possible—perhaps introducing a kind of "angel in the house" cultural benevolence into perspectives of men that would otherwise be cold and unfeeling but are nonetheless the same perspectives. These women writers frequently assumed male pen names such as Currer Bell, Acton Bell, Ellis Bell, George Eliot, and so on and rarely entered polemically into controversy about the place of women in society. Showalter then says this is a phase supplanted by a "feminist" moment in the history of the novel in which novels like the late work of Elizabeth Gaskell, for example, become tendentious, and the place and role of women become the dominant theme. The categories are no doubt porous: Charlotte Brontë belongs to what Showalter is calling "the feminine phase" in the history of the novel, but

Promoting a controversial cause

Woolf had already found in Brontë a proto-feminism that damages the texture of *Jane Eyre*. Showalter, too, is nervous about tendentiousness in fiction, and her history favors the supplanting of the feminist novel by the "female" novel, which simply takes for granted the authenticity and legitimacy of the woman's point of view and writes from that point of view, having shaken off the elements of anger or adversary consciousness in earlier novels.

This history of the novel, which finds partial parallels in historical outlines of the novel offered by African American literary critics, is quite similar to the phases of recent feminist criticism as Showalter chronicles them, though there are only two of these: first the feminist, as she calls it, when the treatment of women by men in fiction is the main focus, and then the gynocritical, which is the development for women of a literary tradition. Showalter points out that much of the most important work of then-recent feminist scholarship, the work of the 1970s, is devoted to the unearthing of and expanding the canon of women's writing, especially that which is not fiction. There had been a time—much of the nineteenth century—when the novel, still viewed as a frivolous and inferior mode, was conceded to women journalistically as an outlet for their compulsion to write, a concession accompanied by the sovereign assertion that they shouldn't, on the other hand, write poetry and plays. The expansion and deepening of the canon Showalter sees as a crucial counterassertion. As she puts it, we need to trace women's writing from decade to decade and not from great book to great book, creating a tradition comparable to the male tradition that one can think about, think within, and draw on as a creative writer oneself. So both Showalter's history of the novel and her history of modern feminist criticism—or modern gynocriticism, one had better say—end at a point when it is still a question of authenticating the woman's perspective.

But this raises a question I've already touched on that has to haunt thinking of this kind. We'll encounter it again and again as we move through other identity perspectives in criticism and theory. If I say that a woman's writing or women's writing in general is of a certain sort, if I identify a woman in a way that I take somehow to be recognizable—as intuitive, imaginative, impressionistic, sensitive, illogical, opposed to reason, a refuser of that periodic sentence that we associate with men's writing—if I appropriate this identity for women like the French feminists, isn't that simply to make a celebration out of men's condescending attitudes toward women in the second chapter of *A Room of One's Own*? If men keep for themselves reason, science, logic, and all the rest of it, saying the head is higher than the heart, has anything been accomplished except to claim that on the contrary the heart is higher than the head? The paradigms of patriarchy remain intact. This is where the theoretical problem arises. It calls for what people who work in the mode of Judith Butler are quite willing to say in theory: *there is no such thing as a woman*. If we work toward the hope that a woman will someday be free to be whatever she wants to be (including, of course, an angel in the house), then it is perhaps best for her to be nothing at all except what she makes of herself. I'm nobody, said Emily Dickinson. Who are you?

Now, of course, this is a very tricky move, one that unhappily proves divisive at times in feminist thought. In real life, there certainly *are* women. Women are oppressed by laws and by the men who are for the most part the same as the laws. The rights and the very lives of women need to be protected with vigilance around the world. The theoretical idea that there's no such thing as a woman cannot for a moment be sustained in life. Yet at the same time, the implications of what the polemics of identity politics are always calling "essentialism," the implications of saying "woman" is one particular thing (often something dangerously similar to what men have always thought her to be), remain detrimental to a more sensitive understanding, even at the practical level, of gender and its possibilities. When I began these lectures, I expressed reservations about the supposition, frequently governing courses like this one, that practice is nothing but applied theory. Stanley Fish, whom we'll be discussing soon, was once seen wearing a T-shirt that said "It works in practice, but does it work in theory?" The dilemma of identity politics shows why that isn't just a joke.

It's all very well to be intuitive and emotional and impressionistic, but one wants to say two things about that. In the first place, a guy gets to be that, too, if he wants to be, no? In the second place, why does a woman *have* to be that? It's perfectly clear in both cases that there are exceptions that go vastly beyond the exception that proves the rule.

As I think Showalter's essay illustrates, this is a bind that feminist criticism around 1980 had not found a consensus solution for. Notice Showalter's animus, at the end of her essay, toward Marxism and structuralism on the grounds that both of them present themselves as "sciences." Of course, I've made the same complaint about those and many other theories from my lectern. But now the trouble is that male paradigms have gendered these approaches male and that feminism accepts this gendering. We want nothing to do with Marxism and structuralism because they are Virginia Woolf's beadle in thin disguise, raising his ugly head again and telling us not to walk on the grass which is off-limits to women. None of that, thank you. Showalter says in effect at the end of her essay (cf. 1385–1386) that what's needed is a criticism that avoids scientific pretension; a form of criticism that engages with the reality of texts and the textual tradition but that doesn't—er, well, but how else to put it?—trouble its pretty head with theoretical matters.

This conclusion would seem to leave feminist criticism in the pleasantly colonized position of doing anything it likes as long as it's not rational. Not a bad thing, actually, I'm inclined to agree, being rather skeptical about the testosterone of reason myself, but as a caveat it would certainly impose limits on feminist criticism—whether harmless limits or a straightjacket may be open to question, but limits nonetheless. Henry Louis Gates, partly through the influence of Bakhtin, will have a very interesting way of showing what's available for a marginalized minority criticism once it avoids the premises and terms of mainstream criticism. I want you to read Gates's essay with that suggestion particularly in mind. We'll return to feminist criticism, to one aspect of feminist criticism since 1980, when we discuss gender theory, especially that of Judith Butler.

CHAPTER 21

African American Criticism

Readings:

Gates, Henry Louis, Jr.. "Writing, 'Race,' and the Difference It Makes." In *The Critical Tradition*, pp. 1891–1902.

Morrison, Toni. "Playing in the Dark." In *The Critical Tradition*, pp. 1791–1800.

The African American literary tradition is rich and long-standing. As Henry Louis Gates tells you, the first important poet in the tradition, Phillis Wheatley, lived during the American colonial period. The flourishing of the slave narrative form begins in the eighteenth century and continues into the nineteenth. In the twentieth century, most conspicuously in the Harlem Renaissance but throughout the century in gathering volume, there has been remarkable work done in all genres. This extended tradition contrasts in duration with the equally rich but also very recent tradition of African American literary theory and criticism.

Certainly there were contributions in criticism and aesthetics from the time of Du Bois and Hughes forward, but very little in the way of theory emerged until the generation of Gates himself. Theory was perhaps avoided at first because of a marked tension within the black intelligentsia. Black criticism and black feminist criticism from the beginning saw that as schools of thought they didn't have quite the same agenda. Critics like Barbara Christian, Barbara Smith, Hazel Carby, and bell hooks were strongly critical of the African American male persona, and male critics for their part found that their attention to race without attention to gender was somewhat limited in effectiveness by these views. For the most part, since the 1980s a sufficient détente has been achieved, however, and African American literary theory moves forward largely unfettered by these concerns.

The role of Henry Louis Gates in African American criticism is, it seems to me, exemplary, although there are some rather harsh moments in the essay you've read, moments that I will to take up in the long run, that may or may not suggest an element of overreach in Gates's thinking. That's the question I'll weigh in conclusion and no doubt maddeningly take both sides about. Harshness is not at all the image that he has projected in general. Not only is he an important mediatory and nuanced voice, he is a superb administrator and program builder. When he left Yale for Harvard, he was able to recruit Anthony Appiah, Cornel West, and others to form a megadepartment. The others have, for the most part, left Harvard owing to friction with the university president at the time, but Gates is an empire unto himself, so perhaps it scarcely matters. Some of his earliest work is what you've been reading for this lecture, and it established his reputation together with the rediscovery of a novel by Harriet Wilson, bolstered by his claim that it *was* a novel, a fictitious slave narrative and an important contribution to our knowledge of nineteenth-century African American literature.

Gates was a perfectly good writer in the first place but somehow suddenly became a master stylist. He started writing for the *New Yorker*, and during this phase of his career, when among other things he produced an autobiography about growing up in West Virginia, Gates became a spokesperson in the public sphere for mutual understanding among races and racial factions. He has been a voice of moderation without incurring any imputation of selling out, although his debates with Houston Baker over the years, as reflected in the exchange you'll find in your anthology, might suggest otherwise. Gates's urbane and judicious contributions to the *New Yorker* during Tina Brown's editorship were, together with Adam Gopnik's letters from Paris, the best work in that incarnation of the magazine.

For Gates, then, as for Elaine Showalter and for Woolf before her, you can see that the conceptual problems bedeviling the category of identity persist. Identity, despite being an important anchor for the thinking of people who feel the need for a place in the literary and cultural firmament, leads nevertheless at least potentially to certain problems in theory. Two problems in particular dog the issue of identity. One of them is "essentializing," which I'll take up in a moment; and there is also the problem of what might be called the identity queue: I am a working-class black lesbian feminist whose nation is Palestine. That gives me a lot of identity options to choose from, but the trouble is that I have to figure out which of them has priority. Which of those identities has the underlying determinate force that motivates and shapes the way I inhabit my other identities? Once I have chosen my *ur*-identity, the others need accordingly to be placed farther back in the queue.

I shall have more to say about this problem, but in the meantime there is the more widely acknowledged problem of essentializing, as its opponents call it in every theoretical debate that concerns cultural history or identity. Gates is very clear on the dangers of ascribing essential characteristics to any group or race (1893):

> The sense of difference defined in popular usages of the term *race* has been used both to describe and *inscribe* differences of language, belief system, artistic tradition, "gene pool," and all sorts of supposedly "natural" attributes such as rhythm, athletic ability, cerebration, usury, and fidelity.

Stereotyping for positive and negative traits alike does nobody very much good, because what is lacking is always implied in what is singled out as a distinctive trait: for instance, "cerebration" here is code for nerdy.

At the beginning of his essay, Gates sees the modern history of race consciousness vacillating between the embarrassed unwillingness to talk about race at all and straightforward racialist determinism with accompanying stereotypes. In contrast with the decorous erasure of race by genteel critics during Jim Crow, the late nineteenth-century work of Hippolyte Taine, arguing that "race," "milieu," and "cultural moment" are the key determining issues in any kind of artistic or cultural production, seems distinctly preferable to Gates, stereotypes and all. Gates is relieved that at least race is being talked about while at the same time he naturally winces away from the racialist thinking that can be traced back from Taine to Montesquieu. (With many others, I distinguish between *racialism*, which is stereotyping by race—alluded to in Gates's list of "'natural' attributes" above—and *racism*, which is discrimination against a race.) As Gates says, the effect of twentieth-century reticence about race on artistic canons was the idea that we all belong to a "great tradition," in the expression of F. R. Leavis, that all worthwhile art belongs within that tradition, and that anything that rejects or ignores or even stands apart from these works can be set aside and neglected. As you will find John Guillory pointing out, it is this commitment to a central canon reflecting "universal" values (but really the values of lately dominant classes and groups) that has united the polemics of the intellectual and political right during the "culture wars" of recent decades.

Yet the problem of essentializing doesn't go away. Suppose you ascribe positive value to what another person might call a stereotype. This is what the Senegalese poet Léopold Senghor did in representing the *Négritude* movement, as Gates says (1901):

> When we attempt to appropriate, by inversion, *race* as a term for an essence, as did the Negritude movement, for example ("We feel, therefore we are," as Senghor argued of the African), we yield too much, such as the basis of a shared humanity. Such gestures, as Anthony Appiah has observed, are futile and dangerous because of their further inscription of new and bizarre stereotypes.

So you can see there are landmines to be avoided in negotiating the discourse of race, and Gates is extremely sensitive to them.

There's also the problem, to return to this, of the identity queue. Gates himself may have a little difficulty with this, at least from time to time, because in this early phase of his career he still works within the uneasy détente with feminism in the African American critical tradition. So, for example, in a somewhat problematic passage in which the identity queue seems to be at issue, he says (1894):

> The sanction of biology contained in sexual difference, simply put, does not and can never obtain when one is speaking of "racial difference." Yet we carelessly use language in such a way as to *will* this sense of *natural* difference into our formulations.

In biological terms, there's definitely a difference between the sexes, he claims, but in biological terms there is not necessarily a difference among the so-called primary races. On this view, the result would be that at least when one speaks of women and men in the feminist tradition, one has to come face to face with the problem of actual difference, an essentialism as it were built in by biology; whereas when one speaks of black and white in the traditions of discourse about race, one isn't actually talking about a genuine difference at all. Therefore the discourse with the stronger justification of the two is the one that concerns merely ephemeral differences, exaggerated and rendered determinate by racism, as opposed to the discourse that is about essential differences, whatever one thinks of them and whatever one wants to make of them.

When we return to feminist criticism, particularly the gender theory of Judith Butler, we'll see that the whole question of the biological basis of sex, the biological difference between the sexes that essentializes the role of sex as the means of reproduction, is profoundly in question, and not just because of so-called transgender issues but also because our very sexual identity is something that we construct. In short, the allegation of difference between the sexes is, after all, as controversial as the allegation of difference between races.

Here we can see the importance of the essay that I've also asked you to read by Toni Morrison. We know her best, of course, as a novelist, but she's also a distinguished critic as well as an influential literary editor. It seems to me that her reflections give us a sideways exit from the predicaments I have been talking about thus far, the problem of essentialism and the problem of the identity queue. What Morrison wants to say, borrowing from the discussion of the master-slave dialectic in Hegel's *Phenomenology of Mind*, is that identity isn't so much a question of what something is as a question of what it is not. It is one thing to be preoccupied with what it is to be black, she says, but another to consider the way being black is inscribed within the white tradition. To be black in that context is to be what *white is not*: black is the absence, the negation or negativity, that *defines* whiteness. For the construction of white identity, for the origins and development of the American cultural tradition, it has been necessary for there to be, as an absence or lack, the African American and, more particularly, the slave.

As Morrison says (1795):

> In that construction of blackness and enslavement could be found not only the not-free but also the projection of the not-me. The result was a playground for the imagination. And what rose up out of collective needs to allay internal fears and rationalize external exploitation was an Africanism—a fabricated brew of darkness, otherness, alarm and desire—that is uniquely American.

She points out further that although her subject is the American tradition, there also exists a European Africanism with its counterpart in its own colonial literature. To reinforce her argument, she takes a remarkable example that must have reminded you at least in some ways of Faulkner's Thomas Sutpen. The historical character William Dunbar rose up not from the swamp but from the Scottish Enlightenment and came to the United States, where according to Bernard Bailyn, the historian Morrison cites, Dunbar became a slaveowner and a completely transformed person. Morrison summarizes Bailyn's information as follows (1796):

> I take [Dunbar] to be a succinct portrait of the process by which the American as new, white, and male was constituted. It is a formation that has several attractive consequences, all of which are referred to in Bailyn's summation of Dunbar's character and located in how Dunbar feels "within himself"—"a power, a sense of freedom he had not known before."

This is in some ways parallel to the rationalization of slavery in ancient Greek culture. The Greeks always said that the reason they had slaves was so they could be free, so the governing population could be liberated from performing the practical daily activities that sustain life in order to think deep thoughts. To be free according to the philosopher-citizen of the Greek polis is to be free from work.

But freedom for Dunbar, as for Sutpen, is not really a freedom from work. It's a broader and more insidious idea of freedom: freedom from responsibility, freedom from the need to acknowledge otherness as human— freedom, in other words, from the sorts of constraint imposed by old world civility in Edinburgh and in London: freedom on this frontier, in this wilderness, in this swamp, simply to be whatever one wants to be. That freedom is achieved on the backs of black slaves. It is in some ways similar, as I say, to the rationalization for slavery in Greece, but it is both more sinister and, as Morrison conceives it, more dialectical. She puts the question of whether a person could *become* white without the availability of a black opposite, objectified as not-free, which functions like the spring in a jack-in-the-box, allowing the white puppet to leap out of the box because of what has been crushed beneath it.

This thesis colors Morrison's controversial reading of *Huckleberry Finn*, which I find strongly compelling, much more compelling indeed that the "N-word" controversy that got the book banned in many school districts— even though we'll return ourselves to question who owns the right to speak words like the "N-word." Morrison argues that the depressing failure to liberate Jim with which the novel concludes would have been the easiest thing in the world because all Tom and Huck had to do was point out the correct fork in the river, yet this failure is an absolute necessity for the only self-definition as a white person that's available both to Tom and to Huck and by implication to Mark Twain himself. We know that Twain couldn't figure out how to end the novel. It lay on his desk for a long time, then he finally came up with this dismal ending. Toni Morrison says it's the *only ending available* because the sentimentality of the relationship between Huck and Jim, which is so strong that it caused another critic named Leslie Fiedler to talk about a homoerotic relation between them in an essay called "Come Back to the Raft Ag'in, Huck, Honey," has obscured the basic structure of consciousness in Twain's novel: it's imperative that Jim remain a slave. If Jim is free, then there is no otherness over against which whiteness can define itself as free.

You can see that Morrison's argument belongs very much to the tradition in which Lévi-Strauss says there can be nothing raw without something cooked. It's a binary argument grounded in negation that we have associated largely with structuralism, but it belongs equally to the dialectical tradition that goes back to Hegel. It is one of the strongest and most characteristic moves of theory, and we'll see it again in Judith Butler, whose sense of the inessentiality of sexual difference differs from that of Gates in the passage we cited. Let's return, then, to Gates.

Before moving back, however, to the key issue of identity construction (as opposed, say, to "ownership"), I want to discuss the account given by Gates and others of the stages of development in the African American literary and critical traditions. First of all, the grasp of the critical tradition as basically a two-step or two-part progression is something that he shares with Elaine Showalter. You remember Showalter says that the first wave of women's interventions in literary criticism is the moment that she calls "feminist," the moment of Kate Millett and other authors who talk about the degradation and unfair treatment of women in male books, the second wave being "gynocritical criticism," or women's appropriation of literary traditions for themselves, the archival work that makes the canon of women's literature not just a matter of leaping from great name to great name but a development from decade to decade. Gates sees much the same development in African American criticism. He doesn't put the two options chronologically, but you could map them onto Showalter's sequence if you wished. He says (1896): "What I mean by citing these . . . overworked terms [he's talking about "the other" in particular] is precisely this: how blacks are figures in literature, and also how blacks *figure*, as it were, literature of their own making."

As Showalter argued, too, the question of the *literary* tradition is more complicated than that of the shorter critical tradition because it passes through more stages. The powers of self-expression available to women from their earliest writings passed through more than two stages, and the same thing is true of African American literature. Gates's account has much in common with work done almost simultaneously by a Yale colleague named Michael Cooke in a book called *Afro-American Literature in the Twentieth Century: The Achievement of Intimacy* (1984). Cooke argued that the history of African American literature passes essentially through four stages. It begins with "self-veiling": the period in which people attempted for the first time to write at all. Of this stage Gates remarks that writing is really writing oneself into the human community, since the ability to write, which slaves in the South were prohibited from learning for this very reason, was considered a proof of being human. In any case, the people who first attempted to write used white models. Phillis Wheatley may have been "signifyin'"—we'll come to this keyword soon—but outwardly she wrote like Alexander Pope. She is an instance, then, of the first phase, which Cooke calls "self-veiling."

The second phase, which Cooke calls "solitude," continues to use white models of prose and narration but takes racial self-definition for its central theme. Here you might want to think of Frederick Douglass and of slave narratives in general, where the emphasis is on being taught by white people, but where nevertheless there is a resistance to subordination that points toward self-liberation. Third, there is what Cooke calls "kinship," a literature in which African Americans reach out to each other, identifying themselves as a community, not as individuals struggling to be free. Cooke links this phase to experimentation with dialect and to ways of narrating and poetizing that emphasize verbal and linguistic difference. The poems of Langston Hughes and much else that's written during the Harlem Renaissance belong to this phase.

When we come to the last phase, we come also to a point of disagreement between Cooke and Gates because Gates doesn't think we've reached the last phase, though I'd imagine that he, too, sees it as an outcome to be desired. Cooke calls the culminating phase "intimacy." This consists in the freedom to expropriate any and all models, not to confine oneself to the aesthetic and thematic choices reflecting a racial tradition but to write as it were postracially, somewhat in parallel with Woolf's ideal of androgyny.

Ellison's *Invisible Man*, for example, is a masterpiece of late modernism. It takes freely from whatever traditions are ready to hand for the work Ellison wants to do. Cooke identifies this aesthetic (which is clearly not reflected in theme) perhaps rather optimistically with what he calls "intimacy": with a finally achieved merger of traditions such that, as in Woolf's argument, one no longer has to write as a spokesperson.

Gates I think rightly feels that we haven't arrived at intimacy, and that's why I deliberately used the word "expropriate" in talking about the way models of writing are taken over in Cooke's fourth phase. The trouble is that if I use models other than those made available by my own tradition, I'm not just pulling them out of the air. I'm using them with a calculated purpose. We're not quite at intimacy because self-definition is still at issue in my very turn to cosmopolitanism. You can talk about the late modernism or even postmodernism of *The Invisible Man* all you like, yet that novel is still about what it means to be black, with a measure of defiance entailed even in the choice of aesthetic.

As Gates sees it, self-definition continues to be the issue. We use other models, but *we need to make them our own*. Otherwise we're just colonized by them, and then after all we're back in phase one. Phillis Wheatley used white models, aspiring indeed to the idea that she was *a poet*, not that exotic spectacle, a young black slave woman who could rhyme. She could write about anything she wanted to write about, she hoped—the tears of Niobe, for example, in the painting by Richard Wilson. But you can see the problem. If intimacy, the dispassionate merger of traditions, is achieved in the fourth phase, well, that's just the realization of what Phillis Wheatley wanted in the first phase; but is it fully realized? A borrowed expression is still the language of the other; hence we have to admit, as Gates insists, that identity blindness is not yet at hand, and certainly for good reason.

This brings us to Gates's key concept: what does it mean to expropriate other people's traditions, more particularly the white tradition, and what is the advantage of doing so? Here at least for the moment, Gates is thinking primarily about criticism, not about literature. How, he asks, can we do theory and criticism in the white man's language? How can we appropriate *for ourselves* the white man's language, terms, theories? The necessity of bending language to one's own purposes is what is emphasized in the remarkable epigraph that Gates takes from Bakhtin. This is a central passage for an understanding of Bakhtin, by the way, as much so as anything that we studied when we were actually reading Bakhtin, and I'd like you to make note of it because I think it can shed light on what we said then. In Gates's epigraph, Bakhtin says (1891):

> language, for the individual consciousness, lies on the border-
> line between oneself and the other. The word in language is half
> someone else's. It becomes "one's own" only when the speaker
> populates it with his own intention, his own accent [and you can
> hear Gates wanting to emphasize that word "accent"], when he
> appropriates the word, adapting it to his own semantic and ex-
> pressive intention. Prior to this moment of appropriation, the
> word does not exist in a neutral and impersonal language (it is
> not, after all, out of a dictionary that the speaker gets his words!),
> but rather it exists in other people's mouths, in other people's
> contexts, serving other people's intentions: it is from there that
> one must take the word, and make it "one's own."

During the course of his essay, Gates echoes this sentiment of Bakhtin by quoting Derrida, too; "We must master, as Derrida wrote, 'how to speak the other's language without renouncing (our) own'" (1901).

How to do this? How do you set about taking over the language you are given? This isn't just a question of negotiating racial difference. It's a question for all of us in relation to each other as speakers. As Bakhtin says in what you have already read, most of the time we're speaking other people's languages. It is rare indeed that we can say, feeling very much like creative writers when we do so, that we have wrenched other people's language out of conventional usage and made it our own, slightly rewritten it so it bears our signature. More broadly speaking, this is the challenge that faces a theoretical enterprise that doesn't want to repeat what other folks have already said.

Gates recognizes, as does Showalter, that the notion of the *sign* is prob-ably the cornerstone of white male literary theory. He recognizes that one must expropriate the sign, and with this end in view he elects to talk about the way one can *signify on* something. He introduces this move very quietly, seemingly just in passing (1900): "Since writing, according to Hume, was the ultimate sign of difference between animal and human, these writers implicitly were Signifyin(g) upon the figure of the chain itself." Notice the "accent," to use Bakhtin's term. You don't necessarily pronounce the *g*: these writers were signifyin' on the chain. Of course, the Great Chain of Being, which is hierarchical, is very different from the chain of the chain gang and, likewise again, from the chain of the signifier in deconstruction. The chain in intellectual history (A. O. Lovejoy's great chain of being) and the chain on the horizontal axis are very different from the chain that binds first slaves and later jailed freedmen together. The critic "signifies on" a term by introducing a reminder that the term also means something that has gone unspoken, unwhispered. At least allegedly, the "signifier" in the white male theoretical tradition is no more than a placeholder in a play of linguistic differences, and the black appropriation of the term can introduce a new dimension to this play.

But what does it mean to "signify on" something? Where does the expression come from? It comes from Africa. Gates takes the concept from the trickster tradition, the tradition of African storytelling in which the weaker is also the smarter, and the monkey or the spider tricks the big, bad guys, the elephant or the lion, over and over again. All of the bad guys get tricked because they are stupider, and the little guy is always able to lie to them without their realizing what's going on. This way of talking about signifying belongs to the tradition of African American folklore, then, and first came to my attention in a song written and sung by the scat singer Oscar Brown Jr. called "Signifyin' Monkey." It was picked up by various instrumental groups and was a soul jazz staple of the 1950s and 1960s. In any case, Oscar Brown Jr.'s riff on the signifyin' monkey helps inspire Gates's idea of taking somebody else's discourse out of its context and bending it to an African American context, a context that is one's own and not just the context one is given.

Signifyin', or signifyin' on, finally, is not just the takeover of a white idea, here in the interest of founding an authentic black literary theory out of white materials; it is also a trick played on the Man. When A talks to C about B in the presence of B without letting B know he's being talked about and in effect lied to, that's the social dynamic of signifyin'. B is a white literary theorist, A and C are black literary theorists who publish in and read B's journal (Gates's essay appeared in the University of Chicago's hallowed journal of theory, *Critical Inquiry*). They share a joke about signifyin' on the signifier, turning a virtual sound in a chain (full of sound and fury, signifying nothing) into an actual social trick that breaks the chain, without B realizing that with this break the rules of the theory game have been changed. That's not "intimacy."

Another example of "signifyin' on" appears in Gates's culminating example from *The Color Purple*, the conversation about "gettin' the man out of your eye." But here there resurfaces the problem that exists, I began by saying, even within the African American tradition. As Gates has been pointing out, Wheatley and later Rebecca Jackson take their models of education and self-development from white male figures who have taught them how to read. In each case, this is pernicious because the existence of the white male figure is very much still in your eye. You got to get the man out of your eye, at least according to the dialogue Gates quotes from *The Color Purple*. Yes, but plainly Shug doesn't just mean the *white* man when she says "the man." *The Color Purple* sustains a feminism struggling to free itself from social constructions of male dominance that aren't just defined by race. Gates rightly says that "the man," which we all recognize as shorthand for "the white man" (just as "Bill" could be anyone's name but used to be signified on by the hipsters as "white man with a square name") can be signified on to become a term of disgust, a speck as well as an offense to the field of vision: "get the man out of your eye." Yet it can be signified on, too, by the *feminist* tradition, making it a term of opprobrium in an overlapping and partially different way: "the man" as all men. Here again we find the slight tension with African American feminist criticism, reflecting détente yet still requiring a choice of emphasis, one way or the other.

Finally I want to take up what to me is the most controversial example in this essay. Gates has been talking about the New Agrarian moment out of which there emerged a number of figures associated with the New Criticism, including Robert Penn Warren, who quite early on repudiated the New Agrarians and became politically progressive in his own writing. You have probably read *All the King's Men* and his poetry as well. Warren was a central figure in the development of the New Criticism, which we have briefly studied.

Warren wrote a poem called "Pondy Woods" in which a black fugitive is hiding in a swamp from a lynch mob and is mocked by a vulture. The black critic Sterling Brown answered a line spoken by the vulture (Gates calls it "Robert Penn Warren's statement"), "Nigger, your breed ain't metaphysical," with the retort, "Cracker, your breed ain't exegetical." I don't think Gates should have followed Brown here (cf. 1893). His "Robert Penn Warren's statement" is like the schoolmaster Mr. Deasy in *Ulysses* saying "What does Shakespeare say? 'Put but money in thy purse.'" Shakespeare doesn't say that, Iago says it. The buzzard is sitting exultantly in a tree, waiting for the fugitive to die. So what one wants to say is that Brown's reading is completely unfair to the author of the poem, Warren, who is writing a movingly sympathetic evocation of what it's like to be a fugitive in this state of terrible and overwhelmed panic.

And yet, while I can't help thinking this a tendentious misreading, I can see the point of it very clearly and feel that this point needs in some measure to be conceded. Part of Gates's point is undoubtedly an attack in advance on the criticism I have been making here. Gates has been discussing the emergence of the New Criticism from the New Agrarianism, as I mentioned. This frequently cited genealogy is itself somewhat misleading, but unquestionably some critics such as Allen Tate, also a poet like Warren, and Cleanth Brooks (to a lesser degree than Tate) did retain the social conservatism of the New Agrarian manifesto to which they had contributed, *I'll Take My Stand*. Gates is saying for his part that being reactionary is inescapably in the grain of New Critical thought, and gives the "Warren"-Brown exchange as an instance of it. When I then complain that Brown's response is unfair to Warren because the poet gave the offensive line to a buzzard I am invoking a New Critical principle, as Gates perhaps anticipated someone would. *It's the New Criticism*, to which Robert Penn Warren contributed, *that tells us we shouldn't confuse speakers with authors*.

Thanks to the New Criticism, this plausible dogma is something we just take for granted when we read poems. All poems for us are to some degree dramatic monologues on the model of Browning and others in the nineteenth century. And yet it's possible to reply that if an author has a speaker in his head, that speaker is part of him, an invention that would have been impossible for someone else to envision. Somewhere in Warren that buzzard lurked. Somewhere in the mind of the canny businessman Shakespeare, Iago's advice to Roderigo lurked. This caveat brings us back to address the well-publicized *Huckleberry Finn* controversy with perhaps greater hesitation than we might have exercised as believers in authorial detachment. We really do need to ask, as signifiers ourselves and perhaps also as signifiers "on," "Who has the right to use the 'N-word'?" If anyone. Despite the fact that in many African American social networks the word is used with jocular fondness in the description and greeting of friends, this practice is strongly discouraged by African American teachers because the word is too badly soiled to be reclaimed. It signifies abjection and degradation in the eyes of others to an extent that simply cannot be *signified on*, or borrowed back and rescued from white hatred and contempt. Perhaps the rule of thumb emerges that words that can't be signified on should be off-limits. We want to exempt Twain and Warren because we owe them so much and also because we don't like book burning. But suppose Toni Morrison were right? Twain couldn't point Jim toward freedom, and Warren couldn't help his fugitive out of the Pondy Woods.

CHAPTER 22

Postcolonial Criticism

Readings:

Said, Edward. "Introduction to Orientalism." In *The Critical Tradition*, pp. 1801–1813.

Bhabha, Homi K. "Signs Taken for Wonders." In *The Critical Tradition*, pp. 1875–1899.

Postcolonial studies is by far the most varied of the identity fields we review in this part of the course: necessarily varied because of the immense variety of the materials and cultures covered, but also because of controversies that swirl within postcolonial studies, or "po-co," as it's affectionately known. In this lecture we are concentrating on one developmental strand in post-colonial studies, a progression from the work of Edward Said to that of Homi Bhabha that can be presented as a matter of contrasting intellectual agendas, each widely influential in turn.

I should mention in passing certain not unrelated topics that won't finally form part of our emphasis, but that you might want to consider if you do have an interest in this field. You might well ask, for example: who *says*, "*post*colonial"? Who says we're necessarily out of coloniality? Just because the provincial viceroy packed up and went back to Europe doesn't mean that things changed all that much in the so-called postcolonial setting, so it might still make just as much sense to speak of "colonial studies." There's also the question of defining those cultures that have been exploited by superpowers or pawns of superpowers during the Cold War (already for the most part a "postcolonial" period), now that the Cold War at least allegedly no longer exists. With respect really to both questions, as national territoriality declines and global capitalist territoriality increases, how has the status of colonized parts of the world changed, if at all?

Another way to put this question—and this does bring us closer to our emphasis today—is to ask whether social, economic, and political crises in the third world are always necessarily to be understood in terms of coloniality. Is it solely the fact that certain parts of the globe were colonized in the past that constitutes them as they are and determines their identity in the eyes of first-world powers and scholars? Said addresses this question when he tries to figure out how it is in the nineteenth century that German Orientalism so very closely resembles French Orientalism, even though the Germans had no colonial interests in the Middle East. During the whole of the early nineteenth century in particular, when German Orientalism is practically indistinguishable from the French equivalent, taking up the same concerns and expressing the same interests, Said wonders how it can be that the French seem undoubtedly to be influenced in their views by their colonial interests, whereas the Germans have no colonial interests at all, at least in the Middle East.

Said solves this puzzle to his own satisfaction. His answer is that German Orientalism derives from the contemporary scholarship of French Orientalism and simply takes on the stamp of French thinking. No doubt the sources at his disposal bear out this claim. Jean-Dominique Vivant Denon's Napoleon-sponsored *Histoire de l'Égypte* in particular exerted a strong influence all over the Continent. Yet Said could have argued, alternatively, that a particular attitude toward the third world, an "ideologeme," to borrow Jameson's term, is simply an aspect of Eurocentrism, regardless whether there happen to be colonial interests involved.

All such arguments, however, leave unanswered the question of how such an attitude comes to prevail. In recent times, speculation has hesitated between national and business interests as root causes. The truth remains uncertain because, as skeptics would argue, the economic basis for coloniality is typically veiled by more or less honestly maintained forms of false consciousness at the national level: liberation of a people from oppression, national security, making the world safe for democracy, and so on. Even before postcolonial times, this recent repetition of the twofold causes for Orientalism was distilled in the history of the British East India Company,

which was both imperialist and a pioneer in global capitalization long before the modern era; that this history has rewritten itself during the modern
transition from colonization to third-world investment makes it all the more
fascinating. What drives Orientalism, we persist in asking? Is it always territoriality, the encroachment of a metropolitan center on a provincial space,
or is it transnational interests in globalization, and how and when can these
motives be separated? It's not enough to say, though perhaps it's tempting,
that nationalism isn't important anymore and globalization is. An ostensibly benevolent nationalism packaged as "American values" continues to
drive American foreign policy, sustained by the broad political agreement at
least of moderates in both parties, with as much skeptical debate in the air as
ever, perhaps more, about the degree to which our anti-terrorist and anti-
dictatorial interventions are pretexts to promote global interests.

Another topic that circulates in postcolonial studies—especially among
those who represent the various colonized peoples of the world, addresses the
question of Gayatri Spivak: "How should the subaltern speak?" Spivak's subtext is, "Can the subaltern speak at all?" and Said raises that question, too, but
there is another aspect of the question to keep in mind: "Which language
should the subaltern speak in?" Suppose, that is, that the subaltern *can* speak.
Suppose Ngugi wa Thiong'o, for example, can write a novel, as indeed he can.
What language should it be written in? Ngugi has campaigned against writing in English and urged other African writers to write in their native languages and not in the language of the colonizer. This opinion is often affirmed
in postcolonial studies, but it is just as often resisted on the grounds that the
circulation of literary influence, which depends on international publishing,
requires the use of languages that are widespread.

Without forgetting these issues altogether, I hope, we turn now to the
trajectory of thought that carries us from Said to Bhabha. In beginning to
think about Said, I thought we'd approach him by thinking instead, once
again, about Virginia Woolf. In the second chapter of *A Room of One's Own*,
the speaker is sitting in the British Library, trying to figure out what scholars
think about women. She thinks she'll just find a couple of books and she'll
be all set. Instead she is overwhelmed by an avalanche of material. "Women"
turns out to be a topic on which *men* have scribbled incessantly. Naturally
these countless men as an aggregate can be seen to have organized their
topic in ways that become visible most clearly in a library catalog or database:

> condition of Middle Ages of; habits in the Fiji Islands of; wor-
> shipped as goddesses by; weaker in moral sense than; idealism

of; greater conscientiousness of; South Sea islanders age of pu-
berty among; attractiveness of; offered as sacrifice to; small size
of brain of; profounder sub-consciousness of; less hair on the
body of; mental, moral and physical inferiority of; love of children of; greater length of life of; weaker muscles of; strength of
affections of; vanity of; higher education of; Shakespeare's opinion of; Lord Birkenhead's opinion of; Dean Inge's opinion of; La
Bruyère's opinion of; Dr. Johnson's opinion of; Mr. Oscar Browning's opinion of.

If we coined the term "female-ism" for all these factoids recorded by men,
we'd quickly see what Edward Said's term, "Orientalism," is getting at.

"Orientalism" is more than just ignorant stereotyping. It is a vast body
of information, some of it scholarly, about peoples called "Oriental" by and
large, especially in the nineteenth-century tradition, none of it compiled by
those peoples themselves. Said's main concern is the peoples of the Middle
East, but he shows convincingly that "Orientalism" (perhaps suggesting to
us the Far East) is nonetheless an appropriate term to use for that tradition
of scholarship and philology in the nineteenth century. Even today, as we
know, "East" and "West" are not always geographically descriptive terms,
and we can certainly say, in the manner we're getting used to, that there
is no "east" without "west." There are endless library shelves groaning under
multivolume treatises on the East, nearly all of them written in the West
about this "other" that haunts the Western imagination. As Said says (1811):
"Orientalism is premised upon exteriority, that is, on the fact that the Orientalist, poet or scholar, makes the Orient speak, describes the Orient, renders its mysteries plain for and to the West." Literature also makes plenty of
contributions, drawing first from the *Arabian Nights* and the lore of actual
travelers like Byron (the nightingale that sings "bul-bul" impales itself on a
thorn as a sacrifice for love, the genie pops out of the bottle, the sultan visits
the harem), and later from Edward Fitzgerald's *Rubaiyat of Omar Khayyam*.

Before edging closer to your excerpt from Said, let me explain what I
mean in saying that Said and Bhabha represent stages of postcolonial discourse. I'm thinking in particular of Elaine Showalter's distinction between
feminist and gynocritical criticism, a distinction that has its corollary, we
saw, in Gates's essay. First there is criticism in which the treatment of women
in literature by men is the focus of attention, then you get criticism in which
a women's literary tradition is the focus. Superimposing postcolonial studies
on this progression, you can see that Said is in phase one. Homi Bhabha, in

turn, focuses his attention on the subject position of the colonized, of the subaltern. He doesn't leave out the subject position of the colonizer, certainly, because he sees the two as radically interrelated, but much of his emphasis is on the traditions and above all the defensive strategies of colonized peoples themselves, which puts him in phase two.

An issue that is not emphasized in either Said or Bhabha is the need to reorient white male literary theory for alternative purposes. There are various, perhaps superficial, ways to explain this apparent difference from Showalter and Gates. Third-world intellectuals have always been educated in high-octane metropolitan institutions, by which of course one means primarily Oxford and Cambridge. To some limited degree, they come to identify—in ways not unrelated to Bhabha's argument about hybridity— with the educational agenda of the colonizer, and to participate in it. That's pure speculation, and as a background scenario it isn't so very different, it must be admitted, from the educational circumstances of feminist and African American intellectuals. Bhabha if not Said, too, may in any case have their own ways of staging raids on "Western" literary theory, as both certainly do make use of its structuralist and deconstructionist moments, respectively, and Bhabha introduces a concept, as we'll see, that's not unlike the concept of "signifyin'."

From the "respectively" in what I just said, we infer another two-stage development that's shared across identity theories. Said's Orientalism works through structuralist premises. Its primary concern is the mutual and interdependent binary opposition of self and other—including the way the construction of otherness is at the same time a means of constructing selfhood, in this case the identity of Being Western. The fundamental binarism of Said's viewpoint has often since been criticized, most often from the standpoint of Bhabha, who participates in the Derridean deconstruction of binarism. Bhabha's concept of "double consciousness" is not just a merger or confusion of two perspectives but an unsettling of perspective as such. Here too, as I say, there is a phase one–phase two tendency that's shared among evolving identity theories. Classical feminism works with a male-female binary that is unsettled by gender theory, and we have discussed the problematic of settling for accepted views of black and white in theories of race.

Turning then to Said, let's begin with a word or two about "truth," the word that was at issue, you'll recall, between the structuralist Lacan and Derrida in his critique of Lacan, "The Purveyor of Truth." Said is at pains to remind his sympathetic readers that his object of scrutiny, the caricature and even the demonization of the Arab world, cannot be dismissed as a mere pack of lies. Much of it is, as one might say, especially in the case of trained scholars and "old Persia hands," true as far as it goes. Said's tone varies somewhat about this, and in balance he does distrust the findings of Orientalism, but it remains clear that for him the fundamental issue is *not* whether Orientalism lies or tells the truth (1802):

> One ought never to assume that the structure of Orientalism is nothing more than a structure of lies or myths which, were the truth about them to be told, would simply blow away. I myself believe that Orientalism is more particularly valuable as a sign of European-Atlantic power over the Orient than it is as a veridic discourse about the Orient. . . . Nevertheless, what we must respect and try to grasp is the sheer knitted-together strength of Orientalist discourse.

A great deal of painstakingly compiled knowledge of a certain kind does exist and has long existed, like the ten volumes of Denon's *Histoire* that I mentioned earlier. Some of it is true, again, as far as it goes. Said draws on a distinction, therefore, between truth and value. It's not that Orientalist discourse is necessarily true or false. It is the case, though, that either way it insidiously devalues its object of attention. Its implicit Eurocentrism Said does not go so far as to consider in all cases a form of stereotyping. Yet even the most meticulous researchers in their very voluminousness still mislead in pretending to be unselective windows on reality (1812): "My analysis of the Orientalist text therefore places emphasis on the evidence, which is by no means invisible, for such representations *as representations*, not as 'natural' descriptions of the Orient."

We had best pause for critique at that passage because at the end of his introduction to *Orientalism*, you'll notice that Said declines to say how it could be done better, while nevertheless holding open the possibility of speaking true. He does not explain how it is that an account of the Arab world by an Arab scholar would be less a "representation" and more "natural" than what he has been criticizing. There is no discussion of whether one can expect the bias of somebody else writing about me to be greater than my own bias—my preconceptions and prejudices—about myself. He admits that he doesn't have an advanced theory that can secure one kind of representation as true or authentic and another kind of representation as biased and inauthentic (1814):

Perhaps the most important task of all would be to . . . ask how one can study other cultures and peoples from a libertarian, or a nonrepressive and nonmanipulative, perspective. But then one would have to rethink the whole complex problem of knowledge and power. These are all tasks left embarrassingly incomplete in this study.

It remains to wonder where the text might be that is "natural." The sign being arbitrary, as we've learned, it does locate us inescapably in the realm of representation, left to *value* one representation more than another while leaving the criterion of truth under erasure.

Said openly announces his own intellectual framework, and it's worth pausing over an idea shared by the two scholar-theorists who matter most to him, Michel Foucault (whose "knowledge and power" gets into the passage cited above) and the Italian Marxist Antonio Gramsci. Said explains his debt to Gramsci as follows (1803):

Culture, of course, is to be found operating within civil society, where the influence of ideas, of institutions and of other persons works not through domination but by what Gramsci calls consent.

You can see the connection with Foucault: regimes of truth are not a matter of having ideas or laws forced down your throat, but a circulation of knowledge, of ideology, which through consent establishes certain attitudes of bias. This is the distinction that Gramsci makes between the way one is imposed on by actual power and authority and the way one is imposed on by the circulation of what Jameson calls "ideologemes."

To continue the passage from Said: "In any society not totalitarian, then, certain cultural forms predominate over others, just as certain ideas are more influential than others; the form of this cultural leadership is what Gramsci has identified as *hegemony*." This is a term that you will frequently encounter, particularly in Marxist criticism, but it is also closely related to what for most Atlantic Basin readers is more familiar from the work of Foucault, the term "power," or sometimes "power/knowledge." As you will learn in the excerpt from Foucault that you'll read for the next lecture, Foucault like Gramsci makes a distinction between power as mere coercion by the police or the law or the dictator and power as the way the entire structure of society makes some form of what passes for knowledge hegemonic and authoritative. Both Gramsci and Foucault, then, make the distinction between absolute power and hegemony or power/knowledge. For Said, following these founders of discursivity, Western Orientialism is a form of hegemony.

For Said, hegemonic opinions construct the postcolonial world and simultaneously reinforce the authority (the being-an-author resisted by Foucault) of those who generate the opinions. Said does, however, disagree with Foucault in one respect, precisely concerning the influence of authorship. I'm not sure Foucault would disagree that authors are, after all, dangerously authoritative if we allow them to be, and feel therefore that Said exaggerates the degree to which Foucault supposes all authors to be negligible even as spheres of influence, but Said's opinion is still worth citing as an index of his sense that power is crushingly oppressive even without a truncheon in its hand (1813): "Foucault believes that in general the individual text or author counts for very little; empirically [that is to say, "based on my experience"], in the case of Orientalism, and perhaps nowhere else I find this not to be so."

In other words, the "author" is in this case the philologists, social historians, explorers, and demographers who have written so extensively on this part of the world and filled our heads with information that goes completely unchallenged by any prior knowledge of any kind. They are unrivaled oracles who can browbeat with impunity. In the case of Orientalism, it is not a question, therefore, of a subliminal drumbeat of opinion expressing itself over and over again—what "they say" when we say that "they say that . . ."—which is the sort of phenomenon that interests Foucault.

So as a circulation of power, the *effect* of Orientalism on the Eurocentric mind is what ultimately concerns Said. He insists on this point somewhat rhetorically because it obviously does concern him, too, that Orientalism also has an effect on the peoples in question. In pressing home his concern, he goes so far as to claim, in the vein of Toni Morrison and others we have encountered, that Orientalism can even be said to *construct* the Eurocentric mind (1806): "[M]y real argument is that Orientalism is—and does not simply represent—a considerable dimension of modern political-intellectual culture, and as such has less to do with the Orient than it does with 'our' world."

Recall what Morrison said. If we are studying the history of American literature and culture, the existence of black as absence needs to be understood as the means of constructing whiteness, liberating whiteness from the forms of constraint under which it would otherwise languish. Perhaps since this motif is starting to recur, I should tell you something about the master-slave dialectic in the fourth chapter of Hegel's *Phenomenology of Mind*. It's clear as Hegel develops the idea that master and slave are absolutely necessary to each other in a structure of mutuality. The master isn't the master, can't define himself as free or superior, without the existence of the slave, whom he has subdued because of his willingness to fight. (Hegel thinks here of the bloodthirsty courage of the feudal German barons.) The trickiness that the slave learns from the need to survive in the position of subordination, which involves the development of complex skills, means that soon enough the master depends on the slave, who has become technologically and culturally superior. The slave becomes master in a fable of class reversal, a situation that reverses itself again and again. This is a philosophy of class relations that structures Morrison's argument about race relations and also structures Said's argument about West and East.

I want to make the transition to Bhabha here, because obviously this dialectic is a form of binarism. The two signifiers need each other as they do in the Saussurian tradition. I can't simply say what a red light is. I know it only in a matrix of relations with what it is not. In a traffic light, red would be nothing were it not for yellow and green. In this semiotic system, red is not-yellow and also not-green. To know it fully is to know its role in two different binaries. I can represent a concept to myself, in short, even the concept *of* myself, only as the negation of some other concept or concepts.

This basic notion of the binary in the Saussurian tradition is what shapes arguments like Said's. That we know ourselves negatively as the not-other is the theoretical principle that undergirds the argument. Nevertheless, Said's thesis about Orientalism does not have a structuralist agenda when presented as an activist social critique. Said uses a structuralist idea to organize what he still considers to be empirical research. He knows he has a structuralist idea, but he believes he can map it directly onto the real world (he is not decomposing in order to recompose, as Barthes put it) because he has seen it play itself out as a reality in the sphere of cultural politics.

The premise, however, is still structuralist. Bhabha openly criticizes binarism of this kind, and in fact identifies this sort of argument with Hegel (1879):

> It is this ambivalence [felt by participants concerning their self-conception] that makes the boundaries of colonial "positionality"—the division of self/other—and the question of

colonial power—the differentiation of colonizer/colonized—
different from both the Hegelian master/slave dialectic or the
phenomenological projection of Otherness.

Here is a moment in which Bhabha is distinguishing himself as clearly
as he can from the project of Said. This passage begins with the word "ambivalence." We shall try to grasp what Bhabha means by this term and see
whether we can work our way into his intricately qualified thinking accordingly. I hope to make things as clear as possible by starting with a historical
example. There is the ambivalence of the colonizer toward the colonized as
well as the subaltern's ambivalence; it's not just one attitude that drives colonization. In the historical experience of the East India Company, for example, there are two distinct phases, phases that have actually succeeded
each other repeatedly throughout the twentieth century. The first phase, in
the eighteenth century, was the period when the East India Company was
governed by Warren Hastings, who had an interest in what we might call
"going native" and encouraged all of his provincial administrators to do
likewise. In Saidian terms, Hastings knew a great deal about the Orientalized
other. He knew all the local languages and dialects, he knew the customs. He
obviously viewed this exotic domain with fascination, and perhaps in some
limited measure even with respect. Yet he was still a ruthless governor, a colonizer who never relaxed his iron grip on authority. Hastings embodied one
form of the ambivalence Bhabha emphasizes, never yielding an inch of authority, while at the same time seeming to become one with the other, and no
doubt laughing up his sleeve at pale English visitors who weren't old India
hands.

Then there is the historical ambivalence that expresses itself in a completely different attitude, the one that surfaced early in the nineteenth century when the East India Company was governed by Charles Grant. There
had been a revival of fundamentalist religion in England, mainly Method-
ism, and evangelical enthusiasm spread itself into the interests of the
empire. Charles Grant and others like him no longer had any wish to go
native. On the contrary, they insisted that a standard of Englishness, especially the standard of the English Bible—the coming of the English book
that Bhabha talks about at the beginning of his essay—be firmly implanted.
The imposition of English values on the colonized was now the announced
agenda of colonization, the ideology that fronted, no doubt often sincerely,
for continued national and business interests. The historian Thomas Babing-
ton Macaulay codified this attitude in a famous—soon to be infamous—

document called "The Minute on Indian Education," which insisted that the education of the Indian people under the regime of the East India Company be conducted strictly according to English models: that missionaries no longer try to adapt their ideas to local customs and folkways but that everything be strictly Anglicized. This is a completely different attitude toward colonization from that of Hastings, and it, too, can be understood as ambivalence. A double standard is obviously in play, yet missionary zeal is often accompanied by genuine benevolence, so the result may be, in individuals, a politics that is more sympathetic than the politics of going native.

There is another instance of what you might call the Warren Hastings moment, a painful example though a fascinating one, in the disturbing masterpiece by John Ford called *The Searchers*. I hope some of you know that film. The John Wayne character is a drifting loner—a stock character in the Western, of course—who shows up at the house of some relatives and hears that a daughter in the family has been abducted by Indians. In this film, John Wayne is an open and vicious racist who obsessively hates the Indians, but he is not an ignorant racist. He has himself, in a certain sense, gone native. He knows all the Native American languages and dialects, he knows their customs. He has made a careful study of the people he hates. This is a volatile mixture to be exposed to in a film because we are much more comfortable with the idea that hatred arises from ignorance. Warren Hastings was a lot like the John Wayne character, and that's just one of the ambivalences that Bhabha is thinking about when he describes the ambivalence of the colonizer. He reminds us that there's no clear parallel between knowledge and sympathy and that the mind of the colonizer comes equipped with more than one attitude. There is the local knowledge mindset, and there is the mindset bent on imposing a superior cultural standard, each of which dictates different strategies, particularly strategies of education.

So that's the ambivalence of the colonizer. Then there is the ambivalence of the colonized, and that, too, like the ambivalence of the colonizer, has to be understood as a complex of attitudes toward assimilation or co-optation. The anecdote with which Bhabha begins is well worth attending to. The protagonist is not a colonizer but someone thoroughly co-opted, a converted evangelical Christian of Indian descent who misunderstands the people he finds sitting under the trees reading the Bible because he believes, and is happy to believe, that the Bible, and for that matter Christianity itself, is "an English gift." But these people resist the notion of the Bible as an *English* book precisely because they suppose a religious idea they are meant to believe in must transcend local origin. They like what they read and want to believe it but wish they could find some accommodation to their own folkways in it. Sure, maybe we'll get baptized one of these days, they say, but in the meantime we have to go home and take care of the harvest. And by the way, if we do get baptized we certainly can't take the Eucharist because that would require eating meat. We don't eat meat because that's who we are.

You can see that these cunningly insinuated provisos to the attitude that the missionary wants to inculcate completely undermines his purpose. They don't think of the book as the English Bible and won't accept it on those terms. They will accept it only as an authority—a universal one, not an English one—that's adjusted to their own values, and this premise would profoundly alter the way they receive the book as a sacred text. This is 1813, as Bhabha points out, precisely the moment when the regime of authority is moving from the Warren Hastings model to the Charles Grant model. It's no longer possible to think of adapting the Bible to local beliefs and circumstances.

What interests Bhabha about this moment, though, is the way it places the complex range of attitudes, the "ambivalence," of the colonized people in relief. There's the attitude of the suborned missionary, and there's the more complicated and interesting attitude of the people he encounters sitting under the trees. In preparing to look at a difficult passage on page 1881, I want to gloss it by suggesting to you that the ambivalence Babha emphasizes—which we might as well identify by the term he uses for it, "hybridity"—is the double consciousness of the colonized, hovering, on the one hand, between submission to authority but with a difference, submission on one's own terms, and, on the other hand, willing acquiescence in authority as given, which is the attitude of the missionary. Here, then, is how Bhabha describes this hybridity in the double consciousness of the colonized:

> The place of difference and otherness, or the space of the adversarial, within such a system of "disposal" as I have proposed, is never entirely on the outside or implacably oppositional. [Not just, in other words, a question of us versus them.] It is a pressure, and a presence, that acts constantly, if unevenly, along the entire boundary of authorization [which is also authority], that is, on the surface between what I've called disposal-as-bestowal [I take that to mean submission—giving in because one has to while covertly retaining one's self-respect] and disposal-as-inclination [which is giving in spontaneously because the regime seems attractive].

Now to give in simply because one sees that one's beaten, as a form of submission, puts one in the position of what Bhabha calls "sly civility" (cf. 1889). This is a position that seems to me closely related to what Gates calls signifyin'. Bhabha gives several examples of this sly civility, but it's all present already in the clever and wonderfully rich ironies one finds in the remarks of these figures sitting under the trees in his opening anecdote. Let me just give you an example of my own to illustrate how sly civility works as a form of signifyin' and as a stance of colonized resistance, a recuperation of the will, which is nevertheless not rebellious, not in any way practiced as an overthrow of authority, but rather as a means of making do within the framework of authority.

Two African Americans are having a conversation in the presence of a white person. Cheerfully they refer to this person in his presence as Bill. Hey, Bill, what's happening, they say. Now as I mentioned in the last lecture, "Bill" has long been a derisive term for white people, as many white people know. The white person has two choices of response in hearing himself referred to as "Bill": he can either take umbrage and ask why they're picking on him like that, in which case the barb has been driven home; or he can play the fool, precisely the sort of fool the name is meant to imply, and pretend he doesn't know that he's being signified on with sly civility. Either way it's a win-win situation for the African Americans. This guy they call Bill is a slave owner, let's say, or the overseer of a cotton plantation during Jim Crow, or a plant foreman; but he feels the ambivalence of the colonizer. He likes to get along with everybody, and because there is an element of good nature in his makeup, he's stuck. He can either complain that his subordinates are treating him unfairly—which of course is neither here nor there in a master-slave relationship—or he can play the fool and pretend that he doesn't notice that he's being made fun of. Either way, this scenario I hope illustrates the sly civility that signifies on the Man. It makes it clear that although the structure of power can't be overthrown any time soon, there nevertheless is a way of subsisting—at least of keeping one's sense of humor within the existing structure of power—while giving the Man a hard time. Bhabha speaks of "disposal-as-bestowal." The sly civility of the subaltern is an attitude that makes the boss feel as though the subaltern's submission has been bestowed as a grudging favor, neither enforced by necessity nor volunteered in admiration.

This, then, is the range of attitudes that Bhabha encompasses in his notion of the hybridity of the colonized. It takes its most colorful and satisfying form in the performance of sly civility, or signifyin' on the Man. The options in relation to the colonizer—himself an ambivalent figure—are not binary but chameleonic, performed in many ways and nuanced, too, by a spectrum of feeling that ranges from sincerity to cynicism. Something like this social scenario emerges in Bhabha's deconstruction of postcolonial binarism.

CHAPTER 23

Queer Theory and Gender Performativity

Readings:

Foucault, Michel. "The History of Sexuality." In *The Critical Tradition*, pp. 1627–1636.

Butler, Judith. "Imitation and Gender Insubordination." In *The Critical Tradition*, pp. 1707–1718.

Although there's much that's new in the reading for this lecture, we'll pause at the end over a review and summing up of what we've done recently, and then continue with that retrospect at the beginning of the next lecture. Let me start, though, with what's new, challenging, and perhaps also subject to criticism in today's materials.

During the course of this lecture, I'll be talking about the slipperiest concept in Judith Butler's essay. It's what she calls "psychic excess," the charge or excess from the unconscious that in some measure unsettles even the many aspects of gender that can be and are performed. We perform identity, we perform our subjectivity, we perform gender in all the other ways we'll consider, but beyond what we *can* perform, there is, in relation to psychic excess, "sexuality" in the untampered-with realm of the unconscious from which it emerges. Sexuality, manifest through psychic excess, suggests therefore a locus of the "authentic," which the grim socio-identitarian dialectic for which Butler is famous makes no pretense to have access to or invade;

but to me, at least, this intimation of an authentic substratum raises a flag or two about the strong structuralism of many accounts of identity that we've discussed, perhaps especially gender theory.

So let's begin with what ought to be an innocent question. Surely we're entitled to an answer to this question, which is: what is sexuality? Now, of course, you may be given pause—especially if you have an ear fine-tuned to jargon—by the very *word* "sexuality," which is relatively recent in our beleaguered language. People didn't talk about "sexuality" in the good or bad old days. They talked about *sex*, which seemed adequate to account for both the normative and aberrant behaviors of which they were aware. But "sexuality" is the more socially sensitive, hence de-eroticized, term that now traverses this field of possibilities. And with this cachet of acceptability concerning an aspect of our lives that's always coming to terms with thought police both to the right and left of us, the word "sexuality" takes hold; yet in doing so it starts to pose a problem for the most brilliant and advanced thinkers about gender. It suggests that there is an aspect of our makeup that's genuine, authentic, something at the least more *our own* than the aspects of ourselves that we can and do perform.

For Foucault, this thing called sexuality—which has in itself an inviolable authenticity that comes as a surprise in his work, too—is something like desired and experienced bodily pleasure. Foucault's social critique insists, however, that this pleasure is always orchestrated by a set of factors that surrounds it, a very complicated set of factors that is articulated perhaps best in the passage to which we turn (1804). He's talking about the difference and the intersection between what he calls the "deployment of alliance" and what he calls the "deployment of sexuality." I want to quote this passage and then comment on it briefly: "In a word," he begins by saying, "the deployment of alliance is attuned to a homeostasis of the social body." The deployment of alliance here—just to get that defined—is the way that in a given culture the nuclear reproductive unit is identified; typically this is the "family," though the family changes in its nature and structure. The way the family is viewed, the sorts of activities that are supposed to take place and be avoided in the family—incest and the conditions that could threaten incest, for example, should not take place in most cultures—are surrounded by veins of discourse conveying all the forms of "knowledge" that make a given deployment of alliance seem natural even though it is constructed and kept securely in place by laws and restrictions. On the other hand, "the deployment of sexuality" we understand to be the way sexuality is talked about and by that means encouraged or discouraged: not dictated by any state apparatus or actual legal system, necessarily, but dictated nonetheless—*talked* about, as I say—simply by the prevalence and force of various sorts of opinion. To continue the passage:

> In a word, the deployment of alliance is attuned to a homeostasis [or a regularization; that's what he means by "homeostasis"] of the social body, which it has the function of maintaining; whence its privileged link with the law [that is, the law reflects current social assumptions about the family—that the family is not a married gay couple with children, for example]; whence too the fact that the important phase for it is "reproduction." The deployment of sexuality has its reason for being, not in reproducing itself, but in proliferating, innovating, annexing, creating, and penetrating bodies in an increasingly detailed way, and in controlling populations in an increasingly comprehensive way.

Notice that a deployment of sexuality, which isn't necessarily a bad thing—these deployments aren't for the most part meant to police outcomes—that accommodated birth control or homosexuality would certainly be a means of curtailing reproduction. Just in that degree, the deployment of sexuality would then come to be, subtly or not so subtly, at odds with the deployment of alliance (except in the case of "the Malthusian couple," to which I shall return eventually). It is just given in Foucault's terminology that *alliance* in most though not all cultures or sociobiological systems is deployed (arranged, institutionalized) to further and ensure reproduction, whereas *sexuality*, shaped undoubtedly by its own circulating currents of opinion for better or worse, is deployed for the distribution of pleasure, subject to the approval or disapproval of interested communities. There is likely, then, to be some measure of conflict between the respective deployments of alliance and sexuality in any culture.

In any case, however, in Foucault's scheme as much as in Butler's, the concept of sexuality continues to elude us because, as the inviolably authentic, sexuality can't be known in a binary relation to another concept. It permeates performance in Butler, hence is not in any sense the opposite of, or "other" in respect to, performance; and in Foucault it overlaps with alliance too extensively to be seen as the "other" of alliance. It is somehow just there in a way that nothing else is. We'll keep wondering about this.

To return to what we said about Foucault in discussing Said last time: Foucault's central idea, the idea he continues to develop throughout his three volumes on the history of sexuality, is the idea of "power" as something other than the power that is openly enforced through legal, police, or state apparatus measures. This kind of power is enforced in its own way, but more insidiously, as the circulation or distribution of "knowledge," which is discursive in nature and imposes its norms on all of us, for better or for worse. Discourse can reveal or constitute sites of resistance as well as reduce us to conformity, and with respect to our present theme it can either promote or inhibit sexuality. Foucault calls this form of power, sometimes hyphenating it, "power-knowledge." I return to power-knowledge now as the concept that governs—and guides you through—the whole text of Foucault. Let me remind you again that even though certain discourses are progressive, with the implication that they are more self-conscious, considered, and reasonable than repressive discourses (you don't have to agree with this, by the way, to accept the structure of the argument), Foucault is at pains never to align a particular form of knowledge with truth—though he often bitterly calls this or that form a "regime of truth." Power-knowledge conditions the way we are or at least the way we think we are—the way we "perform" ourselves, in Butler's parlance—but it never escapes the domain of opinion.

Hence in relation to our question—What is sexuality?—Foucault is being quite coy. He's talking about sexuality, he's writing a three-volume history of it, but he's not talking about it in *itself,* whatever "in itself" might mean in this case. He's talking about the deployment of sexuality, the way power-knowledge constructs it, makes it available to us, makes it a routine performance of libidinal expression, yet without allowing us to stumble upon the essence we continue to seek: the nature of sexuality. It continues to be lost among the vectors of power.

The issue of gay marriage is situated very interestingly, by the way, *between* the deployment of alliance and the deployment of sexuality. While a great many gay activists support gay marriage as a crucial political cause, there are others who see this institutionalization of gay life as a bourgeois redefinition and normalization of who they are. They see it as the imposition of alliance on sexuality that reflects what I earlier described as the tension between these deployments. If sexuality is really just looking around for ways to get itself expressed, taking advantage of deployment where it seems supportive and trying to resist deployment where it seems more like policing, then it would appear not to be particularly interested in alliance. Simply put, gay opposition to gay marriage is opposition to marriage as such, an advocacy of what used to be called free love—or better (perhaps), free sexuality. Perhaps here, then, we can observe, frustrated by continuing to wonder what sexuality actually is, a conflict of mystifications. Free love, whether in a poet like Shelley or as a 1960s "lifestyle," seems to us an Aquarian naivety to which the only possible response is the pop song "What's Love Got to Do with It?" Yet free sexuality, on the other hand, ever and anon, leaves us merely confused.

In reading Butler, we need to admit that to ask the question "what is sexuality?" is, well, something of a false start. We need to see how much of what we thought sexuality might be is excluded from Butler's argument. We thought our question was an innocent one, but we quickly see that in Butler you simply can't *be* a certain sexuality and certainly can't lay claim to being one. You can perform an identity, as we'll see, by repeating, by imitating, and by parodying this identity in drag. You can perform an identity in these ways, but you can't *wholly* perform sexuality precisely because of the element of psychic excess to which her thinking continues very candidly to return. Butler's work, for all the powerful sweep of its demystifications, is not just about "the construction of identity," not just about the domain of performance. It acknowledges that there is something beyond performance that is very difficult to grasp and articulate. The main reason for acknowledging this something beyond is to explain why it is that we perform at all. Why would we bother if our performance were not an effort to achieve a goal we haven't reached? It's nevertheless always clear in Butler, as she returns to the question of the unconscious in particular, that there is something in excess of, or not fully to be encompassed by, ideas of performance.

So let's say we've made a false start. We've asked a question we can't answer, but at the same time we have learned certain things. We've learned that sexuality, whatever it may be, is more flexible and also in some sense more authentic than the identities we perform: sexuality is closer to libidinal drives than consciousness can be. Whatever role sexuality may play in the unconscious, then, it always stands outside any kind of social coding: the sort of coding, for example, that Foucault would indicate in speaking of deployed alliance or deployed sexuality and the sort of coding that Butler refers to repeatedly as "gendering."

Still, for both of them—and this is the other thing we've learned—even sexuality as viewed through deployment, or through the way it can get expressed in relation to gender and performance, is fundamentally discursive. It arises out of linguistic or semiotic formations, formations that Foucault understands as circulated knowledge and that Butler understands, again, as performance. Foucault sees sexuality as the effect of power-knowledge, power as knowledge. Butler sees it as the effect—insofar as it's visible, that is, insofar as it is acted out—of performance.

In order to confront the relationship between what one might suppose to be authentic selfhood and that which is performed, that which is one's gestural quest to become a self, let's take one of the most provocative sentences in Butler's essay (1711): "Since I was sixteen, being a lesbian is what I've been." Now remember that at the very beginning of the essay, she says her whole purpose is to register a politicized intervention in gender studies that takes the form of a philosophical reflection on ontology, on "being." What is it, in other words, she says, to *be* something? What she's doing in this sentence, which is a deliberately awkward-seeming sentence, "[B]eing a lesbian is what I've been," is pointing out to us that to be something is very different from to be "being" something.

For example, I can say I'm busy and expect you to suppose that I really and truly am busy. But you might say anyway, suspecting that I'm not really busy, "Oh, he's *being* busy." In other words, I'm performing busy-ness. I'm going around being busy, imposing on you the notion that this layabout, this potherer, is actually accomplishing something. That's the performance of being busy. But here's the interesting point that Butler is making: the ontological realm is supposed to concern the simple being or existence of things, and in philosophy it's always contrasted with agency, with the performance of actions. But what Butler is saying about her sexuality—and that's why she says that she takes an interest in the ontological aspect of the question—is that an element of the performative actually creeps into the ontological. Even being, she says, is something that in some measure we perform. Hence the doubling up of the word "being" in the sentence, "Since I was sixteen, being a lesbian is what I've been."

In one sense, yes, she just is a lesbian. But in another sense, she has been being one, outing herself as one, taking up a role that can be understood, as all roles can, readily enough as long as they are performed with coherence—"repeated," as she puts it in discussing the performance of heterosexuality. So that's why she puts the sentence that way, and if you made a big mark in the margin and thought you had found the place where she says she really *is* something, not just constructed as something, I think you'll see that she has eluded your capture. She deliberately remains on the fence between the sense of the ontological as authentic and her own innovative sense of the ontological as belonging within the realm of, or at least impossible to factor apart from, performance. She really doesn't want to come down squarely on either side of the fence because for her—and this is what I like best about her work, even though it's perhaps the most frustrating thing about it—what she candidly glimpses beyond the logic of her social critique remains mysterious. She has a great deal to say about it, but she's not pretending that she has exhausted the "subject."

To set this element of mystery aside, then, at least for now, it seems plain that Foucault and Butler have a common political agenda. Foucault is a gay writer who was dying of AIDS in the later stages of writing *The History of Sexuality*; Butler is a lesbian writer. Both of them care greatly about the political implications of their marginalized gender roles, while at the same time they are theoretically very sophisticated about them. As so often, any conflict that arises in their work is the conflict we have often noticed between theory and practice. Their common political agenda is aimed at destabilizing the heteronormative by denying the authenticity, or in Butler's parlance "originality," of privileged gender roles. Who says heterosexuality came first? Butler asks. Who says a given culture's sexual arrangements are natural? Foucault asks. These are the sorts of questions, the politicized questions, that Butler and Foucault raise in common.

So it seems to me that Foucault and Butler are very closely in agreement. But let us pause briefly at the moment when they seem not to agree. You've probably noticed that one text, Butler's, refers to the other author's work in a footnote. Butler notes that the senator Jesse Helms, in having deplored male homosexuality when attacking the photography of Robert Mapplethorpe, simply erases female homosexuality because his diatribe pays no attention to it. It's even worse, she says, to be declared nonexistent or silently outlawed than to be declared deviant. She justifies this position by saying (1712): "To be prohibited explicitly is to occupy a discursive site from which something like a reverse-discourse can be articulated; to be implicitly proscribed is not even to qualify as an object of prohibition."

Here's where she gives us the footnote on Foucault (1712n15): "It is this particular ruse of erasure which Foucault for the most part fails to take account of in his analysis of power." Butler thus argues that in Foucauldian terms, there's got to be *discourse* for there to be identity. Helms's refusal of the category of "lesbian" simply by omission—and of course we know, by the way, that this is a refusal *only* by more or less careless omission—Helms's refusal of this category is, in other words, an erasure of discourse. No discourse, no identity. That is what Butler's footnote suggests that Foucault's position entails, and that would seem to make sense in relation to what we've said so far about Foucault. Discourse creates power-knowledge.

Power-knowledge creates identity. Therefore, where there's no discourse, there can be no identity, and because Helms has erased the lesbian by refusing discourse about it, it must follow that there is no such category as lesbian. To continue the footnote:

> [Foucault] almost always presumes [and we must honor that word "almost"] that power takes place through discourse as its instrument, and that oppression is linked with subjection and subjectivization, that is, that it is installed as the formative principle of the identity of subjects.

In defense of Foucault, however, we should turn to a passage that's fascinating on a number of grounds but especially as a denial in advance of what Butler says here. It's rather long but worth hearing (1632):

> Consider for example the history of what was once "the" great sin against nature. The extreme discretion of the texts dealing with sodomy—that utterly confused category—and the nearly universal reticence in talking about it made possible a twofold operation.

We find Foucault saying as this passage opens that at a certain period, the homosexual identity, understood as sodomy, was a known category, but that *silence* about it (the object of Butler's complaint on behalf of the lesbian) made two things possible. He'll go on to say that sodomy was punishable in the extreme by law; but in the meantime he's saying there was no discourse about it, or almost none. You don't get silence about sodomy in Dante, as I'm sure you know, but for the most part in this period nobody talks about it. So the law persecutes it, yet nobody talks about it. This would *seem* to violate Foucault's own premise that discourse constitutes identity, but it also plainly *does* contradict Butler's claim that in Foucault discourse always constitutes identity.

Let's continue:

> [T]he nearly universal reticence in talking about it made possible a twofold operation: on the one hand, there was an extreme severity (punishment by fire was meted out well into the eighteenth century, without there being any substantial protest expressed before the middle of the century) [Discourse is here

failing also in that it's not constituting a site of resistance, and nobody's complaining about these severe punishments just as on the other hand nobody's talking very much about them], and on the other hand, a tolerance that must have been widespread (which one can deduce indirectly from the infrequency of judicial sentences, and which one glimpses more directly through certain statements concerning societies of men that were thought to exist in the army or in the courts).

In other words, there *was* an identity and that identity was not—at least not very much— constituted by discourse. As you read further along, he'll go on to say that in a way the plight of the homosexual got worse when homosexuality started being talked about, but he will *not* say that homosexuality was not a category when it was not discussed. Yes, penalties for being homosexual were less severe once it became a topic, but the surveillance of homosexuality—the way it could be attended to by therapy, by the clergy, and by everyone else who might have something to say about it—became far more pervasive and determinate than it was when there was no discourse about it. It's hard not to interpret Foucault as saying here that silence was, while perilous to the few, a good thing for the many; whereas discourse, which perhaps relieves the few of extreme fear, nevertheless imposes a kind of hegemonic authority on all that remain and constitutes them as something that power-knowledge believes them to be, rather than something that in any sense, according to their sexuality, they spontaneously are. It occurs to us that in a moment of this kind, we can see why Foucault finds power-knowledge even at its least coercive depressing.

Silence then erases the knowledge of a category but not its existence. It seems to me, then, that Butler's disagreement with Foucault is answered in advance by Foucault and that even there, when you think about it, they're really in agreement with each other. The lesbian may feel slighted in being passed over by Jesse Helms, but she has also escaped his wrath. Foucault's position is more flexible than Butler takes it to be, but that just means that it's similar to her own. They remain, as I've said, very close to each other's viewpoint.

In method, however, they are somewhat different. Foucault is a more historical writer. Historians often criticize him for not giving acceptable historical explanations because he never shows how you get from one moment in history to the next. He talks about differing moments in history, but he sees them in terms of bodies or structures of knowledge—"epistemic moments," as he sometimes says. These moments then are mysteriously transformed into new and different moments. The kind of causality the historian requires tends in Foucault's arguments to be left out. He remains concerned, however, with the way in which attitudes change over time, and it's the changes in themselves that his argument in *The History of Sexuality* tends to concentrate on.

To this end, he pinpoints successive structures of attitude temporally. At the start of the nineteenth century and continuing to the present, for example, there are four intensely scrutinized human types around which power-knowledge busies itself. He describes them as the hysterical woman, the masturbating child, the Malthusian couple, and the perverse adult— meaning the homosexual of whatever kind (cf. 1634). By "the Malthusian couple" Foucault means the couple that is enjoined, according to the precepts of the early nineteenth-century political economist Thomas Malthus, not to reproduce too much because the economy won't stand for it. This is a way of deploying alliance to manipulate and control reproduction, creating a moment in which the deployment of alliance and the deployment of sexuality are surprisingly in league with each other, as obviously birth control and homosexual practices also control reproduction. As you see, it's not always a question of conflict between these two forms of deployment—and it should be added, in any case, that the deployment of sexuality for its part—as when people "just don't care"—may very well take forms that increase reproduction.

These four problematic types, then, are the focus of attention from the nineteenth century to recent times for psychological therapy, the clergy, family or parental advice, and all the other ways that power-knowledge circulates. The hysterical woman is identified as hysterical once it begins to be suspected that her whole being is her sexuality, emanating outward from her womb (*hysteron*), a state of things that's scarcely suitable for the angel of the house. The masturbating child violates the religious doctrine that baptized children are washed clean of sin and challenges, too, the romantic cult of the innocent child of nature that begins at the turn of the nineteenth century. For this and other reasons, this child is a cause of deep alarm and is subject to extreme surveillance and restraint. Power-knowledge declared that masturbation led to impotence, stunted growth, and early death—all opinions that dominated pediatric literature until well into the twentieth century.

The Malthusian couple was primarily an offshoot of "political economy" in the early nineteenth century but has prevailed in our progressive campaign promoting birth control around the world. "We must control population" is a sentiment that may well reflect grim necessities to which we find ourselves assenting, but it's said first in Malthus, who wanted, in the economic interests of families themselves, to police reproduction the way it is policed in China today. Foucault challenges his sympathetic reader on this score, because we liberals eagerly suppose that no form of hegemony would meet with our approval, but this particular focus of power-knowledge, less rigorously endorsed than it is in China, is an ingrained part of secular liberalism. This may have been clearer to Foucault in a nominally Catholic country than it is to us.

And finally, the perverse adult is first openly discussed in the nineteenth century, as the earlier passage that I quoted suggested, and is still of course widely discussed today, quite often by the equivalent of Woolf's male experts on women and Said's Orientalists. But the perverse adult now also has a voice and discourses in his or her own right through a flourishing literature and journalism. The perverse adult is very much in the mainstream of discourse, yet still encounters controversy and at least the remnants of legal and theological prohibition because conflicting "regimes of truth" on this topic quite unashamedly and vocally coexist.

Observations of this sort, then, are what constitute for Foucault a historical project, that of his "history" of sexuality. For Butler, on the other hand, as you can tell from her style, in which I'm sure you recognize a lot of Derrida as you did in Bhabha, it's a question of taking these same issues and orienting them more toward the Continental tradition of philosophy. I've already remarked that she understands the essay you've read as a contribution to that branch of philosophy called "ontology," the philosophy of being. Her basic move, the dialectical inversion of thought that derives from Hegel, is something that I hope by this time you've become familiar with and perhaps even anticipate.

For us, perhaps, the inaugural moves of this kind were the various distinctions made by Lévi-Strauss. Just to review: intuitively, the raw precedes the cooked, as indeed it does in simple chronology. Yet if we understand the relationship between the raw and the cooked to be a discursive formation, we have to recognize that if you talk about eating a raw carrot, you must have eaten or at least heard of a cooked carrot already. Well, this is the Butler move. The heterosexual precedes the homosexual? The heterosexual is the original sexuality and the homosexual is just an imitation of it? Obviously not. If there were no homosexual, who would ever think of the concept of the heterosexual, much less empower the concept as the "heteronormative"? If you're the only person on earth but endowed with language, you may say, looking around, as the case may be for Eve or for another Adam, that you are a sexual being, but you would not say that you're either heterosexual or homosexual. The concepts depend on each other as known, differing practices that define each other negatively. They don't beg the question which came first. In sexuality, the very strong supposition for Butler is that neither came first. They're always already there together in that psychic excess with which we identify sexuality. But in social terms, the idea that what's natural is the heterosexual and what's unnatural, secondary, derivative, and imitative of the heterosexual is the homosexual is belied simply by the fact that you can't have one conceptually without the other.

It's the same thing with gender and drag. Drag parodies, mimics, and imitates gender, but what its performance reveals is that gender is always in and of itself, precisely, performance. If it weren't performance, repeated and coherent as performance is, replete with all the signatures of clothing, posture, gait, and voice, it couldn't be imitated by drag. It may seem demeaning to insist that we perform our identities, but at least as performers we're all virtuosos. Here I am standing in front of you performing professionalism. I'm performing whiteness, masculinity, all those things and more. Perhaps it's hard to focus on my performance in such a way that I'm exclusively performing masculinity as opposed to all the other things I'm performing, but I'm certainly performing masculinity, too, and the drag impersonator wishing to represent me would concentrate on that. I'm insecure about all of these things, Butler argues, about masculinity and everything else I perform, because I would lose possession of them if I did not keep performing them. In other words, I keep repeating what I suppose myself to be, which at the same time is what I hope I am. I'm not comfortable in my skin, presumably, and I don't just relax into what I suppose myself to be. I perform it. My perpetual self-construction does two things at once. It stabilizes my identity, as it is meant to do, but at the same time it betrays my anxiety about my identity insofar as I must perpetually repeat it to keep it going. I am, in a sense, the drag of myself.

Drag brings our self-performance to our attention. It shows us once and for all what's behind the seemingly natural categories of gender that we imagine ourselves to inhabit like a set of comfortable old clothes. Drag, one hallmark of which is its avoidance of comfortable old clothes, reminds us how awkward the self-apparel that we call our identity actually is.

You have probably asked yourself for some time what any of this has to do with literary theory. Fair enough, but I hope you noticed that Butler offers a fabulous textual application at the end of her essay when she says,

"Suppose Aretha is singing to me." "You make me feel"—not a *natural* woman, because there's no such thing as natural. "You make me feel *like* a natural woman," "you" presumably being some heteronormative other who shows me what it really is to be a woman. Suppose, however, "Aretha is singing to me." There's no stress on "like" in this case because now the sense is just that I ("you") make her feel fulfilled in her identity, as though she, a lesbian, were natural. Or suppose she is singing to a drag queen: only a man in drag can bring out what she feels to be natural in herself. This is surely an exercise in reading a song text that's helped by literary theory.

In writing the following sentence—"The philosopher in a dark mood paced on his oriental rug"—I'm obviously thinking of Virginia Woolf's Mr. Ramsay in *To the Lighthouse*. It's a terrible sentence for which I apologize. Virginia Woolf never would have written it. But let's just use it to remind ourselves that what we've been doing *is* literary theory, a set of protocols that not only helps us read but allows us to read with surprising and interesting results.

The Marxist critic would focus on "his" because the Marxist key to this sentence is the possession of a commodity. The African American critic would call attention to metaphors that are color-coded white, insisting that one of the ways literature needs to be read is through a demystification of white as bright, sunlit, and central, and black, as Toni Morrison suggests in her essay, an absence or negativity. A dark mood is bad and needs to be shunned. For the postcolonial critic, the problem is expropriated possession (like the Machu Picchu artifacts) but also undifferentiated commodity: by "Oriental" you don't mean Oriental. You mean Kazakh or Bukhara or Kilim. In other words, the very lack of specificity in the concept suggests the reified or objectified other in the imagination or consciousness of the discourse.

Finally, for gender theory, the masculine anger of the philosopher, Mr. Ramsay—you remember he is so frustrated because he can't get past *r*; he wants to get to *s*, but he can't get past *r*—the masculinized anger of the philosopher masks the effeteness, the pronounced aesthetic sensibility of somebody who keeps an Oriental rug in his study. Or maybe what's being performed is just the effete professorial type. My rug's upstairs.

CHAPTER 24

The Institutional Construction
of Literary Study

Readings:

Fish, Stanley. "How to Recognize a Poem When You See One." In *The Critical Tradition*, pp. 1023–1030.

Guillory, John. "Cultural Capital." In *The Critical Tradition*, pp. 1472–1483.

We've now completed a sequence of theoretical approaches to identity, always with a view—though rather often lately a view from afar—to the way identity is constructed in literature. I'll return to what may have seemed at times the missing link, literature, in a minute. In the meantime, I just wanted to point out something I'm sure you've noticed even when I haven't mentioned it: namely, that each of these approaches to identity has a history in two chapters. Each history arrives at a second chapter that is something like a deconstructive moment, signifying on theory itself, on the claim that theory can offer a clear and distinct concept of identity—in most cases a binary concept of identity, which is the first chapter. Just for example, we find in Bhabha the notion of hybridity as the undermining of cultural binaries through the double consciousness, or multiple consciousness, in which one experiences simultaneously a kind of identification with a state apparatus and a will to subvert it. The resulting behavior is "sly civility" (or "signifyin'," or "drag"—the deconstructive moment in gender theory that comes when gender is no longer considered something essential but something performed).

By the way, I can give you a firsthand example of how sly civility works because people in my walk of life are the objects of it. On talk shows and various public interest panels, they invite people to participate whom they call "professors." Ostensibly that's an honorific title that means the person so addressed is an expert. Perhaps at one time it really did convey respect, and it also had social cachet because professors used to be the offspring of the rich, "dollar a year men." But most of that is now ancient history. Folks don't like to show respect to a "so-called expert" and don't see why they should. Today all it means to be called "professor" is that you're a pedant who doesn't understand the real world. If you're a professor, it's just plain depressing to be called one. This is how it feels to be the *object* of sly civility. You either protest or you play the fool and confirm everybody's opinion. Bhabha probably exaggerates when he says the discourse of hybridity entails an element of terrorism. He wrote that long before 9/11 and thus perhaps uses the term a little breezily for our present taste; but frustrating intimidation is certainly involved. Sly civility is necessary to anyone who thinks he's at least the equal of someone who has real or imagined authority. The subaltern self-confidence and memsahib insecurity that are effected by the exercise of double consciousness is not an actual exchange of roles; things remain as before (I don't hand over my PhD to the talk show host), yet the binary relation of the roles has been subverted.

Each history of identity theory we have considered offers instances of knowledge as negation, as semiotic knowledge, which has been a central theme throughout this course. We don't know what we are except as the obverse of what we are not. I recognize myself only as *not that*. As soon as I objectify or pigeonhole what I am not (and I need to do that if stable concepts of identity, mine or another's, are to emerge at all), I come to understand myself for the first time—according to the argument of a Toni Morrison or an Edward Said or a Judith Butler—as white, Western, and heterosexual, respectively. In short, self-definition is negative in keeping with the tradition of semiotic theories of language and literature.

All this is meant to reassure you that we still are talking about literary theory. The theory of identity in each case is first structuralist and then deconstructive. The turn to social relations in our reading has not been accompanied by a change in the structure of thought we first examined when we took up language as the primary determinant of understanding. We have simply transformed language—viewed now as the determinant of social understanding—into what we call a "social text." Our "center" now, as Derrida would put it, is not Saussure's *langue*, a virtual entity that exists arbitrarily as a synchronic system (the diachronic input that produces it merely obscuring its stable outlines as a scientific object), but rather language that is full of other people's language. It is a space in which society, itself understood as a system of discursive formations, jostles for attention and struggles to shape itself. That's the fundamental change. Of course, structuralism and deconstruction don't understand language as our own autonomous possession either, because the point is always that language is something we can only struggle to make our own in speech; but after our recent readings, we are in a position to understand language more clearly as something given to us as a social formation that in turn forms us if we fail to signify on it.

This brings us to our focus in this lecture, which concerns the preconditions of interpretation. What makes it possible for us to think something, or to think that something is true? How is it that you come to think one thing and I come to think differently? How is it that, on the other hand, there are areas of agreement among us? As your reading indicates, we have arrived at the topic of "interpretive communities."

In order to approach this issue, let's first go back to *Tony the Tow Truck*. We've said all along, I hope not too facetiously, that *Tony* is about whatever it is that we happen to be talking about, and this has been meant as an object lesson in the way interpretation works. As Stanley Fish will insist, though, it's not just a question of "whatever you say is there must be there." ("Very like a whale," says Polonius.) Think of it in Russian formalist historiographical terms. In a given text, all the "devices" that can be identified as auto-functions in literature are present, some syn-functionally dominant and some syn-functionally recessive. The sum of devices is the sum of communally accepted and recognized contributions to the building up of what counts as literature for interpretive communities over time. So it is with critical approaches that always find what they look for—surely a danger signal!—yet are still defensible. (I've convinced myself, in case you're curious, that everything I've said about *Tony* is defensible, even if it's more to the point, more appropriately in scale, to talk about some things, the dominant things, rather than others, the recessive ones.) But certain responses (*Tony* is really about my field trip in sixth grade) don't correspond to any part of what counts as an interpretable object in the public domain, hence don't count as interpretation.

So let's think about *Tony* once again, then, this time as being "about" the forms of identity we've discussed recently. We can say, for example, that *Tony* is a Marxist invocation of class as the social determination of identity. It's a realist text in the canon of Engels and Lukács, as we've said before: no social change is projected, yet it does faithfully reflect the structure of social existence, including—as we'll see—the structure of ethnic and gender difference.

Tony is a global story that reflects hybridity in the American melting pot. It should have been obvious to you all along that Tony is an Italian American with the complex personality of the subaltern. On the one hand, he believes in the American dream: "I like my job." Yet on the other hand, he recognizes that he has his own niche in the world, independent and set apart: the little yellow garage, which partly affords him his identity. Neato, in contrast, is a neurotic WASP, and Speedy is a member of what John Guillory calls "the professional/managerial class." What's interesting about Speedy is that his ethnic origins, his class, and even his gender—he may be a workaholic woman—are not as relevant as one might imagine them to be because the professional/managerial class—as Guillory's source, Alvin Gouldner, points out at length—is an emergent group with common interests that can't be said to share a class or other preexisting identity. It's no accident that Neato comes first in the folkloric triad because Neato represents an older class, a class that is giving way to the professional/managerial class. So Neato comes first and Speedy comes second.

Tony is a gender fable as well. We've said there are no women in it except for those frowning and smiling houses, but it's not just that. Obviously Neato, with his little bow tie in the picture and his prissy "Oh, I don't want to get dirty," is just a bundle of gay stereotypes. And then, of course, Bumpy "pushes and pushes"—you don't want to go there.

So here is the question, and it really does provide us with our transition to today's materials: what have I been doing all this time with *Tony the Tow Truck*? As you can see now, I've been doing exactly what Stanley Fish does with "Jacobs, Rosenbaum, Levin, Thorne, Hayes, and Ohmann." I've been showing that if you bring a certain supposition to bear on what you're reading, you're going to perform a certain kind of hermeneutic act, not with any particular strain but more or less spontaneously, because that's what you're conditioned to do.

Fish's class in the devotional poetry of the seventeenth century had no trouble construing the list of readings in linguistics put on the board for his previous class as a poem, and you can see, of course, that the list offered temptations to be construed that way. Fish admits that the list is a lucky find, but then he runs his finger down the list of faculty names at the college where he's lecturing and says you could just as easily read *those* names as a poem. I think he does make his point, because *Tony* has shown us how extraordinarily elastic texts are when interpretation pulls them this way and that. We can even see that his class missed a few important points. It forgot to mention that an archaic meaning of the word "Levin" is lightning, the flash that comes with any religious revelation. Again, it's hard to understand why the class was stumped by the word "Hayes" because we see through a glass darkly, in a *haze*. That's just how we respond to glimpses of religious truth in the devotional poetry of the seventeenth century.

Fine, you say, enough parlor games, we're still entitled to know what that intentional utterance we call a text is *really* about. You may want to know, for example, whether I think *Tony* has a meaning, not just significance, to recall the distinction of E. D. Hirsch. As a matter of fact, I do. I mentioned it in passing, but it's only an intuition (oddly, I'm less certain about it than I am about the aha! moments that all my "approaches" have yielded up), and it doesn't arise, believe me, out of any predilections I may have for psychoanalysis. I do believe, however, that a story written for toddlers in which the climactic line is "He pushed and he pushed and I'm on my way" is pretty obviously about potty training. A toddler in the anal phase will know what's being pushed and pushed and perhaps will know very little else. Before you scoff, have you never watched *South Park*? So that's "my" interpretation, offered in preference to all the others I've played the ventriloquist for. But what conditions such a conclusion? I've disclaimed a special interest in psychoanalysis, but I do know something about it; psychoanalysis is part of my interpretive community, the part I draw on in this particular case.

We've all been playing the game, just like Fish's class, because we are, as a group, an interpretive community that recognizes a plurality of approaches, evidently so by virtue of the fact that you are more or less willingly taking in what I'm saying. We've been being very knowing about *Tony the Tow Truck*, agreeing that it's about this, that, and the other thing and probably something else on Thursday. At this point, let me offer two caveats about our basic unanimity. First, I would say that within the interpretive community that makes up my audience, a community of people who are curious about interpretation, there has been a suspicion all along that interpretation is a mug's game, and you therefore wanted to experience lectures of this kind to find out just how bad it was. All of us have in common a concern with the potential complexity of those circumstances that surround interpretation. We are an interpretive community that's interested in interpretation, so we play along in the fun house of perspectives.

But second, however, I would hazard that within this interpretive community, there are two subcommunities that grasp the significance of this pluralistic exercise but still want very much to hold out against it. One of them is the community that either always has or has now come to have a very strong commitment to one or another point of view that's been passed in review in this course, and who therefore finds it demeaning to the most important point of view, the true one, that it be treated merely as one in a series. You'll recall that during my introductory apology for giving a survey, I mentioned students and colleagues who have bridled at the very idea of a survey course when, after all, the only thing that matters is Marx's thought, or some other thought. This viewpoint would probably lead you to say not so much that *Tony* is only about this one thing but that plural interpretation is a facile and insulting exercise because the important thing is to take only this one thing seriously no matter what *Tony* is about.

The second subcommunity within our interpretive community is the one that is still committed to "high culture." This community doesn't necessarily deny that there are more ways to the woods than one but insists that we should have been interpreting "Lycidas" or *The Rime of the Ancient Mariner*. According to this view, we have shown a lack of respect for high culture in using *Tony the Tow Truck*. One implication of this view is that multiple approaches to a serious work of literature would yield a measure of consensus about the *best* approach (not necessarily the only one), in contrast with which all the other approaches would stand revealed as trivial. If your commitment is not so much to one point of view as to some idea of high culture, you're not going to say in advance which approach is best, but you *are* going to suppose that a great work of literature will point you in the best direction, yielding perhaps its own terms for interpretation, which should be honored. This is the view, or perhaps a slightly more flexible version of the view, that John Guillory is criticizing when he discusses defenses of a mainstream canon in Western culture.

Nevertheless, we all do have in common, as an interpretive community, the recognition that it's possible to riff on a text as we have done. If somebody does it, we realize that whether we like it or not, we ourselves could probably do it, too—which is proof, from Stanley Fish's point of view and also from John Guillory's, that because we're in a *school* we have a great deal in common. It's what we have in common that brings the text into focus, for all of us and without much confusion or incredulity, in so many ways.

It's high time though that we speak less casually about "interpretive communities" and "schools" and attend more closely to what our authors mean and don't mean in using such terms. Turning, then, to Fish, let's begin with his first sentence (1023). Because this is part of a series of lectures, he begins by saying:

> Last time I sketched out an argument by which meanings are the property neither of fixed and stable texts nor of free and independent readers but of interpretative communities that are responsible both for the shape of a reader's activities and for the texts those activities produce.

I'm not sure he carries his argument all that much farther forward in this lecture, which is why I think it's worthwhile to linger over this sentence.

I'll try to explicate it by sketching in the interesting arc of Fish's career. He has actually changed his mind twice, by his own admission, and those changes are in turn registered in the sentence I just read. So here are his three basic positions, succeeding and undermining each other in turn. When I was Fish's student at the University of California, he firmly held his first opinion. This was just before he published *Surprised by Sin: The Reader in "Paradise Lost,"* a book for which the seminar I was in was a kind of trial audience. To give you an example of what he meant in claiming that *the text produces the reader*, which was his first opinion, I will cite a passage that he cites from Milton. Satan emerging from the fiery lake pulls himself up to his full height, holding a spear: "His Spear, to equal which the tallest Pine [okay: spear, pine, about the same size?] / Hewn . . . / To be the Mast of some great Ammiral [so: mast = pine = spear?] / Were but a wand . . ."! Suddenly you realize that the sequence of sizes is completely reversed and that what you'd already filled your consciousness with—the tallest pine—is just a wand compared with Satan's spear. So what's Milton doing? He's saying you think you know how big Satan is, but you shouldn't mess with him because he is much bigger than you could ever imagine he is. You have *fallen*, being a descendant of Adam, into Milton's syntactical trap, and will fall repeatedly into others, just as the same unwariness of presupposition will make you fall into Satan's clutches until you learn that reading doesn't jump to conclusions but reserves judgment.

What I didn't quote yet, the continuation of the passage, shows that even once we have acknowledged his incommensurable size, we are still seeing Satan only at his weakest. The passage continues, "were but a wand,/ He walkt with to support uneasy steps." He's as weak as he's ever going to be right now, yet he's already a lot more than you can handle. To jump to conclusions, achieving premature interpretive confidence, is to fall, repeatedly to fall. The syntax of *Paradise Lost* teaches us that every time we think too soon that we grasp the point of a text, we prove that we are fallen readers, not yet part of the "fit audience though few" that can benefit from the story of the Fall.

Fish's first opinion was, then, *that the text produces the reader*. Not too long after that, in the course of writing a book called *Self-Consuming Artifacts*, he began to have a different opinion that more or less reversed the first one. He decided it isn't the text that brings the reader into being—into the recognition of a fallen state of being in the case of *Paradise Lost*. It isn't the text that brings the reader into being. It's the reader that brings the text into being. *The reader produces the text*. It's the reader, after all, who performs the *act* of reading, however misguidedly, and it's the reader who finally makes visible the characteristics of Milton's strategy. So Fish reverses his field while retaining from his first position a similar structure of argument and range of insight concerning the dynamic didacticism of the texts that interest him.

This second position seemed sound until Fish remembered that a reader isn't just an autonomous mind but reflects influences. Accordingly, the third revolution in his thinking about "reader response" (the broad field or school to which his theoretical contributions belong, like those of Iser) amounts to this: it's not the text that produces the reader, it's not the reader who produces the text, *it's the interpretive community that produces the reader who in turn produces the text*.

When Fish says (1025), "Interpretation is not the art of construing but the art of constructing. Interpreters do not decode poems; they make them," he's only in phase two of his thinking, because we can still suppose that the interpreter is an autonomous being whose strategies of reading, or constructing, are self-generated. Soon he clarifies, though (1027): "This does not, however, commit me to subjectivity." In other words, it's not just a question of saying that whatever I put into a text is legitimate, of saying we all make different texts because we all have different subjectivities, hence any old off-the-wall interpretation is possible. That's not what he's saying; for the reason he goes on to provide, I can't just say *Tony the Tow Truck* is about my sixth-grade field trip. "This does not, however, commit me to subjectivity because the means by which [texts] are made are social and conventional."

Everything we said about *Tony,* for all its variety and occasional outrageousness, was enabled by some local consensus, some opinion shared by an interpretive community, about what it is possible to say. In other words, I can't have an off-the-wall interpretation of anything if I expect to be understood. If I'm locked in my room, I suppose I can have an off-the-wall interpretation of something (or, rather, produce an off-the-wall text), but no one will publish it. My interpretation, if it's to count as an interpretation at all, derives from the techniques and assumptions of communities that produce, and share, the very *concepts* of "interpretation" and "text."

If only communities armed with conventions are the agents that produce whatever it is that becomes intelligible as a text or some other thing, it follows that there are neither subjects nor objects. This is Fish's way, in parallel with Derrida and deconstruction, of attacking the Western metaphysical tradition. I hope it's clear here, as elsewhere in our reading, that the actual existence of objects isn't at all in question. Fish says colorfully that communities produce objects, but he speaks as a pragmatist, not a Pyrrhic skeptic or a closet idealist. To "produce" an object is to produce the means whereby it becomes intelligible—and recognized in common with others similarly informed—*as* that object. If we retort that a sonnet is a poem of fourteen lines whether we read it ("produce it") or not, we forget that it takes a certain education (differing from the education of other communities) to know, to set forth intelligibly what a poem, a line, a certain quantity of lines, and finally a sonnet might be. This, too, returns us to our first thoughts, in this case concerning "fore-having" in Heidegger and Gadamer and the way we always see something *as* something. Fish departs from this idea, though, in denying the role of subjectivity in the hermeneutic process. Anticipated to some degree perhaps by Gadamer's emphasis on historical horizons rather than romantically conceived individual authors or readers, Fish insists that individuals see, or produce, only what their interpretive communities condition them to make visible.

What, then, is an interpretive community? I have said we all belong to the one that reflects our presence here together and spoke before only of two dissenting subcommunities among us. But there's an obvious complication of these broad commonalities. We understand each other, yet at the same time it's equally true, as I'm sure all of you are thinking, that no one of us has *exactly* the same set of opinions as anyone else. Accepting a weak form of the argument, it's easy enough to agree that we do bring things into being according to certain habits that have evolved through our membership in an interpretive community. But at the same time, each of you says you don't quite interpret Jacobs, Rosenbaum, and the rest of them in the way Fish's class did, nor do you interpret it in quite the way Professor Fry did in supplementing their interpretation. You interpret it a little differently, and your neighbor differently from you. We share productive assumptions, yet each of us produces texts differently.

What would Fish say to that? I think he would say by way of concession, and I do think this needs to be acknowledged because it weakens without undermining his position: granted, in a rough sense we're all in this together—just as John Guillory says in a rough sense we're all in a school—but there's another sense in which each of us is also the sum total, the composite, of all the interpretive communities to which we now belong and from which we have emerged. We're each different because the sum of the interpretive communities to which we belong is always going to be a little different from the sum of the communities to which other people severally belong. The community concept is still in place, but perhaps, some would say, only reductively so, as the atomism of this way of putting it makes it seem as though the sum of communities is as great as the sum of individuals.

Another argument against social constructivism might be called biological constructivism. Sociobiological thinkers like Edward O. Wilson, together with proponents of "artificial intelligence" and some others in the field of cognitive science, point out that the brain is hardwired from birth or nearly so to do and recognize all sorts of things. It has been shown in the lab that aesthetic preference, which was always held up to derision when said to be objective—"There is no disputing tastes," we always say—that even aesthetic preference draws on predilections innate to all of us. We all prefer the so-called golden section, we love arches, possibly because we like shapes that offer shelter or protection. In any case, the fairly conclusive evidence is that we are hardwired to share recognitions and references. Darwin's last book describes how from infancy we recognize each other's expressions as well as the expressions of animals, so that there can be very little question of social conditioning.

I'm not sure Fish's argument is vulnerable to that position, however, because, after all, hardwiring is as communal as social conditioning. And furthermore, arguments from hardwiring harbor no proof that we all *perceive* the same object, showing only, in keeping with Fish's view, that we all *construct* the same object. So it seems to me that although the argument against so-called radical constructivism usually does take the form of pointing to innate predispositions, it actually doesn't succeed; and the argument pointing out that if we are to retain the concept of determinate interpretive communities, they must be almost as numerous as the people who share them is the more telling of the two.

John Guillory's argument, which treats the school as an interpretive community, actually ended the academic canon debate that he expected to intensify and get worse (cf. 1477). He thought the hot-button topic in the academic world for the next twenty-five years or more would be the culture wars: canonical versus noncanonical, cultural versus multicultural—he feared endless quarrels over those terms. Well, it didn't happen because his own argument was so brilliant that everybody came to their senses and realized that the debate was improperly framed. Guillory's book, *Cultural Capital*, did not silence the public version of the culture wars—nothing ever silences the public—but it did decisively silence the debate about "culture" in those "schools" that are his main subject.

Guillory's chief preoccupation, as I say—one that he takes over largely from the sociologist Pierre Bourdieu but also, as he elaborates, from Antonio Gramsci—is with the way the school establishes and proliferates what Gramsci called "hegemony." The school, according to this view, doesn't typically produce minds armed with specific bodies of knowledge or understanding. It produces instead, especially in the humanities—which Guillory thinks are painting themselves into a corner in their obtuseness—people imprinted by a certain quantum of "cultural capital." It repeats, in other words, or in Bourdieu's term it "reproduces," a certain kind of class—"class" here in Marx's superstructural sense rather than class coded by money or even necessarily by family, though of course there are overlaps. Regardless of the specific content that a student supposes herself to have been mastering, and regardless of its emphasis on progressive themes, the school breeds superiority through the possession of culture (symphony tickets, quotations from the poets in after-dinner speeches, but also multicultural enthusiasms) that replicates an orientation to privilege that Guillory says the school in Western culture has always fostered. What the school reproduces is not knowledge so much as *itself*, the attitude that it embodies, its reason for being and for continuation, together with its relation to power and the state apparatus. That's why Guillory says both sides of the culture wars to an equal extent play into the hands of the monolithic ideology reproduced by the school. No text, no matter how progressive or "marginalized" in itself, can effect change as long as it is first processed and later possessed as a cultural commodity.

When you embrace multiculturalism, the "noncanonical," as the only means of inculcating what Guillory calls "progressive pedagogy," you succeed only in deracinating the objects of your attention from the culture to which they belong in precisely the way that "the great monuments of Western civilization" have long since been deracinated from their historical and cultural circumstances. You reduce both Western Civ *and* alternative canons to the same rootless commodification as cultural capital. In the case of Western Civ, it's fodder for after-dinner speeches. In the case of multicultural curricula, it's the opportunity to allude in precisely the same way on parallel occasions, and in either case it has nothing to do with learning anything at all, according to Guillory, about the historical and social circumstances in which any kind of cultural production is grounded.

This argument depends on supposing that the way the great works or noncanonical works are taught under "school" ideology is to view them as vessels of ideas and principles. They're taught as messages. The Western canon distills itself into a message about the superiority of American values as they descend unchanged from antiquity. The multicultural canon distills itself into a contestatory message about the beauty and importance of being whoever happens to be speaking. What all works cease to be is cultural artifacts that both emerge from and articulate the historical circumstances in which they are written.

This argument is ultimately a plea for a new method of teaching. Guillory's own deepest commitment is, in fact, to the great works. He began as an early modern scholar and wrote a fine first book on Spenser and Milton. His later work in literary sociology in no ways discredits or undermines the fact that earlier in his career he was interested in a particular cultural canon. In fact, probably the most interesting chapter in *Cultural Capital* is the one in which he shows how Thomas Gray's "Elegy in a Country Churchyard" came to predominate in English curricula even though it was written in the vernacular, in English. He shows, in other words, how that poem, now itself a cultural monument, undermined the premium placed on the classics, on Latinity, and helped along the emergence of a vernacular national curriculum.

Guillory himself likes the classics, including the ones displaced by Gray's "Elegy," and he actually subscribes to Gramsci's superficially reactionary-seeming idea that all students of all classes should have the opportunity to discuss some common subject matter, not excluding the classics.

Guillory shows, though, how the Western Civ mavens are fooled by the notion that a canon could be "traditional" or permanent. History continuously changes canons. The more books accumulate, the fewer you can read, and the more formerly canonical works must silently drop out of any curriculum, including the Western Civ curriculum. We watch this happen every time we draw up a new curriculum for a standard course. (What would happen to certain theorists in our reading if I decided, as arguably I should, to introduce new ones?) Today we suppose we know the "great classics," having read some Plato, Aristotle, Homer, Virgil, and maybe Thucydides and Herodotus. In former times, people didn't stop with those greats. They read everything there was to read in Greek and Latin, and then they read, because they still had a bit of time, such few books as had then been published in English. Modern languages and literatures have radically thinned out this canon to make room for themselves.

Guillory's argument hinges on the failure of anybody involved in these debates to distinguish between the two forms of "culture." There is the kind of culture that a person without any education at all and the new professional/managerial class can share, the kind of culture in which literature, precisely, doesn't matter. In this culture, Nike is an athletic shoe. Then there is culture with a capital *K*, as we say, featuring the monuments of civilization, but also the alternative canons when they are transmitted as comparable talismans. Guillory says the total disconnect in the way we understand the relations between these two forms of culture is what leads to the deracination in teaching that he complains about. He himself thinks *anything* is fair game to be taught and can be taught progressively as long as it is taught in terms of its social and historical circumstances. He points out that a "great book" is great in part because it can't possibly be reduced to the bromidic confirmation of one's own views that the advocates of Western Civ burden it with (1482):

> No cultural work of any interest at all is simple enough to be credibly allegorized in this way, because any cultural work will *objectify* in its very form and content the same social conflicts that the canon debate allegorizes by means of a divided curriculum.

The Odyssey is full of lying, trickery, class betrayal. In *The Iliad,* one of the more interesting characters is Thersites, who is scarcely an advocate of the values that we associate with Western culture. In any case, this is what

Guillory means by saying that you cannot monumentalize anything in this way if you read it carefully and attentively enough. So ultimately his argument is a program for better reading, one that ventilates the interpretive community we call a school with the living circumstances that produce and express themselves in a culture where Nike is both a shoe and a goddess.

Theory Con and Pro

CHAPTER 25

The End of Theory? Neo-Pragmatism

Reading:

Knapp, Steven, and Walter Benn Michaels. "Against Theory." In *Against Theory: Literary Studies and the New Pragmatism.* Ed. W. J. T. Mitchell. Chicago: University of Chicago Press Journals, 1985.

This lecture concerns an essay written to immediate widespread acclaim and controversy by two young scholars, one of them then untenured, who were still making their way in the academic world. They certainly succeeded with this essay, which was published in *Critical Inquiry*. The editors of *Critical Inquiry* quickly decided to publish in book form, together with "Against Theory," a series of responses to the essay. It's well worth reading in full if you take an interest in the controversies that the article generated—as I hope to persuade you to do.

Steven Knapp and Walter Benn Michaels are "neo-pragmatists," influenced most directly by an important book of the 1970s by the philosopher Richard Rorty, *Philosophy and the Mirror of Nature*; Rorty in turn worked in a tradition that goes back through John Dewey in the 1930s and 1940s, and before then not only to the great philosophical interventions of William James, Henry's brother, but also and perhaps most importantly to the theory of signs worked out by the philosopher Charles Sanders Peirce. Peirce's quirky and difficult theory, which is most perspicuous in his *Letters to Lady Welby*, was not widely known in its day except among a few colleagues, including James. It was taken up, though, by a circle at the University of Cambridge headed by I. A. Richards. In *The Meaning of Meaning*, which published excerpts from the *Letters to Lady Welby* in an appendix, Richards and C. K. Ogden devoted some reflections to Peirce's semiotics that became the introduction to the subject for many later critics. They emphasized "thirdness," or the role of an "interpretant" or human agent between sign and referent, which came to be an influential way of retorting against skepticism that the relation between sign and reference is reliably mediated.

Today, pragmatism, or neo-pragmatism, is increasingly influential in academic literary thinking. Peirce's semiotics is proposing itself as an alternative to Saussure's because it is materially grounded and reflects the dynamics of social interchange, including that of "interpretive communities." I shall try to introduce some of these ideas by way of the Knapp and Michaels essay, concluding by showing, I hope, why Saussurian premises can't be dismissed as easily as Knapp and Michaels suggest that they can. (For a Saussurian rereading of Peirce himself, I refer you to an article by Umberto Eco called "Peirce's Notion of the Interpretant," which sees the interpretant not as a human agent but as an intermediary sign.[1])

1982 was the high-water mark of both the fascination and the frustration with literary theory in this country. It was a hot-button topic—as we've said before—in ways that it is not really today. Our interest in literary theory—or at least in what I might as well go ahead and call Saussurian literary theory—is now at least in part historical, as we have indicated. In 1982, though, where you stood on these matters just made all the difference, and it was in that atmosphere that Knapp and Michaels's "Against Theory" was published.

A neo-pragmatist is as "anti-foundational" (the word is Rorty's) as a Saussurian, offering no account of the objective world as a basis for knowledge and communication, but for the neo-pragmatist the important thing to remember is that we just do know things (for whatever reason: as the essay argues, there is no difference between knowledge and belief); we can't *not* know things; and we *act*, both necessarily and properly, on the basis of what we know, hence playing out the role of *agents* in our social environment. For the neo-pragmatist, speech is a form of agency like all other actions. You can see that by insisting on agency as the central characteristic of being human, at least as a matter of rhetoric the neo-pragmatist guards much more fervently against the supposed crippling effects of nihilism or radical skepticism than does, for example, the deconstructionist.

You encountered roughly these views in the essay of Stanley Fish, who argues that what we believe and reinforce as knowledge through our agency is largely produced by the interpretive community to which we belong. You'll notice now that in the third part of their essay, Knapp and Michaels engage in polite disagreement with Fish. Their broad agreement with him is clear, but they point to him as an object lesson in how easy it is to reproduce bad habits of thought in a casual slip of tongue. To this end, they find a particular passage in Fish where he slips back into the idea that we hold knowledge in relation to belief, not simply as belief. Fish writes one of the responses in the subsequent book called *Against Theory*, but this is really a friendly exchange about a transitory and superficial matter. In this lecture, I'm going to pay a lot of attention to the first two arguments of the three offered by Knapp and Michaels; I'll have little more to say about knowledge and belief, a philosophical issue best reviewed in Rorty.

You'll notice that their tone is very similar to that of Fish. It's a downright, no-nonsense, let's-get-on-with-it tone that, after reading Derrida or Lacan, you may well encounter with relief as a vacation from dialectical tacking and veering. In a way, the tone comes with the territory. It follows from the embrace of neo-pragmatist views because what you're telling your reader is, in effect, you just do what you do and think what you think, don't grope around for rationales, just get on with the business of thinking and doing. As a literary interpreter, you're *bound* to have some opinion about what you're reading; you can't escape having one; so as long as you're interpreting what you read, just get on with it. If you don't want to interpret on your own in the role of an unmediated reader (and since it's hard to forget that interpretation can't be objective, you may prefer to give it up), you can study instead the grounds of interpretation: why other people have said what they said in all the interpretive communities (or "public spheres," to cite the frequently used adaptation of the equivalent term of Habermas) that can be specified historically. The only way you can go wrong is to cobble together some theoretical justification for what you're doing.

Knapp and Michaels argue that people become needlessly and erroneously entangled with problems raised by theory when they make three fundamental mistakes (the third being, again, the factoring apart of knowledge and belief). The first is to suppose that there is a difference between meaning and intention: in other words, that to arrive at a meaning you have to be able to invoke an intention, on the one hand; or, on the other hand, that in the absence of an intention we cannot decide upon a meaning. That's their first argument: people become embroiled in theory when they make one version or another (its theoretical opponent) of the mistake that divides intention from meaning. We'll come back to that argument in a minute. The second argument follows from their insistence that there is no difference between language and speech. They reject the Saussurian idea that language, or *langue*, is virtually present as a database in our heads that produces speech, *parole*, that which is uttered from sentence to sentence. Each of these arguments claims that "theory" enables itself by positing or presupposing a difference between some prior state of things in the mind and the moment of putting that state of things into action, whereas properly speaking there is always only the moment of being in action.

Before I consider these arguments more closely, I should pause over the authors' sense of what theory is and is not. In their first paragraph, Knapp and Michaels interestingly exempt certain quasi-scientific ways of thinking about literature from their general indictment of theory:

> The term ["theory"] is sometimes applied to literary subjects with no direct bearing on the interpretation of individual works, such as narratology, stylistics, and prosody. Despite their generality, however, these subjects seem to us essentially empirical, and our arguments against theory will not apply to them.

This is a little surprising because for one thing, in this course, which is presumably devoted to theory, we've talked about some of these things: narratology; stylistics, which is the science of style and how one can approach it syntactically and statistically; and prosody, an aspect of poetics that works though data to form general ideas about how poems are put together. All of these permissible activities must remind us of the Russian formalists. Narratology, as we studied it, is largely derived from structuralism, indeed also from certain ideas of Freud, and that pedigree makes it sound suspiciously like theory. For Knapp and Michaels, though, those ways of thinking about literature that they exempt from their challenge to theory are what they call "empirical." Without lingering over the distinction between good observational and bad speculative pursuits that seems to govern their exemption of "poetics" for nontheory—a distinction that should be hard for an anti-foundationalist to make (what counts as a fact?)—it may be useful to remark in passing that a better word for what Knapp and Michaels call "theory" is surely "hermeneutics." They are "against hermeneutics," the search for rationales for interpretation.

So: intention and meaning just must be the same thing, and then, too, language and speech just must be the same thing. As we begin to think about these claims, I'd like you to keep in mind the sentence "I can know the meaning of a word, but can I know the intention of a word?" by Stanley Cavell, from his response to this essay in the book, *Against Theory*. That's an invigorating challenge, and we'll be reflecting on some of its implications in the long run.

I'm going to be going a long way down the road in agreement with Knapp and Michaels in what I say now, indeed almost all the way, but I intend to take a sharp turn toward the end of the road that, I hope, saves theory and makes it necessary after all. It's my duty. I can hardly after twenty-six lectures finally confess that the thing we have been talking about should be banished from our vocabulary. So I'll try to slay the dragon, but you're going to have to wait a while because, as I say, it's a very smart dragon with many virtues.

Knapp and Michaels say that before we start troubling our heads with theory, we just take it for granted that any utterance has an intention, and rightly so. Whenever we encounter sounds or marks that we suppose to be language, we accord it an intention simply in so doing; *language is by definition intentional*, they say. Sounds and marks of which we can infer no author, therefore, we deny the status of language because we don't think they are intended.

Knapp and Michaels give us a now-famous example in which this assumption is tested, and make us realize what's at stake in supposing that we know the meaning of something. Ordinarily, we just spontaneously say, "I know what that means," or at least, "It must mean something even though I don't know what it means." That's our normal approach to a piece of language when we believe it to be language. Suppose, then, we're walking on the beach and come across four lines—"lines" is already a dangerous thing to say—that is, then, four rows of marks in the sand, that look an awful lot like the first stanza of Wordsworth's "A Slumber Did My Spirit Seal":

A slumber did my spirit seal;
I had no human fears.
She seem'd a thing that could not feel
The touch of earthly years.

We are not perplexed because we assume some Wordsworth lover has come along and scratched these lines in the sand. There they are, an intended quotation of an intended utterance. It's very hard to know what the utterance means (some of the best critics of modern times have broken their heads against it), but because it's intended, it must mean something. Then a wave washes ashore and leaves what looks like the second stanza on the beach, right underneath the first one, and that naturally throws us for a loop:

> No motion has she now, no force;
> She neither hears nor sees;
> Roll'd round in earth's diurnal course,
> With rocks, and stones, and trees.

Maybe, as Knapp and Michaels help us to speculate, the sea is a kind of pantheistic being that likes to write poetry, in which case the sea intended the stanza. Maybe there are tiny men in a tiny submarine who are conducting an experiment. At a stretch, we can still infer authors for the stanza, then, but it's much more likely that we'll just say it's an amazing coincidence, truly amazing, but just a coincidence. What else could it be?

The point of the exercise is to make us realize that wherever we suppose marks to be writing, we already suppose an intention for the marks. If nobody wrote the marks on the beach that look like words, if no entity or being from God on down wrote them, then the marks are not language but only *like* language, coincidentally so. And even though they look like language, we suddenly realize that it would be foolish to think they have meaning. There is a poem that exactly resembles this bunch of marks that we see in front of us, and that poem has meaning, but this bunch of marks does not have meaning.

Now I think probably most of us would resist the idea that we can't interpret the bunch of marks. We can agree that intention just is meaning, but we want to say that if something *looks* as though it were intended, then nothing prevents us from accordingly interpreting the meaning it looks as though it had. Perhaps a clearer example of the difference between something intended and something merely existent, the former being language and the latter not, could have been found.

For example, some years ago the *New Haven Register* published a picture of two ladies in Milford, near here, gazing in rapture at a scar on a tree trunk that looked like the head of Jesus. Not just these ladies but hundreds of people visited the site. Now of course they believed the scar looked that way because God intended it to be a sign. For them, the meaning was clear. The same thing has happened with toasted cheese sandwiches, as they knew.

But many of weaker faith would say that God didn't make the scar look like that, it was just an accident, and in that case no one would say it is the face of Jesus or a face of any kind, only that it looks like a face. There would be no temptation to interpret the scar, and this is why it seems to me a better example than the accidental simulacrum of Wordsworth's poem, which would still cry out to be read. Granted that in doing so we are positing some mysterious authorship, but notice that we have no such flexibility with the scar. We can't say that "nature" made the marks a face, for example, because we know that only the Christian God acting through nature or by fiat (hence neither wind nor cell growth nor tiny men in lab coats understood as agents) would make a likeness of Jesus.

In short, however you feel about "A Slumber Did My Spirit Seal," in the case of the scar that looks like Jesus you would readily accept Knapp and Michaels's argument. You would say in confirmation of their view that it really does depend on the inference of an intention. No intention, no meaning, but if an intention can be inferred, that intention just is the meaning. I think this an unshakable argument concerning any and all utterances—at least, for reasons that will appear, insofar as we can call them *speech acts*, which we shall do insofar as we can. Perhaps in order to see that intention just is meaning you need only think about it etymologically. When I say "I mean," I mean "I intend you to understand that such and such." It doesn't quite work that way in all languages (in German you have *Ich meine*, I intend, but *das heißt* or *das bedeutet*—*that* means, not I mean), but it does work that way in ours, and it may help us realize that it's against the grain of common sense to factor the words apart.

You may be wrong about a meaning or intention, you probably are wrong, in fact, but that has nothing to do with the question of whether there is a difference between the meaning and the intention in question. If a sentence weren't a sentence spoken intentionally by an agent, human or otherwise, it wouldn't have meaning because it wouldn't be what Knapp and Michaels call "language." This actually carries us into the second proposition of the essay. For an utterance to be understood as language at all, to repeat myself once again, an intention needs to be supposed. Conversely, we ought to be able to recognize, supposing we fail to infer an intention, that what we are looking at is not language but just a simulacrum of language, an effective copy of language like the words produced by monkeys on typewriters.

It makes no sense, Knapp and Michaels would say, to speak of sounds or marks that are not *signs* as language. For C. S. Peirce, who discriminated among hundreds of different kinds of signs, all signs are *active*—that is to say, they have an agency and a purpose, a practical function. Peirce would agree with Saussure that signs are differential, but for him the important point to make about a sign is that it is gestural, it carries out a purpose. And this is the characteristic of a sign in language, not just in speech. The sign in language is already active, fraught with its purpose. Hence, Knapp and Michaels say, there is no difference between language and speech.

This claim should be very hard to accept for anyone who has absorbed from Saussure the idea that language is a synchronic entity in virtual space and speech is a diachronic performance *of* language in actual time. But let us make sure we understand how Knapp and Michaels' claim can be a plausible one. I think they make their best case in a footnote, which, like so many footnotes, may be the most telling moment in the essay: "[A] dictionary is an index of frequent usages in particular speech acts—not a matrix of abstract, pre-intentional possibilities." Think about that. Language, we have supposed until now, in addition to being a set of grammatical and syntactical rules, is also a set of definitions made available for speech acts. Knapp and Michaels deny this premise in their footnote. They're claiming that dictionary definitions are just the sum total, as it were, of *words in action*, hence that any entry defines a word that is *already* a speech act. The *Oxford English Dictionary* gives you multiple definitions of a word, all embedded in sentences, speech acts that can be taken out of sentences and still understood in their agency as performed. Definitions, in this view, are made available *by* speech acts as well as for them. Any word in a dictionary is a fossilized record of the way the word works and has worked in speech acts throughout history. A dictionary is a sum total of speech acts. To distinguish, therefore, between language as something that exists apart from agency and speech as the translation of language into action is a mistake. Language, even in the sense that it's always there before we are, is nevertheless a record of verbal actions that have taken place before our own. A dictionary is just as much a compendium of *intended* speech acts as a compendium of historical speeches would be. "Theory," therefore, should no more seek out a prior verbal medium in which to ground speech than it should seek out an intention to justify a meaning.

We do need to go a long way down the road with this challenge to our thinking, longer than expected, to be sure. It should be said in defense of Saussure, though, that in a way he anticipates this position. (I have not yet begun my rescue of theory; this is just a remark in passing.) Remember I told you that in order to understand structuralism and its aftermath, we need only distinguish between language and speech, *langue* and *parole*, but that in Saussure there's actually a third, intermediate, category that he calls *langage*. That is the sum total of all known speech acts. *Langage* is "empirical," as Knapp and Michaels would say, and not unlike what they mean by *language*. But for Saussure, *langue*, as opposed to *langage*, remains a code, not a gestural archive.

The neo-pragmatist view of language is persuasive for us because Bakhtin and many of our other recent readings have convinced us that language is social, that all of its deployments are interactive, derived from the speech acts of others, appropriated for oneself as one's own set of speech acts, and influential on yet other people as a speech act. If all this is the case, it would just seem to go without saying that language *exists for communication*. Perhaps even after all we've been through it has never occurred to you to think otherwise. Why would you? After all, communication is what we do with language. And if it's true that that's what language is "for," then it makes sense to see it endowed with the agency that speech appropriates. But here is where I'm going to save theory, so sharpen your pencils!

Notice that I said it *would seem* to go without saying that language exists for communication. But what else could it exist for? It won't help much to say that we like to make doodles, or meaningless marks in the sand. Most of us don't, and that's what makes the painting of Cy Twombly, who does like to make meaningless marks that look vaguely inscriptive, so interesting. Most of us like to make marks that communicate. We inhabit a life world in which it is almost inconceivable for anyone to assert that language is not meant for communication. We have refined language to a fare-thee-well as an efficient, flexible, sometimes even eloquent medium of communication.

Yet if I am going to save theory, I need to show that this apparently self-evident premise is wrong. Suppose we approach the subject from a standpoint that I shall call speculative anthropology. Most discussions of "the state of nature"—in Hobbes or Rousseau or Marx on "primitive communism"—are speculative anthropology, conjectures about prehistory, and I shall now take my turn. Let us try to take the art of the down-to-earth remark and turn it in our favor. The purpose of language, then, so they say, is for communicating. Isn't that like saying that the purpose of fire is for cooking? Or, if you object that fire is external to the human organism but language isn't: isn't that like saying that the purpose of the prehensile thumb is for grasping? But, external or internal, I'm not sure it matters even if we could safely make such a distinction. A hole in a rock face is not a cave, not *meant for dwelling*, until we adopt it for that purpose. Stumbling on a purpose is what makes fire a good thing to cook with, the prehensile thumb a good thing to grasp with, and a hole in a rock a good thing to take shelter in, but all of them, in their various ways, are just there, and not just there for us to do with them the useful thing we have discovered. A purpose is what we impose on something that is there already.

Language appeared among us the same way that the prehensile thumb did, as an evolutionary mutation. We "discovered its use," though granted, that's an imperfect way to put it. It might be more circumspect to say that we discovered it had a use for us, which was to communicate, and so once we were able to put this strange capacity to make differential sounds to work, henceforth for us and for our purposes language was there to communicate. Of course, we made an enormous success of it, or a tower of Babel of it, whichever you prefer to think, but in any case we have it, and it has developed among us as a medium of communication.

Suppose that the day after the capacity to deploy varied sounds appeared as a mutation, there was an avalanche or earthquake or tsunami that rendered the possessor of the mutation extinct. In aftertimes there might then have been people communicating, perhaps with incredible eloquence, perhaps even with literary genius, by means of hand gestures or other sign systems that surpass conjecture. Or for that matter, Homo sapiens might have taken a detour in its development such that communication was not anything one could identify as specifically human. All sentient beings communicate in a certain sense, using semiotic systems that are for the most part only metaphorically language, but it's possible that our particular species could have taken a turn in its development after which, no matter what other extraordinary powers we developed, communication remained much as it is among mice or ants.

All of this is possible, you see, when we think about language—an attribute that we use for communication—anthropologically. It exists in such a way that it is, I would think, scarcely relevant to say that its purpose is for communication. It is simply a phenomenon, like feathers, that turns out to be useful for something, unlike mutations for which no use is found.

Notice something about the signs of language to which we give credence if we follow Saussure. Saussure lays every stress on the idea that language is made up of differential and arbitrary signs. He denies that there is such a thing in language as a natural sign. Both Saussure and the Russian formalists—who began their research, you will recall, by discovering aspects of literary language that *do not communicate*—warn us against believing that onomatopoetic devices—for example, "peep, peep, peep"—are actually natural signs derived from sounds or attributes of things or feelings in the world. Saussure argues that onomatopoetic signs are accidents of etymological history. There's a fairly high incidence of onomatopoeia in language because it facilitates communication and it's fun to communicate with, but it doesn't enter language as a natural sign. It only passes through moments, in the evolution of a given word, when the relationship between sound and referent seems to be natural. Bow-wow and *wauwau* are both onomatopoetic in speech, but in the languages to which they respectively belong their differential relations with other signs is what conditions their exact contours and usage.

This is a matter upon which great stress is laid both in Saussure and in the Russian formalists. When you read the passages in which they belabor this seemingly trivial point, you may have wondered why they do so. You can see, though, that a properly semiotic understanding of onomatopoeia is important to them because it anchors their core belief about language—now being attacked by Knapp and Michaels—which is precisely that language is not speech. When we speak, we not only try to communicate; we try to *refer*. In other words, we try to make language correspond to the natural world. We take a system of signs, a code that is not in itself natural but arbitrary, and try to make the signs of language seem natural. In doing so, we reinforce the idea that language exists for communication. But I would say that language isn't for communication; *speech is*.

But this too is a point that needs to be qualified in a way that's crucial for the recovery of theory. We don't always speak, or write, solely to communicate, as the Russian formalists demonstrated. There are peculiar patterns and relations that surface in our speech—unnecessary or uneconomical forms of repetition, for example—that don't seem to further communication. As a matter of fact, they actually seem to impede it. When I really start mixing things up on the axis of combination—for example, in Lewis Carroll's "'Twas brillig, and the slithy toves / did gyre and gimble in the wabe"— I am laying stress on elements of rhythm, pattern, and sound recurrence that cannot be said to have any direct bearing on communication and that thwart understanding.

These are all empirical facts about language as it peeps through speech, hence cannot be dismissed by Knapp and Michaels as mere theory. What we have learned to recognize recurrently is the way language makes itself heard in speech. Those elements of gratuitous nonsense that bubble up to the surface are language's assertion of its evolutionary origin and its refusal to be enslaved altogether by the purpose that Homo sapiens found for it, communication. Similarly in Freud, the Freudian slip—the fact that one can't get through a sentence without making some kind of blunder, often an embarrassing blunder—is the bubbling up of that which the conscious effort to speak intelligibly can't control.

By the same token, we recognize language to be something *else*, something not subject to the control of consciousness, from the empirical study of speech acts in those moments when no dictionary definition could reflect conformance with active usage. We infer language from the erratic behavior of speech. That sense of language, which I'm going to be talking a lot more about in my concluding remarks, is what suggests to me that Knapp and Michaels mislead us in saying that there is really no difference between language and speech. If there *is* a difference between language and speech, as I am claiming, and if this difference is much as we have been taught to think of it by Saussure and his successors down through deconstruction, we have succeeded in rescuing literary theory, and we have incidentally found a way of describing what it is good for, pragmatically speaking: *literary theory is the study of language in speech.*

A pragmatist might respond, though, that even if the point is granted, this is at most a Pyrrhic victory for theory. We're pragmatists, after all, we want to promote human agency and underline those aspects of speech, and of the interpretive process, whereby communication is effected and meaning is arrived at. I would seem to have saved theory at a pretty considerable cost if all I can think to do with it is point out the lapses in economy of expression that preoccupied the Russian formalists in 1914. Even they quickly got beyond that, didn't they? Well, in the next and last lecture I'll try to show that they did not, that their approach expanded to cover every device that could ever be considered literary, including reference itself—and that the tradition they started still has much to achieve.

One last point for now, which takes us back to the distinction between meaning and intention that Knapp and Michaels deny. They argue that two opposed literary camps are hoisted by the same petard. On the one hand, there are people like E. D. Hirsch, who believe that you can invoke an author's intention in order to pin down a meaning. On the other, there are people in the deconstructive camp who say that *because* there is no inferable intention, texts themselves have no meaning. But that's not what deconstruction says. It is not at all the point that texts have no meaning, nor even finally that one can't be sure what the meaning is. What deconstruction says is that you can't *rope off* meaning in a text. Texts have too much meaning; they explode with excess of meaning. You can't corral the way texts produce meaning by inferring an intention, because even an intention correctly ascertained—were that possible—would never account for the eruption of language in and through speech. So the position we have taken in rescuing theory from the claim that there is no difference between language and speech is a position that likewise responds to the claim that there is no difference between intention and speech. Language isn't intended at all. As Cavell says, again, I can know the meaning of a word, but can I know the intention of a word?

The language-speech issue is not really the flip side—as Knapp and Michaels want you to think—of the idea that in order to know a meaning, you have to be able to infer an authorial intention. There is relatively little symmetry between their two collapsed distinctions. It's just not clear that deconstruction, whatever its claims, whatever its perfections and imperfections, has the question of intention in relation to meaning very much at heart one way or another. Speech is intended, as Knapp and Michaels say; it is not speech if it is not intended. But language compromises the intention of speech to the point where intention can play no decisive hermeneutic role in the tracing out of semantic excess. In concluding these lectures, as I've said, I'll try to exhibit the range of coverage that this viewpoint makes available for theory.

CHAPTER 26

Conclusion

Who Doesn't Hate Theory Now?

In the last lecture, we offered theory a reprieve from its banishment by Knapp and Michaels, and we did so by saying that there really is a difference between language and speech. That's a claim that I want to continue investigating in today's concluding lecture. In the meantime, when I keep saying we saved theory, you may well be asking why anybody would bother saving it. We began to wonder last time, especially in view of the neo-pragmatists' claims about the common agency of language and speech—understood on their view to be one and the same thing—whether we have to conclude that theory can't possibly have anything to do with practical objectives. That, too, is a concern that I want to revisit today. Why do we bother to save literary theory? Well, it has something to do, plainly, with discovering the limits of communication.

Speech, as we said last time, is unquestionably "for"—that is to say, we have made it for—communication. Hence the old and frankly shopworn question, "How *well* do we communicate with each other?" is unfortunately one that we in our turn need to ask. I want to say a word or two about what the French during the existentialist period called *la manque de la communication*. First of all, I want to insist that we actually communicate rather well. Congratulations to us! I think that many of the usual ways in which people worry about whether we can understand each other, especially the transculturally sensitive ways, are quite melodramatically exaggerated. My own feeling is that a good deal of the time we understand each other all too well, and that it might be better if we didn't sensitize ourselves to quite such an acute pitch about where each of us is "coming from." I take there to be a measure of bad faith in our efforts to raise each other's consciousness. The supposition is that we treat each other so badly because we don't understand each other's "subject positions" well enough. I'm not convinced of that. Speech is doing just fine, and shouldn't be blamed for our continued ill will. Speech has a rough and ready efficacy, and anybody who denies that, as I say, is more or less unwittingly deflecting attention away from problems that may stem from grounds other than difficulty of communication.

But if this is so, why, then, should *theory* come along and say to the contrary that there's a glitch in communication after all? The problem—denied by Knapp and Michaels as we have seen—is this nagging entity called *language*, which keeps poking up through the communication process, getting in its way, impeding communication, as the Russian formalists suggested, and a good thing, too, from their point of view. Indeed, the slight buzz of language that you can hear in everyday speech isn't so bad, really; we still do communicate pretty well, as I say, so why should theory suppose it can rest its case on this trivial-seeming point of contention with those people who say that language just *is* speech and not something different from it at all?

Part of the function of theory is to gauge the degree to which speech communicates in an unimpeded way, to gauge the level of accuracy and detail at which it can be expected still to communicate effectively. If you still don't consider this matter earth-shatteringly important, I don't blame you; but I do hope to have convinced you by the end of this lecture that it's surprisingly important after all.

In the meantime, we need to remember what theory isn't. We began the semester by distinguishing between theory and philosophy, theory and methodology, even between theory and hermeneutics, and we did so because the whole purpose of philosophy, methodology, and hermeneutics, in contrast with that of theory, is to discover meaning. Theory is more interested in the way meaning is impeded. Certainly, though, even though you're good at theory and you understand the purpose of theory, you can still do these other things. You can be a system builder, explaining the totality of things as a philosopher. Likewise, as Knapp and Michaels say, you can still work empirically with literary data, organized to result in what we call "poetics," a methodology. And finally you can enter the hermeneutic circle and search for meaning; indeed, that is the first thing you do in confronting a text or utterance, and any reflection that succeeds upon this first engagement, including theory, reconsiders the conditions of the interpretive effort. You can do all these things, and you don't have to feel as though theory were standing on the sidelines shaking its fist or wagging its finger at you. Theory doesn't have to be feared as a watchdog. At least in my opinion, and not everyone agrees with me, theory really lets us go our own way and simply reminds us that there are limits or reservations that it's best to keep in mind while thinking through problems of interpretation and meaning.

So theory I would define, and have defined, as a negative movement of thought mapping the legitimate ways—as opposed to the anguished, hand-wringing ways—to be suspicious of communication. Theory is an antithetical counterforce to that which is commonly supposed to be true, posited as true, and—here of course one comes to the point—*spoken* as true: enounced, articulated, spoken as true. If that's the case, why the fuss about language specifically? Why do we so quickly narrow our focus down to language? What I said last time about the relationship between language and speech may have seemed unconvincing to you because it was so narrow. I want now to broaden considerably the sense of what I mean by "language." Theory, I believe, encourages a measure of suspicion about the efficacy of speech, of that which is spoken in keeping with an intention, in three ways.

Last time I mentioned one of these, but now I shall describe three. The first, which I did mention last time, is the way language obtrudes itself on the referential function of speech as *sound*. That is, if we think of speech as a medium of communication, we're forced to ask ourselves, even as we engage in speech, how and why it is that speech is so much burdened, in ways that are of no use whatsoever to us for the most part, by acoustic noise. Sometimes, to be sure, patterns of sound seem to help communication along. You might ask whether sound isn't a reinforcement of meaning. I told you back when we covered the New Criticism that all of you had already done the New Criticism in high school. That's the way you learned literary interpretation. What the New Critic looks for, and certainly finds, is the reinforcement of sense by sound. That's what it says in handbooks about understanding poetry, and Pope said it first in his *Essay on Criticism*. There are plenty of occasions on which we can revel in the complexity of an intentional meaning or intentional structure that is augmented by the way sound patterns are used. The wounded snake in Pope drags its slow length along, swift Camilla scours the plain, and their respective cumbersome and turbo-charged sounds delight us.

At the same time, as the Russian formalists discovered when working with alliterative verse, folklore, and folk verse in the Russian tradition, verse embodying proverbs, there is simply no way of grasping a semantic purpose in the sound elements that are involved. There is a strange pull in our spontaneous utterances toward repetitiousness of sound—it's not *just* that we all for the most part speak in iambics and alliterate without knowing it. Jakobson reminds us in "Linguistics and Poetics" about that moment when a violent event takes place nearby and we identify ourselves as an "innocent bystander." We could have said "witness," not "bystander," but the double dactyl determined our choice. A person is an innocent bystander not because that expression has any particular meaning or semantic valence but because it's catchy. Such functions of sound, which could be called overdetermined appearances of sound in speech, are what an economist might call irrational. They're there, they're doing a job, but it's hard to call it communication.

So much, then, for sound, but it's not only a matter of sound. If it were only that, if literary theory were only about the first two or three years' worth of research performed by the Russian formalists, we probably wouldn't be offering an introductory survey course in the subject. Speech is impeded by language in two other ways. It is disturbed to begin with by the way language produces in what's being said an uncontrollable *semantic* drift that wanders away from the semantic drift of speech. Language seems to have a meaning of its own. It was Saussure who devoted years of research to finding anagrams embedded in Latin and other Indo-European verse. He wanted to build a general theory of poetry out of these discoveries. There was meaning within meaning that couldn't possibly have been planted there and yet, strangely enough, one could find it there. Try reciting a well-known poem— the one that we took up in the last lecture because it was the example given in Knapp and Michaels's "Against Theory"—while reading this:

> Ah slum per dead, um, I spear'd seal. Eye add, know Hume, 'n fierce! Shah seam (duh!) thin; the tic oud-knot fee ill: thud! Uh shover the lee ears. No mo'! Shun hash e'en ow, no fours, shhh! knee th'rears, Norse ease. Role drown, an' hurts, die, urn: all corpse, whither oxen?—sst!-onus entries.

And this is what you will have recited:

> A slumber did my spirit seal;
> I had no human fears:

She seem'd a thing that could not feel
The touch of earthly years.

No motion has she now, no force;
She neither hears nor sees;
Roll'd 'round in earth's diurnal course
With rocks, and stones, and trees.

You can see that to write the "poem" the first way is to perform an exercise that is essentially what Joyce is doing in *Finnegans Wake*. As a matter of fact, as I composed the poem this way, I kept saying to myself that it could be in *Finnegans Wake*. I was quite pleased with myself, as you can imagine. Notice that I have used *only real words*. There's nothing in the transcript that is not a word. I have indulged in some anachronism and used a foreign word or two, but I have also used punctuation to help this discourse make some degree of sense, a certain amount of it concerning death and overlapping uncannily with the sense of Wordsworth's poem. I could have just left it at nonsense—like Lewis Carroll's " 'Twas brillig, and the slithy toves / did gyre and gimble in the wabe"—which is the more obvious way that speech is affected by uncontrollable semantic drift. The amusing point of Lewis Carroll's famous nonsense verse is that we all think we know what it means: " 'Twas blusterous and the slimy toads did leap and frolic in the waves." We think it means something like that, but semantic drift—which is what Lewis Carroll deliberately introduces to overwhelm the plain sense we imagine to be present—prevents us from drawing any secure conclusions about the meaning.

I hope my quasi-nonsensical transcription of Wordsworth's "A Slumber Did My Spirit Seal" can show us the extent to which there *is* semantic drift in speech. Let's say that you are a person far removed from the interpretive community to which all the rest of us belong, as Stanley Fish would put it, and you don't even know what a poem is, let alone that this poem by Wordsworth can be identified instantly by most students of literature. Somebody recites in your presence what I just quoted to you. If you were good at writing and transcribed the thing, you might very well produce something like what I put on the board. In other words, it wouldn't just spontaneously occur to you that what Wordsworth actually wrote was what you were hearing. This kind of semantic drift is present in any utterance.

Utterances are not often mistaken in this way because we're really very good at understanding context. That's one of the reasons why the so-called problem of communication isn't as great as people sometimes claim it is. Hence we're not likely to go badly wrong, yet certainly there are occasions when we do. A speechwriter for Lyndon Johnson wrote the word "misled" in a speech for him, and when Johnson read the speech he pounded his fist on the podium and said "We will not be myzled." I should hope not. As we all know, that's the trouble with spell-check. You put it on, you write your term paper and don't bother to edit it, you turn the paper in. It's full of howlers because, of course, the language is full of homonyms, and spell-check always uncannily gives you the wrong word. You're in the soup, frankly, because your teacher is laughing at your blunders instead of paying attention to your important thoughts. In short, don't use spell-check, just remember that spell-check can show us how much the semantic drift of language permeates speech.

There's yet a third way in which language impedes speech. Remember I have said that language, *langue*, is a *virtual* entity because we could never actually encounter it written down in any codified form. Yes, we have the lexicon in a dictionary, but that's only part of it. So far, notice that we've only been talking about the lexicon when we talk about semantic drift; but in addition to the lexicon, language, *langue*, is a set of rules—the rules of grammar and syntax by means of which, and only by means of which, speech can make sense. Thus in addition to offering sound and word choice, language has a grammatical and syntactical bearing on the choices that we can make while producing speech.

Unfortunately those rules can be slippery. When we talked about the innocuous expression "It is raining" as an illustration of Jakobson's six sets to the message, just for example, we were brought up short by the metalingual function of "It is raining." We asked ourselves, "What on earth is 'it'?" It can lead us in strange directions, this "it": Jupiter Pluvius, God, the cosmos, the clouds. Some of it is plausible, but none of it is definite. We realize that "it" is a placeholder in the sentence that is not doing its job and, believe me, this oddity is not confined to English. As I said before, you can find in other languages: *il pleut, es regnet,* and so on. In all of those expressions, "it" is not doing its job. We start to realize that if we lean too hard even on an innocuous utterance, we're in the presence of what the economists, again, would call irrationality, despite our continuous effort to make sense.

What really conditions the way drift governs any utterance, however, is the way predication works in language. As I said before, any assertion, any declaration of a truth, is at the same time a metaphor. The deep structure of any assertion proclaims that A is B; that is, it is an assertion by definition.

But when "A is B" is the connection of subject and predicate that grammarians call a copula, we understand that the relationship between A and B is not a relationship of identity, a metaphorical declaration that A is B, but rather a connection that de Man, for example, would call metonymic. The problem is that any sentence declaring that A is B metonymically—that is to say, as a grammatical proposition—is at the same time a metaphor. No metaphor stands on all fours but always has an element of what's called catachresis in it. Juliet is not really the sun. Grammar disclaims identity but adheres to a logic; metaphor (or what de Man calls "rhetoric") asserts an identity but defies logic. Every sentence, then, that turns on the hinge of "to be" (and they all do) makes both of these irreconcilable claims at once.

This is the point that de Man is making in "Semiology and Rhetoric": there is a perpetual tension in any utterance between grammar and rhetoric. There's no competent utterance that's not grammatical, there's no utterance of any kind that's not rhetorical, but unfortunately grammar and rhetoric are always openly or subtly at odds with each other, just in the way that predication and metaphor have to be at odds with each other. In other words, there isn't a sentence in which the rules of grammar and syntax are not subtly interfering with what you might call the rules of rhetoric—the ways in which tropes deploy themselves, ways that can be distilled in an understanding of what we call metaphor.

So every sentence, as I say, is shadowed not just by the vagaries of sound, not just by the semantic drift of words and word-echoes, but also by the incompatibility of grammar and rhetoric. All of these warping influences on speech are part of what Saussure and his tradition call language. They are the ways, in other words, in which language—if I can put it this way—speaks through speech, the ways in which anything that we say on any occasion is shadowed by another voice. We've understood this in social terms as Bakhtinian polyglossia. We have understood it in psychoanalytic terms as the discourse of the otherness that inhabits the unconscious. We have understood it in purely linguistic terms as *langue*, but we can also, I think, metaphorically speaking, understand it now as a prior speech that haunts the agency of our intentional speech. *Language is an unintentional speech.*

Keep in mind: nobody—no theorist, nobody in her right mind—would ever try to resist the claim that speech is intentional, that we intend what we say. That's where Knapp and Michaels are right and give us a bracing reminder about the degree to which skepticism about intention is misplaced. The idea that speech is somehow not intended: what could that mean? Speech just *is* intention, but I've been trying to argue that there is a speech, the "speech of language," which is unintentional, which is just there. It can't be factored out. It can be ignored, perhaps, when we focus on the successes of communication, but it can't be set aside as though it were not there. It will always come back. It will always confront us at some point if we take the arts of interpretation seriously enough—if, in other words, we really do bring some pressure to bear on the things that people say: a pressure that goes beyond the pragmatic and enables us to notice the amazing variability that belongs to any utterance on any occasion.

Language speaks through speech partly as its origin. It is as though it were asserting its identity as what it was back before we discovered it was useful for something. Remember what we said about that last time: you have to discover that fire is useful for cooking. Fire is not "for" cooking. A cave is not for dwelling. A prehensile thumb is not for grasping. You have to channel these phenomena for human uses. Language is there in what we say as if to remind us that it wasn't always at our service, to remind us that the history of conscious expression is our never-ending effort to *master* language. It's the professional writer who feels this most acutely. You try to wrestle language into submission. But it's really the ambition of all of us, whether we're writing the great American novel or revising a term paper. We're wrestling language into submission, and we all know it's not easy. I'm just trying to explain why it's not easy.

Language speaks through us, then, as the origin of speech, but it also speaks as the death of speech. It speaks, in other words, as the moment in which the purposeful agency of speech is finally called into question, in a certain sense undermined. I think it's appropriate, I think it's fair, to call language—again metaphorically—the epitaph of speech, the moment at which, in any given speech, the end of its own agency is inscribed even as that agency is asserting itself.

I want to test these assertions by example and also show you a bit more about how semantic drift functions—and also how the perilous relationship between grammar and rhetoric works. Let's look at a couple of epitaphs. If language is the epitaph of speech, why not see what happens in epitaphs?

My favorite epitaph by far will I hope give you a chuckle, too, when you come across it walking through a cemetery. On the tombstone you find written, "I told you I was sick." Now this is a very interesting expression for a number of reasons. For one thing, and one should pause over this, one *can* infer from this complaint a number of speakers who are speaking effectively and communicating a clear message, not just one but many. There's plenty of precedent for posthumous speech in Emily Dickinson and other writers, and of course here the most obvious speaker is the dead person speaking from the grave: "There I was, sitting in the corner all those years telling you I had a headache. You never listened to me."

But the speaker could be somebody else, and I'm *not* introducing a measure of skepticism about intention in saying this. When we posit an intention, we just decide which of several candidates to speak may be speaking, adhering quite properly without question to the supposition that we are in the presence of intentional speech. The speaker could be an apologetic relative, someone acknowledging that they hadn't listened, but with a sense of humor, hence putting in the voice of the dead person the complaint, "I told you I was sick," as a form of apology: "Yes, I know you did, and I could kick myself for it, but I had other things on my mind."

Yet again, the speaker could be someone moralizing over the grave, a frequent habit in eighteenth-century epitaphs. It could be a philosopher saying, "Sickness is the human condition, as I kept telling you. I published many volumes, the whole purport of which was 'I am sick.' I'm Dostoevsky's Underground Man. I am a sick man, a very sick man. Well, let it get worse." Or yet again, the speaker could be a cultural critic, inscribing on the stone, in an allegorical mood, the death of culture. Civilization has been in a bad way for a long time and here, finally, it lies. The way to communicate this colloquially would then be, "I, civilization, told you I was sick. I had many ways of letting you know that all was not well with me: you didn't pay any attention, and here is the result."

I would say that all these ways of reading the epitaph are available to hermeneutics. They are consistent with the effort we make to understand what a speaker means. But suppose we say that "language" must be obtruding itself in this utterance, as in any other. You can see that it isn't here a question of sound. It isn't even a question of semantic drift, although "aye tolled yew eye was seek," if you recite the epitaph to a sight-impaired person standing next to you, might give pause, as might the lurking existential metaphor, "I was sickness," or the recent teenage expression of intense self-admiration, "I was sick." Language makes itself felt in yet another way. It makes us suddenly understand the sentence in a way that perhaps no individual speaker would wish for. It then becomes an allegory, cleverly introduced by *language*, precisely about the inefficacy of speech. That's just the problem with speech, isn't it? "Again and again and again I tell you something," speech says under the spell of language, "and you don't listen." It's because language weakens my speech. That's the problem with being a lecturer.

"You didn't listen," says language's epitaph in my speech. "Oh, well," you say, "his language is just joking."

So it is—according to the allegory introduced by language at the expense of speech, signifyin' on speech—with speech in general. This person sitting in the corner, complaining bitterly about nobody ever listening to her or to him, is actually an allegorist telling us that that's the way speech always is. Thus when I say language is the epitaph of speech, we realize that it is speech itself that's lying here. Having lied in spite of every effort to speak true, here lies speech.

So let's try another one: "Here lies John Doe," probably the *Ur*-epitaph. Let's not even pause over the speaker this time. Let's turn immediately to the problems posed by language. In the first place, John Doe obviously does not lie precisely "here." In fact, if you think about it, it's altogether possible that John Doe could lie absolutely anywhere except "here," because where the sentence is we know John Doe cannot be. He could be anyplace else, as I say. Hence any epitaph is therefore a self-declared cenotaph, an inscription on a place where the body isn't—which of course tells us a lot, too, about the arbitrary nature of language. Language is not comprised of natural signs that attach themselves to the real world. In the case of the body, tattoos are outer-directed speech, what Jakobson would call emotive-conative utterances, not inscriptions, or referential utterances, even if they were to say "my skin is here." Speech is on things, on the outer edge of things, on a piece of rock, for example, but the lie it tells, obedient to language, is even then the dislocation of its referent.

So "here lies John Doe"—except not here, anyplace but here. Hence the interest of the ubiquitous epitaphic word "lies," which we have already noticed. The utterance is a lie, both because John Doe does not lie here but nearby and also because it's not poor John Doe who tells a lie, as the epitaph claims, accusing the deceased. It's language that's making speech lie, and it's doing so on any number of levels, as we've seen. It's a funny thing about epitaphs, something that has been noted by various authors writing in the tradition of what we loosely call "deconstruction": the epitaph is a particularly fruitful locus for the study of the ways language challenges, undermines, and displaces speech.

So speech lies because it can never stop being warped by language, hence we can never possibly mean exactly what we say. We can mean what we say, but we can't mean exactly what we say. That's probably the most commonsensical way of putting the matter. When Stanley Cavell poses the question in the title of one of his books, *Must We Mean What We Say?*, he is actually offering us the possibility that maybe meaning what we say, whether we can do it or not, is not the be-all and end-all of speaking. There is, just for example, what Jakobson calls the "set to the contact" or phatic function. Do I mean, or must I mean, as Cavell puts it, "one two three" when I tap the microphone and say "testing one two three"?

Now you ask—you really should ask, because after all it's been our constant guide—whether language speaks through speech in *Tony the Tow Truck*. Certainly it does. I spoke a while back about the column on the vertical axis of the page that begins each sentence with the vertical "I." As you read the text, there it is, a gift to Lacanian feminism: the phallogocenter pompously getting longer, *I*. Yet *I* is never the first word spoken by an infant. That's another lesson of Lacan. *I* is what you have to learn how to *be*—to put it in Judith Butler's terms—so that *I*, insofar as it is this incredible upright pillar starting one sentence after another in *Tony the Tow Truck*, is the *promise* of autonomy to the toddler: the promise of the glorious kind of identity that stands upright, a successful simulacrum of what is seen in the mirror, and which then develops into what Freud called, referring to the way infants begin to get their way in the world, "his majesty the ego."

But as I've said, this a socializing story about friendship, and the *I* eventually stops coming first. This too, I think, can be communicated as relevant to the toddler in ways that are linguistic yet can't really be called speech. For example, the friendship exists between Bumpy (pronounced BUM-py) and Tony (pronounced TO-ny), in and through the sound of *uh-oh*: long before the baby says "I," it says "uh-oh," and that "uh-oh" echoes in the friendship of Bumpy and Tony. Why "uh-oh?" Because Tony is stuck and his natural response to being stuck would be, "Uh-oh." Along comes Bumpy and—having no doubt thought "uh-oh," too—not only does he recognize the problem, he takes care of it.

Now on the other hand, the problem of self, the problem that's caught up in this vertical *I*, comes into focus for the infant before the mirror as the awareness of otherness, that which is not me. That which is irreducible to the self begins to come into focus, and a way of expressing this is to say, "e-e-e-e," which is perhaps a mask or simulacrum of "he-he-he-he." I think it's for that reason that the two antagonists of the story, the unassimilable others who do not help, are called Speedy (pronounced SPEE-dee) and Neato (pronounced NEE-to). In other words, that sense of otherness— that which is intractable and cannot be reduced effectively to self—is I think articulated in "e-e-e-e." (Bum*pee* and To*nee* provide the third and fourth "e," but now unaccented, owing to the identification with the other enabled by friendship.) Thus what the toddler may hear spoken through the words of the story is not speech, it's language. If you want to hear language in speech, just listen to a baby. That's why nonsense verse has such appeal to young children. They're still hearing language, like the children on the shore in Wordsworth's "Intimations Ode" hearing the mighty waters rolling evermore. They're hearing the hum in the shell of their brains when the adult hears the efficacious sociality of speech.

The history of being human is a history of coming to terms with speech, mastering speech—or, I should say, perhaps, mastering language. So it is, too, in the individual. The individual who is hardwired for language must somehow wrestle that hardwiring into what we call speech. So the first thing we hear in an infant, and maybe what is most predominant in stories for toddlers and in nonsense verse, is language, which can't be reduced to any semantic quantum. Sure, I've just interpreted the language in *Tony* as though it had a kind of meaning, but it's a meaning that comes simply from the observation of feelings and noticing what children actually say on actual occasions, which can't really be called speech but is rather a kind of experimentation with language as it drags itself toward speech. It's not anything that one could confuse with speech, yet it is still partly, as in the mirror stage, an imitation of being adult. When the adult occasionally says, "Uh-oh," there's nothing like the investment in it that there is for the child, for whom it is very often a first articulate sound, repeated therefore with delight. It is the encounter with otherness and the attempt to master otherness, as in Freud's story of Little Hans playing his game of *fort / da*, that this "uh-oh" seems to be expressing.

So much then for *Tony.* I'd just like to confuse—I mean I'd like to conclude—with three theses. Take note, you have to speak very carefully or language obtrudes. I had to say "three theses" very carefully—and of course I had made a mistake just before that. I didn't want to say "confuse," did I? Notice, in fact, that "confuse" was not just any old word getting in the way of communication. It was *precisely* what I did not want to say because I was hoping as always, but especially in concluding, to avoid confusion. I could have said anything else, but I said "confuse." That was language overtaking speech with a psychoanalytic burden, a Freudian slip.

So here are my three theses about language, which I suppose are really only one thesis. First, *it never makes sense.* Language does not make sense. It's arbitrary. It is a system of arbitrary signs that are not natural signs. *You* make sense, not language. You make sense by having an intention and wrestling language into speech, commandeering language for your purposes. Language doesn't make sense; you make sense.

Language in itself, second, says nothing about reality because it is a self-enclosed system, a code, a system of arbitrary signs. I want to put this two different ways to show how our idioms confirm this thesis. You *come to terms*, as we say, with reality. That is to say, you approach reality with words; you come to it with language so that you can identify it in speech. Or again, you *figure it out*. You bring figures of speech to bear on reality just as you come to terms with it.

Third, to adapt an expression with which you're probably familiar, I'll conclude by saying that the road to reality is paved with *your* intentions, be they good or bad.

Passages Referenced in Lectures

For Chapter 1

A commodity is therefore a mysterious thing, simply because in it the social character of men's labor appears to them as an objective character stamped upon the product of that labor . . . : To find an analogy, we must have recourse to the mist-enveloped regions of the religious world. In that world the productions of the human brain appear as independent beings endowed with life, and entering into relation both with one another and the human race. So it is in the world of commodities with the products of men's hands.

    —Karl Marx, *Capital: A Critique of Political Economy*, trans. Samuel
    Moore and Edward Aveling, ed. Frederick Engels (New York:
    International Publishers, 1967), 1:72–73.

What then is truth? A mobile army of metaphors, metonymies, anthropomorphisms: in short, a sum of human relations which became poetically and rhetorically intensified, metamorphosed, adorned, and after long usage, seem to a nation fixed, canonic, and binding; truths are illusions of which one has forgotten that they *are* illusions: worn-out metaphors which have become powerless to affect the senses, coins which have their

obverse effaced and are now no longer of account as coins but merely as
metal.
>   —Friedrich Nietzsche, "On Truth and Lie in the Extra-Moral Sense,"
>   trans. Maximilian Mügge, in *The Complete Works of Friedrich*
>   *Nietzsche*, ed. Oscar Levy (New York: Russell and Russell,
>   1964), p. 180.

Three masters, seemingly mutually exclusive, dominate the school of
suspicion: Marx, Nietzsche, and Freud . . . "truth as lying" would be the
negative heading under which one might place these three exercises of
suspicion.
>   —Paul Ricoeur, *Freud and Philosophy: An Essay on Interpretation*,
>   trans. Denis Savage (New Haven: Yale University Press, 1970),
>   p. 32.

For Chapter 3

When we have to do with anything, the mere seeing of the Things which
are closest to us bears in itself the structure of interpretation, and in so primordial a manner that just to grasp something *free*, as it were, *of the "as,"*
requires a certain readjustment. When we merely stare at something, our
just-having-it-before-us lies before us *as a failure to understand it any more.*
This grasping which is free of the "as," is a privation of the kind of seeing in
which one *merely* understands. It is not more primordial than that kind of
seeing, but is derived from it.
>   —Martin Heidegger, *Being and Time*, trans. John Macquarrie and
>   Edward Robinson (Oxford: Blackwell, 1962), p. 190.

In . . . an interpretation, the way in which the entity we are interpreting is
to be conceived can be drawn from the entity itself, or the interpretation
can force the entity into concepts to which it is opposed in its manner of
Being. In either case, the interpretation has already decided for a definite
way of conceiving it, either with finality or with reservations; it is grounded
in *something we grasp in advance*—in a *fore-conception*.
>   —Martin Heidegger, *Being and Time*, trans. John Macquarrie and
>   Edward Robinson (Oxford: Blackwell, 1962), p. 191.

If, when one is engaged in a particular concrete kind of interpretation, in
the sense of exact textual Interpretation, one likes to appeal to what "stands
there," then one finds that what "stands there" in the first instance is noth-

ing other than the obvious undiscussed assumption of the person who does the interpreting.

> —Martin Heidegger, *Being and Time*, trans. John Macquarrie and
> Edward Robinson (Oxford: Blackwell, 1962), p. 192.

Kant held it to be a foundation of moral action that men should be conceived as ends in themselves, not as instruments of other men. This imperative is transferable to the words of men because speech is an extension and expression of men in the social domain, and also because when we fail to conjoin a man's intention to his words we lose the soul of speech, which is to convey meaning and to understand what is intended to be conveyed.

> —E. D. Hirsch, *Aims of Interpretation* (Chicago: University of
> Chicago Press, 1976), p. 91.

For Chapter 5

There is no art [but one] delivered to mankind that hath not the works of Nature for his principal object. . . . Only the poet, disdaining to be tied to any such subjection, lifted up with the vigour of his own invention, doth grow in effect another nature. . . . He nothing affirms, and therefore never lieth.

> —Sir Philip Sidney, "Apologie for Poetry" (1595), in *The English
> Renaissance: An Anthology of Sources and Documents* (London:
> Routledge, 1998), p. 291.

The pleasant and the good both have a reference to the faculty of desire, and they bring with them, the former a satisfaction pathologically conditioned (by impulses, stimuli), the latter a pure practical [i.e., purposeful or pragmatic] satisfaction which is determined not merely by the representation of the object but also by the represented connection of the subject with the existence of the object [i.e., the subject—or self—either covets or recoils from the object on either sensuous or moral grounds]. [The sensuous or moral disposition of a subject toward an object Kant then calls "interest."]

> —Immanuel Kant, *Critique of Judgment* (1790), trans. J. H. Bernard
> (New York: MacMillan, 1914), p. 53.

Taste is the faculty of judging of an object or a method of representing it by an *entirely disinterested* satisfaction or dissatisfaction. The object of such satisfaction is called *beautiful*.

> —Immanuel Kant, *Critique of Judgment* (1790), trans. J. H. Bernard
> (New York: MacMillan, 1914), p. 55.

Beauty is the form of the *purposiveness* [i.e., the unifying and generative principle] of an object, so far as this is perceived in it *without any representation of a purpose.*

> —Immanuel Kant, *Critique of Judgment* (1790), trans. J. H. Bernard
> (New York: MacMillan, 1914), p. 73.

The BEAUTIFUL is . . . at once distinguished both from the AGREEABLE, which is beneath it, and from the GOOD, which is above it: for both these necessarily have an interest attached to them: both act on the WILL, and excite a desire for the actual image or object contemplated.

> —Samuel Taylor Coleridge, "Essays on the Principles of
> Genial Criticism," *Shorter Works and Fragments*, ed.
> H. J. Jackson and J. R. de J. Jackson (London: Routledge,
> 1996), 1:380.

All art is quite useless.

> —Oscar Wilde, "Preface," *The Picture of Dorian Gray* (1890) (New
> York: Barnes & Noble Classics, 2003), p. 2.

The experience called beauty is beyond the powerful ethical will precisely as it is beyond the animal passion, and indeed these last two are competitive and coordinate.

> —John Crowe Ransom, "Criticism as Pure Speculation" (1941), in
> *Critical Theory Since Plato*, ed. Hazard Adams (New York: Har
> court, Brace, Jovanovich, 1971), p. 450.

For Chapter 8

If we study speech from several viewpoints simultaneously, the object of linguistics appears to us as a confused mass of heterogeneous and unrelated things. [This] procedure opens the door to several sciences—psychology, anthropology, normative grammar, philology, etc.—which are distinct from linguistics, but which might claim speech, in view of the faulty method of linguistics, as one of their objects.

As I see it there is only one solution to all the foregoing difficulties: *from the very outset we must put both feet on the ground of language and use language as the norm of all the other manifestations of speech.*

> —Ferdinand de Saussure, *Course in General Linguistics*, trans. Wade
> Baskin (New York: McGraw-Hill, 1966), p. 9.

Linguistics is only a part of the general science of semiology [which would concern all systems of signs: "the alphabet of deaf-mutes, symbolic rites, polite formulas, military signals," mime, railway semaphores, stoplights, etc.].

> —Ferdinand de Saussure, *Course in General Linguistics*, trans. Wade Baskin (New York: McGraw-Hill, 1966), p. 16.

Language is not a function of the speaker; it is a product that is passively assimilated by the individual.

> —Ferdinand de Saussure, *Course in General Linguistics*, trans. Wade Baskin (New York: McGraw-Hill, 1966), p. 14.

Synchrony and *diachrony* designate respectively a language-state and an evolutionary phase.

> —Ferdinand de Saussure, *Course in General Linguistics*, trans. Wade Baskin (New York: McGraw-Hill, 1966), pp. 80–81.

Synchronic facts, no matter what they are, evidence a certain regularity but are in no way imperative; diachronic facts, on the contrary, force themselves upon language but are in no way general.

> —Ferdinand de Saussure, *Course in General Linguistics*, trans. Wade Baskin (New York: McGraw-Hill, 1966), 95.

For Chapter 11

I have a tendency to put upon texts an inherent authority, which is stronger, I think, than Derrida is willing to put on them. . . . In a complicated way, I would hold to the statement that "the text deconstructs itself, is self-deconstructive," rather than being deconstructed by a philosophical intervention from outside the text.

> —Paul de Man, *The Resistance to Theory* (Minneapolis: University of Minnesota Press, 1986), p. 118.

For Chapter 17

The delight in the moment and the gay façade become an excuse for absolving the listener from the thought of the whole, whose claim is comprised in proper listening. The listener is converted, along his line of least resistance, into the acquiescent purchaser. No longer do the partial moments serve as a critique of the whole; instead, they suspend the critique which the successful esthetic totality exerts against the flawed one of society.

—T. W. Adorno, *Essays on Music*, trans. Susan H. Gillespie, ed. Richard Leppert (Berkeley: University of California Press, 2002), p. 291.

[Great modernist composers like Berg, Schönberg, and Webern] are called individualists [by other Marxists], and yet their work is nothing but a single dialogue with the powers that destroy individuality—powers whose "formless shadows" fall gigantically on their music. In music, too, collective powers are liquidating an individuality past saving, but against them only individuals are capable of consciously representing the aims of collectivity.

—T. W. Adorno, *Essays on Music*, trans. Susan H. Gillespie, ed. Richard Leppert (Berkeley: University of California Press, 2002), p. 315.

For Chapter 18

Let Scott, Balzac, and Dreiser serve as the non-chronological markers of the emergence of realism in its modern form; these first great realisms are characterized by a fundamental and exhilarating heterogeneity in their raw materials and by a corresponding versatility in their narrative apparatus. In such moments, a generic confinement to the existent has a paradoxically liberating effect on the registers of the text, and releases a set of heterogeneous historical perspectives—the past for Scott, the future for Balzac, the process of commodification for Dreiser—normally felt to be inconsistent with a focus on the historical present. Indeed, this multiple temporality tends to be sealed off and recontained again in "high" realism and naturalism, where a perfected narrative apparatus (in particular the threefold imperatives of authorial depersonalization, unity of point of view, and restriction to scenic representation) begin to confer on the "realistic" option the appearance of an asphyxiating, self-imposed penance. It is in the context of this gradual reification in late capitalism that the romance once again comes to be felt as the place of narrative heterogeneity and freedom from the reality principle to which a now oppressive realistic representation is the hostage.

—Fredric Jameson, *The Political Unconscious: Narrative as a Socially Symbolic Act* (London: Routledge, 2002), p. 90.

The Philosophers have only *interpreted* the world, in various ways; the point, however, is to change it.

> —Karl Marx, "Eleventh Thesis on Feuerbach" (1845), in *The Marx-Engels Reader*, ed. Robert C. Tucker (New York: W. W. Norton, 1978), p. 145.

Notes

CHAPTER 2
Introduction Continued

1. Anton Chekhov, *The Cherry Orchard*, trans. Sharon Marie Carnicke (Indianapolis: Hackett, 2010), p. 22.
2. Henry James, *The Ambassadors* (New York: Harper & Brothers, 1903), p. 150.
3. Samuel Johnson, *Selected Writings*, ed. Peter Martin (Cambridge, MA: Harvard University Press, 2009), p. 369.

CHAPTER 3
Ways In and Out of the Hermeneutic Circle

1. Mark Akenside, *The Poetical Works* (London: Pickering, 1835), p. 32.

CHAPTER 6
The New Criticism and Other Western Formalisms

1. In William Butler Yeats, *New Poems* (Dublin: Cualla Press, 1938).
2. William Empson, *Seven Types of Ambiguity* (New York: New Directions, 1966), p. 18.
3. Empson, p. 19.
4. Empson, p. 192.
5. F. W. Bateson, *Wordsworth: A Re-Interpretation* (London: Longmans, Green, 1956).

CHAPTER 7
Russian Formalism

1. Boris Eikhenbaum, "The Theory of the 'Formal Method,'" in *Russian Formalist Criticism: Four Essays*, ed. and trans. Lee T. Lemon and Marion J. Reis (Lincoln: University of Nebraska Press, 1965), p. 111.
2. Eikhenbaum, p. 102.
3. In Roman Jakobson, *Verbal Art, Verbal Sign, Verbal Time*, ed. Krystyna Pomorska and Stephen Rudy (Minneapolis: University of Minnesota Press, 1985).
4. Jakobson, 114.
5. See Matthew Arnold, *The Complete Prose Works, Volume IX: English Literature*, ed. R. H. Super (Ann Arbor: University of Michigan Press, 1973), pp. 52–53.
6. Eikhenbaum, 118.
7. Viktor Shklovsky, *Theory of Prose* (Normal, IL: Dalkey Archive Press, 1991), 20.
8. Yuri Tynianov, "On Literary Evolution," in *Twentieth Century Literary Theory*, ed. Vassilis Lambropoulos and David Neal Miller (Albany: SUNY Press, 1987), 162.

CHAPTER 8
Semiotics and Structuralism

1. Edward Estlin Cummings, *100 Selected Poems* (New York: Grove Press, 1994), p. 79.

CHAPTER 9
Linguistics and Literature

1. Roman Jakobson, "Two Types of Aphasia and Two Types of Language Disturbance," in Roman Jakobson and Morris Halle, *Fundamentals of Language* (The Hague: Mouton, 1956), pp. 69–96.

CHAPTER 10
Deconstruction I

1. William H. Pritchard, "The Hermeneutical Mafia or, After Strange Gods at Yale," *Hudson Review* 28.4 (1975): 601–610.
2. Roland Barthes, *The Eiffel Tower and Other Mythologies* (New York: Hill and Wang, 1984), pp. 3–17 (4).
3. Michel de Certeau, "Walking in the City," in *The Practice of Everyday Life* (Berkeley: University of California Press, 1988).

CHAPTER 15
The Postmodern Psyche

1. Jean-François Lyotard, *The Inhuman* (Stanford: Stanford University Press, 1991).

CHAPTER 25
The End of Theory?

1. Umberto Eco, "Peirce's Notion of the Interpretant," *MLN* 91.6 (1976): 1457–1472.

The Varieties of Interpretation
A Guide to Further Reading in Literary Theory

STEFAN ESPOSITO

Literary theory questions the conditions and assumptions that inform interpretation. This is evidenced in the types of questions that theory asks. How do we interpret the link between an author's thought process and the text that appears on paper? How do we interpret the significance of political and economic factors in a lyric poem? Should the gender, race, or sexuality of an author shape the way we read a novel? The focus of discrete critical schools differs significantly, but all humanistic studies that question the nature of interpretation share a common ancestor in the secularization of hermeneutics. Students wishing to deepen their understanding of literary theory would do well to consider this tradition before branching into other theories of literary and cultural interpretation.

Friedrich Schleiermacher is a foundational figure in the development of modern hermeneutics. In works such as *On Religion: Speeches to Its Cultured Despisers* (1799), *Soliloquies* (1800; 2nd ed., 1810), *Outlines of a Critique of Previous Ethical Theory* (1803), and *The Christian Faith* (1821–1822, rev. ed., 1830–1831), Schleiermacher expanded the domain of serious interpretation from hermetic arguments about sacred texts to all spheres of human communication. Following Johann Gottfried Herder, Schleiermacher argues that all thought is dependent on and bounded by, or identical with, language. Accordingly, he proposed that hermeneutics should be a universal discipline, applicable to law as well as literature, to oral as well as written texts, and to modern as well as ancient sources.

For a good English translation of Schleiermacher's writings relevant to literary and philosophical hermeneutics, see *Hermeneutics and Criticism and Other Writings*, trans. Andrew Bowie (Cambridge: Cambridge University Press, 1998). Schleiermacher is also responsible for one of the first modern treatises on translation theory, *On the Different Methods of Translation* (1813). A summary of the intersections among romantic hermeneutics, literary theory, and translation studies is found in the introduction to *The Translation Studies Reader*, ed. Lawrence Venuti (London: Routledge, 2004).

Following in Schleiermacher's footsteps, but informed by Leopold von Ranke's historicism, Wilhelm Dilthey attempted to turn hermeneutics into a modern experimental science involving the interpretive equivalent of hypothesis testing. In *The Formation of the Historical World in the Human Sciences* (1910), ed. Rudolf A. Makkreel and Frithjof Rodi (Princeton: Princeton University Press, 2002), Dilthey argued that interpretation involves an indirect or mediated understanding that can be attained only by placing human expressions in their historical context. In this account, understanding is not a process of reconstructing the state of mind of the author, but one of articulating what is expressed in the work. Jos de Mul, *The Tragedy of Finitude: Dilthey's Hermeneutics of Life*, trans. Tony Burrett (New Haven: Yale University Press, 2004), is an excellent critical study.

The link between these hermeneutic pioneers and modern literary theory is found in the phenomenological hermeneutics of Martin Heidegger. Heidegger expanded the philosophical scope of hermeneutics by arguing that it is not just a textual, linguistic, or cultural discipline. As Schleiermacher argued, hermeneutics is of universal import. But it is also, according to Heidegger, an ontological imperative. Understanding, or interpretation, is not just a method of reading or the outcome of some experimental procedure. It is not something we do or attempt to do to external symbolic data. It is something we are. Heidegger's magnum opus, *Being and Time* (1927), trans. John Macquarrie and Edward Robinson (London: SCM Press, 1962), inaugurates what has come to be known as the ontological turn in hermeneutics. The following works by Heidegger address the philosophical and existential import of interpretation with more overt reference to how literature, poetry in particular, interrogates the relationship between language and being: "The Origin of the Work of Art," in *Poetry, Language, Thought*, trans. Albert Hofstadter (New York: HarperCollins, 1971); *Hölderlin's Hymn "The Ister,"* trans. William McNeill and Julia Davis (Bloomington: Indiana University Press, 1996). For a clear and probing analysis of the link between art and ontology in Heidegger's work, see Hubert Dreyfus, "Heidegger's Ontology of Art," in *A Companion to Heidegger*, ed. H. L. Dreyfus and M. A. Wrathall (Oxford: Blackwell, 2005). Heidegger's ontological reevaluation of hermeneutics has been most influential for literary theory insofar as it served as a philosophical foil for deconstruction. For a careful appraisal of this legacy, see John Caputo, *Radical Hermeneutics: Repetition, Deconstruction, and the Hermeneutic Project* (Bloomington: Indiana University Press, 1987).

Other important intersections of modern hermeneutics and literature can be found in the following works: Hans-Georg Gadamer, *Truth and*

Method (1960), trans. Joel Weinsheimer and Donald G. Marshall (New York: Continuum, 1994); Gianni Vattimo, *Beyond Interpretation: The Meaning of Hermeneutics for Philosophy*, trans. David Webb (Stanford: Stanford University Press, 1997); Paul Ricoeur, *Freud and Philosophy: An Essay on Interpretation*, trans. Denis Savage. (New Haven: Yale University Press, 1970), *The Conflict of Interpretations: Essays in Hermeneutics*, ed. Don Ihde, trans. Willis Domingo et al. (Evanston, IL: Northwestern University Press, 1974), and *Time and Narrative*, 3 vols., trans. Kathleen McLaughlin and David Pellauer (Chicago: University of Chicago Press, 1984, 1985, 1988).

A number of critiques of phenomenological or ontological hermeneutics are also worth noting. These have been quite influential to various critical movements, including media studies and sociological approaches to literature and the public sphere. Karl-Otto Apel's *Understanding and Explanation: A Transcendental-Pragmatic Perspective* (Cambridge, MA: MIT Press, 1984) attempts to reformulate the relationship between understanding (*Verstehen*) and explanation (*Erklärung*) in pursuit of a more pragmatic, scientific account of language. In works such as *On the Logic of the Social Sciences* (1967), trans. Shierry Weber Nicholsen and Jerry A. Stark (Cambridge, MA: Polity Press, 1988), and *The Theory of Communicative Action*, trans. Thomas McCarthy (Cambridge, MA: Polity Press, 1984–1987), Jürgen Habermas criticizes the ideological implications of romantic and phenomenological hermeneutics, with special focus on Gadamer's conception of tradition and the political implications of Heidegger's ontology. Habermas's work on communication and the public sphere has also been formative for many American scholars working in cultural studies and the rise of print culture. Michael Warner's *The Letters of the Republic: Publication and the Public Sphere in Eighteenth-Century America* (Cambridge, MA: Harvard University Press, 1990) and *Publics and Counterpublics* (Cambridge, MA: Zone Books, 2002) are astute analyses of American literature, culture, politics, and religion through a Habermasian lens.

Reader-response criticism also emerged, especially amongst the members of the Konstanz school of criticism, as a corrective to the ontological turn in hermeneutics. Important works in this mode are: Peter Uwe Hohendahl, "Introduction to Reception Aesthetics," *New German Critique* 10 (1977): 29–63; Norman Holland, *The Dynamics of Literary Response* (New York: Columbia University Press, 1989); Stanley Fish, *Surprised by Sin: The Reader in Paradise Lost* (New York: Macmillan, 1967); Michael Riffaterre, "Criteria for Style Analysis," *Word* 15 (1959): 154–174. Robert C. Holub, *Reception Theory: A Critical Introduction* (London: Methuen, 1984), is a clear primer.

Reader-Response Criticism: From Formalism to Post-Structuralism, ed. Jane P. Tompkins (Baltimore: Johns Hopkins University Press, 1980), is an excellent compendium. For the role played by Hans Robert Jauss, see the introduction by Paul de Man to Jauss's *Toward an Aesthetic of Reception*, trans. Timothy Bahti (Minneapolis: University of Minnesota Press, 1982).

While it has been occasionally criticized as a conservative intellectual movement, the ontological turn in hermeneutics was central to the rise of radical critiques of the Western philosophical tradition. Heavily influenced by Heidegger, Jean-Paul Sartre inspired a whole generation of French intellectuals to reconsider the philosophical significance of literature. His *What is Literature?* (1947), trans. Bernard Frechtman (Cambridge, MA: Harvard University Press 1988), is a foundational text in this regard. Expanding upon the phenomenological work of Sartre, Husserl, and Heidegger, Georges Poulet theorized the act of reading as a hermeneutics of consciousness in his "Phenomenology of Reading," *New Literary History* 1.1 (October 1969): 53–68, and *The Interior Distance*, trans. Elliott Coleman (Baltimore: Johns Hopkins University Press, 1959).

The Russian formalists have been somewhat eclipsed for contemporary students by their successors, Mikhail Bakhtin and his contemporaries, but there is still a substantial literature in English to consult. Two descriptive essays are: Victor Erlich, "Russian Formalism," *The Journal of the History of Ideas* 34 (1973: 627–38) and Peter Steiner, "Russian Formalism," *The Cambridge History of Literary Criticism*, ed. Raman Selden, vol. 8 (Cambridge: Cambridge University Press, 1995): 11–29. For a contemporary survey of the movement similar to Eikhenbaum's, see the translation of an essay by Boris Tomashevsky, "The New School of Literary History in Russia" (1928), *Publications of the Modern Language Association* 119 (2004: 120–132). On Bakhtin, see Caryl Emerson and Gary Saul Morson, "Mikhail Bakhtin," *The Johns Hopkins Guide to Literary Theory and Criticism*, ed. Michael Groden, Martin Kreiswirth, and Imre Szeman, 2nd ed. (Baltimore: The Johns Hopkins University Press, 2005), and Katerina Clark and Michael Holquist, *Mikhail Bakhtin* (Cambridge, MA: Harvard University Press, 1984).

Along with phenomenology, existentialism, and the Russian formalists, Ferdinand de Saussure's structuralism was also a potent intellectual catalyst for literary theory. Jonathan Culler's *Structuralist Poetics: Structuralism, Linguistics, and the Study of Literature* (Ithaca: Cornell University Press, 1975) and Hans Aarsleff's *From Locke to Saussure: Essays on the Study of Language* (Minneapolis: University of Minnesota Press, 1982) are classic studies covering this tradition. Culler's *Ferdinand de Saussure* (Ithaca: Cornell University Press, 1986) is also indispensable. Peter Caws, *Structuralism: The Art of the Intelligible* (New York: Humanities Press, 1988), explores the philosophical significance of structuralism. Terence Hawkes's *Structuralism and Semiotics* (London: Methuen, 1977) is an elegantly written study of the movement's consequences for literary interpretation.

A key figure associated with structuralism was Roland Barthes. His early thinking in *Writing Degree Zero* (1953), trans. Annette Lavers (New York: Hill and Wang, 1977), is a forceful indictment of Sartre's disenchantment with experimental literary forms. Later works by Barthes vacillate among Marxist, structuralist and poststructuralist criticism. *Mythologies* [1957], trans. Annette Lavers (New York: Farrar, Strauss, and Giroux, 1972), attempts to denaturalize the cultural symbols and sign systems at play in quotidian forms of bourgeois society, such as advertising or wrestling matches. *S/Z* (1970), trans. Richard Miller (New York: Hill and Wang, 1975), is a dense and detailed semiotic anatomy of Balzac's story, "Sarrasine." The essays collected in *Image, Music, Text* (New York: Hill and Wang, 1977) gesture toward a radical conception of reading as the enactment of infinite play in the text.

This latter strand of Barthes's thought dovetails with one of the most important figures in literary theory and contemporary continental philosophy, Jacques Derrida. A trio of texts published in 1967 established Derrida as a major intellectual figure and laid the foundation for the rise of deconstruction, a wide-ranging critique of the Western metaphysical tradition that influenced academic work across the humanities and even some of the social sciences. These foundational texts are: *Of Grammatology*, trans. Gayatri Spivak (Baltimore: Johns Hopkins University Press, 1976); *Writing and Difference*, trans. Alan Bass (Chicago: University of Chicago Press, 1980); and *Speech and Phenomena and Other Essays on Husserl's Theory of Signs*, trans. David Allison (Evanston, IL: Northwestern University Press, 1973). Later works by Derrida apply the deconstruction of Western metaphysics to questions of ethics and politics. See, for instance, *Spectres of Marx: The State of the Debt, the Work of Mourning, and the New International* (London: Routledge, 1994); *Politics of Friendship*, trans. George Collins (London & New York: Verso, 1997); and *Of Hospitality*, trans. Rachel Bowlby (Stanford: Stanford University Press, 2000).

Deconstruction in America, championed by the Yale school, has produced a number of critical masterpieces. *Deconstruction and Criticism* (New Haven: Yale University Press, 1979) is a collection of essays by Derrida,

Harold Bloom, Geoffrey Hartman, J. Hillis Miller, and Paul de Man, exhibiting the wide range of approaches that deconstruction has inspired. Hartman's rigorous analysis of Derrida's experimental literary-philosophical collage *Glas* (1974) in *Saving the Text: Literature/Derrida/Philosophy* (Baltimore: Johns Hopkins University Press, 1981) provides a more pragmatic account of deconstruction's place in critical history. Jonathan Culler's *On Deconstruction* (London: Routledge, 1983) is the best review of the theoretical underpinnings and interpretive moves implicit in the movement. Barbara Johnson's *The Critical Difference: Essays in the Contemporary Rhetoric of Reading* (Baltimore: Johns Hopkins University Press, 1980), Carol Jacobs's *The Dissimulating Harmony* (Baltimore: Johns Hopkins University Press, 1978), and Cynthia Chase's *Decomposing Figures: Rhetorical Readings in the Romantic Tradition* (Baltimore: Johns Hopkins University Press, 1986) each enact virtuoso readings of the problematic rhetorical structure at play in literary and theoretical texts.

Arguably, the most influential and controversial member of the Yale school was Paul de Man. His major works, *The Rhetoric of Romanticism* (New York: Columbia University Press, 1984), *Allegories of Reading: Figural Language in Rousseau, Nietzsche, Rilke and Proust* (New Haven: Yale University Press, 1979), and *Blindness and Insight: Essays in the Rhetoric of Contemporary Criticism* (Oxford: Oxford University Press, 1971), have become classics of literary theory. Writing in a dense but more straightforward style than Derrida, de Man artfully demonstrates the indeterminacy of meaning in writers such as Wordsworth, Hölderlin, Shelley, and Rousseau. His work has inspired some equally incisive commentaries, including Christopher Norris's *Paul de Man: Deconstruction and the Critique of Aesthetic Ideology* (London: Routledge, 1988) and Rodolphe Gasché's *The Wild Card of Reading: On Paul de Man* (Cambridge, MA: Harvard University Press, 1998). The controversy surrounding de Man, and by extension deconstruction as a whole, was fueled by the discovery of collaborationist articles he wrote in German-occupied Belgium during World War II. These nationalist and occasionally anti-Semitic articles comprise a small minority of de Man's journalistic output, collected in full in *Wartime Journalism, 1939–43*, ed. Werner Hamacher, Neil Hertz, and Thomas Keenan (Lincoln: University of Nebraska Press, 1988). Reflections, defenses, and theoretical responses from de Man's colleagues, students, and contemporaries are collected in *Responses: On Paul de Man's Wartime Journalism*, ed. Werner Hamacher, Neil Hertz, and Thomas Keenan (Lincoln: University of Nebraska Press, 1989).

The radical critique of Western metaphysics pursued by deconstruction was also an important source of inspiration for a number of French feminist thinkers. Along with Luce Irigaray, Hélène Cixous developed a philosophical critique of patriarchal power structures by combining Derrida's conception of logocentrism and Lacanian psychoanalysis. In "The Laugh of the Medusa," trans. Keith Cohen and Paula Cohen, *Signs* 1.4 (1976): 875–893, Cixous calls for a new mode of feminine writing, termed "écriture féminine." In *Speculum of the Other Woman* (1974), trans. Gillian C. Gill (Ithaca: Cornell University Press, 1985), and *The Sex Which Is Not One* (1977), trans. Catherine Porter (Ithaca: Cornell University Press, 1985), Irigaray espouses the need for a feminine mode of writing that resists the unitary conception of truth that dominates Western philosophy. Another important figure within the French feminist theoretical tradition is Julia Kristeva. In her work on the "semiotic," Kristeva draws attention to the bodily or material experiences of language as opposed to the symbolic, tacitly phallocentric realm of denotative meaning. The principal statement of this theory is *Séméiôtiké: Recherches pour une sémanalyse* (1969) [English translation: *Desire in Language: A Semiotic Approach to Literature and Art* (Oxford: Blackwell, 1980)]. Later works have focused on the distinct challenges faced by female authors. See *Female Genius: Life, Madness, Words: Hannah Arendt, Melanie Klein, Colette: A Trilogy*, 3 vols. (New York: Columbia University Press, 2001).

Many American feminists have expanded upon the marriage of semiotics and psychoanalysis that emerged in France. The work of Jane Gallop is a particularly important and incisive example. See *The Daughter's Seduction: Feminism and Psychoanalysis* (Ithaca: Cornell University Press, 1982); *Reading Lacan* (Ithaca: Cornell University Press, 1985); and *Thinking Through the Body* (New York: Columbia University Press, 1988). Gallop has also written an excellent account of academic feminist literary scholarship: *Around 1981: Academic Feminist Literary Theory* (New York: Routledge, 1991). The work of Toril Moi is widely read and anthologized. Moi provides the clearest argument for the differences between the theoretical work of French feminist theory and its predecessors. In *Sexual/Textual Politics: Feminist Literary Theory* (London and New York: Methuen, 1985), Moi surveys Anglo-American feminism, characterized by the works of such theorists as Elaine Showalter, Sandra Gilbert, Susan Gubar, Kate Millett, and Annette Kolodny. According to Moi, the dominant strand of feminism in academia articulates an essentialist conception of the female self, characteristic of and complicit with liberal humanism. In *What Is a Woman? and*

Other Essays (Oxford and New York: Oxford University Press, 1999), Moi returns to this critique of Anglo-American feminism and pursues an alternative conception of female identity inspired by Kristeva, Cixous, Irigaray, and Simone de Beauvoir.

Literary studies of gender and sexuality, including feminist literary theory, queer theory, and cultural studies more broadly are heavily indebted to the work of Michel Foucault. Foucault's earliest work (1961) is a cultural and institutional history of madness: *History of Madness*, trans. Jonathan Murphy (London: Routledge, 2006). His *History of Sexuality*, 3 vols., trans. Robert Hurley (New York: Vintage Books, 1988–1990), has been extremely influential, both for its analyses of gender and sexuality and for its theoretical insight into the relationships among culture, power, and subjectivity. Late seminars focus on the imbrication of power and knowledge in various societal constructions of the abnormal or pathological. See *Essential Works of Foucault, 1954–1984*, 3 vols., ed. Paul Rabinow (New York: New Press, 1997–1999). An excellent secondary study on Foucault's philosophical significance is Hubert Dreyfus and Paul Rabinow, *Michel Foucault: Beyond Structuralism and Hermeneutics* (Chicago: University of Chicago Press, 1983).

In addition to Judith Butler, numerous theorists and critics have drawn on Foucault to analyze the cultural and institutional construction of gender and sexuality. Susan Bordo's *Unbearable Weight: Feminism, Western Culture, and the Body* (Berkeley: University of California Press, 1993) offers an astute analysis of the power dynamics that guide interpretation of the gendered body in Western society. Eve Kosofsky Sedgwick's two masterpieces of literary and cultural criticism, *Between Men: English Literature and Male Homosocial Desire* (New York: Columbia University Press, 1985) and *Epistemology of the Closet* (Berkeley: University of California, 1990), argue that the homosexual–heterosexual binary develops as an instrument to support heterosexuality and male dominance. Lee Edelman's *Homographesis: Essays in Gay Literary and Cultural Theory* (New York: Routledge, 1994) rearticulates issues of sexual identity and politics through a deconstructive and psychoanalytic lens. In "Queer Theory: Lesbian and Gay Sexualities," *differences: A Journal of Feminist Cultural Studies* 3.3 (1991): iii–xviii, Teresa de Lauretis coined the term "queer theory" and argued for its use as a way of opening up discursive horizons about sex and sexuality.

Many important feminist theorists, including Gayatri Spivak, Shulamith Firestone, and Michèle Barrett, have expanded the scope of feminist theory by yoking psychoanalytic and anthropological critique to Marxist social theory. See, for instance, Barrett's *The Politics of Truth: From Marx to Foucault* (Stanford: Stanford University Press, 1991), or Gayle Rubin's "The Traffic in Women: Notes on the Political Economy of Sex," in *Towards an Anthropology of Women*, ed. Rayna Rapp Reiter (New York: Monthly Review Press, 1975).

The most influential figure in contemporary Marxist literary and cultural theory is Fredric Jameson. After engaging the structuralist project in *The Prison House of Language* (Princeton: Princeton University Press, 1972), Jameson developed his own theory of culture, heavily influenced by Louis Althusser, in a series of works that include *Fables of Aggression* (Berkeley: University of California Press, 1979), *The Political Unconscious* (Ithaca: Cornell University Press, 1981), and *Postmodernism, or, The Cultural Logic of Late Capitalism* (Durham, NC: Duke University Press, 1991). Terry Eagleton's *The Ideology of the Aesthetic* (London: Blackwell, 1991) is a new classic of Marxist criticism. It situates eighteenth- and nineteenth-century aesthetic theories within a heterogeneous array of ideological and political discourses. Ernesto Laclau and Chantal Mouffe's *Hegemony and Socialist Strategy* (London: Verso, 1985) is less focused on literature and art per se but, following the precedent of Antonio Gramsci, analyzes the role of culture in naturalizing imposed power structures.

Jameson's work in particular has been criticized by postcolonial theorists for a claim made in "Third-World Literature in the Era of Multinational Capitalism," *Social Text* 15 (1986): 65–88. Here, Jameson argues that all third-world literature should be interpreted in terms of national allegory, potentially eliding other valid hermeneutic approaches. Aijaz Ahmad argues forcefully against Jameson in "Jameson's Rhetoric of Otherness and the 'National Allegory,'" *Social Text* 17 (1987): 3–25. A defense of Jameson is offered by Imre Szemen in "Who's Afraid of National Allegory?: Jameson, Literary Criticism, Globalization," *South Atlantic Quarterly* 100.3 (2001): 803–827. The classic work on the difficulty of speaking for, about, or as a postcolonial subject is Gayatri Spivak's "Can the Subaltern Speak?" in *Marxism and the Interpretation of Culture*, ed. Cary Nelson and Lawrence Grossberg (London: Macmillan, 1988).

There are a number of excellent critical studies of the heterodox Marxist scholars associated with the Frankfurt school of criticism: Martin Jay, *The Dialectical Imagination: A History of the Frankfurt School and the Institute for Social Research 1923–1950* (Berkeley: University of California Press, 1996); Seyla Benhabib, *Critique, Norm, and Utopia: A Study of the Foundations of Critical Theory* (New York: Columbia University Press, 1986);

Rolf Wiggerhaus, *The Frankfurt School: Its History, Theories, and Political Significance* (Cambridge, MA: MIT Press, 1995); Thomas Wheatland, *The Frankfurt School in Exile* (Minneapolis: University of Minnesota Press, 2009).

Postcolonial studies in general are as varied as the countries that were subject to colonial rule. Nonetheless, some foundational works in this critical vein can be isolated. Aimé Césaire's *Discourse on Colonialism* (1950), trans. Joan Pinkham (New York: Monthly Review Press, 2001), and Frantz Fanon's *Black Skin, White Masks* (New York: Grove, 1967) are important forerunners. Fanon uses psychoanalytical theory to explore the divided self-perception of the colonial subject. A similar model informs his study of the Algerian struggle for independence, *The Wretched of the Earth* (New York: Grove, 1965). Albert Memmi's *The Colonizer and the Colonized* (Boston: Beacon Press, 1965) is a quasi-structuralist account of the interdependent relationship between rulers and subjects. Edward Said's classic *Orientalism* (New York: Vintage Books, 1978) analyzes the interplay of oppressive power and knowledge in Orientalist scholarship and imaginative portrayals of the Middle East. Walter Mignolo's *The Idea of Latin America* (Oxford: Blackwell, 2005) takes a similar tack, exploring the colonial matrix of power behind the invention of the term "Latin America." Achille Mbembe's *On the Postcolony* (Berkeley: University of California Press, 2000) interprets representations of subjectivity—focusing on experiences such as violence, wonder, and laughter—to problematize die-hard Africanist and nativist perspectives, while also exploring some of the key assumptions of postcolonial theory. In *The Black Atlantic: Modernity and Double Consciousness* (New York: Verso, 1993), Paul Gilroy provides a study of African intellectual history and its cultural construction, recasting the peoples who suffered from the Atlantic slave trade as emblematic of the ineluctable cultural hybridity of diasporic peoples. Homi Bhabha's *Nation and Narration* (London: Routledge, 1990) and *The Location of Culture* (London: Routledge, 1994) confront the problematic realities and ambiguities of nationality and identity via an idiosyncratic mix of psychoanalysis, deconstruction, and cultural theory.

African American literary theory is also a vibrant and wide-ranging branch of critical study. In addition to the works by Henry Louis Gates Jr. and Toni Morrison discussed in Professor Fry's lectures, some canonical works in this tradition are: Houston A. Baker, *Blues, Ideology, and Afro-American Literature: A Vernacular Theory* (Chicago: University of Chicago Press, 1984); *The Black Aesthetic*, ed. Addison Gayle Jr. (New York: Doubleday, 1971); Claudia Tate, *Psychoanalysis and Black Novels: Desire and the*

Protocols of Race (Oxford: Oxford University Press, 1998); Robert B. Stepto, *From Beyond the Veil: A Study of Afro-American Literature* (Urbana: University of Illinois Press, 1979). *African American Literary Criticism, 1773 to 2000*, ed. Hazel Arnett Ervin (New York: Twayne Publishers, 1999), is a useful compendium.

While feminist, Marxist and postcolonial studies continue to draw upon psychoanalytic themes, concepts, and thinkers, studies foregrounding the works and ideas of Freud and Lacan have, unfortunately, faded somewhat from the theoretical landscape in recent years. Nevertheless, Harold Bloom's *The Anxiety of Influence* (Oxford: Oxford University Press, 1973) remains a powerful model for understanding the relationship between poets and their precursors. Peter Brooks's works, such as *Reading for the Plot* (Cambridge, MA: Harvard University Press, 1983), *Body Work: Objects of Desire in Modern Narrative* (Cambridge, MA: Harvard University Press, 1993), *Troubling Confessions: Speaking Guilt in Law and Literature* (Chicago: University of Chicago Press, 2000), and *Realist Vision* (New Haven: Yale University Press, 2005), use a focused psychoanalytic lens to examine the rhetorical permutations at play in legal, literary, and aesthetic discourses.

One of the more vibrant developments of psychoanalytic theory is found in the field of trauma studies. Shoshana Felman's collaboration with the physician Dori Laub in *Testimony: Crises of Witnessing in Literature, Psychoanalysis, and History* (London: Routledge, 1992) is a foundational text in this subfield. Like Brooks's, Felman's work often intersects with other disciplines, including philosophy, law, and anthropology. Her *Writing and Madness: Literature/Philosophy/Psychoanalysis* (Stanford: Stanford University Press, 2003) explores the relationship between writing and madness in writers such as Nietzsche, Bataille, and Nerval. *The Juridical Unconscious* (Cambridge, MA: Harvard University Press, 2002) turns to examine trials, especially trials of historic importance, and their relationship to collective trauma.

For a rigorous and thorough close reading of a foundational psychoanalytic text, Phillipe Lacoue-Labarthe and Jean-Luc Nancy's collaborative study, *The Title of the Letter: A Reading of Jacques Lacan*, trans. Francois Raffoult and David Pettigrew (Albany: State University of New York Press, 1992), is indispensable. It is an extended reading of "The Agency of the Letter in the Unconscious, or Reason since Freud." Lacoue-Labarthe and Nancy investigate the rhetorical permutations of systemacity, foundation, and truth in Lacan's text, and psychoanalysis more generally. Slavoj Žižek also expands upon and engages with Lacanian psychoanalysis. His *How to Read*

Lacan (New York: W. W. Norton, 2007) is a clear, accessible, yet incisive look at core concepts and theoretical foundations. An edited collection under Žižek's direction, *Everything You Always Wanted to Know about Lacan (But Were Afraid to Ask Hitchcock)* (London: Verso, 2010), provides numerous lively engagements with classic films, including *Psycho* and *Rear Window*. *The Sublime Object of Ideology* (London: Verso, 1997) develops a line of thought linking Hegel, Althusser, and Lacan that results in a dialectical analysis of the relationship between subjectivity and ideology.

The strange and occasionally impenetrable philosophical interventions of Gilles Deleuze were heavily influenced, in a love-hate relationship, by psychoanalysis. Peter Hallward's *Out of This World: Deleuze and the Philosophy of Creation* (London: Verso, 2006) is an excellent explication of his work. Equally informed by Lacanian psychoanalysis, Alain Badiou has used Deleuze as an intellectual foil while presenting an alternative to both philosophical hermeneutics and traditional aesthetics. See his *Handbook of Inaesthetics*, trans. Alberto Toscano (Stanford: Stanford University Press, 2004), and *Being and Event*, trans. Oliver Feltham (New York: Continuum, 2005).

The various schools and modes of theoretical interpretation mentioned above often present themselves as an alternative or corrective to ideas formulated by the American New Critics. Any student of literature and literary theory would do well to read the revolutionary critical texts associated with this mid-twentieth-century movement. Indeed, the close analysis of cultural discourses enacted by literary theory would not exist but for the methodological and pedagogical innovations of the New Critics. For an extended discussion of the connections between New Critical close reading and various strands of theory, see William J. Spurlin and Michael Fischer, *The New Criticism and Contemporary Literary Theory* (New York: Garland Publishing, 1995).

Cleanth Brooks's essay "The New Criticism," *Sewanee Review* 87.4 (1979), is a clear and incisive statement of the central assumptions, goals, and methods of the movement. These methods are displayed by the virtuoso readings in *The Well Wrought Urn* (New York: Harcourt Brace, 1947) and *Understanding Poetry*, with Robert Penn Warren (New York: Henry Holt, 1938). Mark Winchell's *Cleanth Brooks and the Rise of Modern Criticism* (Charlottesville: University Press of Virginia, 1996) is an astute articulation of Brooks's foundational role in shaping modern literary studies and, perhaps more important, pedagogy in English education. John Crowe Ransom's *The New Criticism* (New York: Harcourt Brace, 1947) reviews the work of I. A. Richards, T. S. Eliot, and Yvor Winters, identifying them as the vanguard of a new way of looking at texts that focuses on semantics and the psychological effect of poetry rather than on taste or the psychology of the author. Richards's masterpiece, *Practical Criticism* (London: Kegan Paul, Trench, Trubner, 1929), is an empirical investigation of the interpretive process itself, using self-report data gleaned from students. For an interesting account of the link between New Criticism in the American South and the conservative agrarian political movement, see Paul K. Conkin's *The Southern Agrarians* (Knoxville: University of Tennessee Press, 1988). The New Critics' chief rivals at the level of theory in their own time were the "Chicago school" of neo-Aristotelian critics who held that interpretation could not be reliably practiced without a well-considered generic framework. See R. S. Crane, "The Critical Monism of Cleanth Brooks," in Crane, ed., *Critics and Criticism: Ancient and Modern* (Chicago: University of Chicago Press, 1952).

There are of course any number of books that have undertaken the survey task of this one (including a book by David Richter, the editor of the anthology we have encouraged readers to purchase in conjunction with these lectures: Richter, *Falling Into Theory: Conflicting Views on Reading Literature*, 2nd ed. (Bedford/ St. Martin's, 2000). Among these, we single out two, the first because it was the premier compendium, in the moment of the New Criticism, of what the theory of literature might be (and in acknowledgment that the title of the present volume is stolen from it): René Wellek and Austin Warren, *Theory of Literature* (New York: Harcourt, Brace, 1949), and the second because it is just an excellent summary of critical movements at its (fairly recent) time, each chapter a lucid and dispassionate summary of a theoretical position until the last page or two, when the Marxist card is played: Terry Eagleton, *Literary Theory: An Introduction* (Cambridge, MA: Blackwell, 1996).

The selections referenced above certainly do not encompass the full variety of theories of literature. Part of the fun and intellectual richness associated with studying theory is the process of discovering new thinkers, and hunting down the sources that inspired them. Coupled with the preceding lectures, Professor Fry and I hope that these readings might inspire students and lifelong learners to chart their own course, rethinking assumptions about interpretation and our experience of literature.

Index